THE MARKET MAKERS

How Leading Companies Create and Win Markets

Daniel F. Spulber

 **BusinessWeek Books**

McGraw-Hill

New York   San Francisco   Washington, D.C.   Auckland Bogotá
Caracas   Lisbon   London   Madrid   Mexico City   Milan
Montreal   New Delhi   San Juan   Singapore
Sydney Tokyo Toronto

Library of Congress Cataloging-in-Publication Data

Spulber, Daniel F.
    The market makers : how leading companies create and win markets/
Daniel F. Spulber.
      p. cm.
    Includes bibliographical references and index.
    ISBN 0-07-060584-X
    1. Success in business.   2. Market share.   I. Title.
    HF5386.S7548   1998
    658.8—dc21   98-6168
                                                    CIP

McGraw-Hill

A Division of The **McGraw·Hill** *Companies*

1 2 3 4 5 6 7 8 9 0 DOC/DOC 9 0 3 2 1 0 9 8

ISBN 0-07-060584-X

The the editing supervisor for this book was Fred Dahl, the designer was Inkwell Publishing Services, and the production supervisor was Sherri Souffrance. It was set in Stone Serif by Inkwell Publishing Services.

Printed and bound by R.R. Donnelley & Sons Company.

McGraw-Hill books are available at special quantity discounts to use as premiums and sales promotions, or for use in corporate training programs. For more information, please write to the Director of Special Sales, McGraw-Hill, 11 West 19th Street, New York, NY 10011. Or contact your local bookstore.

Contents

Preface   *ix*

WINNING MARKETS

1 Introduction   *3*

Winning Markets	*6*
Building Market Bridges	*12*
Market Strategy	*22*
Outline of the Book	*25*

2 The Value of Winning   *29*

Winning	*31*
Intermediation	*37*
Recognition	*38*
Pushing Out the Boundaries of the Firm	*46*

BUILDING MARKET BRIDGES: THE MAIN FRAMEWORK

3 Market Making   65

Price Setting	*66*
Coordinating Exchange	*79*
Market Clearing	*86*
Allocating Goods and Services	*90*

4 Arbitrage   95

Spatial Arbitrage	*98*
Dynamic Arbitrage	*101*
Risk Arbitrage	*107*
Technological Arbitrage	*112*

5 Intermediation   119

Agent	*120*
Monitor	*139*
Broker	*145*
Communicator	*155*

6 Networking   167

Suppliers and Customers	*168*
Matching and Mixing	*172*
Networks and Organizations	*180*
Organizational Boundaries	*191*

MARKET STRATEGIES

7 Entry Strategies   219

Go-Between	*222*
Bring-Together	*227*
Bypass	*232*
Connect	*236*

8 **Indirect Strategies**   *245*

Economy of Force   *246*
Undefended Markets   *248*
The Path of Least Resistance   *252*
The Line of Least Expectation   *256*

9 **Offensive and Defensive Strategies**   *265*

Offense   *267*
Defense   *291*
Innovation   *296*
Overview   *300*

Conclusion   *303*

Index   *307*

Preface

Who are the market makers? They are innovative companies that are continually leading their industry or doing what it takes to become the leaders of tomorrow. They are companies that realize that competition means outperforming all other companies in their industry. Market makers do not view the competitive market as a force beyond their control. They understand that leading companies create and manage their markets by operating the institutions of exchange.

Market makers provide confidence, convenience, and immediacy for their customers and suppliers. They recognize the importance of coordinating exchange and the need to develop effective supplier and distributor networks, and they provide their customers and suppliers with superior transaction services. In short, market makers do what it takes to win their markets.

Who should read this book? Entrepreneurs, CEOs, and venture capitalists will benefit from the new strategic framework presented here. Managers, marketers, investors, strategy consultants, strategy researchers, and management students will find valuable information about how leading companies win their markets.

The book provides a fresh approach to management strategy based on a novel framework. Rather than simply focusing on jockeying for position in product markets, I look at the firm as a bridge between its customers and its suppliers of capital, services, manufactured inputs, and technology. Market makers succeed by building the most effective market bridges, that is, by continually developing innovative transactions. They become the focal point of the industry they serve.

Customers and suppliers benefit from the competitive activities of the market makers. Companies win their markets by delivering superior performance. The results are lower transaction costs, innovative products and services, and economic growth.

I present a new approach to developing a competitive strategy based on creating and managing a company's markets. Each step in the process is illustrated with a practical application. I examine the experiences of many successful companies that are market makers, as well as some less than successful companies.

This book reflects many years of studying how business works. I draw on what I have learned from my work on regulatory and strategy matters concerning major companies primarily in network industries, including telecommunications, electric power, natural gas pipelines, railroads, airlines, postal services, and petroleum refining.

During twenty years of experience teaching students in economics, law, and management, I have been able to test and refine some of the ideas presented here on my outstanding students at the J. L. Kellogg Graduate School of Management at Northwestern University, among others. I am grateful to Dean Donald P. Jacobs and Academic Dean Dipak Jain for their support and encouragement.

I thank my editor Mary Glenn at McGraw-Hill for believing in this project and for her expert help in seeing it through to fruition.

This book is dedicated to my wonderful wife, Susan. I also thank Rachelle, Aaron, and Benjamin for their great enthusiasm and pleasant company.

DANIEL F. SPULBER

THE MARKET MAKERS

WINNING MARKETS

INTRODUCTION

Hugh L. McColl Jr., a former marine, joined what became North Carolina National Bank as a trainee in 1959. As the bank grew, McColl advanced as well, becoming chairman and CEO of NCNB in 1983. He then surprised established market leaders by rapidly changing NCNB from a small regional bank into the powerful NationsBank Corp., with over $280 billion in assets, making it the third largest bank in the U.S. by the late 1990s.

Beginning with the acquisition of First Republic Bank in Texas in 1988 and continuing through the successful purchase of C&S Sovram Corp. in 1991, Bank South in 1995, and Boatmen's Bancshares and Barnett Banks in 1997, McColl grew the Charlotte-based bank into a superregional and then a national bank. McColl, who has been called "America's most ambitious banker," described his vision to shareholders: "We intend to build the nation's preeminent banking company." For over three decades he has pursued the same objectives: "To build leadership positions in the markets and businesses in which we choose to compete and to matter in the lives of our customers and communities."[1]

The head of NationsBank's corporate and investment banking division, F. William Vandiver Jr., summarized McColl's approach by saying, "What you learn in the military is your mission and your men."[2] A consummate competitor, McColl stressed strategy and personnel as he challenged Citicorp and Chase Manhattan for leadership in investment banking.

What are the secrets of the NationsBank success story? First, McColl competes to win. His objective is for NationsBank to win the banking market. Growing through innovative deals, underpricing, and acquisition, McColl has said that "if you stop growing, you die." NationsBank has built a vast network of branch banks and ranks third in total assets among commercial banks, as well as third in loans to big companies.

Second, NationsBank is a market maker, acting as the primary intermediary in a large number of financial markets. As McColl puts it, "Our goal is for our corporate clients to think of NationsBank whenever they face a major financial decision or need an innovative financial solution."[3] The bank is not only in banking for consumers, small businesses, and big businesses, but is entering into stock and bond underwriting and, through its purchase of Chicago Research and Trading, is tackling the market for derivatives.

Third, NationsBank understands the importance of convenience and transaction costs for its customers. Hugh McColl told company shareholders that "our customers are telling us their lives are more complicated than ever. So we are making banking easier," with a network of banking centers in more convenient locations, extended hours, Internet and phone connections, and increased advice and information.[4]

NationsBank has built an organization that provides incentives to its managers and employees for taking necessary action to win markets. The firm provides the information management required to support the bank's market-making activities. Hugh McColl follows the policy of "investing heavily in technology today—so we will still be winning tomorrow."[5]

This success story and many others like it illustrate important principles that I believe can be learned and applied by every company. The key is in devising a successful strategy not simply to maximize short-run profits, but to *win markets*. I explain in this book why winning markets is important enough to be the sole corporate objective. Firms compete to win. They must strive to be the best in their markets. Maximizing shareholder value in itself cannot be the corporation's primary objective. If the firm is successful, the capital markets will take that success into account. Thus, winning markets maximizes the long-run value of the firm.

Many companies have already recognized the fundamental transformation in the global economy that has resulted in increased competition in domestic and international markets. Competitive pressures are forcing companies to pursue ever greater cost efficiencies, to continually improve their production processes, and to speed up the pace of product innovation.

Companies are taking advantage of rapid progress in information processing and telecommunications to create an information economy. The economy is undergoing an information revolution even greater in scope than the industrial revolution. Advances in information processing are altering the shape of organizations, leading to drastic reductions in the size of the central office and to decentralization of authority within the hierarchy. Companies are empowering their employees by pushing decision making and the knowledge required to carry it out further down the corporate ranks. At the same time, they are flattening organizations, slashing layers of middle managers and knocking down functional walls.

Companies are also changing the way they do business, carrying out fewer functions in-house, relying more and more on outsourcing of everything from manufacturing to human resource management. Many have documented the rapid rise of services in the economy, from financial markets to information processing. *Fortune* magazine recognized this shift by eliminating the artificial distinction between its lists of industrial and service corporations. Companies can no longer think of themselves simply as producers of products or suppliers of specialized services. They must develop means of adapting to the pressures of global competition and the accelerating information economy.

How can companies consistently win in their markets? Doing that requires a fundamental change in how companies conceive of their business. New times call for new measures. Companies need to adapt to the evolving business climate by applying strategies that are suited to the challenges ahead. My purpose is to set out a method for developing these strategies.

I demonstrate that firms need to understand their roles as creators and operators of markets. Companies win by building market bridges, that is, by *creating innovative transactions that connect their customers and suppliers.* Using this approach is a significant change from relying on strategies that focus on operations and processes and view the marketplace as an external force beyond a company's control.

In this book, I introduce new types of strategies for winning the market. Adopting these strategies requires rethinking the mission and methods of business. To help companies do this, I introduce a key tool for winning markets that I call the MAIN framework: Market making, Arbitrage, Intermediation, and Networking. Companies succeed by focusing on activities that provide the greatest economic value added. Like NationsBank, successful firms in any industry are *market makers*—they operate the institutions of exchange. They earn economic rents from continually monitoring market forces and then *arbitraging* across markets. They supply *intermediation* services to their customers and suppliers. Finally, companies win markets by creating *networks* of suppliers and distributors. In other words, companies create and manage their markets, earning returns by providing efficient transactions.

Having set up the MAIN framework, I discuss how to apply it to competitive strategy making. I set out four market-entry strategies that are based on the MAIN framework. I then explore indirect methods of competition, through which companies gain strength by serving markets that have been missed by incumbent companies, and finally turn to offensive and defensive strategies for head-to-head competition. Winning markets requires being the best, not only by providing better product quality and lower prices, but by providing more *convenient* service. Convenience means lower transaction costs for the company's customers and suppliers.

I begin this chapter by specifying the goal of the firm: winning markets. Next, I define the basic tool of analysis, the MAIN framework. I then identify novel competitive strategies that are based on market making and other intermediation activities. Finally, I present the outline for the balance of the book.

Winning Markets

We're number one! The excitement that comes with victory is the driving force of business. The desire to win motivates managers and employees and keeps everyone's attention focused on a common goal. Competing to win leads the firm's personnel to make the extra effort required to achieve success in the marketplace. The pressure of fierce competition stimulates innovation, improving product quality and productive efficiency.

Winning markets means that the firm creates and operates the institutions of exchange. The company creates value by making the market through its pricing and coordination activities. The successful firm realizes its role as an intermediary, providing valuable information and coordination services. By continually creating innovative transactions, the firm earns arbitrage profits. The market winner establishes an effective network of suppliers and customers. Formulating a winning strategy begins with building market bridges. Winning markets also means that firms pursue a growth strategy, entering or creating new markets.

Unfortunately, the winning approach of companies like NationsBank has been rejected on many occasions by many companies seeking a quick fix for their current problems. Amid the global competition of the 1980s and the recessionary climate of the early 1990s many companies turned their attention away from effective competitive strategy making and focused instead on operations, busy with downsizing and slashing costs. Many of these companies gave little consideration to their personnel and sacrificed employees through layoffs and the hiring of temps. Although cost efficiency is a necessary part of competition, some companies pursued earnings through retrenchment rather than through growth.

Those companies consolidated around their core competencies, stressing logistics, operations capabilities, engineering, and reengineering. Many companies were benchmarking their rivals, copying their manufacturing and distribution processes. This led to the weakest form of competition, with companies playing follow the leader. Companies were turning inward and revamping their systems. While many companies were reengineering to improve customer service, others become infatuated with acquiring information technology rather than applying advances in computers and communication to the needs of their customers and suppliers.

Many of the downsizing companies were becoming lean and mean to compete more effectively. But others were pursuing less lofty goals, such as short-run profit maximization or manipulating results to improve quarterly financial data. Other managers sought the quiet life, continuing business as usual simply because the company's standard operating procedures had been successful in the less competitive markets of the past. Some firms focused on survival: simply trying to stay in business, minimizing costs, taking few risks, and avoiding the creative strategies that are essential to success. For these companies, the most effective way to cut costs would be to go out of business altogether.

Business has always been guided by the maxim, "Nothing ventured, nothing gained." Winning markets requires aggressive investment and growth. Low costs are not the solution for every situation, and cost cutting cannot replace a winning market strategy.

There is no doubt that state-of-the-art streamlining of operations is important, even essential, to staying competitive. But corporate cost cutting becomes a problem when it causes companies to sacrifice their competitive edge and employee relations. Downsizing will not win markets. Announcing massive layoffs, hiring temps, and continuing with a losing market strategy will destroy management–employee relations and hurt employee morale. It is true in competition as in warfare: Battles might be won with the best logistics, but winning the war requires a strategy for victory and troops with high morale.

Any manager can use the strategies set out in this book to articulate a winning vision of the future. The successful manager need not be an entrepreneur starting up a new venture. Established firms can often benefit from adopting innovative strategies to connect markets. Generally, the Chief Executive Officer (CEO) of the firm is the advocate of an innovative vision. By reviewing and coordinating the activities of the firm as a whole, the CEO repeatedly encounters the challenge of defining the nature of the business. In charting the future course of the business, the CEO must continually formulate innovative strategies to connect markets.

Division managers can bring the strengths of winning strategies to their day-to-day management problems as well as to medium- and long-term strategic planning. The increasing interest in innovation and creativity within large organizations has led to intrapreneurial strategies that use the entrepreneurial approach to start up new ventures within those firms.

Successful intrapreneuring can reinvigorate established firms and make them better competitors.

Market winners outperform competitors along multiple dimensions, including market share, profitability, and shareholder value. Firms achieve success not only by offering better prices and products, but also by reducing the costs of transactions for their customers and suppliers.

The Drive to Win

What is the objective of the firm? The answer is deceptively simple. Companies compete to *win markets.* Companies must strive not simply for excellence, but to be the best in their markets. A more difficult question is how to translate the desire to win into successful strategies and effective tactics. By understanding how to become market makers, firms can devise successful strategies for winning their markets.

Winning a market means that a single firm has significant control over market-making activities. The control a firm gains through effective intermediation gives the firm market power that generates economic rents. Moreover, there are significant economic benefits from having a centralized marketplace. The firm that wins the market earns some of the economic rents arising from centralization. The value of winning markets thus includes returns both to market power and to market centralization.

The thrill of winning markets can stimulate a firm's personnel to further efforts to stay on top, and at the same time the disappointment of defeat can sometimes lead rivals to redouble their efforts. To most managers the objective of winning markets is obvious and not worthy of further discussion. But many managers focus on other goals, including maximizing one's salary and perks, achieving personal power, avoiding conflict or criticism, and maintaining an orderly routine. Some managers are simply complacent, seeking comfort in other measures of corporate performance or choosing to free-ride on the past successes of the firm. However, firms that rest on their laurels soon find that aggressive competitors are prepared to overtake them as market leaders.

Most top managers are driven to win. Listen to Robert Crandall, Chairman and CEO of AMR Corporation, parent company of American Airlines: "I haven't had any fun for the last three years. It's no fun to be confronted with negative trends and to have to say negative things. I work like hell all year and at the end of the year we have a big loss. That makes me a loser. Nobody likes being a loser. So the answer is it's no fun."[6] Crandall, one of the toughest competitors around, found himself facing aggressive, lower-cost competitors like Southwest Airlines as his $20 billion growth strategy failed to turn a profit in the early 1990s.

In the arts and entertainment, the notion of winning is ever present. Musicians try to record a number one hit song and musicals and plays vie for the longest run at the theater. Film makers seek to be tops at the box office and authors look at their ranking or length of time on the best-seller list. Artists compete for Oscars, Tonys, Pulitzers, and a host of other prizes.

There is certainly no doubt about the objective in sports. As the great football coach Vince Lombardi observed, "Winning is not a sometime thing, it's an all-the-time thing." In any sport, athletes strive to win each point, each game, each tournament. Silver and bronze Olympic medalists are justly proud of their impressive achievements, but the objective is always the gold medal. From the National Basketball Association playoffs to the Masters golf tournament to the Superbowl, the ultimate goal is always to be number one.

In international relations and even in war, with its most tragic of consequences, the objective of countries is winning as well. Countries seek to dominate their neighbors, their regions, or broader spheres of influence. Economic rivalries between nations continue to stall cooperative efforts to achieve large markets, such as the common market.

Winning is the sole objective in business, just as it is in sports and international relations. Companies marshall a variety of organizational and market strategies to outdo their rivals, striving to offer their customers the best products and services while earning the greatest returns for their investors.

Some management strategists maintain that winning should not be the firm's objective. They stress the dangers to the firm from all-out competition. They worry that to outperform competitors the firm may take unnecessary risks that might jeopardize its earnings or even its survival. Some analysts are concerned that the pursuit of market dominance will lead firms to compete solely on price or to squander shareholder funds on unnecessary investments that do not add economic value. Others say that the will to win is simply a cultural bias stemming from social pressures to excel or an inappropriate goal transplanted from sports. Many condemn the urge to win as an unfortunate extension of military objectives into the business world. But as we will see, military strategy is an essential part of the manager's planning process.

Those who argue against competing to win are not giving managers useful advice. The manager who is concerned with the firm's sales, profits, or product quality in isolation from competitors will soon be out of business, because the firm will face rivals whose concerns are not nearly so myopic. Companies are increasingly benchmarking the best practices in product quality and cost efficiency. These aggressive competitors will soon capture the market share of firms that operate in splendid, but mistaken, isolation.

The drive to win is much more than competition for its own sake. There are many advantages to be derived from winning markets that reinforce the overriding value of this objective. The winning firm achieves recognition by its customers, suppliers, and investors. Recognition as the market leader creates additional sales that further enhance the firm's market position. Recognition by suppliers enhances cooperative agreements and can lead to favorable contract terms. Investors support successful market leaders through their willingness to supply funds for growth at lower cost. Of course a market winner becomes the preferred target of its competitors and must continually renew its efforts to stay on top. Yet, an innovative market leader is able to set product and service standards and to influence the rules of the game.

Setting the Target

How is winning defined? It is common to identify the winning firm as the firm with the highest sales revenue in a given market. Winning firms include Boeing in aerospace, Coca-Cola in beverages, Du Pont in chemicals, Citicorp in commercial banking, General Electric in electrical equipment, Wal-Mart in retailing, Columbia/HCA in health care, Exxon in petroleum, Alcoa in metals, Procter & Gamble in soaps, or Johnson & Johnson in pharmaceuticals. Winning companies also include niche players that are leaders in their market segment, from the corner drugstore to the consulting boutique. Comparing sales revenue is not enough, however, to define the winners.

Is the biggest firm necessarily the best? Many will object that this sort of winning, that is, achieving the largest market share, is not the best measure of performance and indeed provides little reliable information about performance. Performance can be measured in various ways, including profits, market value of the firm, assets, and rate of growth in sales, profits, market value, or assets.

It is well known that there may in some cases be a trade-off between market share and profits. If there is a trade-off between size and performance, which should the firm's managers choose? While size is certainly an important indicator of success, other performance measures are important as well.[7]

Having the greatest market share is no guarantee of good performance. For example, a number of years ago, the largest computer and office equipment company, IBM, with $65 billion in sales, posted losses of almost $5 billion while smaller companies in computer hardware and software were profitable. In one year, the largest U.S. tire maker, Goodyear Tire, had almost $12 billion in sales and over $650 million in losses, while Cooper Tire and Rubber earned $43 million on sales of about $1.2 billion. At the same time, the largest airlines, American and United, recorded about $14.5 billion and $12.9 billion in sales revenue respectively and almost a billion dollars in losses each; while up-and-coming Southwest Airlines, with sales revenue of only $1.68 billion, earned over $100 million in profits. Even as

United Airlines became profitable, Southwest Airlines, at one-fifth its size, earned more than three times its profits.

Management's objective is not simply to win by a dollar, although that is often enough to claim market leadership. The objective is to win decisively, to attain and sustain a dominant market share, and to be recognized as the leader. Winning is a multidimensional concept. The winning firm must outperform its rivals in organizational efficiency, product quality, innovation, and profitability. But winning does not stop even there. Companies strive for sustainable competitive advantage, outperforming rivals year after year. Good performance also means expanding the company's markets and seeking and creating new markets. Growth is part of winning performance.

NationsBank continually redefined its mission. It grew from a local bank to a regional, a superregional, and finally a national bank. Having attained that status, it sought to transform itself into a financial services marketplace.

Winning markets is a long-term objective since generally, the winning firm earns the greatest profits in its market. The firm earning the greatest profits over time maximizes the value of the firm for its shareholders while providing outstanding service to its customers. Winning markets ultimately means creating greater economic value than other companies in the industry.

Wal-Mart Stores, the leading retailer with over $100 billion in retail sales, is also the profit leader with over $3 billion in profits, far higher than second-place Sears. The market value of Wal-Mart, at over $65 billion, is more than three times that of Sears. In retailing, Wal-Mart has not only overtaken Sears but continues to grow substantially beyond the size of Sears while earning profits that are much greater than Sears'. Wal-Mart's sales are more than triple those of Kmart, but the disparity in profits and market value is even more substantial. Wal-Mart's market value of shares by the mid-1990s was about ten times that of Kmart. The disparity in market value not only reflects the growth potential of Wal-Mart, but the returns that it obtains from its leadership in the retail industry.

Winning markets results from an effective strategy, an efficient organization, and continual innovation. The pursuit of size for its own sake is not generally successful, since size and profits need not be correlated; that is, larger firms may be more or less profitable than smaller firms. However, a successful firm that is more innovative, that attracts more customers, and that operates more efficiently than its rivals will have greater profits, sales revenue, and market value. Size and other performance measures, then, are indicators of the firm's success in winning markets.

Firms strive to achieve a dominant market share, with the ultimate objective of being the primary seller in the market. This objective should not be viewed as being inconsistent with U.S. antitrust laws. Section 2 of the Sherman Act in particular rules out monopolization or attempts to monopolize. But the antitrust laws exist to protect competition, not competitors. Monopolization is prevented by the efforts of competing firms and the continual appearance of new entrants in the absence of governmental or other artificial entry barriers. On the contrary, the antitrust laws set the rules of the game, and rules are necessary to any competition. Vigorous competition is perfectly consistent with the spirit of the antitrust laws. The antitrust laws are not intended to penalize the success that comes from lower prices and innovative products, nor do they penalize firms for the exit of rivals that may be due to the rival firms' complacency, incompetence, or just plain bad luck.

Competition and the will to win are essential to assuring business performance. Competition from its rivals stimulates each firm to improve its products and organization. Consumers are made better off the more intense the competition is. Lower prices, higher quality products, greater variety, better service, and more innovative strategies enhance consumer well-being. The will to win reflects the desire of firms to do the best job for the greatest number of customers. Successful firms generate employment, create opportunities for investors, suppliers, and distributors, and most importantly, provide the best service to their customers.

Building Market Bridges

Winning markets means that a company creates its markets by connecting customers and suppliers and manages its markets by providing efficient transactions. Winning firms are those that customers and suppliers turn to when they want to buy and sell. They are the companies that operate the market mechanism.

The first question that managers ask about their company is, "What business are we in?" Answering this familiar question is one of the most difficult but important tasks faced by managers. Defining the nature of the business is crucial to strategy making and to building a winning organization. What is needed is a method of understanding the firm's activities, its markets, and the types of competitors that it faces. Managers can address this issue in a simple and effective way by applying a fundamental insight: *The firm creates market bridges between its suppliers and its customers.* This approach to strategy making integrates and extends standard analyses of competition and organization.

To win markets, the firm devises the best bridges between its suppliers and its customers. Traditional analyses of strategy and organization stress the firm's products and processes. But thinking of the firm as an intermediary makes it possible to identify a new set of important value-adding activities. This approach is particularly well suited to a growing but highly competitive market in which input and output prices are highly volatile. The firm must act swiftly to earn arbitrage rents.

The market-making approach involves more complex considerations than the firm's marketing channels, which are a useful way to describe the costs and benefits of physical distribution alternatives and manufacturer–wholesaler–retailer relations. Market bridges are not the same thing as the value chain, which is based primarily on internal processes, distribution, value-added manufacturing, and operational efficiencies. Market bridges go beyond basic vertical integration issues such as capturing rent from suppliers and distributors. The market-making approach is a method of strategic analysis designed to generate economic rents.

I call the method of building market bridges the *MAIN framework.* This framework is composed of four basic components:

- Market making
- Arbitrage
- Intermediation
- Networking

To implement the MAIN framework, the firm must first carry out the basic market-making activities. Then the firm applies a number of basic principles to earn arbitrage profits. Further, the firm acts in a variety of ways as an intermediary. Finally, the firm must assess its market networks, both those to which it belongs and those that it wishes to create. These four concepts define the tasks required for building market bridges. Each of the concepts entails a number of steps that are shown in Table 1-1.

Market Making

Firms make the market by creating the institutions of exchange and managing transactions. It is important to emphasize that firms earn profits

Table 1-1.
BUILDING MARKET BRIDGES: THE MAIN FRAMEWORK

Market making	*Arbitrage*	*Intermediation*	*Networking*
Pricing	Spatial	Agent	Suppliers and customers
Market clearing	Dynamic	Broker	Matching and mixing
Coordinating exchange	Risk	Monitor	
Allocating goods and services	Technological	Communicator	Network vs. organizational boundaries

from their market-making activities. The value added by firms reflects not only the transformation of productive inputs into outputs, but also the bringing together of primary suppliers and final customers. The profits earned by manufacturers, wholesalers, and retailers reflect not only a return on production and distribution investment but also the returns to complex intermediation activities. Thus, a clothing manufacturer engaged in fairly standard manufacturing may earn high rents from intermediation between designers and retailers. The profits from manufacturing and distribution are entangled with the returns to managing transactions.

Of the wide range of effective market-making strategies, the firm's four primary market-making actions include:

■ Price setting

■ Market clearing

■ Coordinating exchange

■ Allocating goods and services

Successful firms create value through market making. Intermediation between customers and suppliers often is the primary economic activity of firms, whether they are merchants or manufacturers. Companies coordinate input purchases, production, distribution, and output sales. Most significantly, firms manage trading activities, often setting both output prices and input prices. Certainly, one cannot enter a store or view an advertisement without observing that firms post prices. Furthermore, both large and small companies bid for capital, labor, manufactured inputs, resources, and technology. By setting both the ask prices for their outputs and the bid prices for their inputs, firms centralize trade, clear markets, and establish relative prices across the economy. Comdisco set up a rental and resale market in IBM mainframes and grew into a $2 billion computer company. Markets are created and operated through the price-setting activities of firms.

Consider, for example, the aptly named supermarket. A supermarket chain might sell as many as 50,000 to 70,000 different items. A single large supermarket chain buys from thousands of suppliers and sells to millions of customers. The supermarket sets prices on all of its products, often varying the prices across each of its retail outlets and changing many prices on a weekly or even a daily basis. In addition, the supermarket chain sets many bid prices on the products that it purchases, through negotiations with manufacturers as well as suppliers of its house brands. A supplier to the supermarket can sell a high volume of its output by dealing only with a single buyer. Imagine in contrast the high cost of marketing and sales that would be incurred by a manufacturer of cookies if the cookies had to be sold directly to consumers a few boxes at a time. The customer of the supermarket chain also gains tremendously in terms of the costs of transactions. The supermarket's customer has available tens of thousands of items from which to assemble a market basket, without having to seek out thousands of individual sellers to locate the wide variety of foods and packaged goods purchased by the typical consumer.

The profits earned by supermarkets are not simply returns to their warehousing, distribution, and retail facilities. Rather, a supermarket earns returns from reducing the transaction costs of its many suppliers and customers by acting as their intermediary and centralizing exchange. Consider first a market with decentralized exchange in which there are no intermediaries.[8] Suppose that the market has three consumers and three suppliers. Since there are no intermediaries, if each customer contacts each supplier there will be nine contractual relationships, as shown in Figure 1-1. In general, with N consumers and M suppliers, the total number of contractual relationships required to connect each consumer with each supplier is obtained by multiplying $N \times M$.

Figure 1-1.
EXCHANGE WITHOUT AND WITH AN INTERMEDIARY

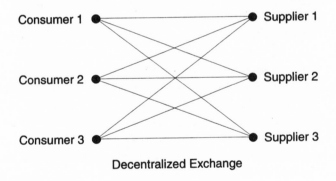

Decentralized Exchange

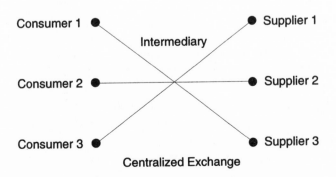

Centralized Exchange

Now suppose that an intermediary such as a retailer or wholesaler is introduced that carries each supplier's product and serves each consumer. Then exchange is centralized and only three contractual relationships are needed for consumers and three for suppliers, for a total of six (see Figure 1-1). In general, with N consumers and M suppliers, the total number of relationships required to connect each consumer and each supplier with the intermediary is obtained by adding $N + M$. If the cost of providing such market linkages were one dollar in each case, the intermediary would reduce transaction costs by $9 - $6 = $3. Generally speaking, the intermediary reduces transaction costs by $N \times M - (N + M)$ dollars.

This is the same logic that drives other well-known hub-and-spoke savings. Telephone companies have long known that the costs of telephone lines could be reduced by connecting calls through a central exchange, with a higher utilization of each line. The airlines discovered the benefits of the hub-and-spoke system after deregulation. Rather than offering direct flights connecting all pairs of cities served by the airlines, the airlines could serve the same number of cities with a smaller number of flights, in the process increasing the number of passengers per flight and increasing the airline's profit. The same benefit is present in intermediation. Not only is there a saving in the number of channels but the degree of channel utilization is increased. In our example of decentralized exchange, each channel carries only one transaction between a consumer and a supplier. With intermediation, each channel to a supplier carries three units of the supplier's product (one for each consumer) and similarly each channel to each consumer carries three products (one from each supplier).

The discussion of market centralization illustrates how the intermediary saves transaction costs. In addition, the importance of winning markets can be illustrated. Suppose that there are two intermediaries in the example, with three consumers and three suppliers. Then, if each of the intermediaries connects each supplier to each consumer, the number of relationships doubles to twelve and there are no clear savings in transaction costs from intermediation, unless there are more consumers and suppliers.[9] The point is that having a single intermediary saves transaction costs for the marketplace as compared to having two or more intermediaries. The situation with multiple intermediaries is best understood as an intermediate case of partial decentralization of exchange, lying somewhere between fully decentralized exchange and fully centralized exchange. The firm that wins the market by outperforming others can earn additional profits as a return to the savings from reducing the number of relationships and utilizing the firm's market bridge to a higher degree.

By their input purchasing activities and their product marketing and sales activities, firms reduce the costs of transactions for the economy. It is costly for buyers to search for products that will satisfy their needs and to search for the seller offering the lowest price for a specific product. It is also very costly for suppliers to search for customers for their products. The Nobel laureate George Stigler recognized that because the efficiency of personal search is low for both buyers and sellers, there arises a need for specialized traders, such as used car dealers, that provide centralization of trading activity. What he may not have realized is that trading activities are often the primary activities of most firms.

The intermediary makes the market not only by establishing a central marketplace but by carrying out the transactions needed to clear the market. The firm's market-making activities include establishing prices, matching buyers and sellers, and gathering and communicating information about prices, products, and consumer requirements. Firms operate markets just as specialists on the NYSE set prices and earn profits from the spread. The firm that wins the market can earn profits by centralizing and coordinating market exchange. These activities will be discussed at greater length in later chapters.

Arbitrage

Building effective market bridges allows the firm to achieve what I call an arbitrage advantage. This forms the basis of the firm's market-making and intermediation activities and is the source of the firm's economic rent. Innovative management strategy applies and extends the basic approach of arbitrage: buying goods and services in one market and reselling them in another. To arbitrage effectively, the firm must have better market information, it must be able to quickly respond to opportunities as they develop, and it must execute exchanges efficiently with lower transaction costs than competitors.

The four basic types of arbitrage allow profit making based on recognizing and taking advantage of price differences arising between markets separated by:

- Space
- Time
- Uncertainty
- Technology

Most competitive activities involve some combination of these types of arbitrage. The value added by a firm is reflected in its market-making activities both upstream and downstream, and in the ways in which productive inputs are combined to address customer needs in downstream markets.

Arbitrage activities make markets work. To carry out arbitrage successfully, a firm must obtain high-quality information about its upstream suppliers and about its downstream customers. Arbitrage requires discerning new opportunities for purchasing and selling goods and services. Through information-gathering, communication, and price-setting activities, firms provide competitive outlets for suppliers and competitive sources of products for customers. Arbitrage activities establish market prices and improve efficiency in the allocation of goods and services. Successful firms recognize the important function of arbitrage in their strategic planning.

Intermediation

In addition to market-making activities, companies provide an important but complex set of intermediation services, acting as:

- Agent
- Monitor
- Broker
- Communicator

These four roles highlight the role of the firm as a bridge between its suppliers and its customers. All these activities are based on information.

Contractual relationships in which one party acts under the delegated authority of another are referred to as principal–agent contracts. The agent can act as a go-between, representing the interests of the principal in interaction with third parties. Companies are often agents for others, acting for individuals or other companies. Wholesale and retail distributors are agents for the manufacturers whose products they offer. Suppliers of products and services often act as agents for manufacturers. Franchise owners act as agents of the franchise company. Many types of companies act as agents for their consumers, including travel agencies, law firms, and accounting firms. In most of these transactions the agent acts as an intermediary. Information plays a crucial role here since it is costly to write complete contingent contracts with agents. Moreover, the principal may not be able to observe the actions or characteristics of the company acting as an agent. This means that rents accrue from being a "good agent," by building a reputation for performance and by communicating information effectively to actual and potential principals.

Companies also intermediate between principals and agents by acting as monitors. The monitor supervises the performance of the agent and acts under the delegated authority of the principal. For example, banks supervise the performance of borrowers, acting as delegated monitors for their lenders. Mutual funds representing investors monitor the activities of the companies whose securities they hold, often taking an active role on the board or in shareholder meetings. Companies are monitors of their own managers and employees, representing the interests of their customers and their investors. The returns to monitoring are based on the efficiency of consolidating monitoring activities.

Companies function as brokers by helping buyers and sellers negotiate contracts and transactions. Contract negotiation is a costly and time-consuming process. It is further complicated by asymmetries in information, when buyers are imperfectly informed about products, prices, and seller characteristics, and sellers are imperfectly informed about buyer preferences and income. This situation can lead to a failure to realize what may be substantial economic rents. A broker, by managing the negotiation, can help buyers and sellers to complete transactions that would not otherwise have occurred. For example, an art dealer who negotiates separately with artists and customers increases the number of exchanges. Similar roles are played by real estate brokers, who not only help buyers and sellers find each other but also participate actively in their negotiations.

Finally, firms function as communicators through marketing and sales, purchasing, hiring and financing, and research activities. The convergence of computers and telecommunications that created the data superhighway has increased our recognition of the crucial place of information in the economy. I have already noted that companies operate the institutions of exchange as market makers. Companies are now beginning to realize that they are important producers and consumers of information.

Networking

Consider the manager's assessment and establishment of market networks. The following simple exercise is very useful for recognizing the role of a firm as a market maker and intermediary. First, divide a sheet of paper into three columns. In the first column list all of the firm's actual and potential suppliers. Then list all of the firm's actual and potential customers or main customer groups in the third column. Now identify the key inputs that are essential to its final product. For a wholesaler or retailer, the key inputs must include the products that are purchased and resold. For a manufacturer, the key inputs depend on whether the firm's activities are labor, capital, or technology intensive. Then, in the middle column, identify how the key inputs are brought to the firm's customers by listing the firm's key market-making activities including pricing, marketing, production, inventory control, and research and development. (See Table 1-2.) If possible, draw lines connecting customers and suppliers through the firm's activities to show the current bridges.

This diagram provides a basic framework for asking what activities of the firm are creating value. What am I adding to the basic products and services of my key suppliers? Would suppliers and customers be better off if they were to transact directly without my help? Can I connect my suppliers and customers in a more efficient way? Could another firm connect my suppliers to my customers in a better way? Are there some supplier products and services that I am currently bringing to one group of customers but not to others to whom they might be of value? Are there customers that I am currently not serving that could benefit from being connected to my suppliers' products and services? Should some of the suppliers be replaced by in-house activities? Similarly, should some customers acting as distributors be replaced by in-house activities? Are there better ways of developing alliances or contracting with my key customers and suppliers?

Table 1-2.
A MARKET BRIDGE DIAGRAM

Supplier 1	Market-making activity 1	Customer group 1
Supplier 2	Market-making activity 2	Customer group 2
Supplier 3	Market-making activity 3	Customer group 3

Identifying the firm's key suppliers may not be a simple task. It is important to identify all of the firm's external sources of finance, including bank loans, equities, bonds, supplier credit, and so on. Next, list the firm's sources of labor services, including the types of employees the firm has, for example temporary service professionals. This can be simplified by generally identifying the types of skills that the firm's personnel has or should have and noting the traditional recruiting methods of the firm. Then, list all of the firm's suppliers of goods and services and the types of purchases made by the firm. Finally, specify the sources of the firm's technology base including licenses, R&D activities, and other sources of the firm's knowledge even if not purchased.

The customer groups served by the company should be defined in terms of their demand characteristics, rather than by the products or services they receive. At the simplest level, the customer groups may be defined in terms of their income, geographic location, or other attributes, such as residential, commercial, or industrial customers. At a more complicated level, the customers should be identified by the types of benefits they derive from the use of the company's products and services.

As a means of simplifying the problem, it is helpful to classify the firm's markets into four categories:

- Finance
- Labor
- Products
- Technology

Finance refers to all forms of financial instruments and assets including loans, insurance, securities, and financial contracts. Labor denotes all types of labor services, managerial, technical, clerical, and production. Products refers broadly to all manufactured goods, services, natural resources, and land. Finally, technology represents all scientific and technical inputs applied by the firm, from basic research to applied business information. These four categories allow a classification of firms in terms of the types of markets that are bridged by their activities. Companies are said to *match* markets if their primary networks are within the same category. Companies *mix* markets if their primary networks cross categories.

Thus, there are four basic types of matching companies. Financial intermediaries include banks, securities brokers, insurance companies, and mutual funds. Labor intermediaries provide temporary workers and specialized services from accounting, legal, and medical professionals. Product intermediaries include all wholesale and retail firms. Finally, technological intermediaries encompass basic research labs, high-tech entrepreneurs, software providers, and other information suppliers.

Manufacturers are the largest group of firms whose bridging activities mix markets. By highlighting important input markets, production processes can be distinguished on the basis of whether they are capital, labor, product, or technology intensive. For example, electric power production is capital intensive; some parts of the textile industry are labor intensive; the chemical processing or computer assembly industries are product intensive; the biotech industry is technology intensive.

A key to building market bridges is to create transactions that link customers and suppliers in new ways. By maintaining product quality and process efficiency, the firm can continue to link existing suppliers and customers. Process innovations are often required to link new types of suppliers with the firm's existing customers. Product innovations are generally needed to link existing suppliers with new customers, while both product and process innovations allow new suppliers to be linked with new customers. These relationships are summarized in Table 1-3. In a dynamic industry, companies continually seek new crossing points between suppliers and customers, as rivals imitate their existing market bridges.

Table 1-3.
INNOVATIVE TRANSACTIONS

Upstream:	Existing suppliers	New suppliers
Downstream:		
Existing customers	Product quality and process efficiency	Process innovation
New customers	Product innovation	Product and process innovation

The insight gained from this perspective is that the firm's market network relationships are at least as important as its organizational structure and internal management. These relationships can be formal contracts, informal working partnerships, or strategic alliances. The relationships a company forges with its suppliers and customers are the source of its added value. This insight needs to be integrated into management strategy. The company must decide which activities should be carried out internally and which should be undertaken in cooperation with the suppliers and distributors. Therefore, the company chooses between extending its organization or further developing its market network.

Strategic recommendations generally fall into two groups: one that views the firm as a merchant and the other, as a manufacturer. These one-dimensional perspectives lead to ineffective strategies. A company that sees itself in these simple terms cannot be poised to win markets.

Much competitive strategy emphasizes the company's marketing activities. The company is seen as engaging in clever pricing and product differentiation maneuvers in its output market. Often, the company's supplier relationships and those of its competitors are neglected. Simply stressing the firm's competitive strategy as a marketer of output will not be effective if a competitor can deliver the same or better products through an end run to the firm's suppliers or through a discovery of superior sources of supply.

Along with corporate downsizing, a great deal of strategic analysis has focused on process reengineering, which stressed the company's manufacturing function. Focusing solely on the firm's production processes is problematic as well, since even the best products will not yield high returns if the firm does not have high-quality customer and supplier relationships. The firm's market-making services can be as important as its manufacturing. The company wins the market by being the best at managing purchasing and sales, setting prices, carrying out a system of payments, and keeping accounts of transactions. The firm stands ready to purchase from its suppliers and to sell to its customers, maintaining inventories and gathering and communicating market information. The market-bridge view provides strategic insights because it integrates the company's merchant and manufacturing roles in a general framework.

The firm seeking to win markets must continually push out its boundaries, extending the size of its organization and its market network. Expansion is carried out through a combination of internal growth, contracts, strategic alliances, and mergers. Market bridges provide a means of evaluating and selecting among the alternative ways to grow.

Market Strategy

Standard analyses of competitive strategy usually restrict their attention to product-market contests. In contrast, I suggest that the firm should view its competition as creators of alternative market bridges. In other words, the company uses its *transactions* to compete against all the other ways that buyers and sellers can interact. Some will argue that advantages gained from these innovative strategies are not sustainable in the face of imitation by competitors. Yet, these strategies provide methods for staying ahead of the game.

Who are the firm's competitors? The competition can be buyers and sellers meeting and transacting directly with each other. The competition can be organized exchanges, from flea markets all the way to organized financial markets. Finally, the competition can be other companies supplying similar economic transactions. Therefore, competition means much more than manufacturing a better widget. It means carrying out the entire set of economic transactions needed to make and distribute that widget.

In the four chapters in Part II, I present a gallery of competitive strategies. The foundation for these strategies is the MAIN framework. By recognizing the importance of market making, arbitrage, intermediation, and networking, firms can devise new competitive strategies. My analysis also draws upon insights from game theory, military strategy, and management strategy. Market strategy augments and extends well-known competitive strategies.

Corporate strategy involves the determination of what markets to enter and exit. The company's market strategies specify how to effect the company's entry plans. The focus of strategy has often been on short-term competitive tactics in the product markets. These tactics include pricing, marketing, sales efforts, product differentiation, and product innovation. While tactical advantage is important, I believe that long-term success is achieved by looking at the company's relationships in *both* supplier and customer markets. A winning strategy requires connecting markets in innovative ways.

I present a new set of competitive strategies by applying the MAIN framework. I set out strategies in the following categories:

- Entry strategies
- Indirect strategies
- Offensive and defensive strategies

First we will consider entry strategies. By considering the costs of creating and managing markets, it is possible to discern four basic forms of market entry. These forms show that it is shortsighted for the firm to look only at the product market, since it is vulnerable to a variety of more complicated attacks. The four strategies for competitive market entry are:

- Go-between

- Bring-together
- Bypass
- Connect

The company competes by lowering market transaction costs. Pursuing the go-between strategy, the firm competes with direct transactions between buyers and sellers, offering them the convenience and lower costs of centralized exchange. Using the bring-together strategy, the company lowers the costs of a fragmented industry by offering the convenience of one-stop shopping. By applying the bypass strategy, the firm leaps over upstream or downstream firms to get closer to customers and suppliers, lowering transaction costs by reducing the complexity of transactions. Using the connect strategy, the firm expands or merges with suppliers or distributors, supplanting organizational allocation for market transactions where the firm's operations can lower costs more effectively than arms-length transactions can.

Next we will focus on indirect strategies, or ways to win markets without incurring the high costs and low returns of direct confrontation. As the firm grows and becomes more successful, head-to-head competition can no longer be avoided. I identify an important secret of success, well known to such firms as Wal-Mart, Southwest Airlines, and NationsBank as well as to military strategists. In some markets, the secret is winning by *indirection*, using the element of surprise by attacking the incumbent's weak points. The firm seeking to win markets should engage in direct competition with a powerful incumbent only when it has the strength and resources to mount an effective challenge. An entrant that engages in direct competition with a strong incumbent without being fully prepared runs a high risk of failure. To win markets, the firm should begin by pursuing markets that the incumbent has ignored, thereby allowing the new entrant to gain experience and to build a substantial customer base.

New entrants can grow substantially and even overtake the incumbent before showing up on their radar screens. Having built up the firm by winning markets where the incumbent is not present, the new entrant will be toughened and ready for direct competition with the incumbent firm for its markets. Companies competing head-on with a stronger rival should seek economy of force, maximizing profits by avoiding costly fights and serving market segments where the company provides the greatest added value. An application of this principle is to serve undefended territory, that is, any market segment that is underserved by competitors. Underserved territory is not limited to geographic areas. It includes customer groups whose needs are not being met by existing products and services or who encounter excessive transaction costs in dealing with competing firms.

Two indirect strategies are taking the path of least resistance (serving the markets through innovative transactions) and taking the line of least expectation (relying on the element of surprise, primarily through rapid market response and new products and services).

Turning from indirect to direct strategies, we will look at how a company competes head-on with major rivals. Offensive strategies present both advantages and difficulties and should only be attempted if the firm brings superior organization, technology, and unique customer and supplier relationships to the marketplace. The firm's offensive strategies emerge from the MAIN framework. The firm must outperform competitors as market maker, arbitrageur, intermediary, and networker.

How do firms compete? Companies entering the marketplace or expanding their market share take on established rivals with offensive strategies. Incumbent firms must be prepared with defensive strategies. Defensive strategies involve the ability to deliver a flexible response to competitive entry and to avoid overextending the firm's product and service offerings. Both offensive and defensive strategies require offering customers lower prices, innovative products, greater variety, and superior services. But more is required: Companies must be prepared to provide customers with greater convenience, in the form of more efficient transactions.

As everyone knows, time is money. Economic transactions are costly because they are time-consuming. The costs of delay are twofold. First, consumers and suppliers have opportunity costs; that is, they have other things to do with their time. Second, the benefits of delayed transactions are reduced because those benefits are received later; that is, consumers and suppliers discount future returns. These two costs lie at the heart of competitive strategy. Supplying a better product with delays may do little to address a customer's needs. The customer places a high value on convenience, immediacy, and transactional efficiency. Reducing transaction costs creates value for customers and suppliers. Creating new markets and efficiently managing existing markets are the two essential parts of a successful, winning strategy.

Outline of the Book

The book is organized into three main parts. Part I, Winning Markets, includes this introductory chapter and a second chapter, The Value of Winning. In that chapter, I explain why managers are rightly concerned with being number one. I examine the activity of competing to win and the economic value generated by winning markets. I show that the firm that wins the market achieves incremental earnings through increased recognition. This allows the market leader to achieve market power, reduced risk, and cost economies. Most importantly, the winning firm earns the returns from operating the institutions of exchange. I consider alternative approaches to competition and contrast those ideas with my framework.

In Part II, Building Market Bridges: The MAIN Framework (Chapters 3 to 6), I show how the firm creates value. The chapters examine market making, arbitrage, intermediation, and networking. Companies make markets by pricing, coordinating exchange, clearing the market, and allocating goods and services. I examine how the firm's market-making activities serve to connect markets, and demonstrate that innovative firms succeed by discovering new connections between their upstream and downstream markets. Next I describe the basic types of arbitrage activities that create value.

Companies act as intermediaries between their customers and suppliers, including investors, service providers, and manufacturers. I show that intermediation involves producing and supplying information to the market. Companies remedy information asymmetries by acting as agents, supervisors, and brokers for their customers and suppliers. Finally, I show that companies grow by expanding both their organization and their market networks. I discuss the options for pushing out the boundaries of the firm: scale, scope, span, and speed.

In Part III, Market Strategies (Chapters 7 to 9), I set out the basic elements of the strategies required to win markets. In Chapter 7, I set out four entry strategies that demonstrate how firms compete against alternative forms of market organization. The company can go between buyers and sellers in the market, it can bring together smaller distributors or suppliers through consolidation, it can bypass distributors to reach customers directly, or it can connect with its distributors and suppliers through contracts and alliances. In Chapter 8, I show how companies can follow indirect strategies to serve markets that are being neglected by major rivals. By serving new markets, the firm is able grow without directly confronting powerful rivals. Once the firm achieves the necessary growth, it is able to switch to a direct strategy and compete for the major markets served by its principal rivals. Accordingly, in Chapter 9, I turn to offensive and defensive strategies based on the MAIN framework.

Companies outdo their competitors by innovative market making. They make the best use of market information to gain the arbitrage advantage. They provide superior intermediation services. Finally, they create competitive market networks. Chapters 3 to 6 present strategies for building market bridges. Chapters 7 to 9 apply these concepts to the design of competitive strategies for winning markets.

Endnotes

1. NationsBank Corporation Annual Report, 1996.
2. Some of the information about NationsBank is drawn from Saul Hansell, "Taking on the Behemoths of Finance," *New York Times*, Sunday July 18, 1993, p. 1, sec. 3; Martha

Brannigan, "Coming on Strong," *Wall Street Journal*, January 28, 1992, p.1; and "Super Banker," *Business Week*, July 15, 1991, pp. 116–120.

3. NationsBank Corporation Annual Report, 1996.

4. Chief Executive's Report to Shareholders, St. Louis, MO, April 23, 1997.

5. Chief Executive's Report to Shareholders, St. Louis, MO, April 23, 1997.

6. The quotation is from S.D. Solomon, "The Bully of the Skies Cries Uncle," *New York Times Magazine*, September 5, 1993, p. 13.

7. There are of course many measurement issues. For example, winning can be measured in terms of the greatest number of units sold, although comparisons across firms become problematical since there are differences in product characteristics and prices across firms. Moreover, substantial discounting could boost units sold without necessarily increasing sales revenue. Therefore, the value of sales is the generally accepted measure of size. Sales revenues vary considerably over the year so that discrepancies in how firms record revenues can lead to different estimates of sales.

There are many thorny issues in defining the market. Should it be local, regional, national, or international? Should the market be defined by product characteristics, by the services that the product provides, by broad classes of product types? It is very easy to justify practically any basis for defining the market and as a result the definitions of markets can be quite arbitrary, particularly when too narrow a specification is used. The definition of the market should generally be as inclusive as possible, identifying potential entrants and product substitutes. Defining a company's market is one of the most important tasks faced by its managers, and a growing company is continually redefining the nature and extent of its markets.

8. The returns from centralization are recognized in marketing channels; see particularly W. Alderson, "Factors Governing the Development of Marketing Channels," in R. M. Clewett, ed., *Marketing Channels for Manufactured Products*, Homewood, IL: Irwin, 1954; and L. W. Stern and A.I. El-Ansary, *Marketing Channels*, Englewood Cliffs, NJ: Prentice-Hall, 1988.

9. With the same number of consumers and suppliers, savings only begin to be realized with five consumers and five suppliers.

THE VALUE **2** OF WINNING

Northwestern University's football coach, Gary Barnett, turned around a program that had long been in the basement of college football, eventually "taking the purple to Pasadena" to play in the Rose Bowl. Barnett inspired his players to continually outdo themselves and showed a genuine concern for their academic performance. A brilliant strategist, his quiet confidence is summed up by his motto: "Expect victory." Successful companies also need to expect victory, devising competitive strategies to win in the marketplace.

Why try to win markets? One compelling reason is that your firm's competitors are doing everything they can to win your markets for themselves. It is the law of the jungle at work: Eat or be eaten. A firm may need to pursue a winning strategy just to have a chance at survival. This applies whether the firm is a successful incumbent or a new entrant.

The traditional recommendation is to maximize the present discounted value of profits, or equivalently to maximize the value of the firm. The question is: How do you know if the actions you have taken have indeed maximized profit? The potential profit of an enterprise is unknown, and in fact, unknowable. Unlike a textbook problem, whose answer is given in the back of the book, the solution to the profit-maximizing problem is a mystery. Clearly, faced with any two specifically defined options, the manager should obviously choose the most profitable alternative. However, the manager cannot know, either in advance or after the fact, whether all possible choices were considered and whether the best choices were made. Faced with this quandary, the only solution is to find a yardstick, which is the performance of other firms. This is why managers try to outperform other firms in their markets in every respect, not just in profitability.

I am asking a more fundamental question, however. Why is winning markets the overriding objective of a firm and its competitors? The answer is that there are additional returns from being the winning firm. It is these incremental returns that justify the investment and risk-taking needed to win. Outperforming rivals brings a host of additional benefits to the company and its shareholders, so the value-maximizing firm will try to win markets. For the same reason, the firm should anticipate that its existing and potential rivals are also trying to win markets. Therefore, firms must compete to win.

This chapter examines the value of winning markets. I identify the significant benefits the firm obtains from market leadership. Winning markets yields important benefits from customer and supplier recognition, cost economies, intermediation efficiencies, and market power. Conversely, firms achieve success by building on brand reputation, achieving cost economies, being efficient intermediaries, and obtaining market power. Clearly, competition is not generally a winner-take-all process. There may be many profitable firms in an industry, with different firms winning markets from year to year. Many firms in an industry may have valuable brand names, cost economies, and market power. The point is that there are economic returns to competing to win.

The intermediation strategy combines value added with market power. As the market winner, a firm has the most recognized brands, which creates additional consumer demand and incremental revenues. Increased demand for the leader's products and services confers cost advantages. A high market share can create market power for the firm to raise profitability. The market leader can more effectively manage the market by supplying institutions of exchange. The strategic implications of winning markets are of critical importance.

Expansion allows the company to achieve economic gains in terms of additional revenues, reduced risk, and cost economies. These result from pushing out the four boundaries of the firm:

- Scale
- Scope
- Span
- Speed

Scale is the company's rate of output production per unit of time, scope is the range of its products, span is the extent of vertical integration, and speed is its rate of innovation. The company pushes out its boundaries through growth, diversification, vertical integration, and accelerated innovation.

Winning

The 200-meter individual medley (200 IM) is a difficult event in competitive swimming. Swimmers must complete 50 meters each of four different strokes: butterfly, backstroke, breaststroke, and freestyle. The swimmer must have a good deal of endurance due to the distance, as well as proficiency in each stroke, to have a chance at winning the event. Most of all, the swimmer has to be fast. The question is, how fast?

There are no absolutes. To win the race, the swimmer has to be faster than all of the other swimmers present that day. To break records, the swimmer has to beat the pace set by other swimmers in different races. There is no point in telling an athlete to train and improve on technique in order to swim as fast as possible. This is not meaningful. What pace is enough? Swimmers train hard, and put in their best efforts, to outperform the other swimmers in the race. While swimmers keep track of their times to monitor their individual progress, the trophies go to those who win the races.

What may be obvious in swimming is less so in business. What should be the objective of the firm? The economically correct answer is that firms should maximize profits. But there are no absolutes here either. How do you know when the highest profits have been achieved?

Clearly, if the company chooses between two actions, say a high or a low price, it should choose the action that yields the highest profit. In a world of uncertainty companies should maximize expected profit, with adjustments for the cost of risk. Even so, the choices of companies are rarely so clear-cut. Companies undertake a multitude of projects. Carrying out strategies requires myriad activities. The question is: What are the consequences for profit of alternative strategic plans?

Keniche Ohmae observes, "[i]n the real world of business, 'perfect' strategies are not called for. What counts . . . is not performance in absolute terms but performance relative to competitors."[1] He emphasizes the distinction between competitive actions that improve the firm's position relative to other companies, and other actions that improve profitability, streamline the organization, or increase the effectiveness of management. The primary purpose of strategy is to achieve competitive advantage.

The objective of the firm is to earn greater economic returns than its competitors. This requires outperforming competitors in many different ways. The company may achieve higher profits through reliable supplier relationships, excellent distributors, superior quality, and innovative products. Greater sales can boost profits if the company is able to take advantage of the recognition and cost economies that come from being the largest company. Moreover, diverting sales from competitors can improve your company's relative performance.

Profits

The firm's performance is measured in terms of economic profit. This means the net present value of the company's cash flow, discounted at the appropriate rate of interest.[2] The appropriate rate of interest is the company's cost of capital, which reflects the riskiness of its business.

Profit maximization does not mean earning the highest possible profit in any given year, but rather earning the highest net present value of a stream of profits. This takes into account the time value of money. Moreover, looking at net present values of cash flows takes into account long-term strategies, not just short-term fixes.

Companies should not rely solely on accounting measures of revenues, costs, depreciation, and cost of capital. Rather, they must develop strategic measures of profits that reflect economic returns, that is, the impact on net present value of cash flows. The advantage of economic measures of profits over accounting measures is that economic profit is *prospective*—it looks ahead to the future effects of strategic decisions.[3] Managers need to develop strategic accounting systems that give them information on their economic performance and allow comparisons with the performance of competitors.

The company's revenues include all of its earnings from sales and other sources of income. The company's costs include all of its expenditures for production facilities and other capital investments, labor costs, purchases of manufactured inputs, raw materials, services, and technology expenditures, such as license fees and royalties. The profit-maximizing firm chooses pricing, products, technology, investment, and other actions to maximize the present value of profits.

The company nets out the cost of capital evaluated as the returns from investing in the best alternative opportunity. The company takes into account all of its costs. It is clear that these include the costs of borrowing money, through debt or through selling equity.

There are a number of reasons to expect that firms will maximize profits. The owners of the firm are interested in the highest present discounted value of earnings they can obtain from the firm. If the firm is managed by its owners, the owners will make management decisions to obtain the highest present discounted value of profits. If the firm is owned by its shareholders, but ownership and control are separate, the market for corporate control will serve to discipline the firm's managers if they do not pursue profit maximization. Maximizing the firm's present value of profits assures that the firm is maximizing shareholder value, since the shares represent ownership of the firm's future stream of profits. The company's shareholders (and bondholders) must be compensated for the cost of capital. So the company must maximize the net present value of the company's cash flows net of the cost of capital. Managers who do not maximize shareholder value will be replaced either through the oversight of the corporate board representing shareholder interests or through a corporate takeover.

What is shareholder value? This is simply the value of the company net of debt, since the shareholders claim the residual earnings of the company. The value of the company is the net present value of expected cash flows. So shareholder value is the net present value of expected cash flows net of debt. The company must compensate lenders for the cost of capital, so the company's debt equals the cost of investment financed by debt.[4] The same holds if investment is financed by a combination of debt and equity. When making investment decisions, the alternative is always to return funds to the company's shareholders or to invest the funds in other projects. Thus, the cost of capital represents the opportunity cost of capital to the firm's shareholders.

Surprisingly, many companies do not take into account the costs of funds obtained from the company's shareholders. Concern over measuring value added is reflected in consulting company attempts to measure the returns to capital.[5] For example, the use of accounting data to estimate annual operating profit net of capital cost and to estimate prospective earnings explains the interest in concepts such as economic value added (EVA) and its extension, market value added (MVA).[6] EVA refers to after-tax net operating profit in a given year minus a company's cost of capital in that year. MVA refers to the company's capital from all sources of debt and equity as well as the capitalized value of R&D investment, minus the current value of the company's stock and debt.[7] Companies such as Coca-Cola, AT&T, CSX, Quaker Oats, Eli Lilly, Briggs & Stratton, Georgia Pacific, and Tenneco use these types of measures in evaluating their strategies.[8] *Fortune* magazine ranked top U.S. corporations in terms of their MVA, with Coca-Cola, General Electric, Wal-Mart Stores, Merck, and Microsoft topping the list.[9] These measures provide some guidance, although they are necessarily imperfect indicators of the present discounted value of cash flow.

These companies achieved additional profits by noticing the capital tied up in expensive production facilities. John Snow, CEO of rail carrier CSX, took account of the capital tied up in locomotives, containers, and railcars, and observed, "[h]ow we use capital determines market value."[10] As might be expected, stock prices closely track EVA for companies such as AT&T. Because of the risks of equity capital, the cost of equity is generally higher than the long-term government bond rate.

Robert Goizueta, CEO of Coca-Cola, had an embroidered cushion in his office that read, "The one with the biggest cash flow wins."[11] He sums up profit maximization with a basic analogy. "When I played golf regularly, my average score was 90, so every hole was par 5. I look at EVA like I look at breaking par. At Coca-Cola, we are way under par and adding a lot of value."[12] He boosted Coke's share price by a factor of almost 15 by shedding some less profitable businesses, reducing the number of plants for producing concentrate, and boosting productivity in the remaining plants.

Capital not only includes the funds tied up in equipment and real estate, it also includes working capital, such as cash, inventories, and receivables. By reducing inventories through just-in-time techniques and improved market information, companies cut their costs of working capital. Emmanuel Kampouris, CEO of American Standard, set a goal of zero working capital. He is approaching the target by using what he calls "demand flow technology."[13] Product manufacturing is closely tied to customer orders, suppliers deliver straight to the production facility, and plants ship the products as soon as they are completed. In this way, manufacturers such as Ford Motor company achieve reductions in capital costs that had been experienced by assemblers such as Gateway and Dell Computer.

The company can therefore measure its profits against market rates of return on capital. The company is creating value if and only if it is generating economic profits, that is, revenues cover all costs including the cost of capital. But is creating value enough? Is generating economic profits sufficient to determine that the company's managers are making the best use of the firm's assets and opportunities? The answer is clearly no. The firm's performance must be compared to that of its competitors.

Tournaments

The success of a strategy is measured against that of competitors. Expected changes in economic profit provide an assessment of the value of the company's investment projects and management decisions. The strategically relevant observation is the comparison of economic performance with the company's market rivals. Competitive strategy requires anticipating rival strategies and taking actions that will be effective in the market.

Investors compare the firm's performance in terms of sales and profits with that of its competitors. This comparison provides a yardstick with which to evaluate performance. Investors cannot be as well informed as managers about market conditions or about the company's costs. Although all companies are different, many of the same forces affect all of the firms in an industry. They potentially have access to the same customers. They can draw on the same technology and can potentially employ similar organizational designs. They often compete for employees and suppliers in the same input markets.

The use of a competitive yardstick spurs managers to put in their full efforts to outperform their rivals. Winning markets is a tournament between managers.[14] The rewards go to the managers of the most successful firms. Competing to be the best spurs both managers and employees to try harder, creating the discipline necessary to continually improve performance.

The relative performances of companies in their industries are reflected in the cost of capital. Investors wish to back companies that consistently top their competitors. The competitive advantage of these companies reflects superior organization, better products, and managerial leadership. Investors cannot determine whether the company is maximizing its profits, but it is fairly easy to determine performance in comparison to competitors.

Is There a Trade-Off between Size and Profits?

In comparing the performance of companies, what weight should be accorded short-run sales and profits? What counts is a long-term result, the net present value of earnings. This is difficult to predict, particularly for outside observers. For this reason, analysts and investors rely on many measures, including market share, profits, and qualitative information about management strategy, R&D projects, and planned investments.

Market share alone cannot be the only measure. There can be a short-run trade-off between sales and profits. Suppose that a firm sells a product that is differentiated from that of its rivals and assume that consumer demand, marketing efforts, product characteristics, technology, and rival responses are relatively stable. The firm can increase the quantity of output sold by lowering its price. If market demand is price sensitive, sales revenues will rise as well. If market demand is not overly price sensitive, sales revenues will decline.

The costs of producing output can increase with output at a constant or increasing rate. Consider a firm for which revenues exceed costs for all output levels below the break-even output. For output levels above the break-even level, costs exceed revenues. For such a firm there is some level of output at which profits are maximized. Increasing output beyond this level reduces profits. Indeed, continued expansion of production until the firm's output is above the break-even level will create losses for the firm.

Faced with these revenue and cost conditions, management must choose its pricing strategy. Clearly, maximizing the firm's output is ruled out since this would lead the firm to an output above the break-even level, resulting in losses. Maximizing sales revenue would under some conditions lead the firm to produce above the profit-maximizing level and in some cases above the break-even level. In other words, the firm would be pricing too low relative to its production costs. In general, the short-run profit-maximizing price will lead to an output for the firm that is smaller than the break-even output. Therefore, choosing the profit-maximizing price will not be consistent with maximizing the firm's market share.

What will the firm's managers do? Since the firm must maximize profits, it cannot maximize its size whenever there is a trade-off between sales and profits. How can we reconcile the economic assertion that firms maximize profits with the frequently observed managerial drive to expand?

I do not believe the answer is that managers behave irrationally. Moreover, I do not find the argument that managers "satisfice" by choosing some mix of sales and profits to be very convincing.[15] The view that managers maximize sales but maintain some minimum profit level to avoid criticism by the firm's shareholders presumes that all shareholders are consistently fooled by such a strategy. Also, to ascribe sales maximization to managerial preferences begs the question: Why would most managers want larger sales? The desire to manage a larger company cannot be a satisfying explanation. Understanding the objectives of the firm cannot be based on the premise of managerial irrationality and shareholder myopia.

The answer to the market share versus profits trade-off must be that achieving growth and profits need not be inconsistent. The simple trade-off between profit and size outlined above, while persuasive, may be a *short-term* phenomenon that does not capture the essential nature of competition. Certainly sales revenue, as well as current profits and other quarterly or annual financial data, are imperfect measures of long-term performance. In the *long term,* such trade-offs may disappear in a dynamic business environment in which competitive advantages come with being the market leader. Thus, managers pursue market leadership with the eventual goal of having the highest profits as well as a dominant market position.

Honda exhibits what James Abegglen and George Stalk, Jr. call the "winner's competitive cycle," which begins as a consequence of pricing, marketing, increased investment, and product innovation. They find that:

> "Once a superior rate of increase is established, a virtuous cycle begins: with increased volume, relative to competitor's volume, comes decreased costs. With decreased costs comes increased profitability and financial strength. More cash is available internally and from external sources to fund growth. This cash is then reinvested in the business in ways that will yield further increases of market share and a replay of the winning cycle."[16]

The possible short-run trade-off between sales and profits need not be reflected in long-run competition. Low prices not only increase current sales but build customer loyalty and expectations of continuing low prices in the future. Companies can build market share upon this basis. Higher sales then reduce unit costs and justify investment in facilities to further lower unit costs. This strategy has proven successful for the giant discounters such as Wal-Mart and the category killers such as Toys-"R"-Us, Builders Square, and Circuit City.

Intermediation

Winning markets improves the firm's effectiveness in building market bridges. By being recognized as the market maker, the firm is able to coordinate its customers and suppliers more effectively.

Market makers provide liquidity and convenience in markets. A dominant market maker handles a high volume of transactions and is better placed to provide immediacy and convenience, standing ready to sell to its customers and purchase from its suppliers. Dominant intermediaries are better able to handle a high volume of transactions. By being a market focal point they can further reduce search costs for consumers who can coordinate their search for the lowest price or the highest variety by going to the market leader.

Blockbuster Video became the principal source of video rentals by providing a reliable and nearly universal bridge between filmmakers and viewers. They have successfully transferred that market bridge to both video game rentals and sales of recorded music. In winning markets, intermediaries gain an inherent advantage in both gathering and communicating information by virtue of taking a larger sample of customers and suppliers and having a correspondingly larger audience for targeted advertising.

This is particularly important in setting prices, which become reference points in input and product markets. Market leaders such as AT&T in long distance play a leadership role in establishing market prices.

Winning markets is crucial in centralizing exchange. The leading computer reservation systems, American Airlines' Sabre and United Airlines' Apollo, represent valuable market bridges for the airline industry. The use of these systems has spread throughout the travel industry including not just international air travel, but car rentals and hotel reservations as well. By handling a greater volume, the market winner is able to clear the market more effectively and to allocate goods and services efficiently.

Market leaders are sometimes able to use their position to enhance their success in arbitrage. The greater the number of transactions the firm handles, the better is their market information. This allows the company to form a better picture of prices across its markets. The firm is likely to be an informed trader. It is also better able to distinguish between informed and uninformed traders among its customers.

Winning markets enhances the company's role as an intermediary. By handling more transactions, market leaders are able to lower the unit costs of processing sales and purchases, thereby increasing market efficiency. Market leaders can achieve efficiencies in monitoring the performance of suppliers in their networks. By achieving a dominant market position, the company is well placed to broker transactions, since it deals with many suppliers, distributors, and final customers. Customers have access to a wide range of services provided directly or indirectly by the company's suppliers. By virtue of its size, the company standardizes transactions, establishing market protocols.

Leading firms are better able to bridge markets by forging supplier and distributor networks. Companies such as Toyota can create vast supplier and distributor networks as a result of the scale of their operations. This allows Toyota to take advantage of the technological knowledge and efficiency of its supplier chains and to benefit from the market penetration of its automobile dealers. Strategic alliances with suppliers and distributors allow leading companies to focus their attention on networking rather than on building costly organizations that attempt to perform all such functions in-house.

Recognition

Why do winning firms advertise that they are the biggest? Hertz, the car rental company, has long advertised its number one ranking, leading its smaller rival, Avis, to respond that "We try harder." CompUSA advertises that it is the largest computer retailer. Ford promotes the Taurus as the best-selling car. There are important advantages in the market that result from being recognized as the market leader. Winning markets confers recognition by customers, distributors, suppliers, and competitors on the winning firm.

Winning markets can be compared to a race between innovators to obtain a patent. The margin of victory does not matter; the patent goes to the first inventor to file the application. Once the firm obtains the patent to the innovation, it obtains the returns to the innovation for the life of the patent. The race is winner-take-all; the second-place finisher does not obtain a share of the rewards and has no advantage over the third-place finisher. In the race for the market, there is a bonus in consumer demand that comes with winning. Firms compete for market share, but customers at the margin become very valuable for the firm, that is, more valuable than the actual purchases of those customers. When a swing group of customers means the difference between being a market leader and being an also-ran, the all-out efforts that successful firms make to gain and retain customers begin to make sense. Those swing customers can help a firm get over the top, and they bring with them a large number of additional customers who shop at the largest retailer or buy the best-selling brand.

Customer Recognition

Markets are subject to imperfect information about prices, products, and services. Being recognized as the leader provides a powerful way of overcoming these informational imperfections. The firm must outperform all others to become the market leader. Many consumers then purchase from the firm because the firm is the market leader, thus yielding incremental revenues for the firm. The incumbent market leader thus gains an important competitive advantage over existing rivals and potential entrants.

Shopping is a time-consuming and tiring process. Consumers may not find it worthwhile to visit many retailers, particularly for products that are not purchased repeatedly. The customer wants to be assured of a large selection, high quality, low prices, and good service, without high costs of search. Yet consumers have imperfect information about the services and inventories of retailers. As a way of resolving this problem, consumers often rely on the shopping efforts of other consumers by going only to the market leader. For example, computer purchases are made infrequently, although after a computer is purchased a consumer may return to the same store for add-on purchases. CompUSA advertises that "More people shop for computers at CompUSA than any other superstore" and "We sell more computers than anyone else, for more good reasons," emphasizing product variety (50 computer models, 5,000 computer products), low prices every day, and customer service. Some consumers may visit only CompUSA, rather than comparison shopping across computer retailers. Leaders in their categories such as Toys "R" Us, Home Depot, and McDonald's get an extra bump-up in sales from winning their markets.

For product manufacturers, brand recognition by customers is of great value. Rather than seeking out new brands and experimenting with products that may not be satisfactory, consumers pay a premium to purchase a known brand. The firm earns economic rents as a return to the customer demand for the firm's brand. Coca-Cola, sometimes referred to as the "world's best brand," generates tens of billions of dollars worldwide by being the most recognized brand. While Pepsico may have comparable sales revenues, Coca-Cola's profits are many times greater than those of Pepsico. In many cases, such as soft drinks and fashionable clothing, being the market winner creates a bandwagon effect with additional sales coming from being the largest selling brand. Thus, a small dominance in market share in a given year can be leveraged into even greater sales in future years.

Brand recognition not only generates incremental revenues over many years but often can be leveraged to sell additional products under the same brand name, thus allowing the firm to expand into new markets. In this way, recognition of Coke paved the way for the success of Diet Coke.

Recognition of the Wal-Mart name should aid its expansion into food distribution.

Brand recognition is important because consumers have high costs of gathering information about products. For many products the attributes are not apparent. Thus, it is difficult or impossible to know the properties of the good simply by shopping or examining the product. Simply purchasing the product and trying it out are prohibitively costly or simply inconvenient. For durable goods, such as vehicles or large appliances, there is a high cost to trying the product on one's own. For most consumers, an automobile represents a significant purchase requiring some knowledge about the product's characteristics before a purchase is made. Yet the consumer cannot determine how a car will perform over the long term simply by observing the car's exterior or even by taking the car for a test drive. Clearly, durability can only be determined by sustained usage. The efficacy of some products will only become apparent after considerable time has elapsed. The performance of house paint may only surface a year after it is applied. For complex electronic equipment such as stereos or computers, the consumer may not have the technical expertise to evaluate the product's performance. First-time buyers of products whose features are not apparent may not have time to test the product if they are trying to satisfy an immediate need.

In addition to brand recognition, the consumer has many sources of information. In combination, the consumer's various sources of market information can be quite useful. It is often the case that the information gathered by consumers is not conclusive. Then, consumers may choose to rely on a simple rule of thumb—go with the winner—by choosing the most popular brand or the most successful retailer.

An important source of information is advertising. The manufacturer advertises the features of the good, touting its durability, safety, sportiness, and other features, but these claims may not be subject to independent verification and are difficult to compare with those of competing manufacturers. All manufacturers of kitchen appliances make claims of reliability. Maytag's lonely repairman is a familiar figure, but the performance of the appliances is difficult for consumers to estimate. Advertisers claims are informative if consumers believe that the market will penalize firms that consistently misrepresent product features. However, many advertising claims are sufficiently general that the consumer requires more detailed information to make a purchase. The firm that is able to advertise that it has the largest sales provides information about the choices made by other consumers. The success of the firm's brand is an indicator of repeat sales—others have tried the brand and found its performance to be satisfactory. Hertz is not only number one in sales but also earns number one rankings in independent surveys of car rental customers.

The level of advertising itself conveys information: Consumers are more likely to purchase a product that is advertised extensively not simply because of the message contained in the advertising, but because the consumer infers from the advertising expenditure that the company is successful. The company is able to spend large sums on a flashy advertising campaign not simply because profits are high but because profitability results from consistent performance and anticipation of future sales. Therefore, the high advertising expenditure itself is a signal of the company's underlying product quality or customer service. The high cost of a conspicuous ad campaign is generally apparent. The firm making the highest advertising expenditures provides an indication of high current sales or confidence in high future sales, which in turn provides consumers with information about the performance of the firm's products and the quality of its service.

Consumers make inferences about the quality of the good from a number of other actions by the manufacturer and the dealer. A higher price may be a signal of higher performance or durability. This relies in part on the judgment of other consumers as well. Consumers infer higher value from a higher price since a manufacturer could not sustain repeat sales at the higher price unless the firm's product delivered sufficient value to justify its high price. This may seem puzzling at first since it seems to imply that the quantity sold may be increased by raising prices, rather than lowering them. Raising prices alone will not work, of course. The higher prices must reflect higher value that either is apparent or has been learned through building brand reputation and a customer base.

Consumers may also make inferences about the quality of products and services through warranties and other guaranties. Consumers may choose a product with a three-year warranty over a product with a one-year warranty not just because the product is covered for a longer period but because the manufacturer's choice of a warranty life indicates a greater confidence in the performance of the product. Consumers rely on the opinions of others in making purchasing decisions. Word of mouth is of vital importance to the success of a business. Consumers also have available independent rating publications such as *Consumer Reports* to help in choosing products. Government regulatory agencies provide information, such as the Food and Drug Administration's testing of food ingredients and pharmaceuticals for safety and effectiveness. In some cases, consumers require expert advice in selecting products. Consumers need prescriptions to obtain pharmaceuticals and may rely on a physician's advice for over-the-counter medicines. Even in the case of pharmaceuticals, however, consumers often choose to purchase a recognized brand name rather than an unknown generic product.

Market information is costly for consumers. As a consumer's time becomes more valuable it is increasingly costly to engage in comparison shopping. Consumers who value a good highly are less willing to defer consumption of a good to engage in additional search. To reduce search costs by relying on the shopping efforts of others, consumers are often willing to go to the largest and best known retailers hoping to find lower prices, greater variety, and better service. Similarly, experimenting with different products to find the best brand can be a costly and time-consuming process. To reduce the costs of experimentation, consumers choose the best known or most popular brand to increase the likelihood of finding the highest value product.

Recruiting Employees

The recognition of the market leader overcomes problems of incomplete information in other markets besides the final product market. The firm that wins the market can obtain benefits in the markets for labor, finance, productive inputs, and technology.

In the labor market, a firm that is a leader in its product markets has an enhanced ability to recruit and retain talented people. Current and potential employees enjoy working for the leading firm. Being with a winner not only suggests job stability and financial rewards but also the personal satisfaction that comes with success. Wal-Mart employees have benefited greatly in terms of job security and financial rewards, but they also enjoy being with the leading retailer. Indeed, even if the firm is not the market leader, employees enjoy the sense of purpose and direction that comes from competition for leadership, to the extent that they will share in the rewards of winning. Hiring and keeping the best workers helps the firm stay on top, since high-quality personnel are essential. As I have already emphasized, in addition to strategy, employee morale is a key element of success. The morale boost that comes from pursuing and winning markets will strengthen employee performance and improve service quality.

Capital Markets

Winning markets also has important rewards in the capital markets. Just as brand recognition increases consumer demand, so brand recognition increases demand for the firm's equity. Capital markets are also subject to asymmetric information problems. Beyond the information available in company financial reports and in the business press, investors do not have available the same quality of information about the firm's future performance as do the firm's managers. Moreover, while investors can monitor the firm's current performance, they cannot monitor perfectly the manager's day-to-day efforts and the quality and direction of managerial decision making.

Shareholders rely on corporate boards to supervise managers and to represent their interests, although in some cases corporate boards do not carry out their supervisory roles conscientiously. Shareholders can turn to independent investment advisors, but there can be conflicts of interest if the advice comes from commission brokers seeking to increase their customers' trading volume. Investors rely in part on the firm's success and reputation in its product markets. Market leadership provides a simple rule of thumb that is useful as part of an overall evaluation of a firm's future profitability. Increased demand for a firm's shares raises the price of the shares and lowers the firm's costs of capital.

Suppliers and Distributors

The firm's distributor and supplier relationships are also strengthened if the firm is recognized as the market leader. A retailer wishes to carry the most popular brands not only for the sale of those brands but because they draw customers who purchase other items. Thus, supermarkets price leading brands such as Procter & Gamble products close to their purchase costs because of the customer traffic those products draw to the stores. Leading brands obtain concessions from distributors including greater shelf space, increased promotion expenditures, additional sales efforts, and additional customer services for purchasers of the brand.

Suppliers also wish to work for the leading firm. A parts manufacturer, for example, wishes to supply the leading firm since the success of the market leader reduces the risks for the supplier. The stability of a manufacturer's leadership position allows it to form long-term relationships with parts suppliers, something that has been used to advantage by the Japanese keiretsu. The supplier will be willing to make substantial irreversible investments in specialized equipment and design technology to serve the unique needs of a successful manufacturer. By reducing the investment risks of suppliers, a market leader can obtain price concessions in return for longer term contracts and larger orders. In addition, serving the market leader enhances the reputation of the parts supplier, which can be useful in obtaining orders from other manufacturers.

Making the Rules

In addition to recognition from customers and suppliers, the market leader is recognized by competitors. This can be highly valuable since the leading firm can be influential in standard setting. Using its position of leadership, IBM was able to set standards for computer design. Most personal computers are referred to as "IBM compatible." Even if Apple computers were easier to use, the majority of users chose to purchase IBM-type computers. The standard was then reflected in software availability and in the design of peripheral equipment. As IBM's leadership has eroded, so has its ability to set industry standards. IBM is forming large alliances with other companies in an attempt to retain an influence over industry standards.

IBM and Apple formed an unsuccessful alliance called Taligent (a hopeful combination of *talisman* and *intelligent*) to try to develop a new operating system standard. The operating system software combined the Unix operating system (IBM's version is called AIX) with Apple's display technology, but failed to win acceptance. The operating system standard is currently set by Microsoft, the leading maker of operating system software. IBM, Apple, and Motorola formed another alliance, called Somerset after the English county in which King Arthur and the knights of the Round Table set off in pursuit of the Holy Grail. The troubled Somerset alliance, which was intended to set a new industry standard for computer chip architecture, began shipping the first chip, the Power PC, in May of 1993, but did not achieve a significant market share. The standard for computer chips is currently set by the family of chips produced by Intel, the leading maker of chips. Intel's chips run most of the 100 million personal computers now in use.[17]

In addition to standard setting, the market leader can exercise price leadership in some cases if the firm's competitors choose to follow its pricing patterns. Thus, if the price leader raises its prices it need not lose market share if its rivals follow its price increases. Similarly, price cuts need not attract new customers if rivals follow price cuts as well. There is, of course, no guarantee that the dominant firm in a market can exercise price leadership. Price increases can create opportunities for rivals to act quickly through increased marketing and even price cuts to unseat the market leader. Price cuts by a market leader can unleash price wars that bring new firms to the fore.

The market leader also becomes the main target of rivals. Thus, as the industry leader, IBM was the firm to beat as clone makers copied IBM's machines and went after its customers. The leading incumbent may face much more heated competition than smaller rivals as new entrants seek to take its place as the market leader. At the same time, the market leader is an attractive merger partner. Market leadership can sometimes be maintained by mergers and alliances while competitors can respond with alliances of their own, as with the IBM alliances directed at Microsoft's leadership in software and Intel's leadership in computer chips.

Motivation

Striving to win the company's markets is the greatest morale booster. It is a crucial source of motivation for managers and employees alike. As companies change the way they reward employees, it is necessary to provide a way to involve employees in the company's activities and to tap into their creativity and initiative.

Increased competition both domestically and internationally have concentrated the minds of management on cost cutting, causing them to shed unnecessary functions within the company and to substitute out-sourcing for many activities that were previously carried out in-house. Companies have slimmed down through massive layoffs and replacement of permanent employees with temps. IBM cut one-quarter of its 400,000-plus workforce.

At the same time, the workplace is undergoing a wrenching trans-formation the likes of which have not been seen since the industrial revolution. The change goes under many names, including reengineering and business process transformation. Taking advantage of advances in computers and communications, companies are drastically reducing the number of middle managers, eliminating layers of authority within the organizational hierarchy. Employees can no longer count on a job in which they will be merely processing information, adding sales figures, and passing them up the hierarchy. These routine functions are facilitated by simple software programs. The focus of employees must be on key decision-making, customer service, or technical functions that cannot be automated easily.

The changes in the activities of employees are of necessity accompanied by changes in the types of performance measures that companies use and in the incentives for performance. Companies are attaching greater importance to the technical skills of their workers, rewarding them for increased training and acquisition of knowledge, rather than focusing on the production-based rewards of the past.

These changes in the nature of the job are reflected in changes in the employment relationship. Fewer employers are offering anything approaching guaranteed lifetime employment. Moreover, companies are relying less on internal labor markets with career ladders and specified ways to advance in the company, a consequence of the flatter organization. They are relying more on external labor markets, so that employees face more frequent job changes and reduced job security. Job descriptions are moving far away from civil service-type gradations, toward general technical functions.

Against this backdrop of change and insecurity, the job changes offer many positive features as well. Companies are increasing the sharing of information at lower levels of the organization and are decentralizing decision making. This increases the responsibility of employees involved in day-to-day operational decisions and increases interest in the job. Employees who continue to develop their skills are rewarded both by providing greater value to the company and also by the personal satisfaction they derive from mastering greater job skills. The replacement of job security with mobility and training will benefit the more creative and entre-preneurial employees.

The difficult problem faced by managers is how to motivate employees to work in the interest of the company. Removal of job security will inevitably cause many employees to pursue their own objectives to achieve career advancement. Others, less loyal to the company, will shirk their duties or interpret company directives in a manner that does not promote corporate interests.

One way of addressing these incentive issues is to present managers and employees with a clear picture of the company's objectives and the proposed means of achieving them. The success of the company in winning its markets can then be tied to increased financial rewards and enhanced job security for employees.

Managers face the difficult problem of coordinating employees, whether in project teams or in entire business units. A common goal of becoming a leader in the company's markets provides a means of uniting employees and directing their efforts. By emphasizing performance relative to the company's actual and potential rivals, a firm can motivate employees to be more focused on the task at hand. Every position in the company becomes a front-line position as the company attempts to outperform others in its industry. Beating market leaders or fighting to stay on top brings forth employee innovativeness and willingness to take risks. The rapidly changing competitive environment further calls for organizational flexibility and responsiveness.

As managers shift their focus from supervising employees and carrying out routine functions, they have increased time available for strategic decision making. It is essential to focus the attention of managers on excelling relative to competitors. Companies are increasingly turning to training exercises in which managers play the roles of competitors, devising marketing plans and entry strategies. By observing the creativity and quick actions of mock competitors and contemplating the possibility that their plans will be thwarted in the marketplace, managers are developing an understanding of competitive strategy. These training exercises serve to define the objective of winning markets and prepare managers for the challenges ahead.

Pushing Out the Boundaries of the Firm

Companies can achieve market power and realize the returns to winning markets by pushing out the boundaries of the firm. The four main boundaries are its scale, scope, span, and speed. *Scale* refers to the size of the firm, generally measured in terms of the rate of output per day or per year. *Scope* refers to the variety of products produced or sold by the firm. *Span* refers to the number of vertical stages of production, distribution, and marketing that are undertaken by the firm. *Speed* refers to the rate at which a technological innovation is developed and implemented. Firms change their boundaries over time. Changes in the scale, scope, span, and speed of the

Table 2-1.
THE FOUR BOUNDARIES OF THE FIRM

Boundaries	*Definitions*	*Consolidation*	*Expansion*
Scale	Size of capacity	Horizontal	Growth
Scope	Product variety	Lateral	Diversification
Span	Production sequence	Vertical	Vertical integration
Speed	Rate of innovation	Dynamic	Accelerated innovation

firm are referred to as growth, diversification, vertical integration, and accelerated innovation. The boundaries of the firm are summarized in Table 2-1.

The returns from consolidation are enhanced revenues, lower costs, and reduced risk. Revenues are enhanced through increases in market power that may be achieved through horizontal, lateral, or vertical expansion or increased R&D. Costs are brought down if the firm can realize economies of scale, scope, sequence, and speed. Risks are reduced if consolidation eliminates some uncertainty about the firm's residual demands or supplies.

There are four main types of consolidation to be considered in this context: consolidation of output, consolidation of diverse products, consolidation of stages of production, and consolidation of new product development. I refer to these types as *horizontal, lateral, vertical,* and *dynamic.* The profits from consolidation are composed of cost gains and revenue gains. In addition, the firm faces risk due to variations in cost or revenue that may be alleviated by consolidation. The revenue gains from consolidation are market power, complements and substitutes, and avoidance of double marginalization. The cost gains from consolidation are referred to as economies of scale, scope, sequence, and speed. The risk reduction from consolidation is due to lower sample variance, diversification, and coordination. The returns from consolidation that will be considered in this section are shown in Table 2-2.

Gains from consolidation are achieved in buying inputs and selling outputs through the exercise of market power. An increase in the firm's market share as the result of a horizontal merger increases the firm's monopoly power, in the absence of competitive entry. A lateral merger with a manufacturer of complementary or substitute products yields revenue gains from coordination of prices. Vertical mergers, when both firms have market power, eliminate the problem of double marginalization, thus increasing profits for the combined firms. Finally, through accelerated innovation, the firm can gain first mover advantages both in cost reduction

Table 2-2.
RETURNS FROM CONSOLIDATION

	Returns		
Consolidation	Revenue	Cost	Risk
Horizontal	Market power	Economies of scale	Reduced variance
Lateral	Complements substitutes	Economies of scope	Diversification
Vertical	Avoiding double marginalization	Economies of sequence	Coordination
Dynamic	First mover advantages	Economies of speed	Development

and market-responsive products. The exercise of market power thus provides a partial explanation for the horizontal, lateral, vertical, and dynamic dimensions of consolidation by companies.

Incremental Revenues

The market power of the firm can be represented by the elasticity of demand, which is the price responsiveness of amount sold at any given price. This is equal to the ratio of the percentage change in the firm's demand divided by the associated percentage change in the firm's price.[18] It is frequently expressed as a positive number. For example, if the price of the company's soft drink rises by 10% and the quantity sold falls by only 5%, the elasticity of demand equals one-half. If consumers have alternatives to the product the elasticity of demand will generally be high as customers will switch away from the firm's products in response to a price increase (or back in response to a price drop). The firm's demand elasticity also depends upon the extent of competition it faces and the costs of entry for potential rivals.[19]

The firm's elasticity of demand varies over time. Demand can be more elastic in the long run than in the short run as customers seek out substitute products and services and as competitors respond to price changes of incumbent firms. A firm with greater market power, that is, a lower elasticity of demand, will have correspondingly higher profits, all other things equal.[20]

Just as there are revenue gains from controlling a larger share of the market for a given product, there are returns from consolidation of goods that are complements or substitutes. The multiproduct company is concerned not only about the effect of a product's price on the sales of that product but also its effect on the sales of all of its other products. This cross-effect is referred to as the cross-price elasticity of demand, which is the ratio of the percentage change in sales of a product divided by the percentage change in the price of another product. The products are substitutes, independent, or complements as the cross-price elasticity of demand is greater than, equal to, or less than zero. For example, a company offering both a diet and a regular brand of soft drink recognizes that a 5% increase in the price of its diet brand can create a 10% increase in sales of its regular brand (accompanied by some loss in sales of its diet brand). The cross-elasticity of demand then is equal to two.

The two-product monopoly increases profit by taking account of cross-price effects, that is, the effect of the price of a product on the demand for another product.[21] Cross-price effects occur because consumers will switch between products depending on the relative prices of the products. These effects help to explain the prevalence of multiproduct firms. A firm producing a wide range of substitutes will consider the competition between its products and the possibility that raising prices for some of the goods will increase demand for its other goods. For example, Procter & Gamble's pricing decisions are influenced by cross-price elasticities for its product lines in soaps. Other companies offering complements, such as cameras and film, balance the revenue effects of prices across products.

Suppose that an upstream input manufacturer and a downstream firm using the input each have market power. The input maker sets a monopoly price following its inverse elasticity rule and the downstream reseller does the same. The result is that on its way to the consumer there are at least two monopoly markups on the product, leading to reduced demand and lower revenues for both firms. This can be shown to be an inefficient outcome in the sense that the two firms could make higher profits through cooperation. If the two were to merge, the internal transfer price of the upstream input would be close to the competitive level and the consumers downstream would face only one markup over marginal cost. The integrated firm could be mimicked by a contract between the upstream firm and the downstream firm that specified a fixed charge to redistribute profits and a lowered unit price closer to marginal cost. This is an advantage of close supplier relationships. However, if transaction costs or legal restrictions prevent the formation of such contracts, then vertical integration may be required as a means of avoiding the distortions of upstream monopoly. Of course, the vertical integration of multiple activities within the firm must be examined within a broader context that accounts for competitive strategies and contracting costs.

Incremental revenues can be achieved through innovative speed, that is, by consolidation of the firm's stream of research and development activities over time. The company's rate of *product* innovation refers not only to the rate of development and introduction of new products but also to the degree of responsiveness to changes in customer requirements. The rate of *process* innovation refers not only to cost-reducing and quality-improving innovations but also the reaction time to scientific and technological progress. Management's choice of the rate and direction of innovation depends on the costs of R&D, competitive introduction of substitute products and new production techniques, and customer willingness to pay for product improvement.

Incremental revenues are obtained from more rapid introduction of new products. By this I do not necessarily mean a rapid-fire series of minor product updates, but rather fundamental changes. There are high returns from product introductions that can be protected through patents or copyrights. Of course, new products can be copied and rivals may try to circumvent patents, so the rate of diffusion must be considered. The substantial decline in new product prices, as occurs for example after a new generation of computer chips is introduced, demonstrates the incremental revenues that are earned early on, because of both demand for novelty and the lags in competitor responses. There are additional gains to early introduction of new products as a result of recognition for the company. By being the first to market, the originator can be identified with the product. This is no guarantee of success, as competitors can learn from the leader's mistakes and capture buyers with relatively minor improvements. Further, competitors can play leapfrog, jumping ahead to the next generation of products, particularly in high-tech industries.

The returns to new products and processes lie in the creation of market bridges. New products allow the firm to connect customers to new types of investments, labor services, manufactured parts, or technologies. Thus, increasing the firm's speed creates innovative transactions that generate rents from exchange. As rents will ultimately be competed away, the firm must continually generate a stream of such innovations, taking advantage of price fluctuations for inputs and competitive products.

Risk Reduction

Consolidation of production and distribution can reduce the risk faced by the firm. If such risk can be diversified away in financial markets or through insurance contracts, then such risk reduction does not explain the size of firms. However, given imperfect financial and insurance markets, or imperfect information about the firm's costs and revenues, there may be risks that are not easily diversified. Therefore, consolidation can be valuable as an alternative means of reducing the costs of risks to the firm.

Size plays an important role in risk reduction as a result of diversification. A larger set of customers reduces demand-side risk, just as an expanded pool of policyholders reduces the risks to an insurance company. If a company has loyal clients that represent a broad cross section of the population, sales fluctuations resulting from individual income and taste changes are reduced. Similarly, a large firm that is able to diversify its suppliers reduces its supply-side risk in terms of pricing, availability, and quality by insuring against idiosyncratic suppliers' problems. Expansion of the company through growth or acquisition can reduce the variance in the firm's demand and costs.[22] Thus, the firm that wins the market may have lower risk than smaller competitors.

The same diversification can be achieved through expansion of the firm's scope. Pooling productive capacity to serve markets in which demands are negatively correlated allows the firm to operate at near full capacity for a greater amount of time, thus reducing average costs. Also, by pooling inventories, firms can smooth the pattern of demands across retail locations, reducing inventories and peak capacity requirements. Just as a retailer supplying many seasonal products can operate more efficiently than specialized retailers, a firm can realize similar gains by providing diverse products. A diversified company can apply technical, marketing, and managerial expertise as needed across a variety of products. The managerial capacity of the firm is employed effectively, despite random fluctuations in individual product sales.

Span plays a crucial role in reducing risk. Vertical consolidation yields returns if coordination can be achieved within the firm at lower cost than through contracts. A manufacturer can reduce the cost of risk due to fluctuations in the availability of productive inputs by manufacturing the parts. A retailer can ensure product availability by integration with a manufacturer. Similarly, a manufacturer can seek to reduce demand risk by entering into distribution.

Many manufacturers have recognized the advantages of just-in-time (JIT) inventories. By not carrying excess numbers of parts and materials, companies avoid the high storage and interest costs. Moreover, the mix of parts that are ordered just before production is necessarily much closer to what is actually needed. These advantages come at a price. There is a substantial risk of stock outs and delivery lags, as well as delayed production if a batch is found to be defective. These risks can be reduced by careful coordination with parts suppliers through long-term contracts and close working relationships. By using bar coding, tracking of parts, and electronic data interchange, delays can be avoided and the flow of new parts can mirror requirements. In industries in which suppliers cannot be relied upon to work closely with the company, or if the firm may need to surrender important technological and market information to a supplier, there are gains to vertical expansion as a means of reducing the risks that accompany JIT inventories.

Speed of response time reduces risk in two fundamental ways. First, rapid product innovation allows a faster response to market conditions and consumer tastes. Stores like The Gap and Benneton, by tailoring their inventory to current fashion and updating their styles with very short production and distribution cycles, reduce the risk of unsold inventory while increasing total sales. These chains have competed away sales from department stores that have significantly longer cycles and are less responsive to market trends. Second, rapid innovation in products and processes reduces competitive risk by beating competitors to market and possibly preempting new entrants. Combining R&D projects also allows for the application of unexpected spinoffs and permits the application of product development efforts to basic discoveries. Increasing speed by investing in R&D reduces the risks associated with the pursuit of blind alleys. By innovating faster, with the inevitable sinking of dry wells along the way, it is possible to correct missteps before it is too late, thus avoiding delays caused by halfhearted innovation efforts. IBM invested billions in basic research leading to important developments in such areas as superconductors and the scanning electron microscope. However, IBM at times failed to take advantage of its speed in basic research by translating the results into marketable products. Returns to speed can only be realized by viewing the company as a bridge between technology and final customers.

Cost Economies

Winning markets confers advantages in terms of cost economies that allow the firm to sustain its leadership position. Achieving cost economies is a potential benefit of winning markets. However, striving for cost economies does not in itself guarantee success. Although Wal-Mart's sales growth was aided by low costs from distribution efficiencies, Wal-Mart did not win the retail market solely as a result of its efficient distribution system. Wal-Mart's expansion strategy, pricing policies, and merchandising ability were primarily responsible for its growth in sales. The growth in sales allowed it to take advantage of economies in distribution. American Airlines, on the other hand, a leader in sales in the 1980s and early 1990s, invested heavily in expansion of its fleet and in the development of airport hubs that potentially yield huge cost economies. American Airlines entered the 1990s with substantial annual losses from overinvestment, forcing it to close down hubs, retire airplanes, and cancel orders for additional planes, as smaller regional carriers with lower costs competed successfully for many routes. The point is that winning markets can yield cost economies, while cost economies alone do not necessarily win markets.

Based on his examination of the origins and growth of large modern industrial enterprises in the United States, Great Britain, and Germany, Alfred D. Chandler argues that companies rarely continue to grow or to maintain their competitive positions without cost reductions and efficient resource use, particularly through taking advantage of economies of scale and scope. He emphasizes that economies of scale and scope are observed *within* the operating units of firms, while transaction costs within the firm generally are incurred through the exchange of goods and services *between* the firm's operating units. He observes that technological change, particularly in transportation and communication, made possible the creation and management of large-scale enterprises in production and distribution.

There are cost economies associated with growth in each of the four boundaries. Cost economies are not guaranteed by growth, however, but depend on whether the management can take advantage of technological opportunities. Large firms such as IBM, General Motors, and many others discovered that bureaucracy, inefficiency, and underemployed personnel can accompany growth. There are diminishing returns to some types of expansion and it is up to management to discern how costs are affected by growth. Moreover, the presence of cost economies does not imply unlimited market opportunities. The firm cannot simply grow to achieve cost economies without recognizing the size of the markets it wishes to serve.

Scale

The primary boundary of the firm is its scale. Firms often define themselves in terms of size, usually quoting the annual value of sales, which provides an indication of total output per year. As I have already noted, firms also compare their success in terms of relative market share, which provides a measure of relative size. While market share need not be an indicator of current or future profitability, firms strive to be the market leader in terms of sales to achieve competitive advantage.

One reason for the focus on size is the presence of technological economies of scale. Economies of scale are said to be present if the marginal cost of the firm is less than the firm's unit cost; that is, the cost of expanding output by one unit is less than the firm's unit cost before the expansion. If economies of scale are present, then expansion of the firm's output lowers the firm's unit cost. The definition of economies of scale given by economists assumes that the firm is using the most efficient technology, so that any gains from implementing technological innovations or from reducing waste have already been realized. Of course, every firm can always find new areas for efficiency improvements. Economies of scale refer to efficiency improvements due only to scale, over and above those due to improving the firm's operating procedures. Identification of economies of scale does not require that the firm have a fixed technology. Rather, an important source of economies of scale is the choice of the most efficient production process for *each level of output.*

The advantages of economies of scale have long been well known. Fifteenth-century merchants in the Mediterranean realized that larger vessels could carry more cargo at lower cost since the volume of the ship increased more than proportionately with its surface area, not to mention the size of the crew. The same scale economy is reflected in modern super-tankers and huge container ships. Volume–surface relationships have also driven the expansion of firms in process industries from chemical manu-facturing to beer brewing.

Adam Smith's famous story of a pin factory illustrated the advantages of the specialization of function and division of labor, which are important sources of scale economies. The benefits of mechanization have been observed since textile mills were established in the early days of the industrial revolution. Mechanized agriculture increased the efficient scale of farms. The advantages of standardization and large-scale assembly were put to good use in making the Ford Model T. Increases in scale allow the use of new materials such as plastics in manufacturing. Many of these economies of scale are production related and are not necessarily sufficient to explain the growth of large corporations.

Economies of scale in the simplest form result from the spreading out of fixed costs across many units of output. If the firm's overhead costs, including accounting, legal, and other management functions, are relative-ly constant, then expansion of output will lower unit overhead costs. Clearly, $100 of overhead contributes $2 to unit costs if there are 50 units of output, but contributes only $1 if output expands to 100 units. The same holds for other types of fixed costs such as capital equipment. By using capital equipment to its full capacity, firms are able to reduce their unit costs. This explains the use of double- or triple-production shifts as a means of making full use of capital equipment.

Another way in which the spreading of fixed costs across many units of output allows for substantial savings is in marketing expenditures. An advertising campaign is a fixed cost for the firm. This is the foundation of franchise businesses such as McDonald's, which can spread the costs of a national advertising campaign across all of its outlets. A smaller competitor making the same advertising expenditure would experience a greater increase in unit costs. Marketing expenditures are sunk costs, so costly ad campaigns pose substantial risks for new entrants or for firms seeking to take on the market leader. This is why the market leader must continue to make marketing expenditures to maintain its competitive position.

Research and development, like marketing, is a crucial overhead cost for which the advantages of market leadership are particularly signif-icant. The market leader can maintain a substantial R&D facility with less effect on unit costs as compared to smaller rivals. Then, a market leader that is cost-efficient can bring to market a one-two punch of low prices and continuous innovation. High R&D expenditures in themselves are no guarantee of success, as IBM found when it could not translate its billions of dollars in research expenditures and cutting-edge discoveries into mar-ketable products. However, if the leading firm's R&D efforts are productive, innovation can be achieved at lower unit costs than it can by smaller rivals.

This is not to say that the largest firms are always the most innovative. Smaller firms may design products that are a closer fit with customer requirements. Moreover, R&D by nature is an uncertain process and smaller firms may have the talent and the good fortune to make path-breaking discoveries before a larger rival. Like marketing expenditures, however, R&D costs are sunk costs and therefore pose substantial risks for competitors. For this reason the market leader must continually invest in R&D to stay ahead of rival innovation and maintain its competitive position.

New sources of scale economies are always being discovered. Computers are replacing routine information processing, calculating, and monitoring of equipment just as mechanization has replaced physical labor since the Industrial Revolution. Moreover, computers have allowed firms to make substantial cuts in administrative overhead costs. Increases in the information processing power of computers have allowed firms to make dramatic reductions in management personnel, resulting in a fall in overhead costs. For example, firms such as electrical equipment giant Asea Brown Boveri were able to reduce central office staff by 90%. Efficiency improvements that reduce total overhead not only lower unit costs, but have the added effect of reducing the firm's minimum efficient scale. In other words, a firm may be able to achieve all available scale economies at a smaller output than before. Thus, increased efficiency may lower the size of firms in some industries as firms are able to achieve the lowest possible costs at a smaller size.

The costs of acquiring and communicating information in large organizations can affect the optimal scale of the firm. The revolution in computers and telecommunications, and the creation of information networks within large companies, will create significant economies of scale. On the other hand, the information costs of monitoring employee performance and observing employee abilities can limit the efficient scale of the organization. To the extent that economies of scale transcend the production plant and are experienced across the organization, economies of scale will yield benefits for the market leader. The principal sources of economies of scale for market leaders must arise from efficiencies in communication, information processing, marketing, and research and development.

Scope

The next important boundary of the firm is its scope, that is, the range of its product and service offerings. In addition to having the largest sales, many successful firms offer greater product variety than their rivals. Not only are there competitive advantages from offering customers more choices, but there can be cost advantages from variety as well. Economies of scope are achieved if the firm can produce two or more products at a lower cost than if the products were produced by separate firms.

As with economies of scale, an important source of economies of scope is due to common inputs or overhead that are spread across the firm's products. Thus, a firm offering many products need not sell large quantities of each product to take advantage of economies of scope. Computer-aided design and manufacturing and the development of the flexible factory imply that the firm need not sacrifice plant-level economies when it expands product variety. The product mix can be adjusted to satisfy individual customer requirements. For example, the Mitsubishi plant in Nagoya is able to produce different models on the same flexible assembly line with minimal adjustments.

Leading firms can achieve companywide benefits of size by diversification into new products and expansion into new markets. The firm can spread the costs of communication, information processing, marketing, and research and development across its products and achieve a smaller unit cost if its total sales are greater than those of its rivals.

The leading retailer, Wal-Mart takes full advantage of economies of scope in distribution. Wal-Mart's superstores take advantage of economies of scope by spreading store operating costs across products. Many economies of scope captured by Wal-Mart are companywide. Offering over 50,000 items, Wal-Mart spreads the costs of a sophisticated computerized distribution system over 20 state-of-the-art regional distribution centers. Wal-Mart employs a sophisticated satellite communications system with video conferencing and centralized inventory control that responds to customer demands and provides detailed sales information to the company's suppliers.

The possibility of achieving economies of scope does not imply that expansion of product offerings will lower unit costs. As with scale economies, limits on economies of scope can stem from the costs of organizing a multiproduct firm. Moreover, many new products can fail to produce a market, or can dilute the sales of the firm's existing products. General Motors has suffered greatly from an unwillingness to reduce its excessive variety of automobile models, offering consumers 7 brands and over 60 models. While there may be scope economies *within* GM's divisions, there are few if any economies of scope *across* GM's divisions. Moreover, the divisions of the company no longer match the market segments that GM serves.

Span

The firm's set of make-or-buy and distribute-or-sell decisions determine the span of the firm. The span of the firm is a crucial aspect of the way in which the firm defines its activities. A characterization of the firm as a service company, manufacturer, wholesaler, retailer, or integrated manufacturer-distributor refers to the span of the firm. The firm's choice of its span is a vital component of its strategy. The trend toward increased vertical integration of manufacturing that has been observed through most of the twentieth century has been reversed in many industries as information technology has allowed firms to outsource a variety of activities, leading to a corresponding growth of the service sector of the economy.

Management's determination of the span of the firm's activities is closely tied to the quantity and variety of the firm's final output. Firms must decide what range of upstream and downstream activities they wish to undertake. Manufacturers choose which steps within the production sequence they wish to undertake. For example, manufacturers may produce all or some of the parts that make up the final product or they may purchase all of the parts and act as final assemblers. Manufacturers can design products internally or contract with independent product designers. Manufacturers can distribute their output themselves or they can sell the products through independent wholesalers and retailers. The span of the firm refers to the number and type of stages in the sequence of activities required to design, manufacture, and distribute a product encompassed by the firm. Thus, the span of the firm refers to the vertical boundary of the firm. It should be emphasized that the notion of the span of the firm does not imply that production and distribution are series of single, ordered steps. Rather, stages of production often involve a complex set of overlapping activities. For each set of activities, the firm must decide whether to carry out the activity itself or whether the activity will be carried out by others, whether customers or suppliers.

Economies of span stem from many sources, including operating cost reductions, securing reliable suppliers, or assuring reliable distribution, resulting in transaction cost savings. Common inputs in a series of production processes often are cited as reasons for vertical integration.[23] Larger firms can more easily achieve benefits from economies of span if there are scale economies at some vertical stages of production. Wal-Mart moves most of its products through its distribution system, so that it is a vertically integrated wholesaler and retailer. Unlike Kmart, which contracts out for its transportation, Wal-Mart owns a fleet of 2,000 trucks.

Economies of span are of particular importance in making markets. A central theme is that firms act as marketing channels for their customers and suppliers. The firm's vertical integration decision is much more than a decision about the stages of production. By choosing its span, the firm chooses the length of the marketing channel that it wishes to provide. A retailer intermediates between its customers and its suppliers (wholesale distributors and manufacturers). A vertically integrated retailer such as Wal-Mart takes on important market-making activities by contracting directly with manufacturers, negotiating prices and product characteristics, monitoring sales, and communicating information about orders.

Speed

Economies of speed can be present in the R&D process. The expected duration of a project can be shortened by increased investment in equipment and additional personnel. If an increase in investment lowers the expected duration of the project per dollar invested, then economies of speed may be said to exist. The presence of economies of speed implies that there may be efficiencies attainable through expansion of specific R&D projects. In addition, there may be cost economies attainable through undertaking multiple R&D projects.[24] Economies of scale and scope in R&D become economies of speed since the output of an R&D program is measured in terms of the rate of innovation.

Innovation plays a central role in competitive strategy and in the firm's organizational design.[25] The presence of economies of scale and scope in the innovation process and the need to structure the organization to increase the rate of innovation imply that innovative speed should be viewed as a boundary of the firm. Firms choosing to increase their rate of innovation must hire scientific personnel, invest in specialized equipment, construct laboratories and testing facilities, purchase technical information, and obtain patents and licenses for technologies useful to their R&D efforts. Increasing the speed of innovation generally will entail changes in the firm's organizational structure and the design of incentives for innovation. Moreover, product innovation will require product market research while process innovation will require research into factor markets. Since changes in the firm's rate of innovation involve fundamental changes in the activities of the firm, speed should be viewed as an important boundary of the firm.

Economies of speed can be achieved if the firm is a market leader in R&D. These economies are not unlimited, however, as evidenced by Ford's investment of $6 billion to design a world car, the Mondeo. The rollout of the Mondeo was slower than expected, as Ford encountered difficulties in coordinating large design and engineering teams.

Firms compare the costs of innovation with the competitive advantages of obtaining the new technology. The costs of technological leadership may outweigh the benefits for some firms. Firms that choose to devote less effort and investment to new product or process development than their customers, suppliers, or competing firms may anticipate that they can successfully compete without the new technology, or that they can obtain new technologies by licensing or copying the innovation after others develop it. As with the other boundaries, the choice of innovative speed by the firm is a choice about which activities are left to the market and which activities are carried out by the firm. Market leaders innovate themselves, while followers must pay for licensing innovations, purchase components from more innovative suppliers, or play catch-up by attempting to duplicate new features introduced by rivals.

Intel, the market leader in computer chips, has maintained its position by continual innovation. Its Pentium chip was introduced even as its 486 family of chips achieved greater than expected success. Intel faced a number of important challenges including the higher-capacity Power-PC chip developed by the IBM-Apple-Motorola joint venture. In response, Intel's CEO, Andy Grove, sought to double the innovative speed of Intel by cutting the intervals at which Intel introduces new chips from four years to two. Changes in the fundamental design of chips have enabled Intel to increase its rate of innovation and even challenge the rate of computer chip development embodied in Moore's Law: that chips double in capacity every 18 months.

The revenue, risk, and cost advantages of consolidation of production are, of course, limited by the organizational costs of a larger enterprise. These benefits must be compared with contractual alternatives. Even taking account of these organizational and contractual considerations, the gains from consolidation provide returns to companies that win markets.

Endnotes

1. Keniche Ohmae, *The Mind of the Strategist: The Art of Japanese Business*, New York: McGraw-Hill, 1982.

2. If the interest rate is r, and expected profit that will be earned in the year t is E_t, the present value of profit is

$$V = E_0 + \frac{E_1}{(1+r)} + \frac{E_2}{(1+r)^2} + \frac{E_3}{(1+r)^3} \cdots$$

The profit stream can be divided into the present value of profit during the planning period, plus the residual value, which represents the net present value of profit in future years. Suppose that there is a five-year planning period, including the current year, and suppose that V^* represents the residual value. Then, the present value of profit is

$$V = E_0 + \frac{E_1}{(1+r)} + \frac{E_2}{(1+r)^2} + \frac{E_3}{(1+r)^3} + \frac{E_4}{(1+r)^4} + V^*$$

3. The problems of using accounting methods as a guide to corporate strategy and their limitations for measuring economic profits are well known. See H. T. Johnson and R. S. Kaplan, *Relevance Lost: The Rise and Fall of Managerial Accounting*, Cambridge: Harvard Business School Press, 1986; Jeremy Edwards, John Kay, and Colin Mayer, *The Economic Analysis of Accounting Profitability*, Oxford: Clarendon Press, 1987; and Alfred Rappaport, *Creating Shareholder Value*, New York: Free Press, 1986.

4. The company subtracts the debt obligation from the net present value of operating cash flows:

Shareholder value = Net present value of operating cash flows − Debt

Suppose the debt is used to finance investment so that the shareholder value is

Shareholder value = Net present value of operating cash flows — Cost of investment

5. For a discussion of how to apply the standard measure of economic profits to accounting data see John Kay, *Foundations of Corporate Success: How Business Strategies Add Value*, Oxford: Oxford University Press, 1993.

6. These terms are due to the financial consulting firm Stern Stewart; see Anne B. Fisher, "Creating Stockholder Wealth," *Fortune*, December 11, 1995, pp. 105–116. See also Shawn Tully, "The Real Key to Creating Wealth," *Fortune*, September 20, 1993, p. 38.

7. Fisher, id.

8. Fisher, id.

9. Fisher, id.

10. Tully, id., p. 39.

11. Tully, id., p. 45.

12. Tully, id., p. 45.

13. Shawn Tully, "American Standard: Prophet of Zero Working Capital," *Fortune*, June 13, 1994, pp. 113–114.

14. The incentive effects of tournaments have been widely studied; see Edward Lazear and Sherwin Rosen, "Rank Order Tournaments as Optimum Labor Contracts," *Journal of Political Economy*, 89, 1981, pp. 841–864; Oliver D. Hart, "The Market Mechanism as an Incentive Scheme," *Bell Journal of Economics*, 14, Autumn 1983, pp. 366–382; and Barry J. Nalebuff and Joseph E. Stiglitz, "Prizes and Incentives: Towards a General Theory of Compensation and Competition," *Bell Journal of Economics*, 14, Spring 1983, pp. 21–43.

15. William Baumol has suggested that the objective of managers may be sales maximization subject to the requirement that the firm make a satisfactory profit. This approach reflects his view that managers pursue a mix of profits and sales revenue. That is, given the menu of combinations of sales revenue and profit that depends on the firm's consumer demand and production costs, managers choose their most preferred combination of profit and sales revenue. William J. Baumol, "On the Theory of the Expansion of the Firm," *American Economic Review*, 52, pp. 1078–1087, and *Business Behavior, Value and Growth*, New York: Macmillan, 1962.

16. Abegglen, J. C. and George Stalk, Jr., *Kaisha: The Japanese Corporation*, New York: Basic Books, 1985, p. 43.

17. See Steve Lohr, "In Pursuit of Computing's Holy Grail," *New York Times*, May 23, 1993, p.1, sec. 3.

18. It is calculated by taking the derivative of market demand with respect to price and multiplying by the ratio of price to demand: $\eta(p) = -D'(p)p/D(p)$.

19. The profit of the company is the markup times the quantity sold, Profit $= (p^m - c)D(p^m)$. By using the fundamental inverse elasticity rule the firm's profit can be calculated based on the elasticity of demand at the profit-maximizing price: Profit $= p^m D(p^m)/\eta(p^m)$.

20. A company with market power can set prices using the inverse elasticity pricing rule. The monopoly price is determined by the fundamental inverse elasticity equation, which states that the markup of the company's price over marginal cost, divided by the price, equals one over the elasticity of demand.

$$(p^m - c)/p^m = 1/\eta(p^m)$$

In this equation, p^m is the monopoly price and c represents the marginal cost of production which is assumed to be a constant level per unit of output. The expression $\eta(p^m)$ represents elasticity of consumer demand for the company's products.

21. A two-product monopoly maximizes profit by choosing two product prices together. The markup over marginal cost for each product depends on the product's own price elasticity and the effect of that price on the other product's demand, known as the *cross-price elasticity of demand*.

22. The economist Frank Knight (*Risk, Uncertainty and Profit*, New York: Houghton Mifflin, 1921, pp. 251–252) long ago observed that, with centralization and unity of interest in an organization,

> The possibility of thus reducing uncertainty by transforming it into a measurable risk through grouping constitutes a strong incentive to extend the scale of operations of a business establishment. This fact must constitute one of the important causes of the phenomenal growth in the average size of industrial establishments, which is a familiar characteristic of modern economic life.

Knight stressed the importance of scale as a means of allowing managers to balance the risks of their errors in perception or judgment.

23. For example, the need to reheat steel is avoided by combining the blast furnace and rolling mill in a single enterprise. Elsewhere, I have introduced the term economies of sequence (Daniel F. Spulber, *Regulation and Markets*, Cambridge: MIT Press, 1989) to refer to the cost savings from combining stages in a production process within a single firm. Chandler (Alfred D. Chandler, *Scale and Scope: The Dynamics of Industrial Capitalism*, Cambridge: Harvard University Press, 1990, p. 37) finds that cost savings from vertical integration were obtained in chemicals, metals, and machinery, but notes that vertical integration occurred in many companies for other reasons such as reliability of input supplies.

24. The widely used S-curve introduced by McKinsey & Company relates R&D effort in terms of investment to the performance of innovation. R. N. Foster (*Innovation: The Attacker's Advantage*, New York: Summit Books, 1986) describes the S-curve as the infancy, explosion, and gradual maturation of technological progress across firms but also speaks of the returns to investment of an individual development laboratory. Thus, for a specific project, the inverse of the S-curve is nothing more than a cost function for R&D with an initial range of performance levels for which there are increasing returns followed by a range of performance levels for which there are decreasing returns.

25. Clark and Wheelwright (Kim B. Clark and Steven C. Wheelwright, *Revolutionizing Product Development: Quantum Leaps in Speed, Efficiency, and Quality*, New York: Free Press, 1992) emphasize competition through new product development and prescribe organizational changes that firms can make to speed product development including integration of marketing, manufacturing, and design. Stalk and Hout (G. Stalk and T. M. Hout, *Competing against Time*, New York: Free Press, 1990, p. 120) of the Boston Consulting Group find that the "structure of an organization that facilitates rapid new product design and introduction is analogous to the structure of a fast-response factory." Harris et al. of Booz-Allen & Hamilton emphasize the importance of technology in management strategy and suggest that "the structure of an organization is vitally important to the effective management of technology resources" (J. M. Harris, R. W. Shaw, Jr., and W. P. Sommers, "The Strategic Management of Technology," in R. B. Lamb, ed., *Competitive Strategic Management*, Englewood Cliffs, NJ: Prentice Hall, 1984, pp. 530–555, at p. 544).

BUILDING MARKET BRIDGES: THE *MAIN* FRAMEWORK

MARKET **3** MAKING

What do firms do? The answer is that they make markets. Managers need to understand their companies' activities as intermediaries between suppliers and customers. This holds true for any industry and for any line of business, whether services or manufacturing. Understanding the firm's role as an intermediary helps managers to determine the value added by the firm and to discern new opportunities for value creation.

Ask most people what a market maker is and they will tell you that it is someone who perpetually stands ready to buy and sell a product or financial instrument. The market maker keeps cash and inventory on hand for buying and selling so that customers and suppliers can enter or leave the market at any time. In financial markets, for example, the market maker provides essential liquidity in financial instruments by allowing conversion of the instrument to cash and back.

I wish to give market making a somewhat broader strategic interpretation. I include a wider range of actions that make markets work. In particular, consider the four main activities:

- Price setting
- Coordinating exchange
- Market clearing
- Allocating goods and services

Companies can compete effectively in a dynamic environment by applying the basic tools of market making.

The hardest task a manager faces is defining the business. The manager must determine what business the firm currently is in and what business the firm will operate in the future. A useful way of addressing this question is to ask what markets the firm is serving and what markets it wishes to serve. The manager's focus shifts away from the particular characteristics of the product that the firm is supplying and moves toward an understanding of the institutions of exchange that the firm provides.

The market-bridge view of the firm focuses attention on the market-making and intermediation services that it provides to its suppliers and customers. A company's suppliers are also its customers when it comes to intermediation services, as is well known in financial markets. A bank serves both its borrowers and its lenders. An insurance company serves both its insured customers and its investors. It is true for firms outside the financial industry as well. A wholesaler serves both manufacturers and retailers. A retailer provides marketing services to a manufacturer by taking delivery of merchandise and conveying information about sales and customer needs to the manufacturer. At the same time the retailer provides intermediation services to its customers by searching for and assembling a variety of products in its stores.

Price Setting

Pricing is the crucial market-making activity of firms. While it is sometimes convenient to say that the market sets the price, price setting is not carried out by an invisible auctioneer. Rather, pricing is often an integral part of strategy making by firms. Moreover, pricing by the firm is an essential aspect of the intermediation between the firm's customers and its suppliers. Pricing is at the heart of competition, so that the prices set by a firm reflect strategic interaction with its competitors. I begin by considering the central aspect of price setting in market making and market clearing. Then I examine pricing as a means of communication with the firm's customers and suppliers, and as a means of gathering information about customers and suppliers. Effective pricing is essential to winning the market.

Living on the Spread

Companies live on the spread between the costs of their purchased inputs and the prices of their outputs. Their objective is to maximize the net present value of these cash flows, otherwise known as economic profit. The method presented here provides the manager with new ways to think about profit and new techniques for increasing the firm's earnings.

The firm's profit is the difference between the present value of its revenue and cost streams:

$$\text{Profit} = \text{revenue} - \text{cost}$$

The firm's revenues are added across its various products. Generally, revenues take into account variations in prices across the firm's markets as well as discounts, promotions, and other pricing methods. The firm's costs are added across its purchased inputs. Costs include the cost of capital and all of the firm's payments for labor, manufactured inputs, natural resources, and technology.

A basic example of a very simple retailer buying and selling a single good illustrates the main ideas. Consider a flower stand that buys and sells roses. To make things simple suppose that the flower stand sells no other flowers and has no other costs besides the roses. The flower stand only sells the flowers by the dozen at a price of $15 and buys the flowers at $10 a dozen. The flower stand's revenue equals the price times the quantity sold and its cost equals the price times the quantity bought. If the flower stand succeeds in selling all that it has purchased its profits are equal to the spread of $5 multiplied by the sales, that is:

$$\text{Profit} = \text{price spread} \times \text{quantity sold}$$

What are the problems faced by the flower stand? A competitor with the same supplier may offer the flowers at $14 a dozen and lure away all of its customers. The stand's manager must be alert to all prices of competitors and be prepared to vary its output price accordingly. A competitor may find another supplier offering roses at $9 a dozen and then offer its roses at $10, effectively driving the stand out of business. The stand's manager must be aware of alternative sources of supply and be prepared to secure lower prices from its supplier or to seek an alternative supplier. In practice, the stand constantly faces fluctuations in both the sales and purchase prices of roses and must be constantly prepared to respond to variations in the spread.

Now suppose that the flower stand purchases and sells a wide variety of flowers, including not only roses but tulips, daffodils, impatiens, carnations, chrysanthemums, geraniums, daisies, and marigolds. The stand now relies on a variety of suppliers and is subject to wide variations in prices and seasonal availability. Moreover, the flower stand offers its customers mixed bouquets combining the flowers in an almost infinite variety of ways. Since flowers are perishable, the manager worries about the possibility of unsold inventory. It becomes necessary to monitor carefully the prices of competitors' flowers and bouquets and the relative prices of alternative sources of supply. The flower stand constantly assembles and reshuffles a portfolio of flowers, taking into account the likelihood of sales and the expected prices. The manager's decisions now must respond to the price spreads for each type of flower. Since the flowers are mixed in some bouquets, all of the stand's purchases depend on each of the spreads.

The main point of this example is that all firms live on the spread between purchases and sales. Retailers offer their customers a wide variety of products, often obtained from many suppliers. Manufacturers produce products assembled, like bouquets, from a variety of inputs. Whether reseller or manufacturer, firms live on the spread.

What is the meaning of competitive advantage in an environment with high levels of price volatility? The main points are as follows: perception, coordination, reaction, and control. First, the firm must be able to *perceive* that it faces a spread. Too often, firms take purchasing for granted. Other firms pay careful attention to purchase costs and sales prices but fail to realize the connection. High purchase prices limit discounts while low sales prices limit bids for inputs.

Second, to strengthen their purchasing and marketing efforts, firms must *coordinate* these activities. The setting of purchase and sales prices should not be carried out in separate divisions of the firm. At the very least, pricing decisions must be closely coordinated with pricing adjustments reflecting changes in both input supply and output demand conditions.

Third, the firm must be prepared to *react* with great speed to changes in the spread, whether from the input or output side or both simultaneously. This concept is familiar to financial firms and other participants in the markets for securities, bonds, derivatives, futures, and currencies. Prices may change in seconds and large amounts of money may be lost or won in the blink of an eye. The speed with which prices change is increasing throughout the economy. Playing at a higher speed must be part of every competitive strategy.

Fourth, the firm must seek to *control* its destiny by setting its bid prices to suppliers and its ask prices to customers. Firms exercise a range of controls over their prices. Some prices of basic commodities the firm may take as givens; that is, they are chosen by the firm's suppliers or customers. Other prices are set through negotiation between the firm and its trading partners. In many cases, the company exercises market power by setting its own prices. For many reasons, this is one of the most important tasks faced by the firm.

Pricing Provides a Service

The prices set by a firm are its "face" to its customers and suppliers. While brand image and reliability are important in the long run, prices are the heart of the contract for all of the firm's ongoing transactions. Many analysts downplay the importance of pricing, suggesting that price wars are to be avoided at all costs and that firms should disguise their pricing policies through complex contract terms or promotional activities. This is a serious mistake because a company's customers and suppliers rely on clear and accurate price information. In fact, setting prices is a service that the firm provides to its customers and suppliers.

Setting prices is not a costless activity. Rather, it is a difficult and time-consuming process that requires the gathering and processing of extensive amounts of market information. Moreover, pricing is an important strategic decision for the firm. As such the overall pricing strategy of the company requires the involvement of the firm's top managers and should not be delegated to the marketing department as an afterthought. Instead, pricing expertise from the marketing department should be made a central part of the firm's strategic plans.

It is often suggested that pricing is a secondary concern and that companies should concentrate on cost reductions, service enhancement, and product differentiation, the notion being that companies that create value can command higher prices, while discounting prices only reduces profits, thus lowering available funds for future quality enhancement and investment. Clearly, if prices are too low, the firm may fail to capture the returns to its innovative activities. However, prices that are too high result in a loss of current sales and encourage customers to seek out competitors, so that future sales are lost as well. Since customer demand is price responsive, setting prices too high can result in revenue losses in comparison with lower prices. High prices result in loss of sales volume, and that can raise production costs or create excess inventories. Commanding a premium makes the company vulnerable to rapid entry of new competitors who can capture market share with small discounts. The company that earns a high return may fail to exercise the discipline required to cut its costs in preparation for competitive attacks.

Some firms face vast computational problems in setting prices, so that getting it right becomes all the more important. A typical supermarket chain, such as Jewel or Dominick's, sets prices on 50,000 to 70,000 stock-keeping units. Not only that, the prices vary across the stores in the chain, reflecting different costs and different local competitors. Also, many of the prices change daily or weekly as the supermarket responds to seasonal availability of fruits and vegetables, changes in customer tastes, manufacturer promotions, and prices set by rival chains. Keeping track of this data consumes company resources. Many chains pay outside tracking services to report on a small number of rival prices that serve as benchmarks.

It is essential that companies such as supermarkets understand that these computational activities also create value. Effectively creating value requires investment in training and information processing equipment, such as scanners, computers, and digital networks that allow close monitoring of current sales and updating of prices with as little delay as possible.

Setting the Spread

Most analyses of competitive pricing in economics and in marketing consider only the prices for the firm's products and services, and neglect the prices paid for the firm's purchases. The purchase prices of goods and services are taken as a fixed part of the firm's costs and play only a secondary role in the firm's pricing decisions. This one-sided approach neglects the firm's market-making activities and can lead to mistakes and missed opportunities.

When firms are market makers, they not only set the prices of the products and services that they sell, they often set some of the prices of the products and services that they *buy*. Firms post wages for new employees and adjust pay levels for existing workers. Depending on the firm's market power with its suppliers of manufactured inputs, the firm either posts offer prices, bargains with suppliers, or takes the supplier's offer as given. Many firms exercise their market power by putting out subcontracts for competitive bidding by potential suppliers. Successful firms *always look both ways*, at the prices they pay suppliers and the prices charged to customers.

It is critical for managers to consider the firm's selling and buying pricing policies jointly. The difference between the firm's ask prices for outputs and bid prices on inputs determines the economic profits of the firm. The price spread is the best indication of the firm's value added. The spread between the bid and ask prices in financial markets reflects the transaction costs of an asset and provides returns to the market-making activities of firms. In retail and wholesale markets, the spread between the purchase and resale price also reflects transaction costs and provides a return to the market-making activities of these types of firms. Competitive pressures narrow the gap and push revenues toward costs. Winning the market requires that the firm perform its intermediation activities at the lowest cost. The firm earns returns from continually finding innovative ways to lower the market's transaction costs. Further, the firm must constantly seek new sources of supplies and new ways of improving contracts with existing suppliers, as a means of lowering purchase prices. Finally, the firm must seek new customers and new ways of serving existing customers to raise sales prices.

The firm should focus its attention on creating correct spreads between its bid and ask prices. Firms can make serious mistakes if they set the ask price as a markup over their input prices, which are taken as fixed. This can lead to over- or underpricing in the product markets and create problems with customers. Conversely, firms can make mistakes if they set input prices in reference to arbitrary output prices, which can lead to over- or underpricing in input markets and problems in relationships with suppliers. The main point is that as a market maker, a company must coordinate its full set of pricing policies.

These ideas are familiar to financial firms such as banks and brokerages who know that the difference between success and failure depends on "living off the spread." Banks must keep track of minute-to-minute fluctuations in the cost of capital, since their earnings depend on the difference between the cost to borrowers and the return to lenders. Every manager should visit a busy trading floor such as the Chicago Mercantile Exchange to see the volatility of spreads and the large gains and losses associated with small variations in the contracts held by investors. Managers should understand that such volatility is no longer confined to organized financial exchanges but is instead a characteristic of almost every market. With the increasing rapidity of communication, consumers and firms monitor daily changes in the prices of computers, peripherals, cameras, and other electronic equipment. With the advent of the information superhighway, daily price changes are becoming the norm in these and many other industries. Therefore, all businesses must become aware that they are living off the spread and be prepared to react accordingly.

The key to winning the market is to provide the best intermediation services. This means that the relative prices of the firm's purchases and sales must be a source of competitive advantage. A retailer that sharply discounts its products can still lose the market to a competitor that has found a way to purchase products at lower cost and can sell for less, even with a higher margin. Similarly, a company with an aggressive purchasing policy may find itself outbid for essential inputs by a competitor. If bidding too low leads to a loss of suppliers, the firm may find it difficult to compete in the product market.

Pricing is a fundamental part of the firm's marketing and purchasing policies. On the sales side, pricing is the most effective means of stimulating customer demand and winning the market from competitors. Pricing is generally regarded as an essential complement to marketing expenditures. Getting the price–value relationship right is one of the most important management tasks, and sometimes the most difficult. On the purchasing side, pricing is also an essential part of competing for scarce supplies and holding down costs. In purchasing manufactured goods such as parts and equipment and outsourcing services, it is also important to get the price–value relationship right to build long-term relationships with suppliers.

Pricing Clears Markets

The most effective means of market clearing is through prices. By raising or lowering product prices, firms can lower or increase their sales. Changes in purchases can depend on the prices offered by the firm to its suppliers. The build-up or depletion of the firm's inventories is affected by the relationship between the sets of bid and ask prices. Fluctuations in demand

and supply faced by the firm can require constant adjustment in prices, promotion, and ordering. If the firm's ask and bid prices are out of balance, the firm runs the risk of carrying costly inventories or of losing customers due to stock-outs. The firm will increase its spread to avoid stock-outs or reduce the spread to reduce excess inventories.[1]

By varying asking prices, firms signal the availability and cost of products to their customers. By varying bid prices, firms signal the value and demand for products to their suppliers. Therefore, the firm's price-setting activities do not simply represent an adjustment of inventories; they coordinate the activities of the firm's customers and suppliers. In this important way, the firm's price-setting activities bring supply and demand into balance, so that customer demands at the posted price are satisfied and suppliers are able to make the desired sales at the posted price. Successful firms devote substantial effort to pricing strategies, realizing that there are substantial returns to this vital market-making activity.

The traditional approach to pricing by supermarkets has opened up the market to new entrants that have a better grasp of market making. To some extent, supermarkets match their pricing and purchasing by establishing margins on particular items. However, for many supermarkets, the marketing and purchasing functions are not fully coordinated. Pricing of products generally involves very low markups on a list of groceries and other products for which competitor's prices are tracked by independent services. Other products such as specialty foods have higher margins. Wal-Mart and Kmart are creating substantial competition for supermarkets in some areas. Large discount wholesale buying clubs are coordinating purchasing and sales prices more closely. Consumers buy in bulk but pay prices that are close to wholesale. As some supermarket chains come to a better understanding of their role as market makers, they are expanding by three to five times the size of individual stores, which have usually been around 30,000 square feet. The chains with larger stores offer greater variety and closer-to-wholesale prices on a range of products. The industry will experience a shakeout of many traditional grocery operations, with innovative chains winning the market.

Pricing Communicates Information

Market making involves more than setting bid prices that reflect demand for the firm's products and ask prices for suppliers. The prices must be communicated clearly to buyers and sellers so that they can make the necessary adjustments in their plans. Thus, the role of the firm as a market maker includes posting prices.

Prices are often the firm's principal means of communication with customers and suppliers. Even for firms with substantial marketing expenditures, prices are important because they represent a credible commitment rather than an assertion that cannot be verified. Prices are offers to buy or sell and thus provide buyers and sellers with information about the firm's opportunity costs and its willingness to pay. A simple statement of the product price in an advertisement is valuable to customers: It allows them to comparison shop easily by comparing advertised prices, avoiding the cost of traveling to various stores.

Clear price information is one of the secrets of success of catalog companies such as Lands' End. Consumers know exactly what each item costs and can compare its price with other advertised prices. The consumer can compare the costs of different items within the same catalog and calculate the cost of the total purchase, something that may be difficult to do in the hustle and bustle of a store. The need to know price information for the purpose of comparison shopping and budgeting is so essential for consumers that new opportunities will be created for companies that can provide this information at the lowest cost, whether through superstores, catalogs, computer networks, or interactive video systems for home shopping.

Prices are generally the most informative part of marketing claims, before product characteristics and brand image. Discounters in particular stress price comparisons with competitors: "We're the low-price leader," "We won't be undersold," "Always the lowest price, guaranteed." By pricing low, discounters signal the efficiency of their operations and their high volume of sales. They let customers know that they are committed to maintaining low prices in the future. Customers understand that the low-price leader is the winner of the market and anticipate that many others will shop at the same store. A continued high volume of sales then allows the store to maintain its low prices in the future, thereby confirming the customer's decision to shop at the low-price leader.

Not all companies understand the value of clearly communicating their prices. Auto dealers traditionally have tried to disguise the prices of vehicles by not being explicit about the level of discounts offered from the list price. Few auto dealers advertise their prices or quote prices over the phone. Indeed, many auto dealers try to raise the cost of learning the price by extended delays, often keeping customers waiting for hours while sales personnel make endless trips to the "back room," ostensibly to check their calculations with a manager. The purpose of such delays is in part a traditional bargaining technique familiar to anyone who has visited a Middle Eastern bazaar. While the salesperson drags out the process, more is learned about the customer's income, preferences, and willingness to pay for the car, so that the discount can be adjusted accordingly to achieve first-degree price discrimination. In fact, the customer's impatience is itself useful as the customer weighs the cost of his or her time versus the cost of making an early price concession. Moreover, the delay detains customers at a particular dealer's showroom so they may not have the time to visit a rival dealer. Exhausted customers may simply agree to a price without a comparison because they are disheartened at the prospect of repeating the costly bargaining process.

While often effective at raising dealer profits, this rather inefficient technique increases the transaction costs for the automobile market as a whole, thereby reducing overall demand for cars. The costs of search and bargaining are so high under this system that in many cases it may affect the consumer's choice of which type of car to purchase. Certainly, it can reduce a customer's loyalty to a dealer despite other efforts at customer service. This situation has created entry opportunities for dealers who post prices clearly, such as dealers selling GM's Saturn. In addition, consumers pay for services such as *Consumer Reports* that calculate likely discounts from list prices.

Prices need not be the lowest in the market to convey useful information. Indeed, higher prices can be a signal of product quality, especially for those goods requiring experience to discern quality. Companies can indicate that the customer value provided by its product justifies a higher price. High prices are set in anticipation of repeat business from satisfied customers, so that new customers can infer quality from the price. In general, prices provide a signal about the company's competitive intentions. Does the company wish to be perceived as a discounter? Does the company wish to target a particular market segment or competitor by matching its prices? Does the company wish to be perceived as a high-end firm, supplying a high-quality product or even providing prestige? In making strategic pricing decisions, managers should always take into account the impression their prices will create.

Pricing Creates Market Information

As a market maker, the firm must constantly gather information about customer demand and supplier costs. Pricing is particularly useful as a means of gathering information. For this reason, one should not waste time in exactly determining the "right" price before introducing a new product and posting prices. Rather, the product should be introduced and the reaction to the posted price observed closely. Reactions to the firm's bid or ask prices provide useful data; delaying the introduction of a product causes lost revenues while small pricing errors only affect marginal revenues. An unexpected demand or supply response can always be met with further price adjustments.

This does not mean that adjusting the price is without costs. On the contrary, it is costly to print new menus, change catalogs, and revise advertising. Also, customer goodwill can be harmed by price increases on repeat purchase items or even by sales if customers who bought before the sale feel they were at a disadvantage. Companies sometimes offer price protection to customers by offering to give discounts if a sale occurs so that the customers will not delay their purchases. By varying its prices, a firm continues to gather information about its customers and suppliers.

Companies experiment with prices constantly to learn about price responsiveness. High initial prices and later declining prices for new products are not due simply to falling costs of production. Rather, manufacturers are able to obtain a fairly complete picture of consumer demand as the price travels downward. Of course, the manufacturer is also able to extract a premium from those customers who are impatient to purchase the latest innovation. The sales observed of a product with a high and declining price provide information about just how impatient those customers are. Often the price changes can be dramatic, as in the case of the introduction of new computers. Prices of some models of notebook computers fell by over half not long after their introduction, not necessarily as a consequence of competition but rather because the manufacturer extracted consumers' surplus from early buyers.

Retailers commonly price higher for seasonal items to sort out consumers who are impatient to purchase goods or who do not wish to risk being rationed by the store if particular products are sold out (e.g., clothing sizes). The end-of-season sales clear out inventories and make use of information about customer price responsiveness.

Another approach is to begin with low introductory offers as a means of testing the waters. Many new products are introduced at a discount or with coupons. This is partly to subsidize the costs of customers switching from existing products and to cover the perceived risks of trying something new. By increasing the price after a product introduction, the company learns about the extent of customer price sensitivity.

A standard marketing tool for analyzing pricing decisions is the price-response function, which determines the relationship between the amount demanded by the firm's customers and the firm's price.[2] The price-response function translates changes in the price of a good, represented by p, into changes in the quantity sold of the good, represented by q. The value of the parameters can be affected by marketing and sales efforts. For example, pricing at $10 yields 100 units of sales while pricing at $20 yields 80 units sold. The price elasticity is measured by the percentage change in sales that occurs relative to a percentage change in the price. If the elasticity is less than one, a price rise increases revenues, while if the elasticity is greater than one, a price cut increases revenues. In the example, the elasticity of demand is less than one since an increase in the price from $10 to $20 increases revenues from $1,000 to $1,600. The highest revenues are achieved in this example at $30, with revenues equaling $1,800. At a higher price, say $40, revenues fall to $1,600.

By varying the price charged for a product a manufacturer can attempt to determine the elasticity of demand. In the preceding example, the retailer may not know the parameters of the price-response function. Careful observation of sales at different prices will allow the retailer to estimate these parameters and then set a profit-maximizing price.

A more complicated aspect of price responsiveness is the effect of changes in the price of a good on the consumer's purchase of another good, known as the cross-price elasticity. There are two possibilities. If a price increase in one product causes the consumer to decrease purchases of the other product, the products are said to be complements. An example is peanut butter and jelly. Increases in the price of peanut butter may lead consumers to make fewer peanut butter and jelly sandwiches, which would reduce the demand for jelly. Other examples of products that are complementary include cameras and film, computers and software, and automobiles and gasoline. If a price increase in one product causes the consumer to increase purchases of the other product, then the products are said to be substitutes. An example is orange juice and pineapple juice. Increases in the price of orange juice will shift some consumer demand to pineapple juice. Other examples of substitutes are ordinary cameras and instant-developing cameras, desktop and notebook computers, and regular and premium gasoline.

Since retailers generally carry a wide range of products, they must be aware of the cross-effect of prices on customer demand patterns. Since customers purchase a market basket of goods at the supermarket, all of the customer's purchases are to some extent complementary. Thus, supermarkets reduce the price of loss leaders, such as dairy products, fresh produce, or national brands, to increase store traffic and thus expand overall sales, particularly of higher-priced specialty items. At the same time, supermarkets have become aware of the profit potential for substitute products, offering low-cost house brands that are substitutes for more expensive national brands.

A fast-food chain such as McDonald's includes many items on its menus that are complements and substitutes. A cut in the price of hamburgers may stimulate sales of both hamburgers and complementary products such as french fries and soft drinks. At the same time, a cut in the price of hamburgers may reduce demand for substitute products such as chicken. Chains like McDonald's amass substantial amounts of information about cross-price elasticities as they vary prices and promotions.

An essential element of winning the market is to have superior information about the price responsiveness of consumer demand. Managers should seek competitive advantage by learning as much as possible about the effects of the product's price and the effects of complementary and substitute product prices on their sales. By knowing more about consumer price responsiveness, the firm can set prices that will win over customers while yielding increased profits for the firm.

Pricing and Market Segmentation

Market making also includes tailoring the firm's prices to fit individual market segments. The extent to which markets can be segmented depends on the quality of the firm's information about customers, the nature of the competition faced by the firm, and the transaction costs of implementing a segmented market strategy. Legal restrictions on price discrimination can also prevent certain forms of pricing.

Individual consumers differ in their willingness to pay for products. Ideally, the firm's profits are maximized by setting different payments for every consumer. This is limited by the accuracy of information about individual customers and the impossibility of identifying the purchase decisions of individual customers. The most effective way of identifying individual customers and assessing their individual willingness to pay is through bargaining. Retailers engage in bargaining over the purchase price of automobiles, as mentioned earlier, and major appliances. Bargaining is also a common feature of decentralized markets with many buyers and sellers, such as the markets for home repair services (plumbing, heating, and electrical work) and real estate markets. Typically, sellers employ the bargaining process to gather information about the customer's income, the customer's knowledge of competitive options, and the urgency of the purchase. This allows sellers to estimate willingness to pay and to price accordingly. Bargaining is a costly process and not always practical.

For firms handling a high volume of purchases, the best way to segment the market while learning about customer willingness to pay is to offer customers various options. The more options offered, the more market segments can be created, if the options are carefully designed. Customers self-select by choosing their most favored option and thus reveal their preferences to the firm. There are many forms of optional pricing.

The most basic form of optional pricing is the quantity discount. By offering a discount based on the quantity purchased, the firm essentially sets out a menu of prices for each quantity purchased. Customers choose the amount to buy by comparing the benefits from an increase in the purchase with the additional discount on the last units purchased. By choosing the size of their purchase, customers reveal their willingness to pay "at the margin," that is, for the last unit purchased. High-demand customers pay a lower per-unit price than low-demand customers. Quantity discounts are common in consumer goods. For example, many types of goods, such as breakfast cereal, laundry detergent, and toothpaste, are sold in a range of package sizes. The per-unit cost decreases with increases in the size of the package. Customer choices of package size depend upon comparing the discount with the benefits of the product, income, storage space, family size, and other considerations. Similarly, multiunit bundles of products carry quantity discounts, such as soft drinks and beer sold by the can or in packages of six, twelve, or twenty-four cans.

Quantity discounts are commonly offered by manufacturers and wholesalers to retailers. In the liquor industry, manufacturers and wholesalers offer somewhat complicated discounts to retailers based on the number of cases ordered. This creates substantial discounts for retail chains as compared with individual liquor stores and small grocery stores. The prevalence of manufacturers' discounts is an important source of economies of scale for retailers. Manufacturers' discounts allow manufacturers to price differently to different marketing channels.

Another form of market segmentation through pricing and customer self-selection is the product line. By offering a product line, firms bundle quality rather than quantity. For example, gas stations offer three choices of gasoline—regular, premium, and super—with increasing octane ratings and other features. While the higher prices in part reflect these product differences, they are also a means of segmenting customers and setting prices for each of the three market segments. Airlines also offer a product line consisting of supersaver, coach, business class, and first class fares. Product-line pricing is a common feature of a wide array of consumer products, including computers, electronics, appliances, automobiles, luggage, and clothing. Consumers self-select by choosing their most preferred product. The pattern of sales reveals information to the firm about the relative attractiveness of product features to its customers.

A more complex pricing method involves offering customers diverse options that can be combined and setting prices based on the bundle of options. For example, computer companies offer a wide variety of options on their basic models, including the type of computer chip (Intel's 486SX, 486DX, 486DX2, Pentium, etc.), the amount of random access memory, megabytes of storage in the hard drive, and the type of monitor. These features are bundled together, and the total price of the bundle is set by the firm, rather than pricing à la carte. Dell offers a product line consisting of the Performance, Dimension, and Dimension XPS series, and a variety of options within each series. Their catalog states that computers are custom built and that "Dell makes it easy to choose and use the computer that's perfect for you." Because there are many options, there is a staggering number of permutations, which allows for a very fine segmentation of the market with corresponding prices for each segment.

Market segmentation, and the adjustment of prices and product features to fit each market segment, is an essential aspect of market making. Winning the market requires gathering accurate information about market segments and tailoring offered prices to meet customer needs.

Firms can win or lose the market segment by segment, and ultimately customer by customer. Improvements in pricing methods, marketing, and information technology have pushed the battle for markets closer and closer to the individual customer.

Coordinating Exchange

A market is a set of buyer and seller relationships and institutions of exchange. Firms act as market makers by establishing buyer and seller relationships, coordinating their activities, and providing the institutions of exchange. The principal characteristic of a market is a centralized exchange where buyers and sellers meet each other or trade through dealers. Firms, acting as dealers, provide a wide variety of central marketplaces.

Since the beginning of civilization, people have met in central marketplaces to trade goods and services. The creation of money allowed individuals to avoid the problem of the double coincidence of wants. Without money, an individual who desired wheat and had wine to trade had to find another individual who desired wine and had wheat to trade. With money, an individual with wine to sell simply had to find a buyer, while an individual desiring wine only had to find a seller.

The search of buyers and sellers for each other created another problem of coincidence of wants. A buyer who wished to purchase a good at a particular time and place had to find a seller who wanted to sell that good at the same time and place. One solution is the farmer's market, in which a town provides a central marketplace and sets a common time for market day, and producers open stands to sell their goods and services. This solution is quite costly since producers have to be at the market at the specified time and devote time and effort to marketing their output. The emergence of specialized dealers solved the problems of both time and place. The dealer could purchase the good from various suppliers when the suppliers wished to sell and build stockpiles of the good. The dealer could then sell the good from stock to buyers when buyers appeared. The location problem could be solved by the dealer traveling between buyers and sellers, or even more easily by the dealer staying in a central location where buyers and sellers could come to the dealer. The central location of dealers in towns and specialized shopping areas further simplified the coordination of transactions.

The Structure of Markets

There are three basic market structures that reflect the extent of market centralization: auction markets, dealer markets, and search markets. Auction markets are highly centralized, with bidding by buyers and sellers who act through market makers. Dealer markets can involve small or large numbers of dealers who set bid and ask prices for buyers and sellers. Search markets do not involve centralized price setting; individual buyers and sellers meet through search or through brokers, and negotiate prices.

The auctioneer image of price setting fits best for organized markets, such as the stock and futures markets, where prices are the result of continual bidding by buyers and sellers. In auction markets for securities, specialists carry out trades that reflect bid and ask prices. Futures are traded in many central exchanges such as the Chicago Board of Trade, the Chicago Mercantile Exchange, the New York Mercantile Exchange, and the New York Futures Exchange.[3] The exchanges provide important intermediation services to their members. Trades are carried out by those who have purchased a seat to become members of the exchange. Traditionally, traders exchanging a particular type of contract meet in trading pits on the exchange floor. Proposed ask and bid prices are announced to the trading pit by traders using a system of open outcry and hand signals. A trade takes place upon agreement between two traders taking opposite sides of the transaction.

In addition to providing a central marketplace, futures markets provide clearinghouse services. All contracts between traders are immediately transformed into offsetting contracts between each of the traders and the clearinghouse. This transfers the risk of contracting with an insolvent trader to the clearinghouse. Using the system of marking to market, the gains or losses on each contract between a trader and the clearinghouse are settled daily. This system makes it convenient to close out a trader's long or short position in a particular contract. Thus, the clearinghouse both reduces the risk of traders and reduces transaction costs.

In dealer markets such as the over-the-counter market for securities, prices reflect the bid and ask prices and completed transactions of many individual dealers and their customers. The NASDAQ service separates price posting from price fixing by providing a record of prices of individual transactions. In futures markets, computerized trading systems, such as the Chicago Mercantile Exchange's GLOBEX system, match buyers and sellers who enter proposed contracts on a network. Most buyers and sellers of stocks or futures act through brokers and other financial intermediaries such as mutual funds. These intermediaries do not set prices for the financial assets but instead set prices for the intermediation services they provide.

Dealers are market makers—they provide a central place of exchange and manage transactions. The central place of exchange greatly reduces the search costs of buyers and sellers who must only find the dealer, and not each other. The management of transactions by the dealer reduces the costs of buying and selling and helps the market to operate smoothly. By buying when suppliers are ready to sell and selling when customers are ready to buy, the dealer provides immediacy to the marketplace.[4]

Many firms specialize exclusively as dealers. For example, used car dealers purchase cars from individuals and from new car dealers who have received used cars as trade-ins, and resell them at a central location. Other dealers buy and sell art, antiques, rugs, or stamps and coins.

Dealers play a prominent role in financial markets. Stocks are sold both in auction markets such as the New York Stock Exchange (NYSE) or the American Stock Exchange (AMEX) and in the over-the-counter market. In auction markets, dealers known as specialists buy and sell particular stocks by matching buy and sell orders and trading on their own accounts, subject to rules set by the exchange. The over-the-counter market is operated by dealers as well. The trade group for major securities dealers operates the National Association of Securities Dealers Automated Quotation system (NASDAQ) that provides a national communications system. Dealers buy and sell stocks directly over-the-counter to individuals. The NASDAQ system records the current bid and ask prices of each dealer as well as posting median prices.

Many search markets involve intermediaries who are not directly engaged in setting prices. For example, in the real estate markets, most buyers and sellers act through brokers. The purchase price of the property results from bargaining between the buyer and the seller, often intermediated by brokers. List prices and closing prices of properties are posted on central listing services provided by brokers' associations. Buyers have different requirements regarding the type and location of house they will buy, and houses have individual features, unlike interchangeable financial assets or commodities. Another example of a search market is the one for highly specialized labor services that must be matched with employer needs. Buyers and sellers, including managers, engineers, actors, and models, obtain matching services from headhunters, agents, and other intermediaries.

Auction markets, dealer markets, and search markets exist for very specific types of commodities. Auction markets generally handle standardized, easily tradable assets. The same holds for dealer markets, which handle trades in assets with lower frequency of trades, and in some cases, smaller numbers of traders. Search markets are at the other end of the spectrum, dealing with unique assets offered by sellers and unique buyer requirements. Most products and services lie in the middle of this range. They are provided by firms who bundle the product or service with their own market-making services.

Market Coordination Creates Value

Practically all companies provide dealer services to their customers and suppliers. They create central places of exchange that facilitate transactions for buyers and sellers. They stand ready to buy and sell products, avoiding problems of the coincidence of time and location. It is essential that companies clearly understand their role as dealers in order to operate efficiently and to earn returns from their market-making efforts.

It is apparent that all retailers act as dealers, whether in food, clothing, furniture, hardware, appliances, computers, or other general merchandise. Customers rely on retailers to have a wide variety of goods in stock at all times. Improvements in computerized inventory control and distribution allow retailers to adjust inventories to patterns of demand and improve availability.

In addition, retailers provide consumers with a central place of exchange, usually a store or chain of stores. The trend toward superstores reflects an understanding of the value of centralization. Superstores in books, such as Barnes & Noble, Borders, and Supercrown, generally carry over 100,000 books. Customers avoid having to search across many smaller bookstores. Customers are assured that the particular book they are looking for will be in stock and that there will be a wide variety of other books to browse through. The success of CompUSA, the computer superstore, and Toys "R" Us demonstrates the competitive advantages that derive from improvements in immediacy and centralization.

As every retailer will tell you, the keys to success are location, location, location. Centralization in location drove the establishment of department stores and shopping malls. The reduction of search costs is best achieved by decentralizing access to a centrally operated network. Thus, a centralized marketplace provided by retailers need not be restricted to a physical location. A good example is the automated bank teller, which can be located in a variety of places, including airports and malls. Customers can access their accounts and withdraw cash at any point in the network.

A catalog is also a central place of business. Increasingly, customers rely on catalogs for a wide variety of products that are delivered by mail, including clothing, electronic equipment, books, and compact discs. While the venerable Sears catalog has been retired, a new set of large specialized catalog retailers has arisen, including L.L. Bean, Lands' End, Eddie Bauer, and J. Crew. These retailers offer a wide variety of products with very rapid ordering and delivery, thus achieving immediacy. A customer can comparison shop through several different catalogs and complete an order in a matter of minutes, without leaving home. Thus, the search costs of customers are drastically reduced.

A phone number alone can provide a central place of business. An increasing number of products can be ordered by phone, including airline tickets, theater tickets, and fast food. A very high degree of centralization is achieved by businesses that offer a national toll-free telephone number for placing orders. Home-shopping channels on television also provide a national central meeting place for customers, who then order products by phone. Unlike shopping from catalogs, immediacy is somewhat restricted in that customers can only observe products when they are scheduled by the shopping channel. However, shopping channels have the advantage of a salesperson who can discuss products and demonstrate how they operate.

Computer networks are significant centralized marketplaces. Computer networks have begun to offer retail outlets for various goods and services and already have millions of subscribers. Computer networks allow two-way communication between companies and their customers that can provide convenience and immediacy.

Retailers act as dealers by providing a centralized marketplace for their suppliers. Manufacturers and wholesalers transact directly with the retailer, not the retailer's customers. Retail chains generally increase efficiency by centralizing purchasing at headquarters and centralizing deliveries for many goods at local or regional warehouses. Wholesalers also provide dealer services to retailers and manufacturers by buying and selling products, carrying out transfers of goods, and centralizing exchange.

Manufacturers act as dealers by providing a central selling place for customers (whether wholesalers, retailers, or final customers). Failure to understand this can be quite costly. IBM relied on others to market its personal computers. It finally responded to faltering sales in personal computers by offering a toll-free number for customer orders, something that had already been successfully done by rivals such as Dell and Compaq. Manufacturers provide central marketplaces for their suppliers of parts, equipment, and other services. Manufacturers are not simply resellers; they also transform the inputs they receive into new products. By transforming productive inputs, manufacturers perform more complex intermediation functions (discussed in depth in Chapter 5).

An important example of market making is the airline computer system. Two prominent systems are American Airlines' SABRE and United Airlines' Apollo. The airlines initially established their systems as a way of keeping track of many thousands of airline fares and all of the available seats and passenger reservations. The computer reservation systems (CRSs) were intended as a means of internal accounting for the airlines to aid in booking passengers. The systems were provided to travel agents to simplify their ticketing and communications with the airline. As a matter of convenience for the travel agents, the computer reservation systems listed the flights of other airlines, who were charged a fee for the service. The convenience was so well received that almost all travel agents signed on to a CRS and soon practically all tickets were written on CRSs. The airline providing the computer system, known as the host, initially listed its flights first on the screen. It was soon discovered that this resulted in substantial diversion of passengers to the host airline and significant incremental revenues. Some airlines charged that travel agents tended to favor the host airline in booking flights, known as the "halo effect," partly as a result of special commissions. Nonhost airlines also claimed that the CRSs were slow to list their fares and allowed the host airline to adjust its fares in response to theirs. The CRS market has been dominated by SABRE and Apollo, with other systems capturing smaller shares of the market. American Airlines and United Airlines were accused of taking unfair advantage of their CRSs. On November 14, 1984 the Civil Aeronautics Board passed a number of regulations governing access and pricing of CRSs, including rules against onscreen bias, and the Transportation Department put forward additional rules in 1991.

As the popularity of CRSs grew among travel agents, airlines observed that listing on the CRS had important consequences for sales. What had begun as an accounting device began to be understood as a powerful competitive tool. Airlines realized that they could adjust prices and seat availability rapidly in response to sales, a process known as yield management. This allows pricing and availability to reflect current market conditions. Moreover, the CRSs are sources of important market information.

The CRSs have grown to become broad travel networks, providing booking for hotels, rental cars, and other services in addition to air travel. In 1990, American's SABRE system formed an alliance with the Amadeus Global Travel Distribution, a network set up by Air France, Iberia, Scandinavian Airlines, and Lufthansa, to provide international services. American also provides extensive CRS services to Canadian Airlines. United Airlines' Covia, which owns the Apollo system, merged in 1992 with Galileo, which was formed by nine European carriers (Aer Lingus, Air Portugal, Alitalia, Austrian Airlines, British Airways, KLM Royal Dutch Airlines, Sabena, Swissair, and Olympic). A third international system called WorldSpan was formed by merging Pars, owned by Transworld Airlines and Northwest Airlines, and the Datas II system owned by Delta Airlines. The CRS business has proven to be profitable even as the airline business itself has suffered losses. American Airlines' SABRE, for example, earned a quarter of a billion dollars in 1993, though the company's airline operations lost money.

Computer travel networks are an important example of market making. The CRSs supplemented the brokerage services of travel agents by providing a central place of exchange for all airlines, hotels, and other travel services. By simplifying the interaction between passengers and providers of travel services, CRSs greatly reduced transaction costs and created immediacy for airlines and passengers. The profitability of the computer systems demonstrates the high economic returns to effective market making.

By providing centralized marketplaces and carrying out transactions with customers and suppliers, firms provide dealer services that reduce the costs of search for their customers and suppliers. Thus, all firms act as market makers, coordinating the actions of customers and suppliers and providing standardized, low-cost transactions. Firms can profit from an understanding of the importance of reducing transaction costs. Winning the market results from providing the best dealer services for both sellers and buyers. The airline computer networks are excellent examples of centralization and convenience.[5] The computer systems provide central coordination of staggering numbers of transactions. They are capable of handling almost a year's schedule of flights, over 15 million, and all the details of passenger reservations on those flights. These systems can be reached by travel agents or by customers directly contacting the airline, and are available on computer networks. Thus, the contact points are extremely convenient for individual customers. The offerings of an airline on the CRS can be adjusted relatively easily, so that transaction costs are lowered for the airlines as well. With the development of electronic commerce, CRS systems are increasingly becoming Web-based, allowing customers to bypass travel agents and access airline CRSs directly over the Internet.

Managers can win the market by creating new dealer services that lower transaction costs. Firms will prosper by finding new ways to centralize and coordinate transactions, particularly through computer and telecommunications networks. Firms that are not providers of transaction services and firms that have not made alliances with operators of these networks could find themselves excluded from the marketplace. It is crucial for managers to develop improved means of transacting with customers and suppliers.

Managing Transactions

By managing transactions, the company creates convenience for its buyers and sellers. Most companies supply merchant services in addition to their manufactured products as part of a bundle. For many, the transactions are means to an end, or even inconveniences, necessary but insignificant parts of a sale. Yet, it is enough to observe the staggering size of the financial sector, including exchanges and brokerages, and the high earnings of the market-making institutions to understand the tremendous economic value of these services. Companies need to recognize that the transactions they supply as part of the deal are also services. By enhancing the efficiency of those transactions, companies can expand their sales in unexpected ways.

Companies handle a variety of transactions. Many of these are internal, as managers allocate capital, human resources, products and services, and technological know-how within the company. It is necessary for companies to look at internal allocation of resources and transfer pricing as alternatives to transactions with suppliers and distributors. Here, information systems are of growing importance. Managers need to look on such systems as sources of value creation, not simply as costs. Other transactions are largely routine, part of long-standing relationships with suppliers and distributors. Increasingly, companies are relying on electronic data interchange to achieve speed and accuracy while reducing paperwork and labor costs. Still other transactions require adapting to new customers and suppliers. The firm must be ready with the appropriate information systems or risk losing customers to competitors offering more convenient procedures.

David M. Weiss, in *After the Trade Is Made*, likens the processing of securities transactions by brokerage firms to production by a manufacturing firm.[6] The brokerage firm carries out a complicated series of market actions and handles many financial instruments including stocks, bonds, commercial paper, banker's acceptances, options, and futures. Weiss describes the sequence of activities that take place in the brokerage firm after a customer makes a trade. Customers give buy and sell orders to account executives or stockbrokers, who pass them on to the firm's order room which then returns a confirmation of the trade and the execution price. The order room executes the order with the securities exchanges and the over-the-counter securities market. Next, the purchase and sales (P&S) department computes payments and interest (figuration), compares the trade with the opposing brokerage firm's transaction (reconcilement), issues a confirmation to the customer, and books the trade in the firm's records. The reconcilement function is carried out through clearing organizations, such as the National Securities Clearing Corporation, that are also intermediaries of a type. Then, the cashiers' department handles the brokerage's transactions with commercial banks, other brokerages, and transfer agents (who reregister the security in the name of the new owner). Five other internal departments handle the margin, stock record, accounting, dividends, and proxy aspects of the transactions.

Notice how the brokerage's entire business is creating transactions between its customers, the exchanges, and other brokers. Since transactions are the brokerage's output, this process is especially transparent. Related procedures exist for manufacturers, but from the perspective of customers and suppliers, the company's intermediation services are mingled with its other products. By enhancing the quality of its transactions, manufacturers can win additional customers and improve supplier relationships. It is essential for managers to realize the economic returns from these valuable services.

Market Clearing

In addition to providing immediacy and a central place of exchange, firms perform another vital market-making service—they equalize supply and demand. Traditionally, economists have emphasized the role of the "invisible hand," adjusting prices in the manner of an auctioneer until the total amount offered by suppliers equaled the total amount demanded by buyers. In contrast, I wish to emphasize that much of the balancing of supply and demand takes place through the actions of firms providing dealer services. Firms play a role in balancing the market through their adjustments of their own purchases, sales, and inventories.

Clearing is an important feature of an efficiently functioning market. This means that when the market is in equilibrium, the total amount demanded by consumers equals the total amount supplied by sellers. Generally, an efficient market is cleared by prices, so that neither side is rationed by limits on the quantities that they can buy and sell. In other words, buyers can purchase all that they want at the ask prices in the market and sellers can sell all that they want at the bid prices in the market. This fundamental aspect of markets is different from the obvious fact that markets are always balanced, since the amounts sold and purchased are always equal.

Market clearing in practice requires action by market makers. For example, on the NYSE, specialists help to clear markets by acting as dealers for particular stocks. The specialist receives buy and sell orders with bid and ask prices respectively, and executes trades by matching orders. Buyers and sellers adjust their orders and bids in response to trades, which helps the market to clear. In addition, balancing is carried out by specialists trading on their own account. While the role of specialists or dealers is evident in a stock market, it is important to understand that companies play a similar dealership role in all markets.

The market-making function is the main source of earnings even in financial markets. A study of over 40 large trading rooms in equities, fixed income securities, and foreign exchange found that the notion that these firms could make profits by consistently beating the market was a myth.[7] The study showed that speculative positioning by trading houses was not a reliable source of profits, whether for major players or smaller operations in regional centers. Speculative positioning yielded profits only if the trading house had proprietary information or sufficient market power to influence prices. On the other hand, the study found that trading firms primarily make profits from trading with customers (including institutional investors) and from interdealer trades if the trading operation acts as a jobber. In trading with customers, trading operations make money from market making, that is from quoting prices and maintaining inventories in illiquid markets. In interdealer trading, profits were made by purchasing high volumes at or close to the bid side and quickly reselling at the offer side. The study observed that in the market for U.S. government securities, the companies with the strongest market-making capacity retained the largest percentage of the spread.

Market making is important in nonfinancial markets as well. Retailers are concerned with matching sales to inventories. If stock-outs occur, with sales demand exceeding inventory, the retailer misses valuable sales and may lose important customers (since availability is vital for maintaining customer loyalty). On the other hand, excess inventory is not desirable either. The cost of holding inventory is not simply the cost of warehousing and shelf space; it includes the interest cost of the investment in inventory. Retailers seek to achieve a high rate of turnover of products. Turnover simply means the rate at which the retailer can sell products and use the proceeds to restock. The faster inventory turns over, at any given price, the greater the rate of return to the retailer's investment. To increase turnover, retailers adjust prices.

In addition to price adjustment, retailers take many actions that help the market to clear. Retailers make innumerable adjustments in the quantity of inventories purchased to increase turnover. Firms order based on demand projections and daily monitoring of the pattern of sales. Items that sell quickly are reordered, while less is ordered of slower selling items. Advances in computerized inventory management and bar coding of products has allowed retailers to monitor sales as they occur, allowing for shorter reordering times and closer adjustment of inventories to demand patterns. This means the retailer can keep fewer inventories at the store or the warehouse and still reduce the likelihood of stockouts. Thus, the amount sold and the amount purchased by the retailer track each other more closely over time, bringing the quantities bought and sold in the market closer to being in balance.

Retailers share demand information with suppliers so that suppliers can adjust production and shipments to satisfy demands without excessive inventories. Wal-Mart has pioneered direct telecommunication and computer links with its suppliers as a means of providing them with detailed information about the sales of their products in individual stores. Some manufacturers restock store shelves themselves, or through jobbers, and thus obtain frequent information about the pace and mix of their sales. For example, bakeries restock the bread aisles in supermarkets and adjust deliveries to the pattern of sales. Retailers adjust their sales efforts to move inventories, advertising and prominently displaying items when excess inventories build up. An interesting example of market clearing can be seen on televised home shopping networks. Viewers are informed of the remaining numbers of an item that is being made available, with the number counting down as sales occur. Promotion of the item ceases at the moment supplies are exhausted.

Another way to synchronize purchases and sales is to pool inventories. Chain stores use central warehouses to pool inventories across stores. This serves to smooth out the demand pattern by pooling the risks from demand fluctuations across stores. This allows the chain store to provide product availability while keeping a much smaller total inventory than it would have to if inventories were kept at each store.[8] Retailers that take orders by mail or by phone and serve customers from a central national location benefit by taking orders from a large pool of customers, which reduces the risk of demand fluctuations in comparison with a decentralized system of local stores and regional warehouses. Wholesalers and other intermediaries earn profits by serving multiple retailers from centralized warehouses, thus effectively pooling inventories.

Electric utilities form large-scale electric power pools, such as the New England Power Pool. To avoid power curtailments or interruptions, utilities must build sufficient productive capacity to meet peak demand. This is quite costly because the incremental capacity lies idle during off-peak periods. Utilities give customers various price incentives to smooth out demand fluctuations but significant random variations in demand persist. Utilities have found that by buying from the pool when their demand is high and selling to the pool when they have excess capacity, they can reduce the need for costly generating capacity. So, by pooling their capacity, utilities are able to bring the supply and demand for electrical generating capacity closer together.

Manufacturers play an important market-making role by adjusting production to changing demand information. Dell and other computer makers assemble computer systems to order, thereby adjusting instantly to demand patterns. Increasing automation of inventories allows manufacturers to reduce their inventories of parts and materials. The use of just-in-time inventory management has often been promoted as a cost-cutting activity. By reducing the time inventories sit idle, manufacturers reduce the time cost of investment in inventories. However, just-in-time inventory management should also be seen as an important market-making activity. The reduction of parts inventories by manufacturers means that the firm's demand for parts is more closely synchronized with the supply of parts, thereby providing clearing services to the market for parts.

Even more dramatic is the development of the flexible factory that eliminates delays in both production and distribution. By producing multiple products on the same assembly line, the flexible factory allows a manufacturer to tailor its production more closely to demand patterns without building substantial inventories or operating multiple production systems with excess capacity. The flexible factory allows a multiproduct firm to achieve the benefits of economies of scope. Like just-in-time inventories, just-in-time production and the flexible factory also perform market-clearing roles by improving the adjustment of production to market demand information.

George Stalk, Jr. and Thomas M. Hout of the Boston Consulting Group describe Toyota's response to the problem of delays in distribution and sales. Toyota found that only 10% of the time a customer had to wait for a car was due to production, while 90% of the delay was due to distribution and sales. Toyota merged its manufacturing and sales companies in 1981 and established an information network that by the end of the 1980s linked several hundred wholesalers and over 4,000 independent distributors. Toyota had changed its strategy from "sell the customers what we have" to "sell the customers what they want."[9]

Retailers such as The Gap have drastically reduced the ordering cycle for clothes relative to traditional department stores. This allows The Gap not only to adjust quickly to the sales patterns in its stores but also to respond rapidly to fashion changes in colors, fabrics, and styles. The Gap is able to outsell department stores that carry a range of products that are less focused on popular styles. Companies that supply clothing to The Gap are able to adjust their manufacturing plans, hiring, and materials purchases in response to more up-to-date information about demand. These new developments represent increased efficiency in clearing markets for clothing.

By adjusting inventories and production to customer demand patterns, firms provide critical dealer services to their customers and help to bring the market into balance. Improvements in computer and communications technology allow firms to closely track customer demand patterns. Just-in-time inventories and flexible production techniques then allow rapid adjustment to customer requirements even while reducing costly inventories and production capacity. These developments are critical to the market-making functions of firms. The market is closer to being in balance since demand and supply are continually brought closer together. Matching demand and supply more closely is not just a question of lowering inventory costs. The key point is that companies make better use of market demand information in determining the quantity and variety of products to be offered. Companies can win the market by improving their market-clearing performance.

Allocating Goods and Services

Firms provide another valuable market-making service: They allocate goods and services. This means that the firm's outputs are delivered to those customers who value them the most. The firm obtains the best inputs in terms of quality and value from its suppliers. The firm carries out this function through pricing, centralization of exchange, and clearing the market. Firms allocate products and services directly in the short run by rationing customers and in the long run by production and investment decisions. The firm bears a substantial amount of risk and reallocates risk across its customers and suppliers. In addition, the firm allocates goods and services internally through its investment plans and human resource policies. These allocation decisions are key components of the firm's market-making strategy.

Allocating Scarce Resources

Classical economics views the market as the mechanism for allocating resources. Prices adjust to shifts in supply and demand. Goods and services are allocated as a consequence of the uncoordinated decisions of many individual traders, each of whose actions has little effect on the behavior of the market as a whole. Within markets, goods and services are consumed by those who value them the most and produced by the most efficient producer. Goods and services move across markets in response to any imbalances in economic rents. This overall picture is accurate for the global economy and for large economies such as the United States. It is a good description for markets in which there are large numbers of small traders, such as commodity markets. However, many industries are characterized by a few very large firms with significant market shares. While these firms are not insulated from price fluctuations and other economic forces (indeed, they may respond quite nimbly), they allocate substantial quantities of goods and services by design. This means that many goods and services travel across the economy and around the world as part of the strategic allocation decisions of large corporations. Much depends on the choices of such companies as Du Pont and Dow in chemicals, Pepsico and Coca-Cola in soft drinks, or Kodak and Xerox in photographic equipment.

How do these companies allocate products? First and foremost by pricing. The variation in prices by location and over time determines to a great extent the size and distribution of sales. Marketing decisions regarding promotion and sales efforts, the choice of distributors, and focusing on particular geographic regions or customer classes determine allocation as well.

But companies do not rely solely on prices to allocate their products. Dennis Carlton observes that, with random demand, there are costs to using the price system because a price that is too high will reduce sales and result in excess inventories, while a price that is too low will require rationing customers and foregoing sales. He suggests that many firms use nonprice rationing methods, and that "firms and organized markets are competitors in production 'allocations'."[10] He observes that for many industries such as textiles, mill products, paper and allied products, steel, electrical and nonelectrical machinery, and fabricated metals, companies rely on such devices as delivery lags to ration customers during periods of tight supplies.[11]

Companies make many allocation decisions in response to anticipated and realized sales. Retailers and wholesalers make purchasing decisions and allocate inventory across locations based on projected sales. Airlines practice yield management by constantly changing the proportion of discounted and full fare seats on flights. Manufacturers vary their production runs and product mix based on the expected behavior of customers and competitors. These short-run decisions determine the allocation of goods and services in many markets.

In some industries the allocation of scarce capacity is built into product offerings. For example, Federal Express offers many categories of mail delivery, including next business morning, next business afternoon, and second business day, which correspond to different priority levels. Customers pay the most for the highest priority, next business morning, which gives their package first access to the firm's transportation and delivery capacity. If capacity is available, lower priority mail can arrive early. When capacity is scarce, lower priority mail is shifted to later in the day when more capacity becomes available. Similar forms of priority pricing are used to allocate electricity generation and transmission capacity. Industrial customers can sign up for interruptible-curtailable service at a discount. In peak periods, such as hot summer days when everyone is turning on air conditioners, the marginal cost of generation is high and capacity shortfalls occur. These customers must then reduce their power usage so that higher priority users can be served.

Companies can earn rents by carefully allocating scarce capacity in markets with tight supplies. The company that provides allocation services essentially makes a market in the product, providing the good to the highest-value user. Moreover, careful planning of pricing and priority contracts allows the firm to make effective use of capacity. Increased use of tracking data and computerized distribution allows the firm to tailor its available capacity more closely to demand and supply fluctuations. This allows the firm to provide valuable immediacy services to its suppliers and customers.

In the long run, companies allocate resources through their investment, production, and distribution decisions. It should be emphasized that large companies allocate resources internally as well. A multidivisional firm allocates scarce capital raised across projects proposed by the firm's divisions. The corporate office evaluates the expected returns and strategic value of the projects and monitors their progress, thus performing capital market functions. Companies also allocate resources and products through divisional budgets and transfer pricing. Human resources are allocated through internal labor markets consisting of job categories, promotional procedures, compensation rules, and performance evaluations. Personnel are continually reallocated through the formation of project teams and the reassignment of employees and managers. Technology is allocated within the firm through decisions on the design of new products and processes, funds for development, assignment of engineers, and the identification of core competencies. It is essential for companies to realize that such allocation decisions are more than bookkeeping, but represent value-creating market-making activities.

It is often noted that financial markets serve to allocate risk across investors. Traders can hedge their risks through a variety of instruments such as futures, options, and derivative contracts. By holding inventories, firms allocate the risks from supply and demand fluctuations for their suppliers and customers. Firms further reallocate risks through their price-setting policies and contract terms. For example, by setting fixed wages and benefits, firms insulate their employees from fluctuations in revenues and costs. Incentive programs tied to sales or profits represent risk-sharing arrangements. Firms reduce customer risk through long-term contracts, service agreements, and warranties. Similarly, risks are shared with suppliers through procurement contracts. The firm's investment decisions involve risk sharing among the firm's bond and equity holders. Thus, large corporations allocate diverse risks as part of their market-making activities. Firms can realize benefits by recognizing the value they create through these implicit forms of insurance.

Endnotes

1. H. B. Garman studies pricing and market microstructure in stock markets. He observes that beginning in 1871 the New York Stock Exchange became a continuous market, and that today all major U.S. securities and commodities exchanges operate as continuous markets. He shows that since demand and supply of securities are subject to random fluctuations, it is incorrect to assume that the market clears at all times. Rather, a dealer should adjust prices to maximize profits from the spread while taking into account the effect of demand and supply fluctuations on the dealer's inventory of securities and cash reserves. See H. B. Garman, "Market Microstructure," *Journal of Financial Economics*, 3, 1976, pp. 257–275.

2. The marketing price-response function corresponds with the economist's residual demand which specifies the demand for a firm's product over a range of prices given that the sales of competitors, or at least the responses of competitors to the firm's prices, are fairly stable. An example of a price response function can be written as follows: $q = 120 - 2p$. I use this function to generate the numerical example in the text.

3. Futures exchanges abroad include the International Petroleum Exchange of London, the London International Financial Futures Exchange, the Sydney Futures Exchange, the Hong Kong Futures Exchange, the Osaka Securities Exchange, and the Tokyo Commodity Exchange.

4. Armen Alchien observed that specialists provide information at a lower cost than search, in "Information Costs, Pricing, and Resource Unemployment," *Western Economic Journal*, 1969, pp. 109–127. The immediacy in financial markets is discussed by Harold Demsetz, "The Cost of Transacting," *Quarterly Journal of Economics*, 82, 1978, pp. 33–53.

5. Note that the CRSs are not dealers, since they do not buy and sell airline tickets. However, by coordinating transactions and providing a central marketplace, the CRSs provide dealer services. The CRSs charge fees to airlines for listing on the systems and for bookings that are completed on the systems. Travel agents pay for CRS services as well.

6. David M. Weiss, *After the Trade Is Made: Processing Securities Transactions*, 2nd ed., New York: New York Institute of Finance, 1993.

7. A. Braas and C. N. Bralver, "An Analysis of Trading Profits: How Most Trading Rooms Really Make Money," in D.H. Chew, Jr., ed., *The New Corporate Finance: Where Theory Meets Practice*, New York: McGraw-Hill, 1993, pp.67–72.

8. See Daniel F. Spulber, "Risk Sharing and Inventories," *Journal of Economic Behavior and Organization*, 6, 1985, pp. 55–68.

9. George Stalk, Jr. and T. M. Hout, *Competing Against Time*, New York: Free Press, 1990, p. 69. The account of the Toyota distribution system is also from Stalk and Hout, pp. 68–69.

10. Dennis W. Carlton, "The Theory of Allocation and Its Implications for Marketing and Industrial Structure: Why Rationing Is Efficient," *Journal of Law and Economics*, 34 (2), Part 1, October 1991, p. 257.

11. Dennis W. Carlton, "Equilibrium Fluctuation When Price and Delivery Lag Clear the Market," *Bell Journal of Economics*, Autumn 1983, 14, pp. 562–572.

4
ARBITRAGE

Firms with superior technological and market information discern arbitrage opportunities. Those opportunities will be seized by competitors, depending on the size of customer switching costs and entry barriers. The speed with which competitors are able to capture or otherwise eliminate arbitrage profits depends on their agility, creativity, and managerial capabilities. Competitive strategy is made possible by the many tangible imperfections in markets and management.

Arbitrage refers to profit-making activities connecting suppliers and customers. The firm obtains financing, labor, products and services, and technology from suppliers and offers products and services to its customers. Profits depend on rapid action, because arbitrage opportunities can be eroded in the blink of an eye in the most competitive markets. The firm must have knowledge of shifting supplier capabilities and customer requirements, and the ability to provide the products and services to realize the necessary transactions.

If markets are perfectly competitive, economic analysis suggests that arbitrage profit cannot exist when the market is in equilibrium. In equilibrium, the law of the single price prevails, with demand exactly equaling supply at the market-clearing price. It is not possible for a product to be sold at a higher price than that at which it was purchased, since there would be instantaneous buying and reselling of such a good. This would cause the bid price to rise and the ask price to fall until the market was in equilibrium, thus eliminating any arbitrage profits. Much of finance is founded on the zero arbitrage profit condition. If prices of assets were such that an investor could earn positive profits from trading those assets, demand would be infinite. However, such high demand would be sufficient to raise the price of those assets and thereby eliminate arbitrage profits. This argument implies that there cannot be any riskless arbitrage opportunity.

The perfect market hypothesis does not always apply, however. It is worthwhile to recall the assumptions that underlie the zero arbitrage condition. All individuals are price takers, that is, buyers and sellers take the market price as given and plan their consumption or production accordingly. The market equilibrium price adjusts perfectly to equate supply and demand, although the equilibrium mechanism is not specified. Firms earn zero economic profits; that is, their revenues equal their cost of inputs, including a competitive return to capital. All prices are known to market participants so that no arbitrage opportunity will go unnoticed. There are no transaction costs that would prevent the market from achieving a single-price equilibrium.

In most markets, imperfections are always present. A variety of frictions exist such as the costs of gathering and comparing price and product information. There are high costs of searching for customers and suppliers. After locating trading partners, additional costs of negotiating, writing, and monitoring contracts must be incurred. There are asymmetries in information in the economy about technology, organizational design, and market opportunities. As a result, there are persistent price differences for the same goods across locations and across companies. Since there are costs to learning about prices, many arbitrage opportunities go unnoticed. While many buyers and sellers are price takers, there are firms that act as market makers, setting prices to clear markets. Moreover, companies exercise market power depending on the level and type of competition that they face. Their actions differ significantly from those firms that take prices as beyond their control. These factors create multiple prices for similar products. In addition, they lead to bid–ask spreads between upstream and downstream markets. This situation contradicts the law of one price. The many transaction costs and resulting market imperfections create myriad arbitrage opportunities. Each time companies engage in arbitrage, the opportunities are reduced or eliminated and the market comes closer to the competitive ideal. In the meantime, companies profit from making the market work.

If firms are price setters, they create a bid–ask spread that reflects the price responsiveness of their suppliers and their customers. The spread is chosen to maximize the firm's profit, which is limited by supplier costs, customer willingness to pay, and the firm's costs of effecting the transactions, as well as other costs of production and distribution. In this chapter, I set out the four basic types of arbitrage. These are based on connecting markets separated by:

- Space
- Time
- Uncertainty
- Technology

Practically any type of arbitrage is a variant or combination of the basic forms of arbitrage. By understanding and employing the techniques described here, a firm can gain an arbitrage advantage.

The role of the firm is to discover and implement new ways to bridge these markets. The firm gains an arbitrage advantage through its ability to connect upstream suppliers of less costly or higher quality products and services with downstream customers in need of those products and services. The connections can be through resale, as with arbitrage across geographic space, or through productive activities, as with technological arbitrage. The market connections can involve allocation of risk, as with risk arbitrage. Finally, the market connections can involve allocation of resources over time, as with dynamic arbitrage. Since most business activities involve combinations of all of these basic forms, winning the market requires understanding and applying the principles of arbitrage to connect supplier and customer markets.

The arbitrage advantage depends on competitors not being able to capitalize on the same opportunities. There are four main reasons why rivals may not seize these economic rents. First, as I have noted, they may not have access to the same information about the opportunity. The purpose of building the market bridge is to be attuned to shifts in demand and supply. Second, competitors can be subject to cost inefficiencies. High costs of transportation and distribution prevent the realization of spatial arbitrage. Costs of writing long-term contracts and of storing products complicate dynamic arbitrage. The costs of writing and monitoring contingent contracts can foreclose risk arbitrage. Productive inefficiency or outdated technical knowledge prevent the implementation of technological arbitrage. Companies cannot successfully carry out arbitrage unless their transaction costs are competitive. Being informed is not sufficient. Third, competitors may be slow to react. Companies need to eliminate organizational inertia to increase the speed of response to market opportunities. Finally, competitors may not have the market relationships in place to take advantage of the arbitrage opportunity. Effective market making and intermediation require a well-developed market network.

Spatial Arbitrage

Venetian traders like Marco Polo set out on trading expeditions to the East in the thirteenth century to exchange goods purchased in Venice for exotic merchandise in India and China. These traders profited from the journey when earnings obtained from selling the exotic goods brought back to Venice covered the costs of the goods originally purchased in Venice as well as the cost of the trip. The trading expeditions were based on the expectation that the price of the exotic goods in Venice would exceed the price of those goods in the East (in terms of the cost of the Venetian goods traded for them).

Successful trading expeditions required knowledge of both the Venetian market and the Far Eastern markets. The traders needed to know what Venetian goods would be desired abroad and what goods were available there as well. They also needed to know how Eastern goods would be valued in Venice. It is obvious that the traders' knowledge of the Venetian market was not unique in Venice, and their knowledge of the Eastern market was not unique abroad. The unique knowledge that the traders possessed was the relationship between values in the two markets. They brought their knowledge of Venetian markets to their Far Eastern dealings and in turn brought their knowledge of Far Eastern markets to the Venetian market. This knowledge provided the source of the arbitrage profits of the Venetian merchants.

Spatial arbitrage provides the foundation upon which all other forms of arbitrage are based. The basic form of arbitrage need not be limited to geographic price differences, but instead is the profitable purchase of a single good in one market and the resale of the good in another market. Suppose that the merchant encounters no costs other than the good itself. Then, if the per-unit resale price is p and the per-unit purchase price is w, the price spread is the difference, $p - w$. The merchant earns a return to arbitrage equal to the price spread multiplied by the number of units sold. The net return is obtained by netting out any transaction costs the merchant incurs.[1]

A firm with market power chooses the profit-maximizing bid–ask spread by taking into account the price responsiveness of customers and suppliers. The firm sets the bid and ask prices to clear the market, bringing together its input purchases and output sales, whether the firm is a merchant or a manufacturer. This means that the firm's input and output prices generally are not set independently but instead reflect the trade-off between the cost of purchasing excess inventories and the cost of leaving demand unsatisfied due to insufficient inventories.[2]

Traditional economic analysis argues that in perfectly competitive markets such arbitrage opportunities cannot exist when the market is in equilibrium. The profits earned from arbitrage cannot be positive.

Otherwise, the argument goes, merchants would wish to sell infinite amounts of the good to continue earning the arbitrage profit on each unit that is purchased and resold. Purchasing more units of the good from suppliers would drive up its price in the upstream market, while reselling more units of the good would drive down its price in the downstream market. These two forces would eliminate arbitrage profit. Moreover, the standard argument maintains that were such arbitrage opportunities to arise, merchants would immediately act to take advantage of the opportunities, so that they would not persist for long.

However, many firms are able to earn substantial arbitrage profits. In some cases profitability is sustained for many years. One explanation is that these firms are simply the lucky few, with many other firms sustaining substantial losses, so that *expected* profits are eliminated or even negative on average. This explanation is consistent with the traditional perfect competition framework. I propose an alternative explanation that departs from the traditional framework but that I believe is consistent with observation of the nature of business.

The explanation I suggest is that firms are able to identify arbitrage opportunities by unique knowledge of upstream and downstream markets. This involves much more than the familiar advice to "buy cheap and sell dear." There is imperfect information in markets about the characteristics of buyers and sellers. Some economic agents are able to obtain better market information than others. Moreover, there do not exist markets for all goods because it is costly to establish markets. Companies incur marketing and sales expenditures as well as all of the expenses involved to introduce new products and establish production and distribution facilities. Transaction costs also include search, bargaining, and forming and monitoring contracts with suppliers and customers.[3] Markets do not spring up magically. Rather, they are created through the skill and insight of companies. Finally, prices are not necessarily taken as given by all traders but rather are established by companies through market-making activities. Successful companies continually create profitable arbitrage opportunities.

The key to identifying and profiting from basic merchant arbitrage lies in forming relationships with unique suppliers that will result in lower than average input prices, or in forming relationships with buyers that will result in higher than average output prices, or possibly both. Arbitrage profit results from making new connections between buyers and sellers. Not only must buyer willingness to pay exceed the opportunity cost of sellers, but the output price agreed to with buyers must exceed the input price agreed to with sellers. The input and output markets may be highly competitive or they may not be. Arbitrage profits can still be earned to the extent that the two markets are separated by incomplete information that the buyers in the output market and the sellers in the input market have about each others' characteristics.

Therefore, companies engaged in arbitrage are building market bridges. They create a new market by connecting previously separated markets, linking sellers and buyers in innovative ways. Their trading activities serve to establish relative prices for the two markets.[4]

It is important to note that basic merchant arbitrage can also be practiced by connecting specific sellers and buyers without acting as a merchant but rather acting as a broker and earning a commission from the sale. The commission earned by real estate agents and other brokers is simply the difference between the effective purchase and sale prices.

Other forms of arbitrage are extensions of the basic variety. Arbitrage generally involves managing a portfolio of products. Retailers and wholesalers carry out a very complex version of merchant arbitrage by purchasing and selling a wide variety of goods. Importers of oriental rugs do not simply purchase rugs in quantity. Rather, they devote considerable effort to assembling a variety of styles and patterns, which allows customers to make a selection that best suits their preferences. Obtaining a range of patterns requires extensive knowledge of available patterns in upstream markets in Pakistan, China, and elsewhere, as well as an understanding of the relative levels of demand for the various styles in downstream markets in America, Europe, and Asia.

Successful use of this type of arbitrage requires knowledge of multiple upstream markets and multiple downstream markets. For example, Wal-Mart sells a wide variety of products in hundreds of stores representing local downstream markets, and deals with over 4,000 suppliers representing many upstream markets. Customers shop at Wal-Mart not only because of the prices of individual items but because of the overall selection of goods available in the store. The success of the enterprise as a whole lies in the coordination of a staggering number of connections between these upstream and downstream markets.

Most retailers and wholesalers purchase and distribute a wide variety of merchandise. By combining products they earn an arbitrage profit that could not be achieved by the purchase and resale of individual products. Often the knowledge gained about upstream suppliers in the purchase of a particular good can be leveraged in the purchase of a related array of products. Similarly, knowledge about customer preferences gained in the sale of some goods can be leveraged into expanded product offerings. For example, Wal-Mart's experience with selling a diverse set of goods ranging from clothing to housewares provides it with detailed information about customer preferences that can be used in setting the spread between wholesale and retail prices.

Dynamic Arbitrage

Beginning in 1688, rice growers met to trade rice on Dojima, an island north of Osaka.[5] According to Albert Alletzhauser, the trading day began at eight in the morning with the lighting of a slow-burning rope that was hung in full view, and ended in the afternoon when the rope had burned out. If trading continued beyond this time limit, the exchange had water men who stood ready to douse traders with large buckets of water, so that the price of the last trade came to be referred to as the bucket price. Farmers and feudal lords sold warehouse receipts and vouchers for crops not yet harvested and established Dojima as one of the world's first futures markets.

Chicago in the mid-nineteenth century was the leading national center for sales of wheat and corn. The grain was stored in elevators and trading began in elevator receipts. These receipts became standardized in terms of the grade of the grain, allowing trading that was not tied to a specific lot.[6] Although forward contracts for wheat were traded in Chicago as early as 1833 according to Bob Tamarkin, the Chicago Board of Trade, an organized futures market, was not established until 1848. Today, futures markets exist around the world, trading everything from agricultural commodities to livestock, lumber, precious metals, currencies, and stock and price indexes. Futures markets provide mechanisms for hedging risks for risk-averse commodities dealers that hold inventories of commodities. Jeffrey Williams argues that this reliance on risk aversion misrepresents the function of futures markets. He shows that dealers use futures markets as "an implicit method for borrowing and lending commodities" and observes that for most commodities traded on futures markets, the "spreads between futures prices rarely cover the known carrying costs of storing commodities."[7] Commodities are stored nonetheless for convenience. Producers borrow commodities, such as wheat, soybeans, or crude oil, because they are needed in the short term as inventories. Inventories of grain and other commodities are needed for the standard purposes of reducing transportation and processing costs and having goods on hand to satisfy randomly arriving customer demands.

Dynamic arbitrage refers to the profitable purchase and resale of goods in markets separated by time. Often, this involves the purchase and resale of contracts. Contracts involve payment or other consideration in return for promises of performance at some future date. If there are organized futures markets for a commodity, the opportunities for dynamic arbitrage for that commodity are swiftly eliminated by the constant activity of many traders. However, for most goods and services, futures markets are not available. The many frictions that characterize most markets create opportunities for firms that anticipate future needs.

The most basic form of dynamic arbitrage is the purchase and resale of commodities over time. Suppose for the moment that there are no storage costs and that the commodity, say crude oil, can be stored without losses. Then, the only cost of holding the commodity is the interest on the current market value of the commodity. Therefore, if current year and next year prices are known, an arbitrageur will only choose to hold the commodity if the present value of next year's price exceeds the current price. Let p be next year's price of crude oil and let r be the rate of interest. Then, the present value of next year's price is $p/(1+r)$. Let w be the current per-unit price of crude oil. Then, the arbitrage profit per-unit held over for future resale is the difference between the present value of the next-period price and the current per-unit price of crude oil, that is $p/(1+r) - w$. The per-unit arbitrage profit is multiplied by the number of units to be resold. The net profit is obtained by subtracting any accompanying transaction costs.

Similarly, if the present value of the commodity's price three years hence exceeds the present value of its price two years hence, the arbitrageur will purchase a contract for delivery in two years and sell a contract for delivery in three years.

The difference between the price at a given date and the price at a more distant date is referred to in futures markets as a spread. Well-known economic models predict that in the absence of uncertainty, the spread between the current (or spot) price and prices at future dates $(p - w)$ must rise at the rate of interest as the future date becomes more distant. This eliminates any potential arbitrage profits and fully determines the entire future path of the commodity's price.[8] Indeed, as already noted, the spreads between prices on organized futures exchanges are generally *below* carrying costs, so that the return to this form of arbitrage would be negative.

For goods that are not traded on organized futures exchanges, a company can earn returns to producing or storing goods in response to a perceived future need for a product, using information about future demand. This basic form of dynamic arbitrage is simply merchant arbitrage across markets separated by time. Since all production of goods and services takes time, manufacturing involves a combination of production and dynamic arbitrage. The manufacturer makes a profit by earning revenues from selling goods at a future date that exceed the costs of inputs purchased today. The manufacturer must combine information about input markets with information about future output markets.

Firms enter into a wide variety of long-term contracts, including financial transactions, labor contracts, purchasing and service contracts, and technology licensing contracts. By transferring income streams over time, all of these transactions constitute forms of dynamic arbitrage.

Wayne Huizenga, the founder of Waste Management and later of Blockbuster Video, said that he applied a basic principle to all of his businesses, namely to always *rent* products to customers since they could be rented over and over, earning a stream of returns for the firm. After dropping out of college, Huizenga began by managing a small trash hauling business in Pompano Beach, Florida that he built into a company with 20 trucks, named Southern Sanitation Service. Waste Management was formed from the merger of Southern Sanitation with Ace Scavenger Service, which began as Huizenga & Sons, a small Chicago trash hauling company founded in the late nineteenth century (by relatives of Wayne Huizenga). An important part of the business involved the rental of trash dumpsters. Renamed WMX Technologies and with over $10 billion in revenues, the company grew by acquiring over 400 companies during the 1980s and also forming Chemical Waste Management to handle toxic waste. Huizenga went on in the early 80s to form Blockbuster Video, the video rental chain.

Renting a product represents a form of dynamic arbitrage. By purchasing an asset today (whether a trash dumpster or the latest Hollywood hit movie) and then renting the product in a future period, the company earns rents from transferring the services of the good over time. Economic theory predicts that in a perfect market the economic rents from such activities would be eliminated and that a company would be indifferent between rental and sales. If renting were more lucrative than selling, more companies would enter the rental market than the sales market, driving down the price of rentals and increasing the sales price of the product, thus eliminating any arbitrage rents. Conversely, if selling a product were to become more profitable than renting the opposite behavior would occur, also eliminating the profits. This implies that rental of a basic commodity such as a video cassette should not yield economic profits.

So why did Blockbuster generate free cash flow of over $1 billion every year or two? Why haven't the high profits generated by renting videos generated a flood of competitors engaging in this form of dynamic arbitrage? Blockbuster has been successful by becoming the market maker in video rentals, making a market bridge between the motion picture industry, as its primary suppliers, and customers renting videos. The stores are ubiquitous, are easily identifiable, have large inventories of videos, and offer many convenient features such as computers and bar coding to speed the checkout process. Blockbuster essentially has won the market for this type of entertainment. Its innovative delivery and rapid growth have made rentals a highly profitable business, without attracting successful entry. The movie rental business is now sharing the spotlight with a growing inventory of video game rentals. Blockbuster stores are fast becoming outlets for music as well. The Blockbuster market bridge allows Huizenga to move out the boundaries by diversifying into music stores, starting the Florida Marlins major league baseball team in Miami, and possibly integrating vertically by acquiring stakes in Republic Pictures and Spelling

Entertainment. This wide array of activities complements the dynamic arbitrage of video game rentals.

Financial Intermediation

Mention arbitrage and financial markets come to mind immediately. Certainly financial markets come close to the competitive ideal. Arbitrage profits are eliminated, sometimes in an instant, in markets for currencies, securities, options, futures, and various types of derivatives. Through application of sophisticated financial models, the increasing use of computers for calculating the returns on complex combinations of financial instruments, and programmed trading, companies can respond to price fluctuations and news. Markets are constantly monitored by traders to detect opportunities for gain arising from price differences in assets with different maturities, risk, or underlying values. However, arbitrage in financial markets need not be confined to the exchanges. There are many opportunities for sustained dynamic arbitrage in financial markets.

The primary function of financial assets is to connect investors with owners of productive investment projects. Financial markets exist to carry out and reduce the costs of financial asset transactions, connecting suppliers of funds with companies and individuals who can employ those funds productively. Financial intermediaries earn arbitrage profits from creating or operating the markets for these transactions.

Investment is essentially a sacrifice of consumption today for a return tomorrow. Financial assets, such as debt and equity, are contracts that promise a possibly uncertain future payoff in return for a transfer of funds today. Investment opportunities can be anything from expansion of established corporations to entrepreneurial startups to individuals purchasing a new home. The market price of the asset depends on the expected returns, the risk involved, and the opportunity cost of funds, that is, what the funds could earn in other investments.

Financial assets are mechanisms for transferring earnings over time. The seller of the asset trades potential future earnings for funds today. The buyer of the asset is attempting to move funds from the present to a future period, and earn a return in the process. For example, corporate securities provide a means for the firm's investors to transfer current income to future time periods. Securities are tradable on stock markets so that investors are always assured of liquidity. This allows for maturity intermediation. The investor can hold the asset for as short or long a period as is desired, even though the company's investment projects may continue for many years.

The value of the stock reflects a share of the firm's anticipated residual returns after the firm has paid its debts. The original owners of the firm choose investment projects to maximize the difference between the present value of the firm and the total investment.[9] The company's owners are attempting to earn discounted returns that exceed the cost of investment. This provides an important insight into the nature of the corporation as a vehicle for raising investment funds. The sale of claims against future income streams is a form of dynamic arbitrage. The firm's owners purchase investment at the cost of shares of the company. They resell the investment by carrying out the investment project and earning the remaining share of the residual returns. This is nicely illustrated by Merrill Lynch's slogan, "We connect investors to opportunities." The ultimate value of the investment projects depends on the value they create for the firm's customers. In this sense, the company is an intermediary between its investors and its customers.

The company bids for funds against its capital suppliers' other investment (and consumption) opportunities. The company competes for investment by providing an attractive rate of return but carries out the bidding in many creative ways. It provides a brand name to investors that represents a basket of past, present, and future projects and their earnings. Investors judge the quality of the firm's products, services, and R&D. Perhaps most importantly, investors evaluate the quality of the firm's managers, as well as its governance structure, relations between the management and the board, the design of the organization, and incentives for employees. The value of the securities fundamentally reflects investor expectations about the company's management strategy.

As many companies know, their bids for capital are enhanced by providing information about their investment projects, their customers, and their competitive opportunities. The corporation thus provides a service to investors, informing them about the firm's product markets and its supplier markets, human resources, purchased goods and services, and technology. Just as mutual funds provide a service to investors by reducing the costs of holding and rearranging a vast stock or bond portfolio, so companies represent collections of many projects for the convenience of investors. Rather than invest in a hundred automobile construction projects, it is far simpler to buy a share of Ford or Chrysler that represents a broad mix of underlying car, van, and truck models and a vast, vertically integrated set of production and technological processes. This does not mean that companies should invest in many diverse activities simply to allow investors to diversity their portfolios. On the contrary, this is precisely the purpose of mutual funds and other financial intermediaries. Instead, companies engage in related diversification, based on knowledge of product or supplier markets or managerial complementarities. By jointly managing the collection of projects for its investors, the company provides the value-added services that create returns from dynamic arbitrage.

So it is important for managers to understand that their companies are financial intermediaries connecting investors with projects and product markets. Of course, securities also provide for residual control of the corporation. This necessarily alters the classical finance view of securities as merely an asset with an uncertain stream of returns. The market for securities provides a mechanism for transferring control over the corporation through mergers and acquisitions, tender offers, sell-offs, leveraged buy-outs, and other changes in ownership structure. Activities in the market for corporate control include corporate raids, premium buybacks or greenmail paid to ward off a raider, proxy contests by outsiders seeking a position on the board of directors, and the company's antitakeover provisions such as supermajority provisions, golden parachutes, and poison pills. The dynamic arbitrage provided by securities thus affords the investor some control over the income stream over time.

Consider the LBO (leveraged buy-out) companies, such as Kohlberg Kravis Roberts & Co. or Forstmann Little & Co. An LBO is an acquisition of a firm that is primarily funded with debt. These types of acquisition were quite popular during the 1980s. An LBO firm manages funds that are used to purchase companies. It transacts with banks, insurance companies, and other financial intermediaries who provide debt funding for the target acquisition. In addition, investors supply capital to the firm's investment funds. The LBO firm engages in dynamic arbitrage in the following way. The firm has knowledge of the market for investment funds, having built long-term relationships with specific investors. This knowledge is useful in negotiating contracts with its investors. It also has knowledge about the market for acquiring companies. This is useful in identifying acquisition targets, in managing the companies once they are acquired, and in identifying buyers when the companies are divested. Combining their knowledge of investor markets and the acquisition market, the LBO firm is able to arbitrage between these two markets, connecting investors with acquisitions. In this way, the investors indirectly tap into the future income streams of the acquired company while it is owned by the LBO firm and when it is divested. Investing in the firm yields a financial asset that represents a future income stream composed of the companies that it buys, manages, and sells.

Another basic form of dynamic arbitrage is intermediation in the market for loans. Two individuals have different requirements for cash over time. This may be due, for example, to different rates of time preference, that is, impatience to consume today versus tomorrow. The financial intermediary charges a rate of interest p to the borrower and pays a lower rate of interest w to the lender for the cash supplied. The financial intermediary receives the spread from buying and selling loan contracts. If Q represents the size of the loan, the profit from dynamic arbitrage is calculated in the same way as basic merchant arbitrage, $(p - w)Q$.

Banks and other financial intermediaries engage in maturity intermediation. By combining funds from investors who desire a short maturity and lending to borrowers who desire a longer contract, they earn the spread from borrowing short and lending long. The short-term lenders receive payments that reflect the risks of long-term lending and the corresponding rates of interest. The intermediaries reduce the costs of complicated transactions by centralizing exchange and combining loan contracts, and reduce transaction costs by handling a large number of contracts. Search costs are reduced because long-term borrowers do not have to look for a succession of short-term loans, and contracting costs are lowered because the intermediary acts as a delegated monitor. Short-term lenders need only monitor the performance of the intermediary, while the intermediary specializes in monitoring the performance of the long-term borrowers, overcoming to some extent the problems of moral hazard and adverse selection for its lenders. These activities create unique information that permits profitable dynamic arbitrage.

Risk Arbitrage

Coffee was introduced into England early in the seventeenth century but became fashionable only after the first London coffeehouse was established in 1652. Coffeehouses became popular places for conducting meetings and business transactions. Lloyd's coffeehouse was founded around 1688 in London. Its founder, Edward Lloyd, published a newspaper with shipping information and as a result, Lloyd's became a gathering place for merchants, shipowners, and ships' captains. By 1710, Lloyd's was the principal commercial auction house in London for vessels and cargoes. In the wake of the disastrous speculation known as the South Sea Bubble that ended in 1720, King George I issued charters for two marine insurance corporations. To compete with these chartered groups, individual insurance underwriters chose to organize, and they centralized their activities at Lloyd's coffeehouse.

At Lloyd's, shipowners and merchants seeking marine insurance would approach a broker, who then sold shares of the total risk to underwriters who were bankers, merchants, and other wealthy individuals willing to place their fortunes at some risk in return for a premium. The Lloyd's of London insurance market was established. In the last century, professional underwriters represented syndicates of investors. While marine insurance continues to be a significant portion of its business, Lloyd's has insured every type of risk from the Bay Area Rapid Transit System to the U.S. Moon Rover to the King Tutankhamen museum exhibit.[10] In June 1992, for the first time in its over two and a half centuries of existence, Lloyd's instituted limits on the liability of its member investors, known as "the names," that are based on a percentage of premiums received.

Lloyd's is an insurance market in which insurance rates are set by the individual underwriters representing syndicates. The underwriters compete with each other to provide insurance policies. Lloyd's itself competes with other providers of insurance. Lloyd's serves as an intermediary between insurance customers and the investors who supply insurance coverage, setting the price of insurance and apportioning the risk between customers and investors. Insurance companies generally are financial intermediaries between investors and customers, although investors do not usually participate directly in particular contracts as in the case of Lloyd's.

The insurance market at Lloyd's is a good example of a business engaged in risk arbitrage. Risk arbitrage involves the purchase and sale of risky assets for a profit. In the case of insurance, investors are willing to take on risk for a premium. Customers are willing to pay a premium to pass on some of their risk. This applies to all forms of insurance: health, life, home, auto, fire, business, and liability.

Risk arbitrage extends beyond insurance to situations in which the production or sale of products entails a reallocation of risk. All business situations involve some type of uncertainty. By recognizing the risk allocation implicit in their activities, companies can successfully engage in this type of arbitrage.

Allocating Risk

What does it mean to allocate risk? It is basically transferring goods, services, and funds across states of the world. We have seen that merchant arbitrage involves price differences across markets, such as different geographic markets. Income is earned by transferring goods and services across those markets. Dynamic arbitrage creates price differences across markets separated by time. Income is earned by transferring goods and services over time through contracts, investment, delayed production, and storage. Risk arbitrage is based on price differences across states of the world.

Consider the case of insurance. Suppose that there are two possible states of the world in the coming year: floods occur, or no floods occur. A homeowner loses $100,000 if floods occur, due to damage to the house and belongings, and loses nothing otherwise. The homeowner would like very much to reduce the size of the loss in the state of the world in which floods occur. Suppose that there is only one chance out of a hundred that a flood will occur. The homeowner's expected loss is only $100,000 \times 1/100 = $1,000. The homeowner, like most individuals, dislikes facing that risk. The homeowner who could make a payment of $1,000 with certainty, that is in either state of the world, would definitely be better off than facing the "flood lottery" with its potential loss of a much larger amount. Aversion to risk is such that the individual would even accept an insurance contract for $5,000. For simplicity, suppose the contract has no deductible, that is, the plan pays for the full amount of the loss if a flood occurs. This contract means that the homeowner pays $5,000 in either state of the world.

An insurance company that sells the contract has expected revenues of $4,000 which equals the premium of $5,000 net of expected damage payments of $1,000. This payment must exceed the returns for undertaking comparable risks. The insurance company is able to reduce its risk by diversification, that is, by writing many contracts whose risk of loss are in part offsetting. It accumulates reserves and averages losses over time.

However, this is only half of the story. The insurance company acts as an intermediary between its investors and the homeowner. The insurance company allocates the homeowner's risk to its investors. Suppose that a single investor is willing to insure the loss at $3,500. On an investment of $100,000 the investor receives $3,500 if a flood occurs and $103,500 if no flood occurs. The insurance company receives a profit of $1,500, that is $5,000 − $3,500, net of the transaction costs required to carry out the investment and insurance contracts. The insurance company has earned rents by buying and selling contracts that transfer income from the flood state of the world to the no-flood state of the world.

Markets for Risk

Companies engage in risk arbitrage whenever there is uncertainty regarding costs upstream, revenues downstream, or production technology. The company profits by purchasing, transforming, and reselling a risky asset when expected earnings exceed expected costs. Risk arbitrage involves some allocation of risk between suppliers and customers. This requires knowledge of the returns required to compensate investors for the risk they will carry, the willingness of the customers to pay for insurance, and the degree of risk associated with the particular projects proposed by customers. Some risk can be hedged through financial markets, but many types of uncertainties are idiosyncratic.

The financial markets serve in large part to allocate risk. Most dynamic arbitrage entails risk because the income streams associated with those assets depend on the state of the world. So financial assets not only connect investors with owners of productive investment projects but they also share risk between the two. Debt holders bear the risk of default but claim the returns before securities holders. Securities holders are residual claimants, with different classes of debt and securities involving different levels of risk. Futures and options contracts are used to hedge the risks of price fluctuations of commodities, securities, interest rates, and exchange rates. The smooth functioning of the financial markets works to eliminate arbitrage rents on financial instruments. Yet, risk arbitrage need not be confined to financial markets. All businesses experience some combination of revenue and cost uncertainty.

Profit from risk arbitrage can be represented in a manner similar to the basic case. In the case of insurance, investors supply a level of coverage Q for which they receive w, which represents an expected return per unit.[11] Similarly, customers contract for an expected payment per unit of coverage equal to p.[12] Then, the expression for the firm's arbitrage profit is identical to the merchant arbitrage case, $(p - w)Q$.

In risk arbitrage as with the other forms of arbitrage, it is important to emphasize that market-making firms set upstream and downstream prices based on the supply of funds from investors and demand from customers, and the returns to bearing comparable risk. Again, there is by no means an opportunity to increase the arbitrage profits without limit by increasing the investment level. Such an increase would require higher expected payments to bring forth more coverage from investors. At the same time, lower expected payments per unit for insurance would bring forth more demand for coverage by customers and would place limits on the profit that could be earned from risk arbitrage.

It is worthwhile noting the many types of risk arbitrage that exist. Consider four types of bridges for matching markets. First, financial assets such as securities provide investors with an uncertain stream of returns that can be held in variable amounts, can be combined with other assets as part of a portfolio, and can easily be resold in capital markets. Financial intermediaries, including all types of banks, finance companies, insurance companies, and mutual funds, reallocate risk by buying and selling contracts with uncertain income streams. They serve to reduce risk through diversification, as the mutual fund holds a basket of securities or as the bank makes a variety of loans and investments.

Second, labor market intermediaries, such as Manpower, Inc., reallocate risks as well. Employers that face fluctuating sales have different needs for labor services across states of the world and are able to contract for these services through a temporary agency. At the same time, workers can have more steady employment by working through the temporary agency. The agency allocates labor services across states of the world and reduces risk by serving diverse employers.

Third, firms face uncertainty in terms of quantity and price of items sold. A firm that purchases or produces to stock will have either insufficient or excess unsold inventories. The firm may adjust its prices to sell its stock. Variations in customer demand will be reflected by changes in the output price. This illustrates risk arbitrage in that the firm is an intermediary between suppliers and final customers. The transactions that the firm enters into with its suppliers and customers result in an allocation of market risks. Similarly, a firm that purchases or produces to order will experience input cost variations due to changes in the cost and availability of supplies. Airlines commit to fares, routes, and schedules on the basis of estimates of the future costs. A small change in the price of jet fuel will raise costs significantly, since fuel costs are a substantial portion of total airline costs. This type of risk can be hedged to some extent. Airlines face myriad other shocks, however, such as inclement weather, labor strikes, regulatory change, and variation in travel patterns. Returns to airline investors reflect the risk of profit variation that they bear.

Product market intermediaries such as retailers and wholesalers engage in risk arbitrage as well. A retail chain holds inventories that insure that customers will have the products available when they are needed. Contracts with suppliers shift some of the sales risk to the retailer. Retailers diversify these risks through central warehouses and a variety of retail outlets. Risks of stockouts or overstocks are also mitigated by offering a wide variety of related products. Further diversification is achieved by servicing a wide variety of customers and relying on multiple suppliers.

Fourth, risk arbitrage is inherent in the research and development process. Firms developing new technologies or new products are intermediaries between investors and the markets for new technologies and new products. For example, entrepreneurs who found biotechnology companies rely on venture capitalists to secure investment funds. R&D on new biotech products involves some risks, which are taken on by investors. Technological intermediaries reallocate risk through licensing and contracts with potential customers.

Companies that bridge markets through complex mixing activities allocate risks among their investors, employees, product suppliers, technology providers, and customers. Risk is, of course, an integral part of the investment process.[13] Securities and debt provide uncertain income streams to investors. Companies mitigate risk for their shareholders not only through careful strategic planning, but also by holding a diverse portfolio of investment projects and engaging in multiple, complementary lines of business. Investors are able to diversify their portfolios by holding combinations of other stocks and financial assets, as well as by buying and selling options on specific securities. The limited liability of owners is often mentioned as an explanation for the existence of corporations. It should be noted that this provides a type of insurance as well, shifting risks to others such as debtors and the company's suppliers.

Companies act as insurers for their employees, smoothing the company's revenue and cost fluctuations through relatively stable wages and benefits and fixed hours of employment. Companies share risk with their employees through performance bonuses, profit sharing, and stock options. Severe fluctuations in the firm's labor requirements are met through layoffs and restructuring.

Companies share risks with their suppliers through implicit contracts, stabilizing orders and payments during demand fluctuations. This type of implicit contract is clearly less in use given just-in-time inventories and arrangements for rapid adjustment of deliveries in response to market conditions. However, it can be replaced by explicit risk-sharing that compensates suppliers for the costs of standing ready, sharing the joint benefits from lower inventory costs. The risks are diversified by relying on a supplier for multiple goods and services.

Companies share risks with buyers through implicit contracts as well, keeping prices and product availability relatively stable despite fluctuations in sales and in the costs of capital, labor, and other inputs. Companies also offer price guarantees to their customers; this is a competitive device but a form of insurance nonetheless. Risks of product failure are insured through return policies as well as formal warranties and guarantees.

Technological Arbitrage

Michael Dell created a computer company in his college dormitory room that was later to become the leader in direct marketing of computers, generating billions in sales. He recognized that personal computers were selling for substantially more than the cost of their components. Since the margin was sufficient to cover the costs of assembly and delivery, this made it possible to arbitrage between the market for components and the market for PCs. He began by assembling the computers himself. Today, Dell Computer continues to tailor each computer to order, usually completing manufacturing and delivery with a week and offering next-day shipping on many systems. Dell's catalog offers computers that are "custom built to do what you need them to do." Customers can also order thousands of software products and peripheral equipment. The company's output matches up exactly with customer orders, avoiding the problem of insufficient stock or costly unsold inventories. This type of rapid response allows the company to take advantage of changes in the prices of components and to take into account competitors' prices.

Dell Computer is an ideal example of technological arbitrage, combining a variety of inputs to take advantage of relative price differences in computer input and output markets. By combining multiple inputs to produce a new product or service, firms connect input and output markets. This type of arbitrage goes beyond spatial merchant arbitrage, since the products are bundled together or altered to form new products. It contains elements of dynamic and risk arbitrage because the production process takes time and involves uncertainties in demand and supply. Profits result from knowledge about production processes or product design. Also, innovations in management and in the organizational design of the firm itself can yield efficiencies that increase profits. The firm's unique knowledge is reflected in the cost of the purchased inputs and in the price of the final products.

The profits from technological arbitrage are simply the revenue generated by the final output minus the cost of the purchased inputs, net of any transaction costs, assembly and production costs, and other production expenses. For example, the company purchases X units of some key input at a per-unit purchase price w. The company transforms the input through assembly or some other production process into Q units of output that are sold at a per-unit price p. Without other costs, arbitrage profits are simply the difference between revenues and costs, $pQ - wX$.

To give a simple illustration, suppose that a computer consists of a chip and a box containing other components. The chip is available wholesale for $40 and the box is available wholesale for $25. The going price for a computer containing these two components is $100, so that without other costs, the arbitrage profit is $35 (that is, $100 minus $40 and minus $25). If assembly costs and other transaction costs involved in purchasing and marketing are less than $35, the firm can arbitrage between the chip market and the computer market. Even though the input and output markets are for different goods, technology, in this case assembly, allows arbitrage between these two markets.

Technological arbitrage can be profitable even if the production processes involved are well known. This can be achieved by securing lower-priced inputs through knowledge of upstream markets, allowing both cost reductions and lower output prices. Higher sales revenue can be achieved though product differentiation. Thus, production arbitrage is a variant of merchant arbitrage, with the intermediate steps of design, manufacturing, assembly, or distribution.

The profit from technological arbitrage is simply another way of looking at economic profit. The change in perspective is useful because it makes clear how the company's production activities provide links between input and output markets. The production activities are means of carrying out the arbitrage. The company need not own the production process. The price spreads between inputs and outputs provide guidance to the firm about the returns to its market-bridging production activities.

In competitive markets, the difference between the output price of a product and the input price of an important input is referred to as an implicit price of the productive activity. In his analysis of futures markets, Jeffrey Williams observes that in the textile industry, "traders are always alert for occasions when the price in the market for spinning services moves away from the price implicit in the difference between cotton and yarn" and states that "only if transactions costs in a set of markets are roughly comparable are all markets likely to be explicit."[14] These price differences reflect the costs of the productive activity and transaction costs. In practice, the price differentials also reflect rents earned by the producer on information regarding upstream markets, downstream markets, and the production process. Companies can earn these rents through arbitrage without necessarily engaging in production.

As the Chicago Mercantile Exchange kicked off live cattle futures trading in November of 1964, its president, Everette Bagby Harris, appeared on the trading floor wearing a ten-gallon hat and accompanied by a black Angus steer lent by Colonel Herman E. Lacy of Shamrock Farms in McHenry, Illinois.[15] Beef futures are contracts for delivery of "cars" of beef, denominated in dollars per 100 pounds. This market effectively established the spread between the prices of feeder cattle and cattle finished for market, providing farmers with insurance against fluctuations in cattle prices during the feeding process. The returns to the cattle rancher represent this spread net of feeding costs per unit.

Gasoline is a bundle of crude oil and petroleum refining. The company producing gasoline, jet fuel, or heating oil is arbitraging between the markets for crude oil and those for refined products. The difference between the returns from gasoline and the cost of crude must cover the production costs, including financial capital, labor, produced inputs, and technology. When both inputs and outputs are traded, futures markets permit the implicit purchase and sale of productive activities. For example, crude oil is transformed into gasoline, so by going long in gasoline and shorting crude oil, it is possible to take a position in petroleum refining, basically buying the production.

Manufacturing and assembly activities involve some component of technological arbitrage. The company's profits equal the implicit price of production activities net of production and transaction costs.

This insight has important implications for the design of the firm. Each productive activity carried out by the firm should be subject to a market test. In particular, can the activity be outsourced for less? It is essential not to restrict the application of this test. Not only parts production but also corporate services such as human resources management, planning, legal, information technology, and marketing can be outsourced. Through electronic data interchange (EDI), companies form a high-speed market that transforms the production activity into a marketable service and allows a continual reevaluation of the components that make up the business. Thus, outsourcing should not be seen as a once-and-for-all decision, but rather as an option that can be exercised or not at any given time as market conditions change. Arbitrage across suppliers and distributors means that such relationships are constantly subject to a market-based reevaluation.

In *Paradigm Shift*, Don Tapscott and Art Caston of the DMR group observe that in the age of network computing, the new enterprise is "modular and dynamic—based on interchangeable parts."[16] Each part of the business can be outsourced or reintegrated as companies become part of multibusiness teams. In fact, the availability of EDI means that while relationships may be stable, the terms of the transactions, from prices to product features, can change continuously.

What are the sources of technological arbitrage? Profits can be earned through unique knowledge of one or more of the following:

■ Input markets
■ Output markets
■ Technology
■ Transaction costs

Through superior information about input markets developed from experience or through supplier relationships, the company can reduce costs and price competitively in output markets. Some productive activities that were not economically viable become so with lower purchase costs of inputs. An example of such arbitrage is the movement of electronics and textile manufacturing abroad in response to lower labor costs. In some cases, lower labor costs allowed new products to be competitive, such as athletic shoes with more elaborate stitching.

Technological arbitrage is made possible by identifying new output markets, superior product design, marketing, reputation, or brand image. Each of these increases the spread with key input markets, allowing the company to cover its production and transaction costs. The high spread between the price of breakfast cereals and the cost of their main ingredients—namely the basic grains: corn , wheat, rice, and oats—reflects the value added by cereal manufacturers such as Kellogg, Post, and Quaker. They achieve the spread through creative product designs, frequent product introductions, brand identification, high advertising investment, nutritional additives such as vitamins, and established distribution networks.

New technologies open arbitrage opportunities in other ways. The firm can introduce an entirely new product or a firm can produce an existing product in a new way, using a different production process or using different combinations of inputs. Indeed, a single innovation may involve new products, processes, and inputs.[17] By achieving productive efficiencies, the company can realize arbitrage opportunities. A process innovation lowers production costs, allowing a company to take advantage of a narrow spread between final and primary goods. At Cray Research in the early 1980s, Steve Chen introduced the X-MP supercomputer, at that time the world's fastest computer. Steve Chen's design used the idea of parallel processing, by putting in tandem two processors from the preceding Cray-1 supercomputer. A significant aspect of the design is that it combined existing inputs, the Cray-1 processors, in new ways. This approach has been extended and surpassed. Today, supercomputers employ many parallel processors to achieve both great flexibility and computational speed, while using low-cost, off-the-shelf computer chips.

Transaction costs are a key component of technological arbitrage. The key input–output price spread must cover not only additional production costs but transaction costs as well. For example, financial intermediaries transform financial assets by creating new ones. Banks engage in maturity intermediation, combining assets to allow deposits and loans of varying duration. Advances in information and communications technology have significantly lowered many types of transaction costs, at the same time shortening the response time of competitors to arbitrage opportunities.

Arbitrage activities contain the seeds of their own destruction. By discerning and taking advantage of a positive bid–ask spread, companies bid up input prices and compete down output prices. Moreover, by acting on the arbitrage opportunity, a company inevitably draws the attention of its competitors, who can copy or improve upon the company's market bridge. Are arbitrage profits necessarily ephemeral then? The answer is generally yes. The company should not count on constantly repeating the same transactions. Unless the company has monopoly power downstream, monopsony power upstream, or patented technology, competition is rapidly attracted to arbitrage profit.

Indeed, the purpose of emphasizing the connection to financial arbitrage is to show that markets for products and services can be subject to the same forces that eliminate arbitrage opportunities for commodities, currencies, and financial assets. Companies must therefore be prepared to seize such opportunities more rapidly than ever before. Factories must be flexible to allow tailoring of output levels, inventories, and product variety to market trends. Supplier networks need to be ready to adapt to changes in the relative prices of inputs that require altering the production mix. Distributor networks must communicate demand information to manufacturers on a continual basis, while posting new prices and presenting new products with minimal lags.

The rapid competing away of arbitrage rents implies that companies must increase their speed of response. There are clear first-mover advantages in earning arbitrage rents. Moreover, companies need to avoid complacency by continually discerning new input markets and establishing new customers for their services. The best insurance is an emphasis on technological innovation as a means of linking markets in new ways that are harder to copy. Winning this race requires a clear view of the company not as a maker of breakfast cereals or copy machines, but as a builder of market bridges. This is the source of the arbitrage advantage.

Endnotes

1. If there are transaction costs per unit equal to t then the firm's profit is given by the expression $(p - w - t)Q$. If transaction costs involve fixed overhead costs equal to M then profit is given by the expression $(p - w)Q - M$.

2. This problem is presented and analyzed more fully in Daniel F. Spulber, "Market Microstructure and Intermediation," *Journal of Economic Perspectives*, 10, Summer 1996, pp. 135–152.

3. On transaction costs, see Ronald Coase, "The Nature of the Firm," *Economica*, 4, 1937, pp. 386–405, and Oliver E. Williamson, *Markets and Hierarchies*, New York: Free Press, 1985.

4. The relative price is simply the ratio of the selling and buying price of the good, p/w.

5. This paragraph refers to an account of the Dojima rice market given in A. J. Alletzhauser, *The House of Nomura*, New York: Harper Collins, 1990, pp. 26–27.

6. Bob Tamarkin, *The MERC: The Emergence of a Global Financial Powerhouse*, New York: Harper Collins, 1993.

7. Jeffrey Williams, *The Economic Function of Futures Markets*, Cambridge: Cambridge University Press, 1986.

8. This is known to economists as Hotelling's rule.

9. The managers of the firm should maximize economic profits which equal the discounted value of cash flow, which equals revenues net of costs. Managers should not maximize accounting measures of profit.

10. The account of Lloyd's is based upon R. Flower and M. W. Jones, *Lloyd's of London: An Illustrated History*, Newton Abbot: David & Charles, 1974; and D. E. W. Gibb, *Lloyd's of London: A Study of Individualism*, New York: St. Martin's Press, 1957.

11. Suppose for example that the investor receives a 6% return with probability 0.5 and a 10% return with probability 0.5. Then, the expected return per unit of investment is $w = 0.6 \times 0.5 + 0.10 \times 0.5 = 0.8$.

12. Suppose that the premium is X dollars for coverage of a loss K that occurs with probability 0.5. Then, the expected cost of insurance is $X - 0.5K$. The expected cost per unit of coverage is thus $p = (X - 0.5K) \div K = X/K - 0.5$.

13. Investors supply an investment X for which they receive an expected payment per unit w. Suppose that the investment project is to produce a good Q that earns an expected return per unit of p. Then, the expression for the firm's expected arbitrage profit is $pQ - wX$.

14. Williams, *The Economic Function of Futures Markets*, p. 44.

15. Tamarkin, *The MERC*, p. 134.

16. See D. Tapscott and A. Caston, *Paradigm Shift: The New Promise of Information Technology*, New York: McGraw-Hill, 1993.

17. The firm's production technology is represented by a production function $Q = F(X)$. This description of the firm's technology applies equally when there are many inputs to the production process and when there are many outputs. The production technology itself is chosen through internal innovation and acquisitions in the upstream technology marketplace.

5
INTERMEDIATION

As intermediaries, companies manage markets by playing four basic roles:

- Agent
- Monitor
- Broker
- Communicator

I use these terms to describe classes of the company's market relationships and the incentives that are involved. They are not intended in a narrow technical or legal sense, nor am I referring to relationships within the organization. Rather, I use the terms to provide a way of understanding activities that create customer and supplier relationships in the marketplace.

"The customer is always right." This statement illustrates the customer's sovereignty over the firm. The company acts in the interest of its customers as their agent. By agency, I do not simply mean that the company performs tasks as the agent, providing services or producing and delivering goods. Companies act for their customers by *transacting with third parties*.[1] The company procures financing, labor, parts and equipment, and technology as a means of delivering a service to its customers. It contracts with third parties for its customers, who then have only to engage in one transaction with the firm itself. As an agent, the company earns a commission equal to its profit margin on every unit sold. Alternatively, the company receives the full benefits of cost reductions relative to any given output price.[2]

As a monitor, the company supervises its employees, subcontractors, and suppliers. Thus, the company not only contracts with third parties, it monitors the performance under those contracts. Investors have the option of lending directly to entrepreneurs. By placing their money in a bank, lenders depend on the bank to supervise the borrowers. But retailers, wholesalers, and manufacturers also provide the service of delegated monitoring to their customers.

Acting as a broker, the company facilitates or replaces costly negotiation between its customers and suppliers, earning its profit margin as a commission. This is closely related to the agent's role of acting for the principal. The problem addressed by the broker function is that incomplete information about the buyer's willingness to pay and the seller's opportunity costs complicates the negotiation process, leading to the possibility of a breakdown in negotiations even when the parties are foregoing gains from trade. The broker allows the parties to realize these gains and takes a commission in the form of the bid–ask spread.

It should be apparent that the company's roles as agent, monitor, and broker depend to a great extent on the presence of asymmetric information in the marketplace. As a communicator, the company tackles this problem head-on by producing and distributing information to its customers and suppliers. Companies have many sources of information. They constantly watch competitors. They learn about market demand by meeting customers and monitoring sales. They learn about the availability of goods through supplier relationships. Finally, they acquire technological information through production and R&D activities.

Companies then communicate information through a wide variety of means, including advertising, pricing and contract terms, and direct contact with customers and suppliers. In this context, I discuss the growing importance of information in the economy and the dramatic implications of the information superhighway for the conduct and content of business. It is essential to understand the economic value of information. Companies can earn significant rents through their communication activities.

Competitive markets are the most efficient institutions for processing economic information. Yet economic actors do not become informed by magic. Rather, companies acting as intermediaries create and transmit information across markets. Thus, intermediation is an essential part of building market bridges.

Agent

Companies are the agents of their customers. They compete to be the best agent in the market. Companies can improve their performance by recognizing the pitfalls of the agency relationship and providing information and contractual assurances to overcome them. To some extent they are the agents of their suppliers as well, but I focus on the company's product market to emphasize the strategic aspects of the agency relationship.

The Principal–Agent Relationship

It is impossible to be in two places at once, and each of us is limited to the same 24 hours of time per day. Individuals are constrained in their capacity to communicate and interact with others by space, by time, or when special expertise is needed to handle a particular legal or business transaction. An important solution to these types of problems is to designate someone else to act for you as your agent. The person who delegates authority to the agent is referred to as the principal.

The use of agents provides many benefits to the principal. An agent can be present at a meeting, freeing the principal for other tasks. A principal can have many agents to represent interests in a wide variety of situations, overcoming the limited capacity of an individual. An agent may possess special skills or knowledge that the principal does not have. Attorneys provide legal proficiency for clients, while real estate agents are more familiar with the housing market than buyers or sellers are.

In law, agency is a fiduciary relationship, that is, one in which the principal places trust in the agent. The agent is expected to act in the other's benefit. The two parties mutually agree that the agent is to act for the principal. The agent is subject to the principal's direction and control, and yet is understood to be able to exercise discretion in choices of actions. Although agency law is concerned with establishing liability for agent actions affecting third parties, I am more interested here in the incentive aspects of the agency relationship than in a literal discussion of contract and tort issues.

The type of agent that I am concerned with here is most similar to the independent contractor. In many cases, the contractor can exercise complete control over the management of the task at hand, and the principal is not liable to third parties for the actions of the agent. The principal is primarily interested in the end result of the agent's effort, namely the service delivered to the principal.

The tasks of the agent generally involve establishing contracts between the principal and third parties.[3] It should be immediately apparent that in many situations *agents are intermediaries* between the principal and another party. For example, a salesperson represents a company to its customers and conveys the customer's desires to the company. A real estate agent represents the sellers of houses. Agents, under delegated authority from their principal, interact with other principals or agents. For this reason, a working knowledge of agency is essential to understanding intermediation.

A good place to start is within the company. Principal–agent relationships are the foundation of organizations. Practically all vertical relationships in an organization involve some delegation of authority, from the CEO to the president, to the vice presidents, to division managers, and all the way down the organization. Managers rely on their subordinates to represent their interests within the organization. Most of these relationships, with the exception of the lowest operatives in the hierarchy, involve intermediation between members of the organization. For example, an executive vice president relies on a division manager to communicate directives and supervise other managers and employees in the division.

Traditional discussions of the span of control recognized the limitations on the number of subordinates that a manager could supervise effectively. By adding a layer of management, supervision activities were divided among middle managers. The upper managers' span of control was substantially lowered since they only had to supervise the middle managers. The middle managers acted as agents by representing the interests of managers and supervising subordinates.

Next, consider interaction between the company and those in its market network. Agency relationships characterize the company's relationships with customers and suppliers. The company delegates authority to its sales staff to transact with customers. The company delegates authority to purchasing agents to connect with suppliers. Company attorneys represent the company to government agencies and in legal proceedings. Shareholders delegate authority to the board, which hires and fires the CEO, who acts as the agent of the company's owners.

Most relationships within the organization involve an agent acting for a principal. In addition, the organization interacts with others in the marketplace and in government by delegating authority to agents who transact with those third parties. In each case, agents are individuals who act for superiors in the organization or who represent the organization itself.

But agents need not be individuals; they can be companies. The company as a whole acts as the agent of its customers. Customers rely on companies to act in their interests, to be where they are not, to meet with others, to perform productive tasks, and to supply expertise. Most importantly, companies represent their customers *by contracting with third parties*. Customers need only purchase the company's goods and services to benefit from these contracts.

The company is also the agent of its owners. Investors in the company exercise residual control rights and obtain the residual returns while delegating authority to management. Management contracts with the company's employees, customers, and suppliers. Investors need only purchase the company's stock to profit from these myriad transactions.

For many companies, the agency role is transparent. Travel agencies are charged with searching for the lowest fare, preparing tickets, coordinating itineraries, and providing travel advice. Travel agencies intermediate between their customers and a host of travel services, airlines, hotels, and car rental companies. By writing tickets, travel agents form contracts with airlines for travelers.

Similarly, a stock brokerage intermediates between its customers and the financial markets. It is charged with searching for investment opportunities, accurately executing trades, keeping records of customer accounts, providing financial planning, and giving investment advice. It enters into stock transactions for its investors.

Most companies play similar agency roles for their customers. Retailers are expected to act in the interest of their customers by continually searching out suppliers for new products. They are expected to provide product variety, convenience, accurate pricing, and other forms of customer service. Also, the retailer is charged with maintaining inventories to provide immediacy and keeping stock in good condition. Customers contract for the services of a variety of companies (restaurants and hotels, transportation companies, gas, electricity, and telecommunications utilities, financial institutions), expecting them to devote effort to producing the desired assistance. The retailer's actions can be interpreted as contracting with suppliers in the interest of consumers.

Manufacturers are agents of customers in a comparable way. They are expected to provide a product that is free of defects, is safe to use, and performs as advertised. They must search out suppliers for high-quality materials and parts and find distributors that explain and service the product. They have the technological expertise to carry out production and to engage in innovation. The customer delegates authority to the manufacturer by purchasing a product, which is a contract for services.

The strategic implications of all this should be apparent. The company needs to view its many actions as that of an independent contractor who is representing its customers. Companies form contractual relationships in their markets as representatives of their customers and suppliers. It would be prohibitively costly for a customer to contract directly with the company's sources of financing, its employees, its suppliers. The company earns economic returns from the agency services it provides.

An individual hires a building contractor to construct a house. Relative to the buyer, the contractor has a comparative advantage in carrying out the project. The contractor has specialized knowledge of the building trades and is familiar with the market for carpenters, masons, electricians, and plumbers. The contractor searches for qualified subcontractors and purchases the materials needed to complete the project. The contractor has experience in bargaining and writing contracts. In addition, the contractor supervises the project to assure that it is completed carefully and within the specified time.

The company coordinates contracting as a means of achieving returns from consolidation and lowering transaction costs. Financing is obtained for a broad range of production and investment activities. The company's contracts with its investors provide a service to the firm's customers. The company enters into financial contracts as a representative of its customers, since the capital provides the means of delivering products and services to those customers. Similarly, the company provides access to the product markets for its shareholders by entering into contracts to make and deliver products.

Can the company be the agent of many principals? The answer is yes, as long as the company fulfills its duties to all of them. This seems to depart from a basic tenet of agency law, namely that an agent cannot represent two principals in the same transaction if they have conflicting interests. Yet, this is not a problem in the sense used here. If both parties are fully informed of the situation, then the agent performs a valuable intermediary role. Returning to the issue of customers and shareholders, how do their interests differ? The customer expects that in return for a payment that is agreed upon, the company will deliver a product or service following the terms of their contract. The investor expects that the company will act to maximize the value of the firm. Each relationship has essential agency aspects.

What are the agent's responsibilities? To begin with, an agent has a duty to inform.[4] The company must report to its shareholders regarding its financial state. Similarly, it must inform its customers regarding the quality and price of its products and its contract terms. In addition, an agent must keep proper accounts. Companies prepare financial accounts and present annual reports, and also keep account of transactions with customers and suppliers. Next, an agent must act in the interest of the principal. The company has a responsibility to act in the interests of its shareholders by maximizing the value of the firm. The company must also act in the interest of its customers, earning profits by delivering value added. It must exercise care to provide customers with products that satisfy health and safety requirements.

It is often noted that the corporation exists to eliminate the liability of shareholders, who cannot be held responsible for the actions of the company. However, it is useful to observe that companies provide very similar services to their customers as well. Just as the buyer of the house is protected from liability for some of the actions of an independent contractor, so the customers of companies are not held responsible for the actions of companies that serve them. For example, even if Exxon harms the environment by spilling oil, customers of the company can continue to purchase its gasoline and petroleum products without bearing any legal responsibility for its actions.

Companies can achieve a competitive advantage by recognizing the market value of their agency services. This requires taking a long view, not simply focusing on the physical or technological aspects of production or the characteristics of service offerings. Rather, the company observes its comparative advantage relative to its customers in contracting with third parties. This perspective allows the identification of a wider range of specialized service offerings that meet customer needs.

Contracting Costs

The advantages of agents are balanced by serious potential problems. Although agents act under delegated authority, they naturally have their own economic interests. These need not be perfectly aligned with those of their principal. Therefore, the actions of agents may be inconsistent with, or in the extreme diametrically opposed to, the interest of the principal.

Indeed, the same conditions that create the need for agents create the opportunity for the agent to take advantage of the relationship. For example, just as the agent is needed to act as a representative at a meeting the principal cannot attend, so the principal cannot be there to supervise the quality of the agent's efforts. Just as an expert must be hired to provide medical, legal, or technical advice, so the principal may not be able to evaluate the quality of the advice.

These problems can presumably be mitigated by careful specification of the contract between the principal and the agent. Both parties are aware that the contract terms create incentives that will affect the agent's actions. However, writing and enforcing such contracts can be costly. This forces a trade-off between creating effective contractual incentives and tolerating some slippage between the principal's objectives and those of the agent.

Table 5-1.
COSTS AND ASSOCIATED PROBLEMS IN THE
PRINCIPAL–AGENT RELATIONSHIP

Cost	Problem
Contract contingencies	Incomplete contracts
Monitoring agent actions	Moral hazard
Observing agent characteristics	Adverse selection

There are three costs in writing such contracts, and each of these is associated with a serious incentive problem. There are costs of writing contingent contracts, which implies that the agreements between the principal and agent will be incomplete. There are costs of monitoring the agent's actions, which can result in the agent shirking duties or not carrying them out conscientiously. This is referred to as the moral hazard problem. Finally, there are costs of observing the agent's characteristics, which may result in misrepresentation of the agent's ability or other information. This is referred to as the adverse selection problem.

Incomplete Contracts

Most of business is fraught with risk. Companies face fluctuations in the level and patterns of demand. The availability and cost of supplies varies unexpectedly. Technological change, competitive entry, and shifting government regulation occur frequently. How do companies share these risks with their customers and suppliers?

A customer is concerned that a product will perform as claimed by the company. It is often too costly to write a contract that specifies the performance of the product under each possible condition, and assessing the likelihood of accidents and their possible severity can be costly. Problems such as this are handled in part by tort law, which assigns liability and provides for remedies, thus replacing the need for costly contracting and negotiation. However, companies have many ways to address this problem. Some retailers offer 100% return policies, with no questions asked, avoiding the need to specify complicated terms in detail to obtain reimbursement or exchange. Some manufacturers and service providers offer blanket guarantees of performance. Federal Express' slogan, "When it absolutely, positively has to be there overnight," does not make reference to weather conditions or other events that impede performance. Rather, the promise is made regardless of potential difficulties.

It is usually not possible or even desirable to take into account every contingency that might arise. So, parties will enter into incomplete contracts, that is, agreements that do not account for all factors that can affect the costs and benefits to the parties. Contract law provides a common set of rules for determining remedies and responsibilities in the event an agreement is breached. This allows all contracts to be simplified because they are written against the background of the law. However, it should be recognized that most contracts must ultimately be incomplete, since it is only worthwhile to deal specifically with the simplest, the most likely, or the most problematic contingencies.

In the absence of transaction costs, contracts could be made to depend more fully on the outcome of market events and other things of interest to the parties. This means that there remains room for additional gains from trade between a company and its trading partners if they can find a way to reduce the costs of contracting. Companies can enter new markets or increase their returns if they can find ways to contract more efficiently, or to offer better contracts that address the risk concerns of their customers. Building a reputation for performance and offering simpler warranties are effective tools for winning customers.

If contracts are incomplete, the two parties have not allocated all risks in a mutually beneficial way, and opportunities remain to structure better contracts that increase value added. This situation provides an entry opportunity for a company that has lower contracting costs or that knows how to design a more effective contract.

Moral Hazard

The problem of risk allocation is compounded when it is difficult to monitor agent actions. This creates the problem of moral hazard that is familiar in insurance markets. For example, fire insurance contracts presume some degree of fire prevention by the insured person. Certainly, limits on coverage and legal penalties usually deter insurance fraud, so that deliberately burning down a building for insurance purposes is relatively rare. In addition, it is unlikely that individuals act negligently as a result of having fire insurance. The question is, will the individual devote sufficient care to fire prevention, or will having the insurance contract lead to some lowering of vigilance? The right amount of fire prevention trades off the benefits of hazard reduction with the cost of care. The individual should invest in additional prevention equipment, alarms, training, and materials, at least to the point that the investment equals the reduction in the expected losses.

But how to guarantee that the individual will make such an investment? The insurance company cannot perfectly observe the individual's efforts. It is costly to visit the site of a business, and definitely not worthwhile for small insurance contracts. Requiring the individual to disclose fire safety equipment such as sprinklers or smoke alarms is useful but provides only a partial picture. It is ultimately not possible to monitor the individual's day-to-day safety efforts. Monitoring after a fire takes place also provides only partial information. An investigation can detect deliberate negligence or faulty equipment but may not give an accurate picture of the degree of care.

This leaves the insurance contract itself as an instrument for inducing the individual to take care. Yet individuals will only take the full amount of care if they bear the full risk of loss. The insurance contract itself reduces some of the incentive to care by reducing the expected loss. This is the basis of the moral hazard problem. Since effort is imperfectly observable, and since contracts involve some sharing of risk, it is necessary to tolerate some departure of care from the most efficient level. In other words, the insurance premium and coverage are adjusted to reflect the fact that most insureds will perhaps take a bit less care in preventing accidents than would be mutually beneficial. As a consequence of insurance, many drivers are slightly less careful, patients engage in a bit less preventive care, and homeowners are somewhat less protective of their possessions.

The general problem of moral hazard begins with the difficulty of monitoring the efforts of agents. Employees may shirk; or they may work hard, but not in alignment with the company's interests. Observing employee effort is an imperfect process requiring the constant presence of managers or production supervisors. It also negates the very benefits of employing an agent—independence of action and individual discretion. It is costly to closely supervise sales personnel. The company must rely on their assessment of the customer's requirements rather than second-guessing their every action.

In a fiduciary relationship, the principal expects that the agent will represent its interest. The agent will negotiate contracts that are beneficial to the principal. The agent will not have an undisclosed financial interest in the transaction. The agent will devote the requisite effort to information gathering. Principals necessarily place their trust in doctors, attorneys, accountants, and other agents.

Moral hazard is also an issue in the behavior of companies acting as agents. The company's actions are only imperfectly observable to its customers. For example, if product quality and safety are not immediately apparent in the firm's product, it is difficult for a customer to determine if the firm has taken sufficient care in production. A customer purchasing medicine cannot easily observe whether the company has followed proper testing procedures in its development. Customers are generally aware that the interests of the company can depart from their own.

The general solution to the moral hazard problem is to base pay on performance, whether measured in terms of profits, sales, productivity, or some other relevant criterion. This shifts risk to the agent who is then induced to increase effort as a means of raising expected performance. However, pay for performance entails additional costs because the principal must compensate the agent for risk to attract the agent's services in the market. Shifting all business risk to an employee is very costly because a substantial portion of the gains would have to be shared as well. Since inducing performance can be costly, the principal must tolerate some departure from desired behavior. The principal trades off the performance benefits from shifting risk to the agent against the costs of compensating the agent for bearing risk.

This suggests that moral hazard problems are not a serious issue in the relationship between a company and its customers, since profits are a pure pay-for-performance system. The company earns the returns and bears the risks of market uncertainty. If the company does not perform as expected customers will go elsewhere. A reputation for low-quality products or service hurts sales as well. However, not all companies respond to such market incentives in the same manner. Some companies have shorter time horizons and are willing to risk poor reputations for short-term gains. Other companies may not supervise employees effectively, or may even offer incentives to employees who promote moral hazard.

For example, Sears' automobile service centers were found to carry out unnecessary auto repairs. They were charged with having defrauded customers in California and New Jersey. Customers answered ads offering low-cost brake jobs. The problem was caused by an internal moral hazard. Service managers were rewarded for the number of repairs performed and engaged in questionable practices to achieve company sales targets for brake jobs, springs, or wheel alignments. This ultimately resulted in customer complaints, charges by state agencies, and reports in the press that were damaging to the company's reputation. The chairman of Sears, Edward A. Brennan, said that the incentive program would be replaced by one that provided rewards for customer satisfaction: "We want to eliminate anything that could even lead to the perception that our associates could be motivated to sell our customers unneeded repairs."[5]

As Sears learned the hard way, companies must do what is necessary to reassure the customer that the moral hazard problem is mitigated to the greatest extent possible. Given the possibility that company actions may depart from the best interest of customers, companies can distinguish themselves from the competition by continually addressing the agency issue.

The unobservable aspects of the company need to be made as transparent as possible. The customer needs to know that employees are rewarded for quality of service. Contracts with customers must be presented in clear and simple terms. The company needs to communicate clearly its commitment to performance in the area of product quality or safety. When there is limited information about relative prices, the company can earn goodwill through accurate price comparisons and transparent pricing terms.

Warranties and product guarantees play an important role in reassuring the consumer. Consumers not only know that they will be reimbursed in the event that the product fails to function properly, but they also know that since the warranty is costly for the company the company has an incentive to produce a better product. This is particularly interesting since the company, as agent, designs its own incentive contract. The consumer, as principal, accepts the terms of the contract based on the incentives for performance they create for the company.

By recognizing that the high cost of observation underlies the moral hazard problem, a company can effectively compete to be its customer's agent by reducing the customer's monitoring costs. The company must audit its own services and provide relevant information to customers. Moreover, the company must structure its contracts with customers such that the company's incentives for performance are evident. Trust lies at the heart of the agency relationship. To be repeatedly chosen as an agent, a company must create contracts that build customer confidence.

Adverse Selection

Not only are the actions of agents difficult to observe, but their characteristics are as well. This creates the problem of adverse selection, a familiar term in insurance markets. It is costly to ascertain the risks faced by an individual seeking insurance. Consider the case of auto insurance. The insurance company may not be able to differentiate drivers who are cautious and skilled from those who are not. The company solicits all types of information from drivers, such as age, driving record, type of car, and number of miles driven to work, as a means of estimating the likelihood of an accident. These measures are useful in increasing the accuracy of the estimate. In addition, the company keeps track of the individual's claims on the company as a basis for determining premiums and coverage.

Ultimately, however, it is not possible to accurately observe individual characteristics. Generally, the individual can be expected to have more information about personal characteristics than does the insurance company. Thus, the company must create contracts that provide customers with an incentive to voluntarily disclose the relevant information. This is done by constructing contracts that allow customers to self-select. If the contracts are not carefully chosen the outcome can be costly for the insurance company. Adverse selection occurs when those who are accident-prone purchase insurance and those who are less likely to have accidents do not.

If the company has designed its contract to reflect the average rate of accidents and it primarily attracts those drivers who are less safe, its contracts may fail to be profitable. For example, suppose that in any given year each customer has at most one accident. There are two types of customers, those who have a likelihood of accident of 50% per year and those who have a likelihood of only 10% per year. The loss from an accident is $1,000 for either type of driver. If there is an equal proportion of the two drivers in the population it may seem reasonable to offer an insurance contract at a cost of $300, which is the average of the expected payments to the unsafe driver ($500) and the safe one ($100). However, while the unsafe drivers will find such a contract very attractive, safe drivers generally will not. If the safe drivers are not extremely averse to risk, they will elect not to buy the contract. If only the unsafe drivers buy the contract, the insurance company will lose money.

The insurance company would most like to offer a higher-cost policy to the unsafe drivers and a lower-cost policy to the safe ones, but how to distinguish between the two? By carefully designing the contracts, it is sometimes possible to choose a combination of premium and coverage levels that cause the two types to self-select into risk classes.

Any contract that pools the two types of drivers is subject to competitive entry by a firm offering a contract that will attract away the safe drivers. However, this would lead the original insurance company to withdraw the contract for unsafe drivers, who would then adversely select by taking the entrant's contract for safe drivers. As a consequence, under some conditions, a market equilibrium could yield contracts that pool diverse types or contracts that separate them. A separating set of contracts might attract the unsafe driver by offering a high-cost, full coverage contract while attracting the safe driver with a low-cost contract that provides only partial coverage.

The problem of adverse selection in markets has been widely noted. The economist George Akerlof described a simple market for two types of used cars in which some proportion were in good shape and the rest were lemons. The problem faced by customers is the difficulty in distinguishing the two. Suppose that half of the cars are worth $10,000 and the other half are worth $2,000, so that the average value is $6,000. If the price of used cars equals their average value, owners of lemons will be quite willing to sell, but owners of good used cars will not, since their cars clearly have a higher value than the average. Customers will understand that only lemons are on the market, and will not be willing to pay a price that reflects average quality. As a consequence, the price falls further and only lemons are sold. With many quality gradations, the process of bad cars driving out good cars would be exacerbated.

Adverse selection is an endemic problem of agency. The principal generally will find it difficult to observe the agent's characteristics. If a skilled agent is required, then those very skills are generally needed to discern whether or not the agent is qualified. Determining the skills of a doctor requires some medical training. Similarly, it is difficult to evaluate an accountant, lawyer, mechanic, or architect. The principal relies on the agent's bargaining ability, integrity, or initiative in carrying out transactions with third parties. These attributes may be unobservable since the negotiations are necessarily carried out without the principal's participation.

In the course of representing the principal, it is to be expected that the agent gathers information that the principal does not have. The agent may be the only one in direct contact with those wishing to contract with the principal. The agent's fiduciary duty requires disclosure of any information that materially affects the principal's interests. For example, an agent may be asked to sell a property at an agreed-upon price. In the course of trying to sell the property, the agent learns that a shopping center will be built nearby that raises the value of the property. It is the duty of the agent to pass that information along to the principal. It would be negligent not to do so, and even worse to seek to profit from the information. The problem is how to structure contractual incentives or penalties that promote full disclosure.

Adverse selection problems are intrinsic to staffing an organization. Each position in the company requires employees who possess a particular set of attributes. The company may want an individual who is intelligent, creative, industrious, patient, persuasive, or personable. How to determine whether the employee meets the criteria for the job? Companies interview prospective employees, obtain letters of reference, require certification or academic degrees, and consult resumes. They subject new and prospective hires to a battery of tests. After hiring, a record of performance and evaluations by superiors is maintained. These are all means to improve the company's imperfect knowledge about the employee.

Employees who perform well according to the company's criteria are often rewarded with pay raises, promotions, and perks. Those who do not perform receive fewer rewards or are dismissed. Yet, anyone would acknowledge that even this process is imperfect. The well-known Peter principle, that individuals rise in an organization to the level of their own incompetence, illustrates how little is really known about employee skills. If people are promoted when they do well, and no longer promoted when their performance flags, they wind up in a position for which they are ill-suited. The organization's stock of knowledge about the characteristics of its personnel is one of its most valuable assets, even though it is nontradable.

Monitoring costs are high, so that information about agent characteristics remains imperfect. The solution to the adverse selection problem is to design incentives that reward individuals for disclosure of their information. Economists refer to these payments as information rents. Consider again the insurance example. Suppose that the insurance company is a monopolist. If the company were perfectly informed about the riskiness of the two types of drivers and other factors affecting their benefits from insurance, it would be possible to design contracts for each driver that fully extracted the amount each was willing to pay for insurance. Such perfect price discrimination is not possible because the drivers are better informed about their chances of having an accident than is the insurance company. The contracts must cause the drivers to sort themselves out, each selecting the contract that was designed for that driver. Offering contracts that extract all rents could lead to adverse selection, with both types of drivers selecting the contract intended for the safe driver.

To design contracts that separate out the two drivers it is necessary to set contract terms (coverage and premiums) that do not fully extract the amount each agent is willing to pay. Rather, at least one of the agents must receive positive gains from trade in an insurance purchase. Then, by their choice of a contract, the two drivers will reveal their types.

The point of all this is that the principal must make implicit payments for revelation of information. This implies that overcoming adverse selection is costly. There is a trade-off between the benefits of acquiring better information about the agent and the costs of paying agents to reveal themselves by offering them better contract terms. As a result, it is generally necessary to tolerate some imperfections in contract terms in order to obtain more information. The possibility of adverse selection implies that contract terms will not be as efficient for the parties as they would be in a world of perfect information or, equivalently, one with costless monitoring.

As I have already observed, the company is an agent of its customers. As agents, companies are not immune from adverse selection incentives. There are myriad sources of information asymmetries. The lemon problem can drive customers from the marketplace or cause low-quality producers to proliferate. Customers are acutely aware of their lack of information. To become the customers' agent of choice, a company must overcome the information asymmetry as much as possible.

Companies have private information about the quality or safety of their products. There are several varieties of customer uncertainty. First, the characteristics of a company's products may be apparent upon examination. However, the customer must engage in costly search to observe each company's products. Competitive advantage can be gained by reducing customer search costs through informative advertising and alternative channels of distribution such as catalogs and direct mail. The costs of shopping can be lowered by expert advice, accurate product labeling, and voluntary disclosure of prices and other contract terms. Second, evaluating the performance of some products requires consuming the product. The process of trial and error entails the cost of purchasing the good and the opportunity cost of not having purchased a substitute product. Companies can ease these concerns through guarantees and return policies. Finally, it may take years to observe the performance of some products, for example, the durability of appliances. In this case, building a reputation for reliable service and replacement of defective products reduces the expected costs of purchase.

Multiple Principals and Agents

Companies generally serve many customers and face the challenge of making each one feel important. Customers have the task of choosing among competing sellers. Therefore, in most markets, agents compete to serve principals and principals compete for the services of agents. This has important consequences for the types of incentives faced by firms and the nature of their contracts.

Agents with Multiple Principals. Since the firm has many customers, it is an agent with multiple principals (see Figure 5-1). To some extent the principals compete with each other for the agent's time and attention. The agent's actions may not always be directly aligned with each principal's interests because of conflicting demands on the agent's resources.

Figure 5-1.
PRINCIPALS COMPETE FOR THE AGENT'S SERVICES

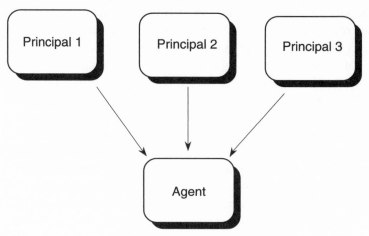

For example, a real estate agency represents many sellers (who are customers for the agency's selling services). Sellers are concerned that the agency might devote more effort to selling the houses of others, resulting in their receiving a lower sale price due to delays. The agent must take care to assure each principal that its house is important and that it is receiving the necessary attention. The agency assigns an individual agent to represent the house, who frequently contacts the owners with information as it becomes available. It promises to hold a certain number of open-house showings of the property and specifies how the house will be advertised. Sometimes, the realtor prepares a marketing plan that is tailored to the house.

The presence of uniform commissions has been said to address the multiple-principals problem.[6] The agency receives a percentage commission of, say, 6% rather than a flat fee to give it an incentive to seek a higher price for the house. A higher commission on any given house would increase the agency's sales effort. Yet, were commission arrangements to vary from one house to another, a seller would have greater cause for concern that the agency would be spending more time on a house that would yield a greater return. Still, properties differ in terms of the asking price (which of course determines the commission), the ease of sale, distance, and other attributes. These will inevitably affect agency incentives. This situation is similar to that of other agents with multiple clients including lawyers, talent agents for actors and athletes, and advertising agencies.

The market for consulting companies is booming. The market leader is Anderson Consulting, with a multibillion-dollar consulting practice. Anderson and the other companies in the top ten (Coopers & Lybrand,

McKinsey, Booz Allen & Hamilton, Gemini Consulting, CSC Consulting, Boston Consulting Group, A. T. Kearney, Mercer Management Consulting, and Monitor) provide management advice to many Fortune 500 companies, including AT&T, GTE, DuPont, GM, Sears, and PepsiCo.[7] Each consulting company deals with many clients. To address the issue of divided attention, the companies create project teams that stay with a single client until their task is complete. This provides an assurance that the project team is devoting its efforts to the problem at hand. According to *Business Week*, "Consultants are no longer just parachuting in, observing, and bailing out. They're forming teams with executives at client companies and working together to analyze problems and develop solutions. Assignments that were once narrowly focused have evolved into 18- to 24-month efforts that encompass strategy, operations, organization, and technology." By working closely with the consultants in teams, management can direct the project more carefully, assuring that the efforts of the consultants are monitored more closely.

This provides some general lessons for companies, whose customers know that they are competing with each other for service. To serve as their agent, companies must stress procedures that will result in individual attention, rather than a one-size-fits-all approach. This means using account representatives, establishing customer service numbers that minimize delays in response, retaining additional personnel to meet periods of peak demand, and offering personally tailored services. Dell Computer's customized computer configurations make customers feel that the company is carrying out assembly and ordering to meet their individual needs.

Principals with Multiple Agents. Competitive markets can be seen as contests between agents (see Figure 5-2). To be chosen as an agent of its customers, the firm must provide superior performance compared to other agents. It needs to understand that while it is acting under delegated authority, the principal has alternatives. Competition between agents serves to alleviate the problems of moral hazard and adverse selection.

In the case of adverse selection, establishing competition between agents reveals information. The best-known example is the procurement auction. A buyer wishes to choose among several sellers, each with unobservable production costs. Of course, the buyer wishes to be served by the lowest-cost seller and asks sellers to submit sealed bids. The lowest-cost seller will submit the lowest bid so that the auction process reveals the identity of the lowest-cost seller, and thus relieves the information asymmetry between buyers and sellers.

Price competition between sellers with unobservable production costs is very similar to the sealed bid auction. Suppose that companies have

Figure 5-2.
AGENTS COMPETE TO SERVE A PRINCIPAL

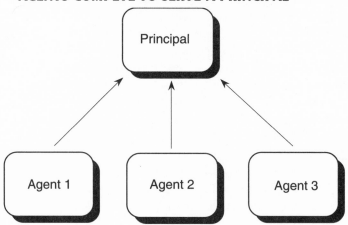

relatively constant operating costs per unit of production, so that a single firm could serve the market. If potential customers are able to accurately observe prices without search costs, the lowest-cost firm will win the market by offering the lowest price and supplying all of the output demanded.[8]

Price competition with unobservable costs works as follows. The firm's expected profit is equal to the profit contingent upon winning the market multiplied by the likelihood of winning the market. This implies that a firm choosing its pricing strategy faces two diverging incentives. On one hand, the firm wishes to charge a price as close as possible to the monopoly price to maximize profits contingent on winning the market. On the other hand, the firm must lower its price to increase the likelihood of undercutting the prices of rival firms. A price cut becomes less attractive the higher the firm's marginal cost is. The firm will trade off the effect of price on marginal profit against the effect of price on the likelihood of capturing the market demand.

As a result, the price set by each firm is always strictly less than the price that the firm would charge if it were a monopoly. Starting from the monopoly level, if the firm slightly reduces its price, it incurs a relatively small loss in profit but enjoys a more significant gain in the probability of winning the market.

The greater the number of companies in the competition the lower is the likelihood that any individual company will win the market. Recognizing this, companies moderate their markups in anticipation of bids that might undercut theirs. The number of firms thus affects expected profit both through the likelihood of winning and through the equilibrium pricing strategy. The greater the number of companies entering the price competition, the closer each firm's price will be to its unit cost. In this way, price competition elicits cost information from companies.

Competition reveals many other types of information as well. If the characteristics of products are imperfectly observable, companies will compete to disclose any information that is to their advantage to disclose. There are many who believe that product labeling should be required by law while others feel it should be voluntary. Although there may be a role for regulation in specifying product labeling standards, there is good reason not to rely on forced disclosure. If no manufacturers label the content of their products, there are returns to a manufacturer that unilaterally discloses its product features and challenges others to do the same. The company that discloses will gain a competitive advantage even if the products are otherwise identical. Moreover, if the products differ and some producers disclose contents while other do not, consumers will be able to infer that those failing to disclose have products with inferior features.

Maintaining competition between agents relieves the moral hazard problem as well. Many companies contract with multiple parts suppliers. Second-sourcing guarantees that low bids by any supplier do not reflect temporary cost advantages. Contracting with multiple suppliers ensures that the suppliers will continue to invest in cost reduction and will keep improving product quality. Even if the suppliers' efforts are not directly observable, the company is able to induce effort by establishing yardstick competition. For example, the company can divide its procurement needs into a large and small share. The company that performs best in a given year can be awarded the larger share in a subsequent year. Alternatively, the company can award a cash bonus to the company that delivers the highest quality parts or turns in the best on-time performance. The maintenance of multiple sources allows the company to avoid future costs of search and contract negotiation.

Companies can alleviate the moral hazard problem for suppliers by a technique known as paying efficiency wages. The suppliers are paid above their market opportunity costs, but face termination if their performance falls below some standard. The above-market payment must at least cover the cost of performing well plus the supplier's alternative prospects. To avoid losing this premium, the suppliers then will devote substantial effort and investment to making sure that their expected performance meets the targets.

This reasoning extends to product markets. In some cases, companies can price above market if they consistently deliver high-quality products or service. For services whose quality or reliability are at a premium and where effort is difficult to observe, there are gains from the product differentiation strategy of higher quality at a higher price. In markets where moral hazard problems are present, the customer can infer that high-price manufacturers will perform well because they have an incentive to seek repeat business. This explains the oft-repeated observation, "You get what you pay for."

To illustrate the agency role, consider Microsoft Corporation's entry into electronic publication on CD-ROM.[9] CD-ROM, which stands for *compact-disk read-only memory*, refers to disks resembling music CDs that contain the equivalent of 250,000 pages of text. The disks are played on special machines and displayed on computer terminals, and provide a combination of text, pictures, sound, and video images. Computer companies offer product bundles that include CD-ROM players and stereo speakers packaged with computers and monitors.

Microsoft ranks only fourth in the consumer edutainment market, with only 8% of the market behind Compton's New Media (owned by the Tribune Company), Software Toolworks, and Interplay.[10] The company's titles include Microsoft Encarta, Complete Baseball, and Cinemania. Encarta is a multimedia encyclopedia that allows users to look up an entry, such as Mozart, that can be supplemented with pictures and a musical interlude. Complete Baseball includes statistics, details about players and major league teams, and video clips of great plays. It comes with an on-line network service for updating scores and batting averages.

Electronic publishing requires forming contracts with third parties: authors, musicians, illustrators, photographers, movie companies, and text publishers. Microsoft's success in the CD-ROM market depends on its ability to form strategic alliances.[11] Without these alliances, Microsoft cannot perform the vital agency function required to connect its customers with producers of content. To address this need, Microsoft began to enter into alliances with publishers, for example, with Scholastic, Inc., to produce children's titles. To help it address difficult contracting issues, Microsoft hired the former president of the encyclopedia company, World Book International, as director of intellectual property development. Microsoft has formed alliances with wholesalers, such as Ingram Book Company, but to increase its share of the electronic publishing business it will have to continue to establish a wide range of contractual relationships with publishers and independent CD-ROM producers.

To compete effectively as agents, companies need to demonstrate that they bring access to a greater number of third parties. This requires providing product variety and continually updating the types of products offered to keep up with changes in supplier markets. Most importantly, competing agents provide convenience. It is costly for their customers to negotiate with third-party suppliers. The company that is able to form these contracts more efficiently adds value. By saving its customers the costs of negotiation through its intermediation efforts, the company can attract the greatest number of principals.

Monitor

I have emphasized that by contracting with third parties, companies act as the agents of their customers. After contracts are formed, the parties enter the performance stage. In this stage it is often necessary to assess whether the actions of other parties satisfy the terms of the contract. The agency role of companies thus carries with it the need to monitor contractual performance.

Indeed, monitoring is an extension of the agency role. The monitor acts under the delegated authority of the principal, and has a fiduciary responsibility to accurately report information that affects the interest of the principal.

Monitoring and Contracts

Monitoring is essential to reducing the costs of contracting, because it alleviates moral hazard and adverse selection problems. Recall that the moral hazard problem arises from the cost of observing agent actions. As a result, the principal writes incentives for performance into the contract that trade off the benefits of rewarding performance with the costs of compensating agents for the risk they bear. As I have mentioned, it is necessary to tolerate some inefficient performance to reduce the risk that is shifted to the agent. The contract is based on available information about the agent's performance and effort. The better the principal can get a handle on effort, the more effective the contract will be, so better monitoring means better contracts. For example, an insurance company can write better policies if it is better able to monitor the care taken by its insured customers in preventing accidents. Therefore, more costly monitoring is justified if it yields benefits from improved contracts.

The same argument applies for adverse selection. If testing, observation, and certification procedures yield improved information about agents, then more efficient contracts can be written. Recall that when principals and agents have different information, it is necessary to write contracts that tolerate some inefficiencies to avoid giving excessive information rents to the agent. Any improvement in the principal's information about the agent's characteristics leads to better contracts.

It has often been noted that financial intermediaries specialize in delegated monitoring.[12] Rather than directly lending to companies, investors place their funds with a financial intermediary who then lends to companies. There are obvious advantages to be gained from consolidation. The intermediary is able to diversify risk by lending to a variety of borrowers, and there are efficiencies in managing the payments system. But there are additional gains to the consolidation of monitoring itself. By monitoring many borrowers, the financial intermediary is able to reduce the costs of monitoring.

Debt creates moral hazard problems in a manner similar to insurance contracts. Suppose that a company is partly debt financed. Since the company can default on the debt by going bankrupt, the company shares the risk of loss with its creditors. This somewhat reduces the incentive to avoid losses. Moreover, it affects the types of technologies and market strategies pursued by the firm. The firm may wish to take greater risks than would be preferred by the lender, perhaps in the form of new product introductions or application of more speculative production processes. In fact, higher interest rates can encourage more risk taking and a greater probability of bankruptcy. This can lead lenders to ration creditors by limiting the number and size of loans rather than raising the cost of borrowing.[13] The effects of debt on borrower incentives are offset by the transaction costs of bankruptcy and the loss of reputation of the managers who led the firm into reorganization.

Lending also involves adverse selection, the problem of distinguishing good borrowers from those that pose high credit risks. For this reason, lenders review borrower credit histories, gather information about future income, and secure loans with collateral. These steps provide only imperfect protection, because bankruptcy entails transaction costs for both borrowers and lenders. Since information gathering is costly, the lender has an incentive to structure loan contracts so as to give borrowers an incentive to self-select in a way that reveals their creditworthiness. As in the case of the moral hazard problem, imperfect information can lead lenders to ration credit.[14]

Banks develop routines for keeping track of borrowers that create monitoring efficiencies. Through learning by doing, they gain expertise in distinguishing credit risks and in evaluating the performance of borrowers. In the event of bankruptcy, which entails high transaction costs, the bank has established procedures for liquidating assets and recovering funds. Therefore, acting as intermediaries, banks earn rents from their monitoring activities.

An LBO partnership provides delegated monitoring for its investors. The LBO serves to mitigate moral hazard by improving the performance of managers in the acquired company. The LBO imposes a substantial amount of debt on the acquired company so that the managers do not have much free cash flow; this limits managers' ability to waste resources on perks and reduces the temptation to pursue marginal investment projects. Moreover, the managers often invest in their companies and so have a greater incentive to be effective competitors. Consider the LBO company, Berkshire Partners. Berkshire has invested about $100 million in the acquisition or recapitalization of more than 25 companies. It closely monitors the management of acquired companies through monthly management meetings, planning meetings, sales meetings, and board meetings. Members of the LBO partnership serve on the board of the acquired company. The LBO partners are involved with the acquired companies' capital expenditure and other resource allocation decisions.[15]

Just as financial intermediaries provide monitoring services, so do all kinds of companies, from retailers to manufacturers. First and foremost, companies monitor the performance and characteristics of their employees. Monitoring employee activities is an essential part of management. Designing the organization to carry out delegation and facilitate supervision is crucial to effective monitoring.

Armen Alchian and Harold Demsetz emphasized the role of the firm as a "specialist" that monitors team production efforts, designs incentives, and receives the residual rewards.[16] This observation has turned out to be prophetic, as companies increasingly turn to team production and team-based organization. Teams provide a means of reducing the costs of monitoring and improving assignment of personnel to productive tasks in the organization.

The increasing use of outsourcing makes monitoring contractual performance even more important. Manufacturing tasks that are performed under contract become reclassified as services. Companies have become increasingly creative in farming out not only production, but all manner of corporate services including legal, accounting, personnel, and strategic planning. As tasks are shifted out of the organization, the management role changes from organizational supervision to monitoring supplier performance. Fewer managers are needed for day-to-day supervision of subordinates. When a productive task is farmed out, there is no longer any need to manage the employees involved, to purchase supplies for that task, or to make technology choices. Rather, managers need only evaluate the services their company receives. The nature of management thus evolves to include greater interaction with the company's service providers.

I have already noted that manufacturers act as agents for their customers by forming contracts with their parts suppliers. This reduces the transaction costs for their customers. It would be prohibitively expensive for a customer who wished to buy a car to contract with all of the parts suppliers of, say, General Motors. The manufacturer achieves returns from consolidation of production by writing a single contract for all of the firm's purchases from a given supplier. Moreover, the company builds the relationship with the supplier through repeated contracting over time. This repeated contracting further lowers the transaction costs with the supplier as transactions become routine. Long-term contractual relationships with the supplier help build the trust necessary to alleviate opportunism, so that both manufacturer and supplier have an incentive to invest in cost reduction and in product innovation. Clearly, through contracting, the manufacturer gains a significant cost advantage over an individual customer. This is an important source of the company's value added.

Just as the manufacturer has an advantage in forming contracts, so it brings special expertise to monitoring contractual performance. The manufacturer communicates with the supplier repeatedly regarding on-time performance and technical specifications, and the manufacturer and supplier share technological information. More importantly, the manufacturer has the knowledge to evaluate the product and service quality delivered by the parts supplier. The supplier acts as the agent of the manufacturer, whose monitoring relieves the moral hazard and adverse selection problems inherent in their relationship. Another way to view this is to see the suppliers as agents of the final customers, with the manufacturer playing the role of intermediary (see Table 5-2). By monitoring the supplier, the manufacturer certifies that the parts produced will perform as desired. For example, an automobile manufacturer provides warranties covering parts—air bags or car stereos—that were designed and built by third parties.

Table 5-2.
THE MANUFACTURER AS MONITOR OF ITS SUPPLIER

Principal	Final customer
Supervisor	Manufacturer
Agent	Parts supplier

Retailers and wholesalers also function as monitors, searching out low-cost suppliers and certifying product quality for their customers. In some cases retailers provide product guarantees, while in other cases the manufacturer's warranty applies. Often, the customer can return a product to the retailer if it is found to be defective quickly, but must deal with the manufacturer after the product has been in use. Retailers have an incentive to monitor manufacturers' performance, then, since this affects the value of the products they sell. When distributors carry out product servicing they have an additional incentive to monitor the manufacturer. The retailer that sells a variety of competing brands can react rapidly to changes in product quality by providing the information to its customers and inducing them to switch brands.

This type of monitoring is quite significant since it can serve to alleviate the lemon problem in some product markets. Recall that the instance of products that were lemons lowered prices, causing bad products to drive out the good. Gary Biglaiser argues that introducing an intermediary into a market with adverse selection enhances efficiency.[17] A retailer buys in large quantities from a manufacturer, so the retailer has a greater incentive to invest in monitoring quality than does an individual buyer. Again, there are efficiencies in consolidating monitoring in the hands of the retailer. In addition, the retailer has an incentive to report the quality of goods accurately to customers, stemming from the returns to building a good reputation. The performance of the products reflects on the retailer. This means that over time, manufacturers with products of different quality levels will sell through different marketing channels, or retailers that stock various quality levels will target different customer groups. As a result of the actions of intermediaries, multiple products of varying quality are sold but at different prices and sometimes through different channels. The retail intermediaries improve the ability of their customers to distinguish between the good products and the lemons.

Retailer Hammacher Schlemmer is able to sell products at what appear to be higher than average markups by acting as a monitor of its suppliers. In its catalog, the company touts its product offerings as "the best" electric shaver, "the best" clock radio, "the best" leaf blower, and so on. It guarantees that the products are superior according to the "Hammacher Schlemmer Institute best test." This assures customers that the retailer is monitoring supplier performance. The company earns rents by finding interesting products and introducing innovative ones, saving its customers the costs of searching and then testing all available products in any given category.

Monitoring the Monitors

As the Roman poet Juvenal asked: Who guards the guardians themselves? How can we be sure that monitors do their jobs? Monitors are subject to moral hazard problems: They may not be diligent in observing contractual performance or in reporting their observations. Monitors are also subject to adverse selection: It may be hard to distinguish effective monitors from incompetent ones.

One answer to this question is that monitors compete. There are many potential monitors. For instance, the market for financial intermediation is very competitive. Commercial banks that are the best monitors of borrower performance will prosper and drive out less competent monitors. Lenders seeking security, liquidity, and higher returns will move funds to the financial intermediaries that are best at monitoring investment.

There is some reciprocal monitoring. While a manufacturer is concerned about a supplier's production performance, a supplier is concerned about the manufacturer's marketing, product design, and efficiency. Since the supplier's success depends on the success of its customers, it has an incentive to assess the manufacturer's market prospects. The supplier may be unwilling to make specific investments to satisfy a manufacturer whose prospects are not impressive. Thus, while the supplier competes to be a manufacturer's agent, the manufacturer competes with other principals to obtain that agent's services.

Similarly, manufacturers monitor their distributors to make sure that they provide customer service and accurate product information. In addition to product information, the manufacturer also wishes to make sure that the distributor provides warranties, advertising, employee training, spare parts, or customer instruction.

The incentives of the manufacturer and distributor need not always be aligned. Manufacturers of certain types of products are concerned that retailers may not provide sufficient technical explanations of product characteristics and customer service. These types of marketing support are useful in building market share over the long term, particularly for such products as cameras or stereo equipment, whose attributes may not be apparent. However, if some stores provide customer service and recover the costs by marking up the products, it is likely that discount stores will benefit. Customers can go to the high-service store to become educated about the properties of various models, and then go to the discount store that offers no customer service to take advantage of the lower prices. Unless the sales of the high-service store are sufficient to cover its service costs, it will have an incentive to reduce its service or to stop selling the product altogether.

Manufacturers employ a wide range of vertical contracts as a means of monitoring and influencing their distributors. Lester Telser points out that suggested retail prices provide a means of limiting distributor competition as a way of eliminating the free rider problem.[18] By limiting the discounts that stores can offer, this pricing scheme provides them with sufficient margin to offer additional customer service. Similarly, offering exclusive contracts to specific retailers or awarding exclusive territories allows the manufacturer to set service requirements for its distributors as a means of building brand image and market share.

Vertical contracts and monitoring performance are intrinsic to building the market bridge. The contractual relationships between concentrate producers Coca-Cola and Pepsi-Cola and their bottlers are a good case in point.[19] The concentrate producers delegated both manufacturing and merchant roles to their independent bottlers. They relied on the bottlers to perform a wide variety of important tasks. The bottlers were expected to invest in plant and equipment and to improve facilities to keep up with changes in technology, packaging materials, and an increased range of products. Rapid growth in industry sales required additional investment by bottlers to keep up with demand and achieve economies of scale and scope. Bottlers were expected to expend considerable effort in marketing to supermarkets, convenience stores, restaurants, and other retail outlets. (Interestingly, Coca-Cola handled distribution for fountain sales while Pepsi-Cola depended on its bottlers to reach this vital market.) Finally, bottlers were expected to maintain product quality and to refrain from selling substitutes or imitations.

The concentrate producers faced important monitoring and control problems, particularly as the market grew and competition increased. The vast network of independent bottlers increased the costs of monitoring performance to the concentrate producers, particularly in the area of marketing. There were substantial transaction costs in negotiations between bottlers and retail outlets, and difficulties in coordinating national product promotions. As a means of improving monitoring and reducing contracting costs, the concentrate producers moved away from independent distribution to using captive distributors.[20] Through Coca-Cola Enterprises and Pepsi-Cola Bottling Group they consolidated control over bottlers. Pepsi-Cola extended its fountain distribution through its purchase of fast-food chains Kentucky Fried Chicken, Pizza Hut, and Taco Bell. These significant changes in industry structure illustrate the importance of vertical monitoring.

One might say that monitors have monitors who have other monitors to bite 'em, and so on, ad infinitem. For example, shareholders rely on corporate boards to monitor the performance of management. By investing through pension funds and mutual funds, the fund manager intermediates as a monitor of the board. While smaller investors only have the option of selling out or remaining silent if management does not perform as desired, the funds can exercise influence on the board. Since they can own a significant percentage of the shares of a company, the funds can question the board and its management decisions and even help to overthrow CEOs. Brokerage companies such as Charles Schwab offer a wide selection of mutual funds to their customers and provide performance statistics that allow monitoring of fund performance. So, the monitors are themselves monitored.

Broker

After serving in World War II, Johnnie Bryan Hunt went to work as a truck driver in Little Rock, Arkansas.[21] He saw rice farmers burning rice hulls after the harvest and realized that the hulls could be processed and resold as chicken litter. Hunt drew on the knowledge of the market he acquired when he sold chicken litter as a young man. To carry out his project, he established the J.B. Hunt company, which was to become the world's largest producer of poultry litter.

In 1969, J.B. Hunt bought a small trucking business consisting of five trucks and seven trailers and established it in Lowell, Arkansas. The company, J.B. Hunt Transport Services, grew into the second largest long-haul trucking company in the U.S., with 5,500 tractors and 12,000 trailers.

In 1989, Hunt formed an innovative alliance with the Santa Fe Railway to carry Hunt's trailers piggyback. This alliance was followed by other arrangements between Hunt and Burlington Northern, Southern Pacific, Union Pacific, and Conrail. Shippers negotiate directly with Hunt Transport, which both originates and terminates the shipment. Thus, Hunt acts as an intermediary between shippers and the railroads. By combining trucking and rail for each shipment, Hunt is able to take advantage of the speed and cost differentials between rail and trucks to obtain an arbitrage profit. Hunt's company brings together knowledge of the characteristics of downstream markets, particularly the requirements of shippers, and knowledge of upstream markets, particularly the suppliers of rail and truck transportation. By originating and terminating shipments, Hunt acts as a transportation broker, vastly reducing the transaction costs for shippers.

Brokerage is an important component of intermediation. The broker brings together buyers and sellers and assists in their negotiations. Shippers going through Hunt Transport have the benefit of one-stop shopping and avoid the need to negotiate with multiple truck and rail carriers. Companies can act as brokers even if their customers and suppliers do not meet directly. It is useful to think of the company as brokering between its customers and its investors, employees, and suppliers of services and manufactured inputs. Thus, both manufacturers and merchants provide brokerage service.

By coordinating exchange between buyers and sellers, the broker reduces their costs of search, and by mediating exchange, the broker reduces the costs of bargaining. In the presence of asymmetric information, buyers and sellers may fail to reach agreement even when they are foregoing gains from trade. Brokers can increase the likelihood of profitable trades by supplying information to both parties. The broker's value added is equal to the gains from trade between its customers and suppliers. The broker's bid–ask spread or commission is a share of these gains from trade.

Negotiation

Negotiation can be a costly process. Because negotiation is time-consuming, there are direct costs of personnel involved in bargaining. There are also indirect costs of delay in obtaining the benefits of the negotiation. Since future benefits are discounted, increases in the cost of capital raise the cost of delay. In addition, delays can result in missed market opportunities, costly inventory holding, and payments to retain the services of suppliers while negotiations continue.

Negotiation is not necessarily successful even when the parties can achieve gains from trade if an agreement can be reached. There may be frictions between the personalities involved in the negotiation or between the personalities they represent. One reason for this is a simple failure to communicate effectively. Another is that the parties may be pursuing other objectives that are inconsistent with the negotiations. Sometimes, the parties to a negotiation may wish to demonstrate toughness to others. Some receive personal gratification by extracting concessions, even at the risk of not concluding an agreement. Many have emphasized techniques for achieving agreement, including carefully listening to the other side's concerns. It can be useful to make concessions on some points in order to induce the other party to make concessions elsewhere.

Yet, imperfect communication in negotiations is a familiar occurrence. Labor strikes are an example of the breakdown of negotiations. Clearly, both the company and its employees are harmed by a strike. The two sides are fighting over the division of a pie that represents the company's earnings. Since a strike reduces earnings it leaves a smaller pie to be divided. The company loses whether or not employees extract pay or benefit concessions. Baseball players have gone on strike to change pay or contract terms. The results are dissatisfaction by fans, lost ticket sales, and lost television revenues. Players and management alike justify a strike as a means of establishing a precedent and point to the lack of reason by the other side.

Most tort cases are settled out of court. The reason is that both parties stand to gain by avoiding the court costs and other legal expenses and the time involved in a trial. Yet some cases go to court because of the failure of settlement negotiations. In some cases, plaintiffs are unsure of the defendants' degree of negligence, which affects the expected legal damage remedy, and defendants are unsure of the extent of the injury suffered by the plaintiff.

An important cause of the breakdown of negotiations is asymmetric information. The buyer is unsure of the seller's opportunity cost and the seller does not know the buyer's willingness to pay. Each side worries that it could be making a better deal and is willing to risk losing the benefits of an agreement.

Consider the following seller's dilemma. Suppose that a seller wishes to make an offer to a buyer. The seller knows that the buyer's willingness to pay is either $150 or $200. The seller believes that there is a 50% chance that the buyer has either a low or a high willingness to pay. If the seller offers the buyer $150, then the exchange is made, since both types of buyer would be willing to pay the price. If the seller offers the buyer $200, the offer will only be accepted with a 50% probability. Clearly, the seller will prefer a sure thing equal to $150 over a risky offer with an expected return of .50 × $200 = $100. So in this case, the seller offers the low price and negotiations are successful.

Now suppose it costs the seller $140 to serve the buyer. Then the seller makes the following comparison. If the low price is offered, the seller earns $150 − $140 = $10 with certainty. If the high price is offered, the seller earns $200 − $140 = $60 with a 50% probability. This has an expected value of .50 × $60 = $30. Unless the seller is extremely averse to risk, the higher price will be offered to the buyer. This means that half the time, the seller's offer will not be accepted and negotiations will fail. Notice that the two walk away from the deal if the buyer has a low willingness to pay, even though there are still $10 worth of gains to be had from the exchange.

A natural question to ask is: Why do buyer and seller in the example walk away after one round? Having noticed that the first offer was not accepted, would not the seller make a second, but lower, offer? The answer depends on how the negotiation procedure is structured. The seller can extract the most concessions from a buyer if the seller can make a credible commitment to a take-it-or-leave-it offer. If the seller were to make a second offer after its first offer was refused, it would be in the interest of both types of buyers to refuse the first offer, in anticipation of receiving a lower second offer. This is an illustration of the adverse selection problem from the point of view of the seller, since both buyers would attempt to portray themselves as having a low willingness to pay. The seller would not wish to lower the offer.

Even with multiple rounds of offers, it is possible that negotiations can fail even though the seller's cost of service exceeds that of both types of buyers. This problem can be worsened if each side has imperfect information about the other, or if there are many different types of buyers and sellers. Finally, as I noted previously, it may be costly to engage in multiple rounds of bargaining.

The presence of imperfect information creates an opportunity for intermediation. Suppose a broker posts a bid price for the seller of w and an ask price for the buyer of p, earning the bid–ask spread, $p − w$. The buyer and seller have the option of entering into an uncertain negotiation process. Even if negotiation were costless, they are not sure that it will be successfully concluded. In contrast, dealing with the broker is a sure thing: The posted prices are known in advance. Buyers with a willingness to pay above the posted ask price and sellers with an opportunity cost below the bid price thus will deal through the intermediary. By attracting high-value buyers and low-cost sellers, the intermediary reduces the attractiveness of entering the decentralized bargaining market.[22] This allows the intermediary to set a bid–ask spread that earns a share of the expected gains from trade of the buyer and seller.

Buyers and sellers not only face bargaining costs, but also must engage in costly search to find the right trading partner. Brokers reduce the costs of both negotiation and search by centralizing exchange. Search costs are lowered since many buyers and sellers can search across a much smaller number of intermediaries. In addition, by dealing with many buyers and sellers, the broker can bring about matches to meet diverse requirements. Just as a specialist on the New York Stock Exchange clears the market by matching buyer and seller offers, so other types of brokers can match buyers and sellers with positive gains from trade. For example, real estate brokers connect home buyers with sellers of houses that have compatible prices, locations, and other characteristics. Then the brokers often inter-mediate in the bargaining process to establish the sale price.

The interposition of companies as brokers between buyers and sell-ers reduces the costs of negotiation in a number of ways. The presence of asymmetric information and the possibility that negotiations will break down in direct negotiations creates a role for intermediaries. Moreover, intermediaries bring experience and special skills to the bargaining process that reduce the costs of negotiation.

Most companies, whether merchants or manufacturers, negotiate with suppliers and customers. A company's costs of negotiation with a sup-plier are spread over all the items purchased, so that there are economies of scale and scope in negotiation. This reduces the costs of bargaining between individual buyers and sellers.

Companies generally have formal or informal long-term relation-ships with their customers and suppliers. A publishing firm may have implicit contracts with printers and designers. A manufacturer may rely on a set of parts suppliers or a preferred group of distributors. These relation-ships are founded upon past records of performance and anticipation of future performance. There may be unwritten agreements that a manufac-turer will continue to purchase some percentage of its needs from the parts supplier. The buyers and sellers may maintain their relationships through frequent contacts and sharing of information. To the extent that the rela-tionships are profitable ones, buyers and sellers will have an incentive to maintain their level of performance and to be concerned with the prof-itability of the relationships for the other parties. The value and reliability of the relationships will also determine the extent to which the parties will invest in the relationships. A parts manufacturer will invest in new tech-nology to upgrade its performance for a large buyer in anticipation of con-tinuing their relationship.

Repeated contracting between companies and their trading part-ners reduces the costs of negotiation through established procedures. Long-term relationships help to build trust, which also reduces the chance that negotiations may fail. The reduced costs of negotiation enhance the com-pany's position as an intermediary.

Reputation is another significant aspect of the set of buyer and sell-er relationships that constitute a market. I use the term *reputation* in a broad sense to refer to the information that buyers and sellers in a given market have about each other. Information includes knowledge of pricing practices, product quality, reliability of service, and competitive strategy. Clearly, the information that buyers and sellers have about each other extends beyond ongoing transactions and contracts. Sellers invest a great deal in building a reputation for product quality or reliable service that is known to actual and potential consumers and to actual and potential rivals. Reputational considerations enter into the contractual performance decisions of buyers and sellers. For example, Sears has widened its selection of suppliers of major appliances. Sears brings to its supplier relationships a reputation based on existing long-term relationships with other appliance manufacturers such as Whirlpool. This further reduces the costs of bargaining by alleviating information asymmetries.

Value Added

In brokering trades, companies create value added equal to the difference between the buyer's willingness to pay and the seller's opportunity cost. Suppose that the company brokers a trade between a single buyer and a single seller. The buyer's willingness to pay for the good equals V dollars and the seller's opportunity cost equals C dollars. Then, by brokering the transaction, the company creates value equal to the difference between the two amounts,

$$\text{Value added} = V - C$$

This provides a simple but important characterization of the economic contribution of the firm as broker.

To create and then capture as much value added as possible, companies engage in the full range of market-making and arbitrage activities. The value created by the firm depends on the market alternatives of the buyer and seller. The rents earned by the firm also depend in part on its ability to bargain with both sides of the market and on the value created by competitors.[23] The returns to bargaining depend on the number of customers and suppliers the firm is dealing with and the costs of bargaining, such as the costs of communication and the time costs of delay. Because of the complexities of bargaining, companies can gain from posting bid and ask prices. By coordinating exchange, companies widen the markets they serve, thus increasing the combined willingness to pay of their customers and increasing their base of suppliers.

The value added created by the firm is divided into three components. The first is the net benefit to the buyer, which is the difference between the buyer's willingness to pay and the firm's ask price,

$$\text{Net benefit to the buyer} = V - p$$

Next is the profit to the firm, which is equal to the bid–ask spread,

$$\text{Profit of the firm} = p - w$$

Finally, the seller earns a net return equal to the difference between the bid price and the seller's opportunity cost,

$$\text{Net return to seller} = w - C$$

Clearly, the firm's profit is limited to the total value added by the transaction.

Generally, the company faces many diverse buyers and sellers. The firm's value added is the sum of buyer willingness to pay levels net of total seller opportunity costs. Suppose for the purpose of illustration that each customer only buys a single unit and each supplier only sells a single unit. The buyers have different willingness-to-pay levels and the sellers have different opportunity costs. These are represented in Table 5-3.

Table 5-3.
BUYER WILLINGNESS TO PAY AND SELLER OPPORTUNITY COST

Buyers	Willingness to pay	Sellers	Opportunity cost
Buyer 1	100	Seller 1	30
Buyer 2	90	Seller 2	40
Buyer 3	80	Seller 3	50
Buyer 4	70	Seller 4	60
Buyer 5	60	Seller 5	70

From Table 5-3, it follows that to maximize its value added the company should arrange the exchange of four units of the good, since the costs of the fifth seller are $70 while the willingness to pay of the fifth buyer is $60. Thus, the *marginal* value added is $10, which is the difference between the lowest willingness to pay and the highest opportunity cost. The value added to the market would then be $160, which is (100 + 90 + 80 + 70) minus (30 + 40 + 50 + 60).

One way to maximize value added is to take a percentage commission on trades. For example, suppose that the broker takes a commission of 10% of the sales price negotiated between buyer and seller. The market clears with four trades. Suppose that buyer 5 and seller 5 do not participate in trading and that each buyer and seller negotiation results in a price that splits the difference between the buyer's willingness to pay and the seller's opportunity cost. Then, no matter how buyers and sellers are paired, the broker earns $26.

Suppose that the company buys and resells the good, bargaining with both sellers and buyers. As the broker, it is assumed that the company itself has no use for the good except reselling it to a consumer. Suppose that the broker purchases to order, that is, bargains first with the buyer and then with the seller. Suppose also that the broker negotiates first with the highest-value buyer and then with the lowest-cost seller. It is then straightforward to show that the buyer, seller, and intermediary split the value added evenly.[24] That is, the ask price of $76⅔ and a bid price of $53⅓ yield a bid–ask spread of $23⅓. This is one-third of the difference between the buyer's willingness to pay of $100 and the seller's cost of $30. The broker's total surplus for the four trades (no matter which buyer and seller are paired) equals $53⅓, one-third of the value added to the market.

If the company cannot negotiate separately with each customer and supplier and it must set uniform ask and bid prices, the outcome will differ substantially. The profit-maximizing company sets an ask price of $90 and a bid price of $40, yielding a spread of $50. At these prices, the company buys and sells two units and earns $100. Increasing the number of transactions requires more complicated pricing policies that target different trader characteristics.

The broker is able to create more value by distinguishing between customers with different willingness to pay and between suppliers with different opportunity costs. This allows the company to increase value added by pricing differently to the market segments it serves. This depends on the quality of information available to the company about its trading partners. Companies improve their information through repeated transactions and pricing policies that induce buyer and seller self-selection.

Gathering Market Information

To understand the firm's customer markets, it is also helpful to recognize that customers have imperfect information about the characteristics of the firm's product and service offerings. The popular advice to "get close to the customer" reflects the constant need to improve communication between a firm and its customers. I use the word *communication* because marketing and sales are a two-way street. The firm must get to know customer needs in choosing prices and product features, and the firm must let its customers know what prices and products it has to offer.

The basic unit of analysis of market demand is the individual customer. There are many characteristics of individual customers that may be of interest to the firm. It is not always enough to rely on such generic characteristics as age and income. Knowing consumer preferences is one of the most important parts of any business. Information about consumer preferences is gathered in a variety of ways, including statistical analysis of sales data and reports from sales personnel.

Economic analysis of consumer preferences begins with the most basic question, not much different from the Pepsi taste test. Independent of prices and budgets, the consumer is presented with two different bundles of products (or product features), say bundle A and bundle B. The consumer is asked whether bundle A is preferred to bundle B, or bundle B is preferred to bundle A, or whether the consumer is indifferent between having either bundle A or bundle B. This most basic of frameworks can be used to specify preferences of surprising generality. For example, the product bundles can represent two market baskets of goods for a consumer: clothing, food, housing, recreation, and so on. Such market baskets are used by the government to calculate the consumer price index. The bundles can represent sets of product features such as the memory, speed, battery life, and durability of a portable computer.

The products in the bundles can represent different quantities of goods at different points in time. The consumers' ranking of the two products then reflects their patience or impatience, referred to as the rate of time preference. Decisions about consumption versus saving or about purchasing durable goods such as appliances are affected by the consumer's rate of time preference.

The product bundles can represent different proportions of goods in different states of the world; that is, the bundles may include goods that are contingent on future events. For example, bundle A can represent one insurance plan, consisting of a premium and deductible, with bundle B representing another. The consumer's ranking of the two bundles then reflects the consumer's attitude toward risk, referred to as the degree of risk aversion.

A consumer's demand for products is determined by the consumer's preferences, budget, and information about the product. Consumer demand for products is affected by the consumer's income and location, in addition to the prices and availability of rival products.

Product pricing must take into account the price sensitivity of the consumer's demand. There are many statistical techniques for measuring the price sensitivity of individual consumer demand. One important source of information is price and purchase data for a set of consumers collected by marketing research companies and referred to as panel data. The advantage of panel data is that individual consumer information is available, often with considerable detail on individual products purchased and on what prices were actually paid. Panel data is accurate to the extent that the consumers on the panel are a representative sample of the population of potential customers. Another technique has the firm experiment by varying its own pricing and promotions across its customers and applying statistical analysis to the resulting changes in customer purchases. Purchase and experimental data can be supplemented with survey data and information gathering from the firm's existing and potential customers.

Information about individual consumers can be pieced together to obtain a set of market segments. This is useful to the firm in targeting products and advertising toward each segment. However, great care must be taken not to rely exclusively on aggregate data, that is, summary information that describes how all customers in a given market behave. For example, while market share data provides a good snapshot of the current sales of competing firms, it is not necessarily a guide to future sales patterns. Indeed, reliance on market share data alone can be very misleading, since a completely new product with little or no market share today may sweep the market tomorrow. The measurement of market share itself is problematic: A company may have a very high market share if its market is narrowly defined and a very low market share if its market is broadly defined. For example, a company may have a very high share of sales of cheese-flavored popcorn but a negligible share of the sales of snack foods.

The popular product life cycle is a very imperfect guide to understanding customer markets. The product life cycle purports to describe the sales of all products as if they were living creatures with a period of growth, maturity, and decline. One problem with this approach is that not all products experience such a simple pattern of growth and fall in sales. Even if they were to follow such a simple pattern, it is not possible to know in advance how much growth will occur and when maturity and decline will set in, because the success (and failure) of a product is dependent on the price, features, and marketing of the product and of rival products, as well as on changes in technology and consumer preferences. Changes in pricing and marketing can give new life to an old product, while technological change can render a previously successful product obsolete.

The aggregate or market demand function, which relates total quantity sold to each price level, is a sum of individual consumer demand functions. Using the market demand function, it is possible to calculate the aggregate price elasticity of demand for a given good. Price elasticity is a measure of the price responsiveness of consumer demand. Price elasticity is measured by taking the percentage change in the quantity purchased as a result of a price change, divided by the percentage change in the price.[25] The market price elasticity is very useful for setting prices on established products and estimating the resulting sales revenue. However, the aggregate market demand function is less useful for estimating the effect of product changes or as a guide for new product introductions. The ultimate goal must be to obtain data about individual consumers.

In building the market bridge, the firm is implicitly supplying information along with the product. For example, by reselling a product purchased elsewhere, a firm earns a return to the information that it has about price differentials across the two markets. Any product offering by a firm implicitly reflects the firm's information about production technology and characteristics of upstream suppliers and downstream customers. Companies are able to lower prices by access to superior technical information that increases productivity or by discovering lower-cost suppliers. Products can be tailored to better address customer requirements by improved knowledge of their preferences.

I have already mentioned Theodore Levitt's useful insight that managers are subject to marketing myopia, focusing on product characteristics rather than customer satisfaction.[26] Asking what *services* the product provides to the firm's customers can be a difficult exercise for experienced executives. The product may have achieved its success on the basis of various technologically advanced or other unique features. However, it is important to look beyond these temporary advantages to see their ultimate value in terms of consumer preferences.

Consider for example the market for desktop printers. The first definition of the product that many will give is in terms of price, as in "printers costing less than three thousand dollars." Price is not in itself sufficient as a description of a product. The next definition that some will point to concerns the specific characteristics of the product: It prints using laser or inkjet technology, it sits on the desktop, and so on. A more sophisticated definition views the printer as a component of a computer system that provides information retrieval or desktop publishing services. This type of definition is more creative since it focuses on ultimate usage by the customer, and also suggests different features that might be applied to different end uses.

A definition of the desktop printer that pushes beyond the boundaries of the product's features is perhaps the most useful; note that since the printer is a means of taking data out of a computer, it can also be a means of putting data into a computer. At Xerox, researchers have developed a set of computer symbols that can be read by a computer from a piece of paper much as a supermarket scanner reads a bar code. In this way a printer with reading capabilities could function as a means of entering and retrieving data from a computer. Standard documents can have an area reserved for the new code that can be used to route the document in a computer network. Already, printers have been combined with facsimile machines to improve the quality of fax printouts. Using the coded documents, a fax machine could correctly route a document to designated recipients. It is not difficult to imagine printers playing an important role in computer networks as means of entering and retrieving data on paper.

By looking beyond the characteristics of a product to the services it provides, the firm can achieve a deeper understanding of its customers. This new information leads to a broader characterization of the product's actual and potential performance. Companies can then deliver innovative services that effectively address customer requirements.

Communicator

As agents, monitors, and brokers, companies alleviate information asymmetries in markets. By reducing the costs of contracting to its customers and suppliers, the company provides agency services that increase the net returns to its customers and suppliers. Through monitoring, the company reduces transaction costs that arise from moral hazard and adverse selection problems. Acting as a broker, it reduces the costs of search and negotiation.

As a communicator, the company earns returns from gathering and conveying information in the marketplace. There are returns to producing and distributing information, as well as arbitrage profits that are based on taking advantage of differences in information across markets. Information is transmitted by intermediating between customers and suppliers. By building market bridges, the firm informs customers about new products or price changes and informs suppliers about customer requirements.

Communication is an essential aspect of buyer and seller relationships. Albert O. Hirshman identified three types of actions.[27] A consumer can choose to demonstrate dissatisfaction with the relationship by exit, that is, by making no further purchases. Alternatively, a consumer can remain in the relationship but voice a complaint. Finally, a consumer can indicate satisfaction by loyalty, that is, by continuing the relationship. By tracking exit, complaints, and loyalty, the company learns valuable information about the characteristics of its customers. Similarly, companies gather information about the products and prices of their suppliers and about the abilities of their employees.

Companies transmit information to consumers through formal advertising as well as pricing, contract terms, brand image, and a host of informal contacts. Companies communicate with suppliers through repeated transactions, contract negotiation, and other meetings. While these activities have always played a crucial role in the operation of markets, the importance of information processing and communication has been enhanced by the development of new technologies. The information superhighway has increased the speed and capacity of information transmission and is fundamentally altering the role of companies as market communicators.

Supplying Information

Information is a product as much as any other. Companies supply information directly as well as bundled together with their products and services. It is both a productive input for companies and a consumption good. The growth of the information economy is impressive. The rising returns to production, transmission, and processing of information have led to rapid growth of companies in computers, software, and telecommunications. The information economy creates opportunities for companies as information providers.

Consumers. The economic information of interest to consumers concerns the prices and characteristics of goods and services, ranging from health care to financial services to groceries. Providing market information is a highly valuable service. In addition to market information, consumers purchase many services such as books, periodicals, reference data, computer software, movies, and video games that can be delivered as information on electronic networks.

Consumers have many sources of information about producers and products. Consumers shop by visiting stores and consulting catalogs, and are targeted by tens of billions of dollars worth of advertising. Consumers learn about products from television, radio, and publications as well as from specialized private agencies such as the Consumer's Union, publisher of *Consumer Reports*. The information superhighway provides a new set of high-speed, interactive information services.

Consumers obtain market information directly from manufacturers as well as from market intermediaries such as retailers, wholesalers, and brokers. Consumers receive advice from specialized consultants, including accountants, lawyers, and physicians. For example, consumers purchasing pharmaceuticals are advised by doctors and pharmacists. Consumers are informed by the actions of public regulatory agencies, such as the Food and Drug Administration, the Consumer Product Safety Commission, and the National Highway Traffic Safety Administration. In addition, they observe the purchases of friends, relatives, and acquaintances.

Consumers also make inferences about product quality by observing product attributes, manufacturer brand image, contract terms, and pricing. Any of these product characteristics is a market signal that reveals information about the company's product. For example, a product warranty conveys a signal about the product's quality, while an excessive number of exceptions in fine print warns the buyer to beware.

The time and expense involved in acquiring product information and making a purchase decision is an important part of the cost of buying products. By knowing what information is available to consumers, the firm can design its product offerings in a manner that is responsive both to customer needs and customer knowledge. It is not worthwhile to offer a costly, high-tech product such as a camera or stereo system unless the product's advantages over rival products are conveyed to consumers in a meaningful way. Companies must give at least as much thought to the pricing information and technical assistance they provide their customers as they do to production cost and product design.

The service provided by the firm can be highly valuable to the consumer if it simplifies the consumer's search process. Some firms, such as travel agencies, earn economic rents entirely by providing information services. Information services are provided by retailers with specialized sales staffs. Many retailers earn rents by providing convenience and selection to their customers, thereby reducing the need to search across many stores. Some firms deliberately raise consumer search costs; for example, many auto dealers refuse to give price information over the telephone, requiring travel and negotiation before the price is revealed. This has created customer dissatisfaction and opened the door for some automobile manufacturers to increase sales by offering new pricing policies that are more easily observed.

Companies need to focus on providing products and services in a manner that improves the information available to consumers. This includes the provision of product information in a manner that allows for easier product comparisons and emphasizes the special features of the firm's products.

Producers. Information is not only a service for final consumers but is also a productive input for most of the activities carried out by companies. Information increases the productivity of employees as companies increasingly turn to the "infomated factory."[28] Technical workers, including computer programmers, medical technicians, laboratory technologists, and engineers, are the largest occupational category in the U.S. and will soon represent a fifth of the labor force, forming what *Fortune* calls the "new worker elite."[29]

Increased technical training is not sufficient to prepare employees to handle complex automated equipment. Companies have found it necessary to give employees current information about the factory's day-to-day operation and to involve them in decision making. This not only improves the way in which employees operate smart machines but increases overall efficiency. At Weyerhaeuser Company's Longview, Washington plant, workers saved millions of dollars in energy costs in computer-operated sodium hydroxide manufacturing. At G.E.'s Salisbury, North Carolina electrical distribution equipment factory, increased information-sharing has boosted employee productivity by decentralizing decisions regarding parts procurement, maintenance, hiring, and production scheduling. Self-directed worker teams operating automated factories are also being employed by IBM, Motorola, Digital Equipment, General Motors, Xerox, and other Fortune 500 companies.[30]

Advances in information processing and communications have fundamentally changed organizations and the nature of the workplace. Vast increases in computer power and the falling cost of equipment have eliminated the need for managers to handle purely clerical tasks, such as adding up sales reports or production data and communicating them to the next level of management. Fewer managers are needed for data analysis and preparation of strategic plans. Moreover, lower-cost computing and communication have improved the efficiency of supervision, allowing managers to expand their span of supervision. These developments, combined with competitive pressures to lower costs, have caused substantial elimination of layers of management in many companies, resulting in flatter organizations with fewer total managers. Management personnel have been shifted out of headquarters to the company's divisions with up to 90% reductions in central staff, as occurred at the electrical equipment company, Asea Brown Boveri. The ranks of managers have been pared throughout the organization with shifts of personnel to marketing, customer service, and other areas, as well as considerable layoffs.

Communications and information processing act as substitutes for many productive inputs. Bar coding and electronic data interchange with suppliers and distributors reduce the need for costly inventories. A faster response time allows manufacturing to be tailored to sales and changes in fashion, further reducing inventory and production costs. Computer-controlled manufacturing reduces materials and energy usage. Moreover, automated flexible manufacturing reduces the need to duplicate costly capital equipment to produce multiple products, allowing factories to increase product variety within a given facility. By investing in computer-aided design and manufacturing (CAD/CAM), companies enhance the productivity of designers and reduce the need for costly prototypes, shortening the path from design to production.

Enhanced communications capabilities allow personnel to work at home or in the roving office, reducing the need for company office space. Thus, communications are a substitute for real estate, reducing the costs of land and buildings. They also substitute for travel, with telecommunications, video conferencing, and electronic mail replacing costly travel time and expenses. Transportation costs are also reduced by electronic delivery of some services, including sales support, technical advice, data analysis, and product design.

Information Networks

Driven by the great westward expansion in the United States, the railroads changed the economic landscape, creating towns and new industries in their wake. Companies such as the giant grain trader Cargill grew by following the railroad, setting up warehouses and building a market bridge between farmers and shipping agents. Later, the interstate highway system changed the fortunes of entire regions and aided the growth of the auto industry, the petroleum industry, and transportation of products and materials by truck. Just as these developments benefited vast numbers of new businesses while destroying others, so enhanced communications services are drastically changing the shape of the economy.

The information superhighway is a catch-all phrase for the burgeoning information and communication networks. The information superhighway consists of four basic elements: distribution, transmission, switches, and software. *Distribution* refers to the means of access, the on-ramps to the highway. These are as diverse as technology allows and include copper wires, coaxial cables, fiber optic lines, and wireless communications such as cellular and personal communications services (PCS). *Transmission* refers to the backbone or main lines of the system, which are primarily fiber optic trunklines but also include satellite and microwave transmission. The data transmission capacity of the highway is measured in terms of bandwidth. The carrying capacity of lines need not be symmetric. The ratio of downstream to upstream bandwidth determines whether the system is designed for data delivery or communication. The signals are routed through the transmission and distribution system by means of computers that provide *switching*. Finally, switches are operated by *software*. The system depends on protocols for voice, data, and video signals, including the Internet standard TCP/IP and Asynchronous Transfer Mode, a circuit-switched and packet-switched hybrid better suited for multimedia.[31]

The number of companies involved in the data highway is staggering. It includes suppliers of equipment for distribution, transmission, switching, and communications software: the long-distance companies (AT&T, MCI, Worldcom, and Sprint), the regional Bell operating companies, cable television companies, telecommunications equipment manufacturers, computer manufacturers, and software companies (including Microsoft, IBM-Lotus, and Oracle). There are also companies that produce customers' on-premise equipment, including telephones, computers, fax machines, television receivers (set top boxes), and other types of receivers and transmitters. Finally, there are companies providing content, including publishers, movie studios, on-line services, databases, game manufacturers, and other forms of software.

The Internet connects tens of millions of individual computers on tens of thousands of networks in at least 170 countries. Internet connections have astonishing growth rates of 10 to 15% per month. Tens of millions of people have access to e-mail on the Net, and eventually access will be nearly universal. The Internet connects well over 100,000 networks, combines about 20 million hosts (computers with an IP address accessed by remote users), includes over 1.5 million domain names, and links more than a million World Wide Web servers.[32]

A crucial intermediation role is played by the companies that provide access to the Internet network. Thousands of companies known as Internet Server Providers provide Internet connections.[33] Companies such as market leader America OnLine supply access to home shopping, banking, electronic mail, and a variety of interactive information services.

The development of the information superhighway reflects a fundamental shift in computing away from the use of individual computers—whether a personal computer, workstation, or mainframe—toward the use of computers connected to networks. Computers in a network are able to share memory and data processing, so that the network becomes a large computer with many terminals and decentralized processing power. The computers share data with each other, and the definition of data is broadened to include video and voice as well as text. People in a network can interact with each other simultaneously in a workgroup or through delayed communications such as e-mail. This close interaction within local area networks or across broader networks goes far beyond isolated transmission of information between computers. The computer network itself is the locus of data storage, retrieval, and processing.

Moreover, the Internet represents a shift away from isolated proprietary networks. What began as small groups of linked computers has evolved toward a system of communication in which computers are intelligent terminals that are used to transmit and receive information. The computer has become a vehicle for traveling along the Internet to exchange messages, data, sound, and images.

The network is a fundamental change in computer technology that perhaps can be best understood in terms of organizational design. The large mainframe computer represented the ultimate in centralization. The mainframe contained all of the computing power and memory. Individuals wishing to use the central computer competed for scarce access time, which was controlled by information systems managers. Applications, software, and data were handled centrally. At the other extreme lies the use of a personal computer (PC), representing a fully decentralized system with each user controlling the operation of a single computer. All computing power, data, and memory are separate for each individual user. Each PC has its own software and data files. In some companies, the PC system retains some elements of centralization if information system managers control the selection of equipment and software and monitor individual usage. Yet, individual control of the PC remains decentralized.

Neither the centralized mainframe system or the decentralized PC system involves computers directly in communication. In the case of the mainframe, individual data entry and withdrawal allows for limited interaction. This is analogous to communication in a hierarchy. Individuals in different parts of the organization must communicate by sending information up the organization to its center and then back down to reach the other party. In the PC system, individuals can exchange printouts and disks, and even data files through telephone wires. However, communication remains informal and outside of the computer system, relying instead on informal channels established by the organization.

The shift from isolated host computers to networking has a number of implications for software companies. It means that applications such as word processing and spreadsheets, which have generally been used with a single host computer, can be replaced by networking software. The software operates sets of computers and permits them to interact. Data need not be resident on one's computer, but can reside on someone else's computer or on a server on the network. For example, the software company Novell defines its business as "providing system software that manages and controls the way applications and data are accessed across computer networks." Their objective is "to be the leading vendor in the emerging workgroup and networked applications marketplace."[34]

One type of software, known as middleware, is designed to help individuals retrieve data and travel the network. Mosaic, which was developed at the National Center for Supercomputing Applications in Illinois, was the first browser software for the World Wide Web. Its growth has been phenomenal, with over a million copies distributed in the first year and a half.[35] Mosaic Communications Corporation of Mountainview, California, which soon changed its name to Netscape Communications, was founded by James Clark, the Stanford University professor who established Silicon Graphics Inc. The rapid success of Netscape not only demonstrates the high economic value of information, but also the returns to companies that provide software bridges to that information.

Networks create a new communication system that bypasses the traditional hub-and-spoke pattern. There is no longer a need for a central exchange. Rather there is what Peter Huber, writing about telecommunications, has termed a geodesic network in which everyone is connected to everyone else along a "path of minimum length."[36] George Calhoun forecasts that future telecommunications technology will not be confined to a single form but will include many forms of access,

> some on a small scale (e.g. microcell radio), some of global proportions (VSAT), some optimized for narrowband transmissions, others for broadband, some for vehicular communications, others for fixed or portable, some for data-dominant traffic, others for voice-dominant traffic, and still others for the transmission of image-based traffic—all rather imperfectly stitched together.[37]

He calls the many-faceted communications system a "laminar network."

Many transmission and access technologies are needed because they vary in terms of their suitability for carrying out these diverse transmission tasks, including fax, data transmission, interactive services, video transmission, and mobile communications. And many different switching and computer technologies are involved because they vary in terms of their costs and performance in supplying various services. This means that there are continual opportunities for innovative companies to create new types of electronic bridges within the information networks.

Electronic Market Bridges

The information superhighway has spawned businesses devoted to producing and supplying innovative information services. Companies are grasping a new set of opportunities not only by building and operating the new networks but by providing access and intermediating between customers and suppliers of information services.

Electronic information has the potential to vastly reduce the costs of search for buyers and sellers. One important application is shopping by computer. When fully implemented, consumers can search at low cost across many companies, and then can search through the company's offerings. Companies can maintain central inventories and avoid the cost of retail outlets. Moreover, companies can update product offerings and prices in real time as new products arrive or as inventories are depleted. This allows companies to respond rapidly to volatile price changes and obtain arbitrage rents.

Computer shopping offers many advantages for consumers over existing methods of retail distribution. Shopping at the store entails travel costs and time. While window shopping may be fun for many, others dislike the crowds, traffic, parking, and indifferent sales personnel. But the advantages of shopping at stores are that consumers can handle the good itself and enjoy personal service. This suggests that brand names and increased product information must accompany computer shopping, and that sales personnel must be available on-line to answer questions that may arise. Catalog shopping is convenient but requires delivery of a catalog by mail, which creates delays between the time the catalog is printed and an order is placed. Television shopping channels such as QVC and the Home Shopping Channel are growing rapidly in popularity but customers are limited to viewing the item shown on the screen at any moment, and cannot browse through a wider selection.

Information technology is altering all forms of retailing. A number of companies are acting as communicators in the auto industry. J.D. Power & Associates, which made its name providing market information through automobile quality surveys, extended its business by providing sales information through the Power Information Network.[38] A national computer network, it allows automakers and dealers to receive information daily about individual auto sales including location, per-vehicle profit, and dozens of other facts. Companies are able to adjust production rapidly to consumer preferences, and competitors can monitor some measures of rival sales. A U.S. subsidiary of Aucnet Inc. of Japan established a satellite system to allow used car dealers to exchange vehicles. A marketing research company, Dohring, set up a computer system for dealer showrooms that surveys customers on dealer performance.[39] Circuit City, the largest consumer electronics and appliance retailer, established a new and used car distribution system called Carmax. Consumers enter the desired features of a car into a computer, which then displays pictures of the available choices and the locations of the cars on the lot. Circuit City brought techniques used in consumer electronics to the used car market, such as warranties, repair service, clearly posted (no-haggle) prices, financing, and large selection.[40] Thus, Circuit City made a market bridge in used cars while providing market information.

Many new types of market bridges are made possible by information networks. The costs of a wide range of basic transactions are reduced, earning rents for companies reducing those costs. Consider automatic teller machines (ATMs) and point-of-sale (POS) terminals. These networks deal in a form of electronic money that provides convenience and increased security for buyers and sellers. There are over 139,000 ATMs in the U.S. handling over 29 million transactions per day, at half the unit cost of using a teller. Similarly, there are well over 875,000 POS terminals at gas stations, supermarkets, and other stores, handling over 3 million transactions daily.[41] Mastercard International operates the Cirrus System that connects networks of ATMs, with over 265,000 ATMs in 83 countries.

These developments were harbingers of substantial innovation in business. Electronic networks have certainly created vast new capacity for the transmission of information, including voice messages, data, and video. Advances in computer and communications technology are changing the organizational structure of companies. Market institutions are in flux as well. The information superhighway links households with all types of businesses around the world, allowing shopping from home and electronic commuting to work as well. This will substantially increase the extent of competition as the boundaries between markets are erased. Companies will face more rapid price changes and product innovation, because electronic menus are widely seen and easily revised.

Market bridges increasingly have significant electronic components. Electronic networks allow for rapid communication and very low-cost interaction among large numbers of people who are separated geographically. The speeding up of business and the transcending of distance for many services are important developments. Companies need to recognize this shift as they design and adapt their market bridges. The roles of companies as agents, monitors, brokers, and communicators are significantly enhanced by the expanding information economy. The intermediation strategies I have outlined are particularly well-suited to the information economy.

Endnotes

1. The discussion in this part of the chapter departs a bit from standard economic analyses of the principal–agent problem. Economists usually model the problem as one in which the agent performs a task for the principal such as work requiring costly, but hidden, effort or disclosure of information. In contrast, I follow the legal perspective and stress the role of the agent as an intermediary that negotiates contracts with third parties.

2. Of course, having purchased inputs, it can be said that the company earns a 100% commission on increments to the resale price. This simply demonstrates the two aspects of intermediation.

3. *Black's Law Dictionary* (abridged 5th ed., St. Paul, MN: West Publishing Co., 1983) states that an agent is "One who deals not only with things, as does a servant, but with persons using his own discretion as to means, and frequently establishing contractual relations between his principal and third persons."

4. Robert N. Corley, Peter J. Shedd, and Eric M. Holmes, *Principles of Business Law*, 13th ed., Englewood Cliffs, NJ: Prentice Hall, 1986, pp. 306–307.

5. Lawrence M. Fisher, "Sears's Auto Centers to Halt Commissions," *New York Times*, June 23, 1992, p. C1.

6. This point is made by Saul Levmore, "Commissions and Conflicts in Agency Arrangements: Lawyers, Real Estate Brokers, Underwriters, and Other Agents' Rewards," *Journal of Law & Economics*, 36, April 1993, pp. 503–540.

7. John A. Byrne, "The Craze for Consultants," *Business Week*, July 25, 1994, pp. 60–66.

8. The accompanying discussion draws on Daniel F. Spulber, "Bertrand Competition When Rivals' Costs Are Unknown," *Journal of Industrial Economics*, 43, March 1995, pp. 1–12.

9. Information about Microsoft's CD-ROM business is drawn from Laurie Flynn, "Now, Microsoft Wants to Gather Information," *New York Times*, July 27, 1994, p. C1.

10. This is based on sales figures for 1993, when Microsoft sold only $30 million. By comparison, Microsoft's Consumer Software Division earned $300 million, and the company as a whole earned $4.65 million for the fiscal year ending June 30, 1994; see Flynn, "Now Microsoft Wants to Gather Information."

11. Richard Brandt and Amy Cortese, "Bill Gates's Vision," *Business Week*, June 27, 1994, pp. 56–62.

12. See for example Douglas W. Diamond "Financial Intermediation and Delegated Monitoring," *Review of Economic Studies*, 51, 1984, pp. 393–414.

13. This point is made in the classic paper by Joseph Stiglitz and Andrew Weiss, "Credit Rationing in Markets with Imperfect Information," *American Economic Review*, 71, 1981, pp. 393–409.

14. Ibid.

15. Cynthia A. Montgomery, "Berkshire Partners," Harvard Business School Case Study, 9-391-091.

16. Ronald Coase's analysis of the firm compares the cost of transacting across markets with the benefits of allocating resources within the firm. Armen A. Alchian and Harold Demsetz, in their article "Production, Information Costs, and Economic Organization," *American Economic Review*, 62, 1972, pp. 777–795, suggest that Coase's analysis neglects the potential advantages of team production and organization, the difficulties in metering outputs, and the problem of shirking in teams. They argue further that residual rewards are given to the firm's owners as a means of preventing shirking, as in standard principal–agent relationships. They state (p. 793) that "the firm serves as a highly specialized surrogate market," since the firm collects and "sells" information to employees by organizing their production activities.

17. Gary Biglaiser, "Middlemen as Experts," *Rand Journal of Economics*, 24 (2), Summer 1993, pp. 212–223.

18. Lester G. Telser, "Why Should Manufacturers Want Fair Trade?" *Journal of Law and Economics*, 3, October 1960, pp. 86–105.

19. See Timothy J. Muris, David T. Scheffman, and Pablo T. Spiller, "Strategy and Transaction Costs: The Organization of Distribution in the Carbonated Soft Drink Industry," *Journal of Economics & Management Strategy*, 1, Spring 1992, pp. 83–128.

20. See the discussion of transaction costs in Muris et al., "Strategy and Transaction Costs: The Organization of Distribution in the Carbonated Soft Drink Industry."

21. The account in this paragraph is based on Agis Salpukas, "When Trucks and Trains Unite," *New York Times*, June 21, 1992, Business Section, p. 5.

22. See the analysis of Thomas Gehrig, "Intermediation in Search Markets," *Journal of Economics and Management Strategy*, 2 (1), 1993, pp. 97–120.

23. Adam Brandenburger and Harborne Stuart emphasize the connection between the gains from trade and the firm's value creation. Their discussion is concerned with the importance of bargaining between the firm and its customers and suppliers. They further observe that the company with a competitive advantage is the one with the greatest value-added

gap, whether due to higher buyer willingness to pay, or lower costs, or both. A greater value-added gap allows the firm to supplant a competitor by charging less to its buyers, paying more to its sellers, or both. See Adam Brandenburger and Harborne W. Stuart, Jr., "Value-Based Business Strategy," *Journal of Economics & Management Strategy*, 5, Spring 1996, pp. 5–24.

24. To calculate the ask and bid prices, proceed as follows. First, the bid price negotiated with the seller splits the difference between the resale price and the seller's cost: $w = \frac{1}{2}(p + 60)$. The ask price negotiated with the buyer splits the difference between the buyer's willingness to pay and the bid price: $p = \frac{1}{2}(100 + w)$. This example is based on John Harsanyi's joint bargaining paradox. In his example, the intermediary purchases the stock and is subject to hold-up by the buyer so that the ask and bid prices are different than in the present example of purchasing to order. For further discussion see Ariel Rubinstein and Asher Wolinsky, "Middlemen," *Quarterly Journal of Economics*, 102, 1987, pp. 581–593.

25. The consumer's demand is represented by a function, $Q = D(P)$ where Q is the quantity demanded and P is the price. The elasticity of demand with respect to price is the ratio of the percentage change in the amount purchased divided by the percentage change in the price (times negative one):

$$\text{Elasticity of demand} = - \, dQ/Q \div dP/P$$

26. Theodore Leavitt, "Marketing Myopia," *Harvard Business Review*, 53, September-October, 1975.

27. Albert O. Hirshman, *Exit, Voice, and Loyalty*, Cambridge: Harvard University Press, 1970.

28. See Doron P. Levin, "Smart Machines, Smart Workers," *New York Times*, October 17, 1988; and Shoshana Zuboff, *In the Age of the Smart Machine*, New York: Basic Books, 1988.

29. This is based on forecasts by the Bureau of Labor Statistics; see Louis S. Richman, "The New Worker Elite," *Fortune*, August 22, 1994, pp. 56–66.

30. The experience with information sharing at Weyerhaeuser, GE, and elsewhere is discussed in Levin, "Smart Machines, Smart Workers."

31. The trunk line capacity varies between a T1 rate (1.544 Mbps) to OC-48 (2.4 Gbs). The Internet backbone is at a T3 rate (45Mbps) which is operated by MCI. A bottleneck is created by local access which varies from 2400 bps to 19.2 Kbps. Increased capacity can be attained over leased lines operating at 56Kbps to T1 (1.544 Mbps). The carrying capacity of conventional copper lines can be enhanced up to T1 using ADSL (Asymmetrical Digital Subscriber Line) technology. A. Reinhardt," Building the Data Highway," *BYTE*, March 1994, pp. 46–74.

32. Robert H. Zakon, "Hobbes' Internet Timeline," info.isoc.org/guest/zakon/Internet/History, 1997.

33. *Boardwatch* Magazine, July/August 1997, lists over 4,000 Internet Service Providers.

34. Novell Fiscal Highlights, 1994.

35. John Markoff, "New Venture in Cyberspace by Silicon Graphics Founder," *New York Times*, May 7, 1994, p. C1.

36. See P. W. Huber, *The Geodesic Network: 1987 Report on Competition in the Telephone Industry*, Washington, D.C.: U.S. Department of Justice, Antitrust Division, 1987.

37. George Calhoun, *Wireless Access and the Local Telephone Network*, Boston: Artech House, 1992, p. 527.

38. James Bennet, "A Way for Car Dealers to Squeeze Out the Lemons," *New York Times*, March 6, 1994, p. 11.

39. Ibid.

40. Michael Janofsky, "Circuit City Pins Growth on Sales of Used Cars," *New York Times*, October 25, 1993, p. C1.

41. *Statistical Abstract of the United States, 1997*, U.S. Department of Commerce, Economics and Statistics Administration, Bureau of the Census, p. 522, table 802.

6 NETWORKING

A crucial step in building market bridges is the creation of customer and supplier networks. Market networks are interlocking economic relationships between sets of buyers and sellers, coordinated by individual companies or associations. The fundamental problem faced by the firm is the trade-off between expanding the organization and interacting with the network. Should the company carry out an activity in-house or should it rely on suppliers and distributors? In this chapter, I set out some tools for making these crucial decisions.

In identifying the networks that the firm belongs to and wishes to establish, the manager should take an inventory of the company's current and potential suppliers and customers. Successful firms earn economic rents by making markets and intermediating between their trading partners. This requires a determination of the types of products and services that will create innovative market connections.

Market definition is a difficult but important task for managers. A company's markets should be defined by the services it provides, even while they transcend any simple categories and evolve continuously with technological advancement and changing tastes. Nonetheless, for our purposes it is helpful to begin with four general categories of markets: finance, labor, products, and technology. These allow for a simple classification of market links that can be divided into two main groups: *Matching* refers to market connections within the same category of markets, while *mixing* involves market connections that cross market categories.

Next, the manager determines the location of activities—within the organization or in the network. One criterion for this determination is a comparison of the costs of internal versus external transactions. In this context, I examine the vertical linkages within the Japanese keiretsu and their implications for market networks. Another important criterion is the value of the information gathered and distributed, whether the activity is internal or outsourced. Markets are primarily a form of communication, as they provide a mechanism for learning about prices, product characteristics, contract terms, and the quantities to be bought and sold.

Winning the market means that the firm provides the essential connections within its network. As I observed in Chapter 5, successful companies benefit from expansion in terms of size, product variety, degree of vertical integration, and rate of innovation. The returns to consolidation include incremental revenues, reduced risk, and cost economies. In some cases there is a trade-off between the gains from expanding the network and the returns to consolidation. Companies can expand efficiently by recognizing that there is a variety of methods for pushing out their boundaries. I conclude this chapter by comparing alternative ways to grow: expansion, contracts, alliances, and mergers.

Suppliers and Customers

Innovative management strategy is founded upon information about markets. The firm establishes relationships with both customers and suppliers. These relationships are valuable not only as ongoing sources of business transactions, but also as sources of market information. The firm uses this information to bring together its customers and suppliers in new ways. The manager determines in which upstream and downstream markets the firm currently operates and decides in which markets the firm should operate in the future.

A useful picture of the firm is obtained by determining the types of markets that it serves. I classify markets into four categories:

1. Finance
2. Labor
3. Products
4. Technology

Finance refers to markets for venture capital; bank loans and deposits; financial instruments, including equities, bonds, futures, and options; and insurance contracts. *Labor* refers to markets for labor services, including production workers, technical workers, professionals, and clerical and management personnel. *Products* refers to all outputs and services provided by firms, ranging from capital equipment to consumer goods and data processing. *Technology* includes markets for patents and licenses, computer software, and knowledge embedded in capital equipment. This category broadly represents the marketplace of ideas, including the output of commercial, government, or university research centers.

The basis of the classification lies in differences in contracting for productive inputs. Contracting in the four types of markets has implications for ownership and control of the company. The intermediation activities of companies in these markets can differ as well. This classification is useful even though all markets have fundamental similarities.

Consider first financial markets. Most transactions involve simply buying and selling financial assets that provide uncertain income streams over time. The financial sector is distinguished in part by its sheer size, the efficiency and rapidity of its markets, and the existence of major centralized exchanges. The corporate financing process has unique qualitative features. To obtain financing, companies not only provide returns to investors but surrender various degrees of control to new debtors and shareholders. The securities markets allow transfers of assets providing residual returns after the claims of the company's debtors have been satisfied. They are also markets for corporate control, since securities confer control rights on shareholders. The debt that companies obtain from banks and other lenders also confers some rights of supervision and control, particularly when agreements are renegotiated or in the event of bankruptcy. This implies that the company's financing decisions are not simply purchases of capital in return for payment of a share of profit or interest. Rather, they entail choices about the ownership structure and control of the firm by investors.

The company's purchase of labor services is not simply a set of spot transactions at a fixed wage, as in the traditional economic model of labor markets. The company's employees form the organization, managing and staffing the firm. Certainly, the company has a legal identity that is distinct from its employees. However, the company's knowledge and skills generally rest with its personnel. The employees do not represent simply a flow of services that passes through the firm, although that may be the case for individual workers. Collectively, groups of employees have substantial bargaining power, whether through unions or internal divisions of the firm. Since most employment contracts are of long duration, the purchase of labor services is a long-term agreement in which the provider of labor services has a stake in and an influence on the decisions of the firm.

The company's input purchases are carried out through spot and contractual exchange, without necessarily affecting the firm's ownership or organizational structure. The procurement of productive goods and services is a crucial part of any business, whether the company is a manufacturer or distributor. A manufacturer must decide whether to make or buy each productive input. If the input will be produced by the company, the organization must expand through investment and hiring or through mergers and acquisitions. If the input is to be purchased, the company must choose between multiple sources and determine what types of contracts with input providers are needed. These procurement decisions determine the company's degree of vertical integration.

Markets for technology and other informational inputs have unique characteristics. Information may be scarce and costly to produce, but particular know-how can be used repeatedly without being depleted. It can be almost costlessly reproduced, and in some instances it can be easily copied. Ownership rights to intellectual property are notoriously difficult to define, complicating market transfers and contractual arrangements. Companies can obtain technological knowledge through in-house research and development, association with universities and research laboratories, and technology transfers from other companies. Information has become the primary driver of the economy. The creation, processing, and transmission of information is a pervasive activity that is reshaping every type of business. The information economy does not mean simply an increased usage of computers and telecommunications. Rather, it represents fundamental changes in the design of organizations and the structure of market transactions.

Most companies operate in all four markets upstream.[1] They must obtain financing, hire personnel, purchase products and services as productive inputs, and select productive technology. Winning the market requires an effective financial strategy to obtain the funds for growth and to invest in cost-reducing projects. Companies must out-invest rivals either through capital expenditures or effective leveraging through alliances. Companies must have a coherent employment policy, hiring the most talented people and investing in training and employee development. They need to develop an effective network of suppliers and distributors to obtain low-cost inputs and distribution. Finally, investment in product and process innovation is essential to keeping and holding a competitive lead.

Downstream, firms can act as sellers in any of the four markets. The firm connects its suppliers and customers through a variety of activities, including retail and wholesale distribution, production of goods and services, and research and development.

Innovative strategy continually identifies new combinations of upstream and downstream markets. Some activities may appear to be directed only at a single market, and some activities are focused upstream. The firm may identify and obtain new sources of finance, new sources or types of skilled labor, new productive inputs, or new technologies. Other activities appear to be focused exclusively downstream. For example, the firm may introduce new products or it may identify new customers for its products. The firm can engage in efficient wholesale, retail, and marketing activities, devise new methods of production, and create innovative products. However, to be successful, these activities must be carried out in a manner that effectively connects the firm's markets. For example, a retailer that identifies lower-cost suppliers than its rivals will not succeed unless it also has good customer relations downstream. Similarly, a manufacturer with good marketing channels nonetheless may be constrained if it does not have the required skilled personnel or has not invested sufficiently in research and development to keep up with technological change.

A great deal of attention has been given to competitive strategy in the product markets.[2] Firms have been encouraged to pay attention to competitive interactions with immediate rivals and potential entrants. The focus has been on predicting rival actions and on selecting best responses to the anticipated actions of rivals. Competitive strategy often involves devising sophisticated plans for product market rivalries. Strategic interactions involving pricing policies over time, product introduction and design, and the erection of entry barriers are certainly of great importance, particularly when rivalry is very intense and the actions of rivals matter a great deal. Firms earn monopoly rents as a consequence of entry barriers in downstream markets. The competitive strategy approach is pathbreaking in that firms are able to analyze industries and competitors in a systematic way using economic tools.

Another set of approaches to strategy stresses the resources of the firm.[3] Firms are advised to build up and take advantage of unique internal resources, whether special production skills, technical knowledge, management skills, or unique access to productive inputs. The focus of the resource-based approach is on identifying and applying the firm's unique characteristics to sustain a competitive advantage. The resource-based view underlies many related strategy prescriptions, including the admonition to develop a company's core competencies or to emphasize its capabilities.[4] These are supposed to be difficult for a new entrant to imitate or acquire and therefore confer lower costs or higher revenues on the incumbent. These approaches suggest that the firm has unique resources as a consequence of entry barriers in upstream markets, whether capital, labor, products, or technology. A firm can earn monopoly rents in the product markets as a consequence of these upstream entry barriers.

Yet, these two approaches each tell only half of the story. The competitive strategy view is basically a downstream approach, while the resources of the firm view is an upstream approach. These two types of strategic advice are complementary. Innovative management strategy should build on both of these approaches in a number of ways. The firm should be encouraged to look at *both* its upstream and downstream markets, according importance to both of these market activities. Rather than exclusively focusing on interaction with downstream rivals, I would focus more on the activities that connect upstream markets with downstream customers. The manager then is concerned with creating new supplier relationships, new production processes and products, and new customer relationships that will connect the firm's markets.

Our approach differs in a more fundamental sense. The focus is not on creating entry barriers in either upstream or downstream markets to earn monopoly rents. While such a strategy can be effective, it may not be perfectly suited for every industry. The reason is that these strategic approaches reflect in some respects a particular view of how markets function. The traditional economic models of perfect competition show that competition drives the economic profits of firms down to zero.[5] The only source of profit is a return to entry barriers. In that framework, the firm can only earn positive economic profit from either monopoly power in downstream markets or monopsony power in upstream markets. Such an approach overstates the likelihood and importance of entry barriers.

In contrast, the view taken here is that economic profit can be positive in the absence of entry barriers, as a consequence of various market frictions. Markets do not function by themselves, but instead depend on the intermediation activities of firms. Asymmetric information about prices and products, customer needs, and supplier abilities creates opportunities for rapid response and makes available information rents. By taking advantage of arbitrage opportunities within and across the market categories, companies make markets operate more smoothly, creating economic rents as a return to their market-making activities.

Matching and Mixing

The market networks created by companies can match buyers and sellers within the same category or mix them across categories. While firms generally interact with all four categories of upstream markets (so that no pure matching really exists), it is useful to examine firms whose *primary* activities connect the same category of markets (see Tables 6-1 to 6-4). I first consider matching activities in the markets for finance, labor, products, and technology. Then I briefly describe more complicated mixing activities.

Matching is especially important in financial markets. There are many types of financial intermediaries, including commercial banks, savings institutions, brokerage firms, mutual funds, insurance companies, and firms providing diversified financial services. The sheer size of the financial sector is staggering. It is important to understand the dimensions of this sector since the intermediation role in finance is so evident that it can serve to provide a model for other types of businesses. These firms purchase and sell assets and create new financial assets. They collect and supply information about the supply and demand for assets and establish market prices. The profits of financial intermediaries are based on the spread between the ask and bid prices for financial assets. Financial intermediaries earn significant economic rents from their market-making activities.

Commercial banks earn rents by connecting their various depositors to a variety of borrowers. Leading commercial banks including Citicorp, BankAmerica Corp., NationsBank Corp., Chase Manhattan Corp., and J.P. Morgan & Co. are primary providers of business credit and make consumer, real estate, agricultural, and government loans as well. They invest in Treasury bills and municipal bonds and raise money through various types of checking, savings, and time deposit accounts. The largest 100 commercial banks command trillions in assets, earn tens of billions in profit, and employ over one million people.

The commercial banks are highly diversified market makers, setting prices, providing liquidity in the market for loans, and coordinating exchange. They handle the payments systems, keeping track of deposits and withdrawals through checks and other instruments. The commercial banks earn the spread between the borrowing and lending rates of interest, engaging in dynamic and risk arbitrage. They reduce risk through a diversified portfolio of loans and investments.

As managers of the payments systems, commercial banks cooperate and compete with credit card companies. Mastercard and Visa have created a vast worldwide network linking customers, merchants, and banks worldwide. The network, which is so familiar that it operates almost unseen, works as follows. A customer presents the Mastercard or Visa card to a merchant to pay for a purchase. The merchant then gets approval for the charge from the merchant's bank, and ultimately submits the charge to that bank. The merchant's bank submits the charge to the credit card company, which charges the customer's bank that issued the card. The customer's bank bills the customer and payments flow back to the merchant, passing through the credit card company. Mastercard and Visa obtain fees from both banks along the way. The two cards are accepted by over 10 million merchants worldwide, generating many times that number of transactions per day. Mastercard connects the two banks directly through 14 regional nodes while Visa processes all transactions in computer supercenters in Virginia and Britain.[6]

Diversified financial institutions provide a wide variety of services, including stock brokerage, insurance, and credit. The 10 largest diversified financial institutions, including the Federal National Mortgage Association, Morgan Stanley, Dean Witter Discover & Co., CREF, Travelers Inc., and American Express, manage about 1.5 trillion dollars of assets. Travelers bought

Table 6-1.
MATCHING: FINANCIAL INTERMEDIARIES

Supplier markets	Customer markets
Finance ———————————→	Finance
Labor	Labor
Products	Products
Technology	Technology

Salomon for $9 billion to create a financial supermarket offering a full range of financial services. Travelers connects Smith Barney's retail brokerage network with Salomon's experience in bond trading and investment banking.

Savings institutions primarily provide mortgage loans, engaging in both risk and dynamic arbitrage. The 50 largest savings institutions have several hundred billion dollars in assets. These include H.F. Ahmanson, Great Western Financial Corp., Golden Western Financial Corp., Glendale Federal, and California Federal Bank. They also act as market makers, providing liquidity and coordinating exchange for mortgage loans. They compete with many other institutions that provide mortgage loans including commercial banks and specialized mortgage companies. Traditionally, the savings and loans have provided all intermediation services between depositors and real estate borrowers. Market bridges have become highly segmented, as each step in the process of granting and servicing the loan has been divided among market intermediaries. Three companies operating under government mandate act as intermediaries, pooling individual mortgages and allowing mortgage-backed securities to be traded on a secondary market. These are the Federal National Mortgage Association (Fannie Mae), the Government National Mortgage Association (Ginnie Mae), and the Federal Home Loan Mortgage Corporation (Freddie Mac). These agencies have taken on some of the risk diversification and pooling functions of the savings and loans. Thus, the savings and loans also act as intermediaries between borrowers and the financial markets, originating loans and reselling them to investors.

Insurance companies are also financial intermediaries. By investing the premiums, they stand between those they insure and financial markets. Insurance companies pool the risks of their customers and allocate risks across markets. They manage a complex set of financial transactions. Insurance companies originate and monitor complex, contingent insurance contracts. Among the biggest insurers are Prudential of America, Metropolitan Life, Teachers Insurance and Annuity Association, New York Life, and Aetna Life & Casualty. The 50 largest companies have more than a trillion dollars in assets and employ almost half a million people.

Matching is also widespread in the market for labor services, where many firms organize the provision of various services. These firms act as

Table 6-2.
MATCHING: A SERVICE INTERMEDIARY

Supplier markets	Customer markets
Finance	Finance
Labor ⟶	Labor
Products	Products
Technology	Technology

intermediaries in the labor market by writing contracts with individual employees for the supply of their labor services. Customers then contract with the firm to obtain labor services. This includes all organizations that provide accounting, legal, medical care, architecture, and consulting services, and firms that provide temporary services of technicians, secretaries, nurses, and computer specialists. This category also includes private schools and training facilities. Many small businesses resell labor services, such as general contractors, electrical contractors, auto and appliance repair shops, appraisers, and beauty salons. These firms earn rents on the basis of their knowledge of the upstream market for individual labor services and the characteristics of customer demand for labor services in the downstream markets. By organizing the contracting process for labor services, firms that engage in matching act as market makers.

The best example of labor market intermediation is the temporary service agency, which coordinates buying and selling of labor services. The agencies handle hiring, salaries, and benefits for their employees, and manage the payments for the companies that employ their temporary workers. These companies provide immediacy for workers and employers. The workers have a greater chance at employment by working for a variety of companies, and companies can easily adjust employment based on their production requirements. Among the largest temporary services are Manpower, Olsten Corporation, and Kelly Services, with sales in the billions of dollars. The over 1,600 companies belonging to the National Association of Temporary and Staffing Services handle a daily average of over 2.3 million personnel.

Health care companies are primarily labor intermediaries, organizing and delivering the services of doctors, nurses, and technicians to patients. Health care consumes over 14% of GNP. Among the largest hospital and managed care chains, each with billions of dollars in revenue, are Columbia/HCA Healthcare, National Medical Enterprises, Humana, and U.S. Healthcare. These companies are market makers, establishing prices and coordinating exchange of services. They also intermediate between doctors and insurance companies. Insurance companies organize preferred provider organizations that are networks of physicians. The PPOs act as market mak-

Table 6-3.
MATCHING: A WHOLESALE OR RETAIL INTERMEDIARY

Supplier markets	Customer markets
Finance	Finance
Labor	Labor
Products ──────────────→	Products
Technology	Technology

ers, setting prices through negotiations with doctors, and coordinate exchange by handling claims and informing patients of member doctors. Health maintenance organizations mix financial and labor market intermediation by supplying physician services bundled with health insurance.

In product markets, wholesalers and retailers perform market matching by purchasing and reselling goods and services. These firms' earnings depend on the spread between the prices of the goods upstream and downstream. Retailers and wholesalers act as intermediaries between suppliers and customers, supplying demand information to suppliers and providing price and product information to customers. Retailers and wholesalers earn rents on the basis of their knowledge of upstream and downstream markets. Wholesalers and retailers are among the most important market makers in the economy. About one-third of the 100 largest diversified service companies can be classified as wholesalers. Among the largest with billions in sales are Fleming, Supervalu, McKesson, Sysco, and Bergen Brunswig.[7] The shoe companies Nike and Reebok also act as wholesalers, concentrating on design and marketing while contracting out practically all of their production.[8]

The largest retailers account for almost half a trillion dollars in sales and employ over four million people. Many of these companies are market winners in their category. Certainly the largest retailer at over $100 billion in sales, Wal-Mart is the dominant general retailer. Kroger, at $25 billion in sales, is the largest supermarket chain, although it faces strong local competition in many areas. Toys *"Я"* Us, Home Depot in hardware, and Circuit City in electronics exemplify the category killers.

In technology markets, companies that engage in basic research and development or engineering and design as their primary activity can be described as connecting technology markets. These firms include research laboratories, engineering companies, software companies, and computer services companies such as Electronic Data Systems. Leading software developers, such as Microsoft, IBM, and Novell, deliver advances in computer technology by recruiting top personnel and incurring substantial development expenses for desktop computing, network software, database management, and interactive media.

Table 6-4.
MATCHING: A RESEARCH AND DEVELOPMENT INTERMEDIARY

Supplier markets	Customer markets
Finance	Finance
Labor	Labor
Products	Products
Technology ⟶	Technology

Acquisition and sales of technology refers to licensing as well as to purchasing and selling of products that embody technological innovations. Technology markets should be broadly defined to include dissemination of new discoveries through scientific publications, conferences, and other types of communication. A large share of research and development is carried out by units within companies that pursue many other objectives. It is helpful to think of the research and development unit within the company as connecting upstream technology markets with downstream technology users, including the company's other divisions.

Mixing refers to the market-connection activities of firms that connect upstream markets from one or more categories to downstream markets in different categories. The preceding discussion of matching noted that no firms are engaged purely in matching, since all firms must obtain financing, hire labor services, purchase products, and employ technologies. Mixing refers to primary activities that span market categories.

Practically all manufacturing firms are engaged in creating market connections that mix categories. For example, Ford Motor Co., with over $26 billion in shareholder equity, must have extensive knowledge of financial markets. With over 300,000 employees, the company must have a clear understanding of its labor markets. The company purchases parts from a large network of suppliers. Finally, the company must follow technological change in design systems, manufacturing, and automobile components (engines, suspensions, brakes, electronics, and materials).

Hewlett-Packard printers are built around components manufactured by Canon, so that Hewlett-Packard provides intermediation services to the printer market. Computer makers such as Dell assemble components including Intel chips, thus acting as intermediaries between customers and component suppliers. IBM suffered from failing to understand the importance of the market-making aspect of computer manufacturing. IBM did not realize that the companies providing cheap clones of its machines were providing intermediation services to computer users and component manufacturers. Rivals such as Compaq perfected customer service, while Dell and others provided mail order convenience. These computer companies prospered not simply because their clones were cheaper, but because their market-making services were superior.

Table 6-5.
MIXING: A MANUFACTURING COMPANY

Supplier markets	Customer markets
Finance	Finance
Labor	Labor
Products	Products
Technology	Technology

Companies building market bridges identify key arbitrage connections between upstream and downstream markets. This can be done using a simple matrix listing of the firm's markets in which the columns denote the firm's upstream markets while the rows denote the firm's downstream markets. To apply this method, one should successively refine the market classifications. First, identify the main connections in terms of the four types of markets—finance, labor, products, and technology. These are the upstream and downstream markets for which the manager has specialized knowledge about the market or innovative ideas about market networks. Second, subdivide the key markets to identify the crucial market segments. Third, identify the suppliers and customers within the crucial submarkets. Firms can leverage market-matching activities to more complex mixing activities. This was done by an innovative firm called Comdisco, Inc.

Comdisco, Inc. has $5 billion in total assets, over $2 billion in revenues, and over $630 in shareholders' equity.[9] The company operates 42 sales offices around the world. Founded in 1969, Comdisco began as a broker of IBM mainframe computers, playing a market-making role for a very specific product and a restricted set of customers. From this matching service, Comdisco has expanded into a wide variety of areas. Comdisco is the world's largest independent lessor and remarketer of high-technology equipment. The company leases not only mainframes but all types of computer equipment. In addition, Comdisco leases many types of high-tech equipment including satellite earth stations, point-of-sale devices, automatic teller machines, and telecommunications equipment such as PBXs. The company controls over 4,600 mainframes, 145,000 terminals and modems, and 30,000 tape and disk drives.

Comdisco's domestic and international computer and high-tech equipment purchasing, selling, and leasing business offers a great example of the high returns to market connecting activities. The company represents over 3,500 manufacturers, including IBM, Hewlett-Packard, Digital Equipment, Unisys, Apple Computer, Sun Microsystems, ROLM, AT&T, and Xerox. On the customer side, Comdisco services a majority of the Fortune 1000, with equipment installed in almost 55,000 locations worldwide.

Comdisco has expanded its market-making services in a number of ways. First, it provides technical services to its customers including transportation, repair, and maintenance of high-tech equipment. Second, it provides asset management services for its customers through software that allows users to keep track of their equipment and its costs, and through equipment upgrade programs that adjust customer equipment to meet changing requirements. Third, it provides consulting services to help customers with strategic and financial planning of high-tech leasing and purchasing. Comdisco also started a medical equipment leasing business in 1991 aimed at the $10 billion a year medical equipment market.

The largest subsidiary of Comdisco, CDRS, provides disaster recovery services to over 3,000 subscribers in the U.S. and abroad. They have helped companies keep operating during Hurricane Hugo, the San Francisco Bay area earthquake, the power outage in New York's financial district, and the great downtown Chicago flood. With the slogan "Business as usual . . . no matter what!" CDRS offers disaster planning for firms as well as computer hardware and software, recovery facilities with computers and office space, and computer and telephone networks to allow businesses with multiple locations to continue operating.

Table 6-6 lists some of the key upstream and downstream market connections supplied by Comdisco, Inc. through its many market-making activities. The table selects four key downstream markets of Comdisco: equipment leasing, disaster recovery, asset management, and medical leasing. Then, four major upstream markets are listed: software, telecommunications services, telecommunications equipment, and computers and high-tech equipment. It is important to observe that while Comdisco is concerned with maintaining its high-quality customer relations, its vendor relations are also important. For example, it maintains close relationships with long-distance telecommunications companies, since telephone links are an important feature of its disaster recovery services. Comdisco also relies on a very strong labor input, with emphasis on sales personnel and innovative computer and telecommunications technicians. Comdisco must

Table 6-6.
SOME KEY MARKET CONNECTIONS FOR COMDISCO, INC.

Downstream	*Upstream*			
	Software	Telecom services	Telecom equipment	Computers and high-tech equip.
Equipment leasing	X		X	X
Disaster recovery	X	X	X	X
Asset management	X	X		X
Medical leasing				X

also have a financial markets strategy not only to finance its rapid rate of growth but also to allow its international operations to function smoothly. The company established a credit facility that allows it to borrow in a wide range of currencies. It closely follows technological innovation to keep in touch with developments in computers, software, high-tech equipment, and network technology.

Market connection activities are easily seen in a company such as Comdisco. These activities lie at the heart of most successful companies. A favorable competitive position can be sustained by a focus on learning about the characteristics and needs of customers and suppliers. This type of information gathering requires establishing durable relationships with customers and suppliers. Firms then can earn arbitrage profits by providing market-making services that reduce the market search costs and decision costs of customers and suppliers. Innovative management strategy is concerned with matching and mixing markets to create new market connections.

Networks and Organizations

Thus far, I have stressed the importance of creating customer and supplier networks. Does this mean that the firm is simply a conduit for the goods and services created by others? Are market making and intermediation the sole source of the firm's value added? To the contrary. The market-bridge perspective leaves room for the firm to engage in primary manufacturing, basic research, and many other activities besides. The key issue facing managers is when to carry out activities within the organization and when to move the activities out to the network.

Usually, the firm is presented with a simple trade-off: Do it yourself or use the market. I suggest that this choice is not framed correctly. Companies have a choice between carrying out an activity within their organization, building a market network of suppliers and distributors through contracts and alliances to carry out the task, or relying on the market-making services of other firms. Just as organizations can involve ongoing relationships, so can market connections. Carrying out the activity internally or through purchases and contracts should perhaps be viewed as different market-making alternatives. Internal activities require hiring specialized labor and contracting with primary parts and equipment manufacturers. Contracting out for production requires a different type of network. Thus, the choices are among alternative networks as much as they are organizational choices.

Two important considerations that enter into this important decision are transaction costs and information. These will determine both the boundaries of the organization and the characteristics of the firm's network. In either case, the firm plays the role of coordinator and intermediary, but the structure of production and distribution will differ fundamentally. A good illustration of coordination in a network is provided by the keiretsu. I examine the benefits of the keiretsu in this light, although market networks need to be continually reconfigured. The outsourcing decision is also highly dependent on the acquisition and diffusion of information. Rapidly growing communication capabilities are changing the costs of communication, both within and between firms, as market networks move toward electronic interaction.

Transaction Costs

Managers continually face the question of which activities the company should carry out itself and which ones should be farmed out to suppliers and distributors. Should the company make its own parts? Should it provide wholesale services and retail outlets? These types of decisions determine the boundaries of the firm *and* create the firm's market network. Taking on an activity grows the company, while contracting out expands the network.

The obvious answer is to compare the cost of undertaking the activity with the prices offered by suppliers and distributors. The problem is that this simple comparison can hide hidden costs or benefits of the alternatives. Carrying out market transactions entails costs for the company, including the gathering of market information and negotiating deals.[10]

For example, a firm must decide whether or not to manufacture a part at the cost of $100. A supplier offers the part at $50 which appears to dominate the firm's costs, but the hidden costs of dealing with the supplier equal $60, for a total of $110. An additional problem arises if there are hidden costs within the firm as well. Suppose that setting up the part manufacturing operation takes up management time and effort and managers also need to spend time supervising the activity once it is set up. If these costs are $40, then the total costs of making it yourself are $140, so that contracting out once again becomes worthwhile.

In comparing contracting out with vertical integration it is also necessary to take into account the costs of monitoring contractual performance. There is also the possibility that suppliers or distributors can take advantage of the company's sunk investment to strike better deals after the investment has been made.[11] Oliver William identifies "opportunistic behavior" as a major issue in contracts and organizations alike.[12] *Opportunism*, also known as contractual hold-up, refers to the situation in which one party to an agreement takes advantage of the irreversible investment of the other party. Parties to formal or informal long-term contracts often make investments that are specific to the transactions, what Williamson calls asset specificity. Not only can the investment not be recovered, such as an R&D or product design expenditure, but it cannot be applied to providing the service to another customer. If some portion of the investment can be recovered, the remainder represents sunk costs. These costs would suggest that if there are technological advantages to combining two production processes, companies will choose vertical integration rather than combining the two processes through procurement or joint production contracts. Similarly, transaction costs can explain why firms diversify to obtain the benefits of multiproduct production if it would be costly to combine firms making related products.[13]

To illustrate opportunism, suppose that a buyer and seller enter into an agreement for the purchase of a service at a price of $130. To provide the service the seller must make an investment of $100 that cannot be recovered. The operating cost of providing the service is $20. After the seller has made the investment, the buyer has an incentive to renegotiate the contract and offer the seller a far lower price for the service, say at $25. The seller cannot recover the irreversible investment but still has an incentive to supply the product because the new price of $25 covers the $20 operating cost.

Opportunistic behavior can occur if contracts are incomplete. Contract law plays an important role by providing remedies for breach and some rules for renegotiation. Opportunism may also be limited by social norms of trust between transacting parties, so that incomplete contracts can be consistent with efficient performance. Finally, reputation effects can limit opportunism in markets and encourage buyer and seller performance. Yet, these factors may not serve to limit opportunism in organizations, as managers and employees take advantage of the commitments of others. For example, employees may not respond to incentive bonuses if they are paid in advance of completed work. Accordingly, Williamson emphasizes the need for a complex hierarchy to manage vertically integrated companies so as to "harness opportunism."[14]

On the other hand, there are management costs within vertically integrated companies. These costs can limit the growth of the firm and affect the shape of its organization. The presence of trade-offs between market contracting and vertical integration implies that management choices that determine the span of the firm are crucial strategic decisions. It is interesting to note that computers and advances in communications have impacted both the costs of contracting out and the costs of doing it yourself. Since electronic data interchange allows improved coordination with both external and in-house suppliers, it is worthwhile for most companies to reassess the make-or-buy decision.

Viewing companies as market intermediaries takes the transaction cost perspective a step further. Firms, by acting as intermediaries, create market relationships and organizational forms that minimize transaction costs. Firms produce transactions for customers and suppliers to reduce the costs of searching for a trading partner and negotiating contracts. In turn, firms can carry out transactions only if the cost of doing so is less than the relevant bid–ask spread. The intermediation theory extends the transaction cost perspective by viewing all transactions as created by firms. The notion that an individual firm decides between using the market and forming organization contracts based on transaction costs is consistent with intermediation. In this view, using the market refers more specifically to engaging in transactions that are produced by intermediaries, which might include the firm itself, its customers, or its suppliers. Transaction cost analysis takes the individual transaction as a unit of analysis. The intermediation approach taken in this book looks more broadly at the set of transactions produced by the firm.

I do not draw such a sharp distinction between internal production and the costs of using the market. Rather, I view market transactions as the product of the activities of the firm. The fact that there are costs to creating transactions implies that those transactions must be produced by firms acting as intermediaries. Firms make the market or rely on the market-making activities of others. I do not conceive of markets as entities that exist separately from the buyers and sellers, as in the traditional invisible hand framework. The costs incurred by a firm in transacting with buyers and sellers are the costs of operating markets. These costs are no less internal to the firm than the firm's other productive activities. Thus, I view the market-making activities of retail and wholesale intermediaries as comparable with those of manufacturing firms. The make-or-buy decision represents a choice of the firm to undertake market making at different levels of the vertical production process. The firm is thus not defined simply by what production activities it chooses to carry out, but also by its choice of market-making activities.

Just because a firm chooses to rely on suppliers and distributors for goods and services does not mean that the activity is carried out in an impersonal marketplace. Such may be the case for standardized commodities such as energy resources or the purchase of financial assets. For other goods and services, companies rely on the intermediation services of others, obtaining temporary help from service agencies, financial advice and credit through financial intermediaries, and so on. For customized products and services, the firm continues to play an organizing role by coordinating the activities within its buyer and seller networks.

Information

Transaction costs provide a useful criterion for deciding whether certain activities should be internalized or outsourced. Companies should compare the costs of purchasing from suppliers at different levels of the industry. In-house production entails purchasing of primary inputs, while outsourcing entails production of intermediate goods and services. The market transaction costs or the alternatives should enter into the accounting of total costs.

Consideration of the implications of knowledge gained and lost provides an additional set of costs and benefits. The cost of information exchange within the organization and across networks is an essential ingredient.

In comparing the benefits of production with those of outsourcing, the company must determine whether it has the technical knowledge to produce the product. Superior information about technological processes will be reflected in lower costs. The company may wish to acquire the information through learning-by-doing, which then justifies in-house production at a higher cost than outsourcing to suppliers. Delegating production to suppliers of nonstandard items further requires sharing detailed technical information with them. This can result in diffusion of information to rivals.

Similarly, distribution should be delegated to others with superior market information unless the company wishes to acquire more direct knowledge about its consumers. Many have observed that franchising firms such as McDonald's operate company-owned outlets as a way of gaining a window on the market.

Sharing information with suppliers and distributors creates the risk of a different kind of opportunism. Suppose that the information shared is not transaction specific. Then, there is the possibility that the other party will achieve substantial benefits outside of the transaction. It may not be possible to adjust the terms of trade in a way that compensates the company for the full value of the information.

Private procurement of goods and services generates spin-offs just as government procurement in defense and aerospace created microchips and other innovations. Private contracts cannot easily anticipate or provide for innovations. This suggests that companies would contract out more if they could capture the economic rents from related innovations. It also provides an incentive to carry out R&D in-house or to establish research joint ventures.

Employees often benefit from training programs that are not firm specific to achieve higher wages and salaries elsewhere, often by working for a rival. The competitor gains an advantage by free riding on the training program, paying the employee a premium based on the additional productivity value of the training. Such opportunism can be addressed in part by paying employees a lower wage to reflect the benefits achieved by training, but this makes the firm even more prone to raids by competitors. The employee training problem is being addressed by increasing use of knowledge-based rewards within companies. Knowledge opportunism explains in part the extensive reliance on independent organizations, particularly colleges, universities, and technical schools, to provide training.

Knowledge opportunism is a problem of dealing with parts suppliers that can be addressed through contracts that prohibit sharing information with others. Technological knowledge can be passed on through licensing and royalty arrangements. However, what cannot be controlled is the learning of rivals as they perform the needed service. IBM provided tremendous learning opportunities for its chip maker, Intel, and its operating software provider, Microsoft, that were later to be leveraged into a much wider set of activities. One approach is to enter into long-term contracts or stable, informal arrangements with suppliers to attempt to capture the full value of the information. This helps to explain the stability of supplier and distributor arrangements observed in some industries.

Closely related to the issue of information opportunism are the comparative costs of communication within the organization and with suppliers and distributors. These costs are coming down with increased application of computers and advances in telecommunications. Lower costs within the organization have led to substantial reengineering, slimming down the ranks of middle and upper management that had been occupied with very standard data gathering and analysis. This has flattened the hierarchy, increased delegation of authority, and strengthened the interaction of top managers with marketing and production personnel.

At the same time electronic data interchange has increased the information flow between manufacturers and suppliers and between retailers and manufacturers. This will change the shape of market networks just as it has altered the shape of organizations. As the cost of creating market networks falls, there will be increased usage of these networks. One of the key questions is whether this means that companies should expand their organizations or rely more on their market networks. The answer is that many types of in-house production are no longer desirable because they can be more cheaply farmed out as the costs of supplier and distributor coordination fall. Companies that provide networking services will prosper and expand.

Are information networks qualitatively different from well-established methods of communication? These include telephones that already transmit voice, fax, and data; cable TV systems; wireless communications; and express mail service. The answer is yes; high-speed, high-capacity data interchange is changing business fundamentally, by improving communication within organizations and across market networks. Just as railroads changed the landscape, creating new cities, businesses, and marketplaces, so the electronic highways are altering business geography.

The global marketplace has developed rapidly since the 1970s, thanks to economic growth, particularly in Asia, and international trade liberalization. Advances in transportation and communication have increased trade by lowering costs worldwide. The creation of information networks has created new opportunities for communication that will greatly lower costs and boost national and international commercial activity.

Jim Manzi, then Chairman and CEO of the Lotus Development Corporation, observed that American companies were creating "electronic keiretsu" by linking up through computer networks, electronic mail, relational and document databases, and mobile computing.[15] He noted that computer groupware allows Compaq Computer to keep in touch with its worldwide network of distributors, Johnson & Higgins (the world's largest privately held insurance broker) to exchange market and price information with its brokers, and Fort Howard Corporation to communicate with its brokers, distributors, and final customers for its paper products.

Business is undergoing a complete transformation as it recognizes the increasing importance of information, both as an input to production, distribution, and management and as a product. Information provides a substitute for other inputs that are used by the firm. This means that by some increase in the application of various information technologies and a corresponding decrease in other inputs (notably capital equipment, labor, energy, and manufactured inputs), companies can maintain or increase productivity. As the cost of information processing and communication falls, this implies that companies will continue to substitute information for other inputs. This does not mean that companies will shrink; rather it will lead to growth as overall costs fall. Indeed, since information increases the productivity of other inputs, it can ultimately stimulate the demand for those inputs.

Because information is a substitute for labor services, including management, the increased effectiveness of word processing and spreadsheets has improved the productivity of clerical and accounting personnel. Advances in automation have increased the productivity of operations and warehousing, while computerization and mobile communications have boosted the effectiveness of sales personnel. Computer-aided design not only saves on the time and materials required to produce models, it improves the productivity of design personnel.

Companies can boost the productivity of their experts in a variety of areas, including engineering and product design, by increased use of communications. This allows a given number of technical personnel to provide services throughout an enterprise as needed, thus reducing slack. Enhanced telecommunications act as a substitute for a variety of other services. Data interchange, electronic mail, and faxes have reduced the demand for express mail. Videoconferencing and on-line communication reduce business travel, which is costly and time consuming.

I have already observed that information and communications technology allows companies to reduce inventories by adjusting parts manufacturing and stockpiles to patterns of market demand. Moreover, companies can reduce materials usage through computer-aided design and manufacturing. Computer controllers reduce energy in smart buildings and materials usage in processing industries. Companies are increasingly relying on electronic transmission for handling customer and supplier transactions.

There is a widening list of new communication and information services. The creation of information networks provides a means of delivering these services. Delivery of news and financial data on data networks competes with newspapers, magazines, radio, and television. Electronic home shopping for almost all types of products competes with stores as well as with mail-order catalogs. Electronic networks provide a means of delivering a variety of services including health care diagnosis and treatment recommendations, education, and entertainment. Many of other services such as accounting and legal advice and technical expertise can also be supplied electronically.

The increased effectiveness of communications and data processing technology have greatly reduced the cost of building market networks. This means that market networks will expand and high returns will be obtained by the companies that create and operate the networks, creating new market bridges.

Keiretsu

The Japanese keiretsu provide an example of coordinated networks of companies. The term refers to a large grouping of industrial companies whose economic activities are interrelated in a variety of ways. The keiretsu are the descendants of the large, privately owned and highly diversified companies, called zaibatsu, that were partly dismantled during the U.S. occupation after World War II.[16] There are two kinds of keiretsu, horizontal and vertical. The horizontal keiretsu is a group of large firms in different lines of business united by a central bank and trading company. The vertical keiretsu refers to an alliance between a major company and its suppliers and distributors. While this distinction is useful, the horizontal keiretsu is actually bound together by many vertical contracts. Both aspects of the keiretsu illustrate the Japanese approach to building market bridges.

The horizontal keiretsu dominate the Japanese economy, with the six major ones comprising a total of 189 companies; almost all of those companies head their own vertical keiretsu, thus involving thousands of additional smaller firms.[17] The six big groups are: Mitsui, Mitsubishi, Sumitomo, Fuyo, Sanwa, and Dai-Ichi Kangyo (DKB). The members of these groups are all large firms in their own right. For example, the Mitsui group of 26 companies includes Sakura Bank, Mitsui & Co. (a trading house),

Mitsui Fudosan (real estate), Toyota, and Toshiba. The Mitsubishi keiretsu of 29 companies had combined sales in 1990 of $360 billion, while DKB with 48 companies had sales of $416 billion.[18] As a comparison, the latter exceeds the combined 1994 sales of the top four U.S. Fortune 500 companies (General Motors, Ford, Exxon, and IBM), which comes to about $403 billion.

There is little competition within the keiretsu. In the horizontal ones, the companies are involved in distinct businesses, such as automobiles, equipment manufacturing, mining, chemicals, and banking. The vertical form might appear to involve some competition between suppliers of similar parts and equipment, but the stability of the relationships precludes more intense rivalry. The members of a keiretsu compete with the corresponding members of another that are in the same industry. Due to the supportive nature of the groupings, the keiretsu to some extent compete with each other.

The members of a keiretsu are separate firms, operating distinct businesses each with its own management, company name, and corporate identity. Yet members of the group cooperate closely with each other and engage in a large number of interfirm transactions. The horizontal keiretsu are bound together by tradition, a vast web of interpersonal relationships, a common sense of purpose, and numerous institutional ties. They are further united by formal councils of company presidents, extensive cross-shareholding, and interlocking directorates. Taken together, it would be easy to believe that the members form a gigantic, diversified conglomerate. But there are substantial differences between these groups and the conglomerate that transcend the disparities in size.

To understand these differences, it is essential to examine the two types of companies that are at the center of the horizontal keiretsu: a main bank and a general trading house (sogo shosha). They are the primary glue that holds the group together. These companies are of particular interest to the present discussion. They provide institutions of control and coordination that are distinct from those in a conglomerate.

The main bank performs a wide variety of roles. In part, it takes on the task of capital allocation of the corporate office of a conglomerate, by funding company projects. The bank secures credit for the group members and provides a host of additional financial services. It is also an owner, holding large amounts of stock and actively monitoring its investment, thereby acting as a mutual fund. It places directors on company boards and guarantees the solvency of companies. The bank goes further by coordinating the activities of the member companies. Most significantly, the main bank provides financial intermediation for all of the companies in the keiretsu, acting as lender and shareholder as well as monitor of company performance.[19]

Therefore, the main bank constructs a very large financial market bridge between its depositors and the firms in its keiretsu. The bank is a market maker in terms of credit for the firms, although not necessarily in its securities as a consequence of long-term shareholding. It is in this sense that the main bank provides vertical ties for the keiretsu network, increasing its vertical span as a financial company.

The general trading company's activities are particularly fascinating. The shosha are major importers, exporters, and distributors, and act as financial intermediaries between the large banks and the small- and medium-sized members of the group. Paul Sheard has observed that the shosha act as intermediaries in many transactions, essentially providing trade credit by handling all of the payments between companies. The buyer sends an order to the seller and takes delivery of the goods on credit. The buyer issues a bill to the shosha which in turn issues a bill to the seller who uses the bill to obtain financing from a bank. The buyer pays the shosha when the bill is due, and the shosha in turn pays off the bank. The size of the general trading companies is startling. Itochu Shoji of the DKB group is the largest, with $160 billion in sales in its 1992 fiscal year. Miyashita and Russell point out that the profit margins are very slim, in this case only one-twentieth of a percent.[20]

The trading company therefore provides intermediation and market-making services for the members of the group. The general trading companies are a clear example of how companies operate markets, handling payment systems, coordinating transactions, and connecting buyers and sellers. By extracting small profit margins from very high trading volumes, they operate the institutions of exchange for a substantial segment of the Japanese economy. The trading companies are very large market bridges in the import–export and trade credit markets.

The major companies in Japan operate vertical keiretsu. This is a pyramidal system of subcontracting based on "inter-firm (often inter-personal) relationships cultivated through years of mutual trust and cooperation (though early on, the relationship was of a feudal type of domination and subordination)."[21] Ozawa describes the auto industry as eleven core companies at the top of the pyramid (Toyota, Nissan, Honda, Mazda, Mitsubishi, Fuji, Daihatsu, Isuzu, Suzuki, Hino, and Nissan Diesel) that assemble the vehicles. Next, there are 168 primary subassemblers and subprocessors. Then there are 4,700 secondary subcontractors and 31,600 tertiary producers. Typically, the tertiary producers are small enterprises with fewer than 30 workers and wages that are 40% of the average at the top of the pyramid.[22]

For example, the leading company, Toyota, with $72 billion in sales in 1992, had 10 subcontractors, as well as minicar maker Daihatsu Motor and truck manufacturer Hino Motors, in its first tier.[23] These 12 companies comprise over 110,000 employees and over $61 billion in sales. In the middle level are 248 second- and third-tier contractors. At the lowest level are

Figure 6-1.
TOYOTA'S MANUFACTURING AND DISTRIBUTION HOURGLASS

Manufacturing

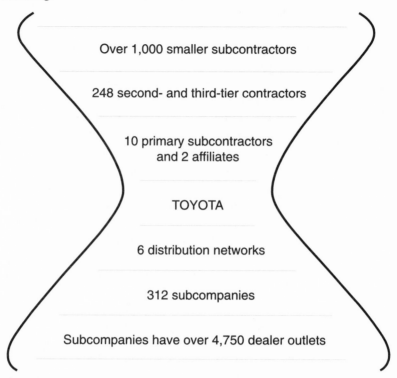

Over 1,000 smaller subcontractors

248 second- and third-tier contractors

10 primary subcontractors
and 2 affiliates

TOYOTA

6 distribution networks

312 subcompanies

Subcompanies have over 4,750 dealer outlets

Distribution

perhaps over 1,000 smaller contractors. Then, Toyota is at the top of a huge distribution pyramid with six distribution networks including Tokyo Toyota Motor, Tokyo Toyopet, Osaka Toyopet, and Toyota Tokyo Corolla. These networks have 312 subcompanies and 117,000 employees. With the subcompanies, Toyota has over 4,750 dealer outlets. Combining Toyota's manufacturing and distribution networks creates an hourglass structure that highlights its role as a market bridge between its suppliers and distributors. This is represented in Figure 6-1.

In comparison, the American auto industry, including General Motors, Ford, Chrysler, and Japanese companies that manufacture in the U.S., is served by about 6,000 suppliers, mostly through direct formal contracts. The automakers act like defense procurement agencies by providing the specifications and even the designs of parts to their subcontractors, who then competed on the basis of price. Automakers are changing their relationships with parts producers by involving them in the design process. This is partly due to the success that Japanese manufacturers operating in the U.S. have achieved with this approach. Companies such as Nissan are creating networks of primary and secondary vendors through longer-term partnerships and shared engineering and design knowledge.[24]

The main lesson of the keiretsu is that companies can profit from the creation of manufacturing and distribution networks. By establishing these networks a company plays a facilitating role, providing technical information to suppliers and receiving in return high-quality parts, design ideas, and on-time performance. Similarly, the company coordinates the activities of its distribution network, from which it obtains sales effort and market information. Of course, these networks need not be bound by interlocking directorates and other restrictive practices to be effective. Rather, they should depend on the creation of gains from trade for all the members. In response to competition, even the Japanese keiretsu are becoming more open in terms of increased trade with companies outside the group. The success of manufacturing and distribution networks ultimately must depend on the quality of the intermediation services provided by the leading firms, and the flexibility of network organization in response to changing markets.

Organizational Boundaries

Winning the market requires that the firm push out its boundaries. Growth allows the company to realize the revenue, risk, and cost gains from consolidation. The question is how best to grow—by expanding the organization or by expanding its market network? Choosing among alternative ways to grow determines the type of organization and the shape of market networks created by the company. The main choices are internal expansion, contracts, strategic alliances, and mergers.

Growth involves more than vertical make-or-buy decisions. Managers must also choose scale, scope, and speed, as well as other aspects of the firm's span. Accordingly, a more general strategic analysis is required. Understanding market bridges provides a set of guideposts. These are outlined in Table 6-7.

Scale

Growth is a very important part of winning the market. Operating costs can be reduced through increased investment, allowing lower prices. Investment also allows product quality improvements, creating increased sales. Expenditures for additional personnel can improve service quality and bring new skills into the company.

Table 6-7.
ORGANIZATIONAL BOUNDARIES

Boundaries	Growth	Contracts	Alliances	Mergers
Scale	Expansion	International partnerships	International alliances	Horizontal
Scope	Diversification	Joint ventures	Product standards, horizontal keiretsu	Lateral
Span	Vertical integration	Supplier and distributor contracts	Supplier and distributor networks, vertical keiretsu	Vertical
Speed	Accelerated innovation	Licensing, technology transfers	R&D joint ventures	Dynamic

The firm seeking to increase its size and market share has four main options. First, the firm can grow by *internal expansion*, increasing its investment, employment, and production. Second, the firm can grow through *contracts* and *alliances* with other firms. It is apparent that contracts with rivals, whether explicit or implicit, are anticompetitive and ruled out by antitrust law. However, this need not preclude contracts and alliances with foreign companies in the same industry that result in an expanded role in the global marketplace. Finally, the firm can grow through *horizontal mergers* with rivals, again to the extent permitted by antitrust law. What should determine the firm's choice among these three options?

Expansion builds on the existing strengths of the firm, allowing it to apply successful organizational ideas, production methods, and marketing styles. Wal-Mart grew almost entirely by expansion, improving and refining its distribution and pricing systems. The company made substantial investments in large retail outlets, realizing the gains from economies of scale at the store level. Moreover, the company created a massive distribution network, capturing the cost savings from automation and large-scale warehouses and the benefits of coordination through a centralized satellite communications system. It was able to build the distribution network efficiently by carefully choosing where to expand its retail operations. Finally, Wal-Mart established a vast network of primary suppliers. Thus, Wal-Mart is both a retailer and a wholesaler, capturing economies of sequence from vertical integration. It might not have achieved such success from an innovative system without internal expansion. Mergers might not have allowed the optimal integration of retail outlets, nor would the design of stores and warehouses from other companies have fitted so easily into its system.

Yet, internal expansion entails costs of adjustment, production delays, and construction lags. Managers must continually oversee the hiring of new employees and the establishment of new facilities. Growth can take time. The company must build up customer demand by investing in marketing and brand reputation. Even if the expansion is demand-driven, the company must adapt its organization to deal with expansion.

Horizontal mergers create a rapid increase in market share, avoiding the adjustment costs and delays from internal expansion. Consolidation through mergers can also create efficiencies as companies eliminate duplicative overhead expenditures and retire redundant production and distribution facilities. By consolidating productive capacity, companies can increase their size without going through a costly duplication and shakeout process. The industry capacity remains constant after the merger so that the market power of the merged firm can increase, particularly if the capacity is operated efficiently and if potential entrants are reluctant to add further plant and equipment in the industry. Sam's Club, which grew primarily by internal expansion, acquired the Pace Membership Warehouse business sold by Kmart for just these reasons.

One way to win the market is through a large-scale merger, as Fleming of Oklahoma City has done in U.S. wholesale food distribution. From its position as the number two wholesaler, Fleming acquired the number three wholesaler, Scrivner, at a cost of over $1 billion from its German owners, Franz Haniel & Cie, G.m.b.H. The combined company, with about $19 billion in sales, was able to leap-frog the previous number one, Supervalu Inc. of Minneapolis. The merged company will have a market share of over a third of the $100 billion food wholesaling industry. This need not be the end of growth by merger. In fact, Supervalu Inc. had reached its number one position through a $1.1 billion acquisition of Wetterau. The merger also realizes scale economies. The company will eliminate one of the headquarters, and close or consolidate 8 of 52 distribution centers. Before the merger, Fleming had already planned to close five regional offices and five distribution centers.[25]

The companies competing in food distribution are building competing market bridges. The merger widens Fleming's market network. The company will expand from 2,100 to 5,800 independent and chain supermarkets and go from 900 to 2,800 convenience stores. The merger has an important vertical element as well. The new Fleming will own 315 retail stores and have 15% of retail sales. This type of growth is required to stay competitive, as wholesalers extend their reach into retailing and retailers expand into wholesaling, and hybrid discount warehouse stores like Sam's Club enter the business. As the chairman and CEO of Fleming, Robert E.

Stauth, states, "Fleming was the last of the major wholesalers to get into retailing. For the wholesale side of the industry to be viable, wholesalers have to be into retailing."[26]

One benefit of mergers and acquisitions is a gain in information about technology or customers. In this sense, what appear to be horizontal mergers have important vertical elements. The merged firm may then take advantage of the distribution system or R&D capabilities of one of the partners.

This does not mean that acquiring competitors is always the best means of market dominance, since it does little to prevent the entry of companies offering lower prices or better products. Excess capacity in itself is not a deterrent to a potential entrant with superior performance or improved distribution. Rather, growth through horizontal acquisition is recommended only when it brings benefits unattainable through expansion. There are high transaction costs in the market for companies, just as in other markets. The acquiring company must search out potential targets, considering the complementarities with the existing business. The market for corporate control itself can exhibit substantial transaction costs. The acquiring company must negotiate the terms of the merger or acquisition. This can take time away from managing the business. The merger and acquisition process can lead to conflicts with the firm's existing owners, its board, and its managers.

Mergers are not always successful because the companies must integrate their management and operations. Much has been made of cultural differences and friction between corporate managers and employees. In addition, the presence of antitrust challenges to horizontal mergers can raise the costs of the merger or prevent it altogether.

International alliances and joint ventures can provide the best of both worlds. They permit the firm to gather information from partners about markets and technology, while instantly expanding the size and global reach of the network. Transaction costs are reduced because alliances are easier to form and maintain than a full merger. The partners can leverage relatively small investments to create vast international networks. The members maintain their corporate identity, management, and ownership structure intact, and alliances are less likely to raise antitrust concerns.

International alliances provide access to new suppliers and customers as well as technological information, as in the Toyota-General Motors alliance. This demonstrates that many horizontal alliances also have vertical elements. Joel Bleeke and David Ernst of McKinsey & Co. suggest that cross-border alliances and acquisitions are a form of arbitrage, for example, "with Fujitsu trading capital and manufacturing skills for Amdahl's expertise in mainframe design and architecture."[27]

The strength of an alliance is that companies can rapidly expand their market networks without much loss of flexibility. The alliance can be dissolved or refocused as market conditions change. Additional partners can be added to expand the market reach. Alliances may be necessary for smaller firms to catch up and overtake larger companies or other alliances.

A case in point is the global telecommunications industry, in which companies are forming a series of national and international strategic alliances. Customers seeking seamless communications want suppliers that can provide integrated worldwide networks. Sprint, for example, formed a strategic alliance in 1994 with France Telecom and Deutsche Telekom. The alliance has over $70 billion in combined annual revenues and $155 billion in assets. The telecommunications partnership combines knowledge of many national markets with technological expertise in the transmission of voice, video, and data. In this way, Sprint is better positioned to compete against AT&T and MCI in the U.S. market while challenging them abroad as well. In response, MCI and British Telecom formed a competing alliance named Concert to provide international communications services. AT&T pursues international alliances through a consortium called World Partners, which includes the Japanese long-distance company KDD and Singapore Telecom. Through this consortium, AT&T has allied itself with the telephone companies of the Netherlands, Sweden, and Switzerland, who form another consortium called Unisource.

Among the drawbacks of alliances is that they can create incentive problems for the partners. There is always the possibility of free riding on the other members or of one partner pursuing objectives that are inconsistent with the partnership. A partner can use the alliance to gain valuable information and then act opportunistically by using the information to compete against alliance members in the future. As a consequence, partners may be reluctant to share information fully with each other. It is important to structure alliances as joint ventures to build a specific market bridge so that the incentives of the partners are consistent.

Scope

Expanding the company's range of products offers many advantages. Investment in product development yields increased sales as consumers respond to product variety. Flexible manufacturing and sales that tailor products and services to customer requirements create competitive advantages. Product variety allows growth through entry into new markets. This is particularly important if the company's sales are constrained in its existing markets by the level of demand or competitive entry. As we have seen, the company can achieve revenue, risk, and cost gains to consolidation by branching out into new products.

Again, the question is how to increase the scope of the firm. The main ways to grow are through *diversification, joint ventures* and *alliances* with companies producing different products, and *lateral mergers*. Each of these options entails different strategic benefits and costs. These options also have different effects on the size of the company's organization and the reach of its market networks.

Diversification refers to a company increasing the range of products that it offers through increased investment and the development and marketing of new products. For the purposes of the present discussion, I distinguish this type of growth from lateral mergers which also result in diversification. Growth by diversification is recommended if the company can leverage its knowledge and abilities into new markets.

The company can achieve the benefits of offering customers increased variety by essentially repeating well-established production and marketing procedures. For example, a company such as Coca-Cola offers a wide range of soft drinks, including Coca-Cola Classic, Coca-Cola, Diet Coke, Sprite, Diet Sprite, Cherry Coke, Tab, and caffeine-free versions of several varieties. The production and marketing of each brand is similar, so skills and market networks are readily transferable.

Coca-Cola relies on the same network of bottlers, including company-owned operations, independent bottlers, publicly owned franchises, and those owned by large companies such as Procter & Gamble. There is no need to search for new bottlers. The process of contracting with bottlers is basically the same across brands, so existing agreements can be expanded. The delivery of concentrate is similar as well. The company does not incur high set-up costs, as a company introducing its first brands would. These bottlers in turn have established networks of retail outlets including supermarket chains and restaurants. The distribution networks generally remain the same across the company's brands. Moreover, Coca-Cola uses the same supplier network for most of its products. The company negotiates with the suppliers of plastic bottles and cans and makers of sweeteners to obtain better terms for its bottlers. These activities are relatively similar for each type of soft drink that is being produced. Coca-Cola relies on its knowledge of advertising companies to market its various brands.

Coca-Cola has diversified further into other types of drinks, including orange juice, wine, spring water, and sports drinks called PowerAde. Under the Minute Maid label, the company has added sodas containing juice and a line of sweetened fruit juice blends called Fruitopia. These activities are not a major departure from the basic concentrate business. The product development, marketing, and distribution activities are closely related and draw on the company's existing skills.

Increases in scope can be achieved through lateral mergers. These provide a means of taking advantage of cross-elasticities of demand by allowing the merged firm to coordinate pricing across product lines. Recall that *substitute* products compete with each other, so that an increase in the price of a product's substitute increases the demand for the product.

Consumer benefits from a product are enhanced by using another product that is a *complement*, so that an increase in the price of a complement reduces the demand for the product.

Lateral mergers reduce the fratricide across substitute brands and increase revenues for the merged firms. Similar to a horizontal merger, lateral mergers allow firms to expand their product lines without increasing productive capacity in the market by creating competing product lines. If two companies produce complementary products there are also benefits to a merger: The combination of brands can have greater customer recognition, and the companies can bundle the products together.

Companies can expand their scope through joint ventures to produce or distribute a new product. This is particularly desirable if the partners bring complementary technological or marketing skills to the joint venture. The costs of such contracts are the transaction costs involved in searching for partners, writing the contracts, and monitoring the performance of the venture. Joint ventures have the advantage of information exchange, but there is the risk that partners can benefit from information that will allow them to compete more effectively in the future. It is therefore important to choose partners carefully on the basis of the type of information that will be exchanged and the types of goods and services the partner currently produces and is expected to produce.

Joint ventures can be carried out for both substitute and complementary products. By forming an alliance with makers of substitute products, companies can fill in gaps in their product lines while eliminating redundant variations in product features. More commonly, though, alliances are between makers of complementary products.

It is important to observe that complementary products are themselves a type of network. If complementary products are used together, such as cameras and film or computers and software, any improvement in the quality and variety of one product increases the benefits to users of the other products. These products form a network because they are interconnected by compatibility. For example, companies selling compact disc (CD) players and suppliers of compact discs form a network. Availability of a greater variety of music in the CD format enhances the value of CD players. Similarly, the general adoption of VHS format (over Betamax) by producers of video cassettes created a market for VHS video cassette players.

One problem that must be surmounted in establishing a network is coordination. Vendors of complementary products need to adhere to a common technological standard that allows ease of interconnection or joint use of the products. There are significant returns to market makers that can play this role and earn some share of the economic benefits of coordination.

The next problem is that there are network complementarities. This means that a company that introduces a new complementary product provides benefits for other companies in the network, but the sales revenues that are earned by the company do not capture all of these benefits. This implies that the company might not invest as much in the development of the new products as it should from the point of view of the other companies in the network. Another way to view this problem is that since the members of the network are free riders, fewer innovations or new products are introduced than would be the case if one owner could capture all of the benefits of the innovation.

There are a number of ways to solve this problem. One company could diversify and try to create all of the network by itself, preventing others from interconnecting to its system by creating impenetrable technological standards. Another solution is to merge with all potential members of the network. These solutions are not appealing, since they tie up substantial amounts of capital and require the firm to build a system that cannot flexibly respond to new business conditions. Moreover, an exclusive approach denies the firm access to the creativity of other companies that might join a network, and the company loses the potential marketing and customer networks of other network members.

A more appealing solution is to form joint ventures and alliances to coordinate standards and to capture the economic rents from product networks. In other words, market networks can be created to achieve the benefits of complementary product networks.

An example of a wide-ranging alliance that attempted to coordinate technical standards and internalize network complementarities was built by Oracle Corp. around its multimedia technology. Oracle offered database software modified to manage thousands of hours of video and audio as well as text. This software was the basis of an alliance that included General Instrument, Scientific Atlanta, Kaleida Labs, 3DO, General Magic, Sega America, Sharp, and Apple Computer.[28] General Instrument provided a module that was an add-on to a television set-top decoder box that would run Oracle's software. Scientific Atlanta's set-top box would work with the media server, Kaleida Labs would integrate its media player, 3DO would establish an interface with its cable and network licenses, and Apple would develop a set-top box that used Macintosh technology to work with the media server.

Headed by its CEO and founder Lawrence Ellison, a college dropout from the south side of Chicago, Oracle grew from a $5 million company in 1983 to revenues of over $4 billion in 1996. Its success is due to its relational database management system that allows users to retrieve data from many computers and servers as if it were stored in a single database. This is particularly important as companies move away from mainframes, linking many computers through local area networks and storing data in various locations throughout the system. The technology applies to large-scale networks of the type that are used to form information superhighways. By working closely with producers of complementary products, the technical standards can be harmonized. Network complementarities can be captured through joint ventures that share the returns from new product development.

Another way to appropriate the returns from complementary products is to bundle them together. Practically every product is a bundle of features. An automobile, for example, is a package containing many parts, such as engines, brakes, and suspensions, and many distinguishable characteristics, such as mileage, speed, and styling. Companies that combine a product with service or transportation are also offering bundles. A company that sells products in a bundle, rather than a la carte, is in some cases able to extract more revenues from consumers. These incremental revenues are not attainable if the products are supplied by different companies. This explains the significant trend of bundling together packages of software. Software suites such as Microsoft Office offer a set of programs, including a word processor, spreadsheet, e-mail, presentation graphics, and relational database.

If the complementary products are offered by different companies, one approach is to enter into an alliance to bundle the products together. IBM's bundling of the DOS program with its computers was responsible for the early success of Microsoft. Oracle Corp. and Novell bundled the Oracle 7 database management software with Novell's NetWare and the UnixWare operating system. This not only coordinated their marketing efforts but created a more valuable product because the different software products interacted more easily and allowed users to work with databases on networks.[29]

Companies that expand their scope through diversification or lateral mergers can harmonize the substitutes in a product line through pricing and selection of product features. In the case of complementary products they can take advantage of network effects by designing components that work well with each other but not necessarily with the products of competitors. Alternatively, through joint ventures and strategic alliances, companies can coordinate product development to create a network of companies producing related products. Network complementarities can be controlled through licensing and bundling arrangements. Thus, there are both organizational and network approaches to increasing the scope of the firm.

Alliances should be focused on technological or marketing complementarities. The horizontal keiretsu, while certainly successful in the Japanese economy, does not provide a model for expanding the scope of market networks. The horizontal keiretsu unites large-scale firms in an unwieldy conglomerate with limited benefits beyond coordination of interfirm trade and joint financing.

Joint ventures and strategic alliances should take advantage of the technical strengths of the member firms, particularly in an industry where widely diverse sets of skills are required. It is unlikely that one firm can be proficient in all areas. In the computer industry, it is rare for a firm to master both hardware and software. Alliances reap the gains from specialization and division of labor across firms. Moreover, alliances are flexible, allowing members to be added as new companies make discoveries or as new requirements arise. The company that wins the market will be the one that establishes the network and coordinates the efforts of its members.

Span

Companies can increase their span through vertical expansion or vertical mergers to achieve incremental revenues, reduced risk, and economies of sequence. Alternatively, they can make formal contracts with suppliers and distributors. In addition, companies can create supplier and distributor networks, as in the Japanese vertical keiretsu. The choice of the span of the organization determines the type of market network the firm creates. Perhaps more than any other set of decisions, choosing the span of the firm is crucial to building market bridges.

A company's market-making activities—pricing, coordination of exchange, market clearing, and allocating goods and services—connect its suppliers and customers. By choosing which suppliers to connect with which customers, the company determines what productive steps are to be performed by its organization. Therefore, the choice of market connections is mirrored by the span of the firm.

The company selects its span by determining its value added at each stage of production from input production to R&D, product design, manufacturing, and marketing. The firm compares the potential spread between output and input prices with its production, processing, and transaction costs.

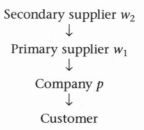

Secondary supplier w_2
↓
Primary supplier w_1
↓
Company p
↓
Customer

The company has the following choice. It can build a market bridge between its customer and its primary supplier, earning the spread $p - w_1$. Alternatively, it can expand its organization to include the tasks carried out by its primary supplier and build a market bridge between its customer and its secondary supplier, earning the spread $p - w_2$. The choices also entail different operation and transaction costs.

The company determines its distribution network in a similar manner. It can build a market bridge between its supplier and its primary distributor, earning the spread $p_1 - w$. Alternatively, it can expand downstream into distribution by taking on the role of its primary distributor and building a bridge between its supplier and its customer, earning the spread $p_2 - w$.

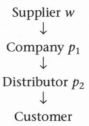

Supplier w
↓
Company p_1
↓
Distributor p_2
↓
Customer

The price spreads set by the firm depend on the elasticities of demand or supply at each stage, the extent of competition, and the long-term strategy of the company.

Growth does not necessarily require vertical expansion. As I have emphasized, there can be significant returns to market making and intermediation. It is evident that companies are increasing their use of contracts. They are outsourcing not only production activities but also corporate services that were once thought to be intrinsic to management, including strategic planning, human resources, legal services, data processing, accounting, and real estate. Outsourcing allows companies to leverage their investment and technical skill to create a large company by only carrying out essential assembly or key manufacturing processes in-house. Companies can invest in personnel training and customer service. Furthermore, they earn returns to market making by coordinating the activities of their subcontractors and suppliers. This trend is reshaping organizations.

William Roberti, the chief executive of Brooks Brothers, which now outsources production of suits, slacks, and sportcoats and plans to outsource production of shirts and ties, says, "Today we want to be a merchant and a *marketer*, not a maker." This allows for greater investment in design and marketing. Brooks Brothers, owned by the British retailer Marks & Spencer, is also outsourcing distribution, moving its brand through catalogues, factory outlet stores, and luxury boutiques.[30]

Outsourcing allows companies to transform internal production activities into products and services that can be farmed out. The company that is outsourcing is able to interact with many suppliers, bringing diverse skills into its market network. Competition among the firm's suppliers maintains cost efficiency and product quality and stimulates innovation. Independent suppliers are able to increase their production by providing outsourcing services to multiple customers. This permits suppliers to realize scale economies and to invest in cost-reducing capital equipment. The suppliers themselves are outsourcing some of their manufacturing and other activities, creating a network of suppliers similar to the vertical keiretsu.

Suppliers reduce risks by serving a variety of customers. This allows them to operate near full capacity, thus lowering average costs. Texas Instruments (TI) produces two types of semiconductors for its outside customers, low-cost DRAM memory chips and expensive customized microprocessors for mainframes and workstations, with 90% of the production process identical.[31] Shawn Tully notes in *Fortune* that TI is able to run at full capacity by using the memory chips as a buffer, varying production of the low-cost chips to accommodate increases or decreases in the demand for specialized chips. Similarly, he observes that Solectron, which manufactures circuit boards, monitors client sales projections and operates flexible factories that allow it to vary the product mix for its portfolio of major customers.

Transaction costs are certainly important determinants of the span decision. The company must compare the costs of carrying out an activity within the organization with the costs of contracting or creating market networks. Managers must ask whether there are any inherent cost advantages to internal transactions and incentives as compared with forming contracts with suppliers and distributors.

Clearly, the growth of electronic data interchange and other advances in information processing and transmission lowers the costs of communication between firms. While organization costs have fallen as well, I believe that the cost balance is tipping in favor of market costs. This suggests that companies should begin to shed many inessential activities that can be farmed out to subcontractors and coordinated at lower costs than ever before. It is incorrect to conclude that a company can gain a competitive advantage simply by finding lower-cost subcontractors. This option may be available to competitors as well. Moreover, it may not be desirable to move plants abroad to employ lower-cost labor and resources if the savings are erased by higher communication costs. The advantage is obtained by combining low-cost suppliers and distributors with more effective communication and coordination systems, thus lowering the total of production and transaction costs.

The risk of supplier and distributor opportunism can be factored in. The company must determine the extent to which its contracts with suppliers or distributors are subject to hold-up. Do these contracts involve substantial transaction-specific investment? To what extent can companies switch suppliers and distributors? The bargaining power of the company's trading partners, both before and after investment expenditures are made, determines the desirability of contracting. For readily available products and services, vertical integration is becoming less and less desirable.

Companies are increasingly divesting themselves of activities that can be readily contracted out.

Vertical integration is not necessary to create incentives for performance by vertical trading partners. Companies can induce suppliers and distributors to perform effectively by carefully designing contracts. The span decision then depends in part on the limits of contracting as compared with organizational incentives. Incentive contracts with suppliers have the advantage of competition between suppliers and greater ease of adjustment. Incentive contracts within the organization have the advantage of greater ease of monitoring. However, the company must contract with many individual employees and coordinate their activities. This entails organizational costs but allows observation of individual performance. External contracts permit the company to monitor only final performance, leaving management of the task to the subcontractor.

Informational considerations are essential in the vertical integration decision. The company should vertically integrate, rather than turning to contracts and alliances, if it is able to leverage unique marketing and technological knowledge into upstream or downstream activities. A manufacturing company with knowledge of how to design essential parts will expand into specialized manufacturing. Similarly, knowledge of distribution may indicate the need to expand into wholesale or retailing. Companies may choose to vertically integrate as a means of learning about the company's markets or developing its technological base.

Informational considerations often call for vertical mergers and acquisitions. Ownership creates conditions for more complete sharing of information than could be achieved through contracts. If suppliers and distributors possess essential market knowledge, vertical integration is desirable as a means of information gathering. By sharing market and technical information with vertical partners, companies run the risk of informational opportunism. Subcontractors and distributors can use information from contractual relationships to engage in bypass competition. Ownership mitigates the risks from sharing proprietary information.

Mergers are desirable if the acquired company has scarce resources, whether patents or skilled personnel, whose value can be enhanced by the acquiring company. Alternatively, the company making the acquisition can bring better management practices or new markets and technical applications to the combined company. Mergers and acquisitions also avoid the duplication of capacity that might occur if the company were to choose to expand internally. By purchasing suppliers or distributors, companies avoid increasing upstream or downstream competition.

In some industries in which bypass competition is less of a concern, joint ventures are a good mechanism for information exchange. Vertical joint ventures are a good vehicle for developing new products, such as computer chips or capital equipment. Often, joint ventures are narrowly defined relative to the business of the partners.

Vertical alliances are desirable if a company's suppliers and distributors possess essential knowledge, and they in turn can benefit from the company's knowledge. Vertical alliances have the advantage of flexibility. The company can vary its distributors as market conditions change. Suppliers can be changed as the company's input requirements and technology evolve.

Vertical alliances are means of developing supplier and distributor networks. The Japanese vertical keiretsu illustrates the benefits of stable, long-term relationships. These create incentives for manufacturers to share market and technical information with their parts producers. Distributors have an incentive to share sales information and to maintain service quality.

Speed

Winning the market is a process of successive leadership, with new companies continually rising to prominence, providing customers with better value, novel products, and creative services. The key to leapfrogging opponents is to increase the rate of innovation. Success depends to a great extent on beating competitors to market with a better production process or an inventive product. A faster market response time leads to products that more closely approximate customer needs. The question is how to boost innovation.

Companies seeking to increase their rate of innovation can pursue both organizational and market network approaches. Targeted investment in R&D and product design accelerates innovation and heightens market responsiveness. Companies can increase their rate of innovation by contracting with independent labs and purchasing technology licenses. Alliances with other companies through R&D joint ventures allow the costs and benefits of R&D to be shared. Companies can enhance their innovative performance through mergers with companies that can provide needed skills.

To increase the expected rate of innovation, companies can grow their R&D by increased investment in equipment and research facilities and by hiring skilled personnel. The likelihood of completing a project by a given date can be increased by adding specialized equipment and scientists and engineers. Companies can increase innovation as well as productivity through training. Companies like General Electric, U.S. Robotics, and Motorola incur training expenditures that are above 4% in proportion to payroll; Motorola established a course on how to reduce product development cycle time.[32] Companies continually strive for increased efficiency in the R&D process.

Ford Motor Company increased its rate of new product introductions with a new or substantially updated model every three months through 1995. Its largest R&D project was the $6 billion dollar world car named Mondeo, which sells in the U.S. as the Ford Contour and the Mercury Mystique. That amount is double what the company spent developing the successful Taurus.[33] The project took eight years from beginning to sales of the cars in the U.S., longer than many product cycles. *Fortune* called the Mondeo "clearly the biggest, most complex global car project ever attempted." The project included the design of two new powertrains (engines and transmissions). Economies of scope were achieved by combining the design of both the American and European models. According to then chairman of Ford Europe, Jacques Nasser, this made more efficient use of scarce product development engineers.[34] The development team was truly international with the V-6 engine, automatic transmission, heating, and air conditioning designed in Detroit, the interior, steering, suspension, electronics, and four-cylinder engine designed near London, and the structural engineering in Cologne.[35]

Yet, just like dry wells in the oil industry, costly projects often fail to yield results. Pharmaceutical companies investigate many preparations that never go to market. For the enterprise to be viable, the expected returns on the successful projects must exceed overall R&D costs for all projects. The payoffs from R&D are often substantially delayed. The costs of R&D are paid up front, and the future benefits are discounted. R&D expenditures by biotechnology companies such as Chiron Corp., Biogen, or Genentech exceed half of sales.

Choosing the level of expenditures in R&D is a difficult decision for managers because it represents investment in future markets. Moreover, the outcomes of R&D are by their very nature unknown and unpredictable. If the timing and type of outcomes were known in advance, they would not be innovations. Thus, the investment decision is fundamentally different from constructing a new plant to expand capacity, with its attendant cost and demand uncertainty. An R&D program should produce surprises.

It is easy to be misled by predictions of the rate and direction of innovation. An example of a successful forecast is Moore's Law, named after Intel Chairman Gordon E. Moore, who predicted in the mid-1960s that computer chips would quadruple their number of transistors every three years, although even that prediction is being surpassed. For a dozen generations of chips, there has been a quadrupling of the capacity of dynamic random access chips (DRAMs) and growth of four or five times in the performance of microprocessors every three years. These gains are achieved by reducing the size of the transistor circuits etched in silicon by 10% per year. A Pentium microprocessor offers the processing power of a 1988 Cray Y-MP supercomputer. The Semiconductor Industry Association projected that the 16-megabit DRAM chip that became available in 1993 would continue to double its capacity every three years, reaching 16 gigabits in the year 2008, the equivalent of eight sets of Encyclopedia Britannicas. The transistors will shrink to only 0.10 microns thick. The microprocessor speed, at 150 megahertz by 1993, will increase to 700 megahertz by 2008, far exceeding current mainframes.[36] This growth in processing power is making possible the creation of personal supercomputers with new abilities for learning, speech and pattern recognition, and artificial intelligence.

These projections presume an averaging of the delays and quantum leaps that characterize the innovative process. For example, there is the crucial assumption that the 4-gigabit limits of current lithography using UV light will be surmounted by other methods such as the use of electron beams and other speculative technologies. Even if technically feasible, the cost of achieving the projections may be prohibitive; the current cost of a wafer factory is over $1 billion.[37] And there may be fundamental changes in production methods. For example, *Business Week* reports that Texas Instruments has developed a $30 million factory with a faster cycle time that matches the productivity of a current wafer factory, essentially a minimill for chips.[38] The design of chips may change in a fundamental way, perhaps using new materials or changing from electrical to optical transistors. Finally, there may be other solutions to the problem of supplying memory and computing power, for example, by providing them through computer networks rather than only through chips housed in unconnected boxes.

Growth of the company's R&D efforts is indicated if it has particular skills that can be applied or developed further. In-house R&D also has the advantage of being precisely targeted toward the company's specific needs. If these benefits cannot be realized, companies can enhance their R&D capabilities by associating with universities and independent research labs.

The company's R&D efforts can be enhanced by close collaboration with suppliers and customers. Eric von Hippel questions the common assumption that product innovations are always made by product manufacturers. Instead, he shows that the functional source of innovations can often be customers or suppliers. For example, he examines specialized scientific instruments—the gas chromatograph, nuclear magnetic resonance spectrometer, ultraviolet spectrometer, and transmission electron microscope—and finds that most innovations are created by users. Alternatively, most of the innovations in process machines used in electric wire and cable termination are not due to the manufacturers of the machines, but rather to the suppliers of connectors.[39] These observations suggest that customers or suppliers can be an important source of accelerated innovation.

Many innovations can be licensed by developers lacking the manufacturing and marketing capabilities. Pharmaceutical companies outsource R&D by contracting with biotechnology companies. For example, the best-selling diagnostic test in the U.S. is a blood test for hepatitis C marketed to hospitals and blood banks by Johnson & Johnson and Abbott Laboratories. Johnson & Johnson receives a royalty from Abbott and splits its profits and the royalty with Chiron Corp, the developer of the test.[40] Companies like J&J are technological intermediaries, earning above-market returns from making markets for innovations.

Research consortiums provide a means of reducing the costs of R&D duplication and costly racing to be first. A consortium yields results that can diffuse immediately without the need to copy or reverse engineer rival innovations. It achieves economies of scale and makes efficient use of scarce scientific and engineering talent. Consortiums also have the advantage of being isolated from short-term pressures within the company to develop greater basic research. On the other hand, they are focused on a specific set of industry problems and therefore are better positioned to develop useful solutions than is a general research lab. Consortiums benefit from public subsidies. Of course, R&D consortiums are no panacea; they are as subject to free riding and disagreements as any partnership. The partners must each receive a gain in information and reduced costs that outweighs the competitive advantages of homegrown innovation. The partners must also discern that rivals do not receive an advantage through cooperation that improves their relative market position in comparison to independent R&D.

IBM worked on a network of technology alliances in the early 1990s. For example, it collaborated with Toshiba to make large flat-panel color computer screens. The company designed microprocessors in Austin, Texas with Motorola, Apple, and Groupe Bull to create chips based on reduced instruction set computing. It worked with Siemens and Toshiba to develop 256-megabit memory chips. IBM played a key role in forming the Sematech research consortium.

Research consortiums can be particularly important as a competitive response to the formation of rival consortia, as is the case in the HDTV battle between three alliances: Zenith Electronics and AT&T; General Instruments and M.I.T.; and Thomson Consumer Electronics, Philips Electronics, Sarnoff Research Center, and NBC. It should be noted that the first two groups entered into cross-licensing arrangements to mitigate the effects of racing.

General Motors, Ford, and Chrysler have formed 12 research consortia, on electric vehicle batteries, wiring, auto safety, and parts recycling.[41] Hewlett-Packard and Canon have a long-standing partnership in printers, with Canon providing the printer engines and Hewlett-Packard providing software, control technology, and distribution.

Informal industry alliances are mechanisms for increasing innovative speed. Von Hippel observes that informal proprietary know-how trading can occur even among competitors. He notes that among U.S. steel minimills this occurs through "an informal trading network that develops between engineers having common professional interests."[42] Minimills produce steel from scrap that is melted in an electric arc furnace, cast in continuous casters, and rolled into the desired shapes. Von Hippel considers the four largest firms, Chaparral, Florida Steel, Northstar, and Nucor, and another seven smaller companies. He observes that technical know-how about the steelmaking process is of value to the firms and that technical abilities vary across them. He characterizes informal trading as a means of reducing transaction costs because it is an "inexpensive, flexible form of cross licensing."[43]

Mergers provide an effective means of acquiring R&D capabilities and transferring technological knowledge. As I have already emphasized, ownership can provide greater incentive for information sharing than can be achieved contractually, as a consequence of information opportunism and the difficulty in writing contracts based on the outcome of research projects. Mergers permit the company to rapidly expand its R&D scale and scope. R&D can be subject to racing as companies compete to obtain patents or to be the first to market. Mergers can alleviate the overinvestment associated with racing. Mergers allow companies to rationalize their research efforts, eliminating unnecessary duplication. In addition, the risk of imitation and diffusion can be reduced. Vertical mergers allow companies to combine basic research knowledge with product development skills. This is a concern for companies that have found their basic research brought to market by others without sharing in the economic returns.

The preceding discussion shows that there are many ways to increase innovation. Companies can create innovative products and processes by mixing the basic options. Companies can increase speed as well as all the other boundaries by growing both their organizations and their market networks. However, there are limits to the formation of alliances and networks. The company can become overextended, focusing on empire building rather than linking suppliers and customers. The discussion in the next section of the strategic moves of the software company Novell provides a cautionary tale that illustrates how investment, joint ventures, alliances, and mergers and acquisitions can expand the company's boundaries without yielding strategic benefits.

Novell and "Coopetition"

In 1982, a small personal computer maker called Novell Data Systems was close to going out of business.[44] A group of programmers was at work on a network operating system. One of its features was that it allowed PCs to share a disk or a printer. The company could not even afford a booth at the Comdex industry trade show in Las Vegas. So the programmers, led by Drew Major, rented a hotel room to exhibit their software. Ray Noorda, an electrical engineer born and raised in Utah, who happened to stop by the hotel room, joined the company as its president. Major was to become the company's chief scientist.

Noorda began by halting hardware production to focus on software. He made a series of acquisitions and alliances to grow the company. Noorda called Novell's business philosophy "coopetition."[45] The growth strategy initially proved successful as acquired companies brought new technology to Novell. Ultimately, the acquisition strategy proved less successful as the company stumbled in its attempts to meet Microsoft head-on.

Novell Inc. prospered in the booming network software market, and its Netware software reached 85% of the market. How did Novell rise, phoenixlike, from a near failure, even challenging the software giant Microsoft in the network market? What are the general lessons for winning the market? The initial success of Novell illustrates the tremendous value of building market networks and working with customers, competitors, and suppliers. The company's eventual problems outline the limits of the strategy.

Ray Noorda explained his evolving strategy as follows:

> We always realized that the only differential value we had was in the software. To begin with our aim was Netware somewhere; just get it sold. Then it was Netware everywhere, distribute it broadly. Then, we said it has to be Netware anywhere, so we'll sell it through a lot of O.E.M.'s [original equipment manufacturers]. Now, we say it has to be almost invisible, so people buy it out of necessity—Netware underware.

In April of 1994, Robert J. Frankenberg moved from Hewlett-Packard, where he had built the software and network business, to become president and CEO of Novell, with Ray Noorda remaining as chairman of the board. Frankenberg observed that "no other company has the combination of network market presence, technology resources and customer and channel relationships that Novell has," adding, "network software will transform every aspect of information systems."[46]

What began as a program for PCs to share peripheral equipment such as printers was the beginning of software that allows PCs to be linked with each other and with department-level minicomputers and mainframe computers. Netware accommodates not only IBM-compatible computers, but also Apple's Macintosh and Unix-based computers such as Sun workstations. While almost universal compatibility is a first step in building alliances, Novell made a number of key moves in distribution.

Novell benefited from having the right product focus at the right time, namely network software, but also earned returns from crafting a market network. The company distinguished five types of partnerships:

■ Distribution

■ Systems

■ Service and Support

■ Development

■ Application

Novell built a vast set of market relationships in each of these areas.

In *distribution*, Novell pursued a multichannel strategy, working with a variety of resellers. First, Netware was sold through more than 13,000 independent distributors, called value-added resellers (VARs). The VARs, such as CompUSA, Egghead Software, and Anderson Consulting, provide training, information, and network installation. In Europe, Asia, and Latin America, Novell sells through authorized distributors who sell to retail sellers. Novell also enlisted competitors as sellers of Netware by leaving gaps in its product line that were filled by other software companies who marketed the operating system along with their software. Therefore, Novell chose to rely on contracts rather than building a large sales organization.

Novell partnered with companies that have complementary hardware and software *systems* including IBM, DEC, and Hewlett-Packard and system integrators such as Memorex Telex, Electronic Data Systems, and others. Novell worked with third-party service vendors to supplement its own *service* personnel and those of its resellers. Thus, it contracted out for service as well.

Novell relied on *development* partners to aid in the development of new products, combining its own network expertise with the partner's product expertise to speed up innovation. Finally, Novell's *application* partners provided marketing and software support for end users.

What is perhaps most interesting about the Novell approach is the use of strategic alliances and acquisitions (see Table 6-8). The acquisitions served as a means of acquiring information about markets and technology and provided a way of developing new products. Joint ventures allowed Novell to invest in and acquire emerging technology.

Novell acquired distributors Microsource and Cache Data to expand its markets. It then built technological connections to IBM, Macintosh, and Unix through a series of acquisitions. At the same time, Novell built up its information about databases and networking through joint ventures, including Softcraft (database/programming tools), Excelan (Unix and Macintosh networking products), DaVinci Systems, (e-mail), and Cooperative Solutions (transaction processing).

Novell earned almost half of its revenues abroad. It formed Novell Japan together with partners Canon, Fujitsu, NEC, Sony, Toshiba, and Softbank. It was able to leverage its 54% share to achieve substantial market acceptance in Japan. It also formed an alliance with Onward Technologies in India to develop Netware products.

Through its acquisitions of Software Transformation, Inc. and Serius Corporation, Novell built its Appware systems group to provide tools to developers of applications for networks. The objective was to develop software tools that are "portable across different operating systems, including Unixware, Apple Macintosh, DOS, and Microsoft Windows."

To take on Microsoft simultaneously in many markets, Novell set out to build expertise in word processing, spreadsheets, and other applications software. By purchasing WordPerfect Corporation, Novell gained access to a market with software sales of $700 million a year and word processing expertise. Combined with its purchase of Borland International's QuattroPro spreadsheet business, this allowed Novell to offer a software suite that connected to Netware and Unixware while competing with other software suites, particularly Microsoft Office.

Novell was divided into three business units. The Netware Systems Group developed server-based network operating system products including file and print, communications, messaging, database, multimedia, and network and systems management. The AppWare Systems Group aided in the development of network-based distributed applications. These are tools for use by software developers of network applications, libraries for use by commercial software vendors, transaction processing technology for companies, and operating systems and network access software for connecting into local area networks. Finally, the Unix Systems Group linked Netware services to the open industry standard Unix software through an operating system for deploying applications across networks.[47]

An important market for Novell is "managing and sharing information in workgroups."[48] The company's Groupware software is designed to provide a wide range of foundation services including information transport, directories, monitoring, and database management. In addition, workgroup applications include messaging, directories of personnel, monitoring of projects, document handling, electronic forms, and tools for managing teamwork. Groupware is intended to interconnect to as many operating systems as possible, while connecting users to all potential gateways including electronic networks, on-line services, messaging, voice, paging, and fax.

The Novell strategy differed from those of competitors Microsoft and Lotus. Microsoft's strategy for its client and server architecture was based around Windows as its principal system platform. Lotus, in contrast, based its workgroup architecture on the proprietary database technology of Lotus Notes. Novell characterized its strategy as centered around documents and information. It is both platform-independent and database-independent, to "allow workgroup computing to work interchangeably across multiple operating system platforms and across multiple information

Table 6-8.

NOVELL INC.'S ACQUISITIONS AND STRATEGIC ALLIANCES

Year	Acquisition	Alliances and joint ventures
1985	Microsource (distributor)	
1986	Cache Data Products (distributor)	
	Santa Clara Systems (disk tape drives)	
1987	CXI (connections to IBM mainframes)	Softcraft (database/programming tools)
1988	Dayna Communications (connections to Macintosh)	Dayna Communications (Macintosh connectivity software)
1989		Excelan (Unix, Macintosh networking products)
1990	Indisy Software (IBM messaging)	Novell Japan (Canon, Fujitsu, NEC, Sony, Toshiba, Softbank)
		Onward Novell Software India
		Gupta Technologies (database, software)
1991	Digital Research (operating system developer)	DaVinci Systems (messaging software)
		Cooperative Solutions (transaction processing)
		Univel (Unix Systems)
		Serius Corp.(writing programs)
1992	International Business Software (virtual server	Reach Software (workflow automation software)

Table 6-8. (continued)

NOVELL INC.'S ACQUISITIONS AND STRATEGIC ALLIANCES

Year	Acquisition	Alliances and joint ventures
1992 (cont)	Annatek Systems, Inc (automated software distribution services)	
1993	Unix Systems Laboratories (Unix developer)	Unix alliance (Digital Equipment, Hewlett-Packard, IBM, SCO, Sun Microsystems, X/Open; standards organization, 30 Unix vendors)
	Univel (Unix Systems)	Oracle partnership (OracleWare System) IBM (Netware for OS/2)
	Software Transformation, Inc. (Appware systems group)	Lotus Development Corp. (Lotus Notes on NetWare)
	Serius Corporation (Appware systems group)	Hyperdesk (object-based services interface)
	Fluent (multimedia software products)	Compaq (Enterprise Computing Partnership for joint marketing and sales)
1994	WordPerfect Corp. (word processing)	Geoworks (operating system for small computing devices)
	Borland International's QuattroPro (spreadsheet)	National Semiconductor (strategic agreement to develop and brand hardware and software products)

Sources: Based on information from Novell public documents and company reports.

stores."[49] The "competitive objective is to see its market-leading system services become the infrastructure for the next generation of networked
applications."[50]

Within two years of acquiring Wordperfect, Novell was forced to
sell the WordPerfect word processing program, the QuattroPro spreadsheet,
and the Perfect Office Application Suite for a small fraction of what it had
paid. WordPerfect had lost market share to Microsoft's Word, Microsoft
Office dominated the market for software bundles called suites, and the
QuattroPro spreadsheet lost out to Microsoft Excel and IBM's Lotus 1-2-3.
Novell had not sold the programs effectively through its marketing channel of value-added resellers. A joint marketing agreement with Borland
failed to sell QuattroPro effectively.[51]

Novell was later to encounter problems in adapting its software to
Internet applications. Its problems highlight the perils of building large
organizations rather than expanding *market networks*. The problems it
encountered with applications software stemmed from the fact that it
relied on its existing distribution networks, instead of creating market networks appropriate to the applications software markets. Value-added
resellers were not well suited to developing customer markets for the software, so the company was at a disadvantage in competing with Microsoft's
distribution networks. The coopetition approach was not a sufficient strategy to compete with Microsoft in the desktop applications market.
Acquiring companies provided technology, but technology alone could not
substitute for the need to develop flexible market networks. Ultimately,
Novell shed its desktop applications to focus on the battle for the network
computing market.

Endnotes

1. This framework applies even if the firm does not participate in all types of upstream markets. The firm may self-finance from retained earnings. It may manufacture many of its
productive inputs. It may rely heavily on its own research and development.

2. The pathbreaking work of Michael E. Porter has revolutionized the field of management
strategy. Porter's books have made major contributions to the study and practice of man-
agement strategy; see *Competitive Strategy: Techniques for Analyzing Industries and
Competitors*, New York: Free Press, 1980; *Competitive Advantage: Creating and Sustaining
Superior Performance*, New York: Free Press, 1985; and *The Competitive Advantage of Nations*,
New York: Free Press, 1990.

3. The resource-based approach is surveyed in J. Mahoney and J. R. Pandian, "The Resource-
Based View within the Conversation of Strategic Management," *Strategic Management
Journal*, 13, 1992, pp. 363–380. See also C. K. Prahalad and G. Hamel, "The Core
Competence of the Corporation," *Harvard Business Review*, May-June, 1990, pp. 79–91; and
George Stalk, P. Evans, and L. E. Shulman, "Competing on Capabilities: The New Rules of
Corporate Strategy," *Harvard Business Review*, March-April, 1992, pp. 57–69.

4. See Prahalad and Hamel, "The Core Competence," and Stalk, et al., "Competing on
Capabilities."

5. Economic profit refers to the earnings of the firms over and above the cost of productive factors including a competitive return to capital. This differs from accounting definitions of profit.

6. This is explained in R. E. Calem, "Taking the Worry Out of Paying with Plastic," *New York Times*, November 14, 1993, p. 9.

7. See *Fortune*, May 30, 1994.

8. Shawn Tully, "The Modular Corporation," *Fortune*, February 8, 1993, p. 106.

9. Information about Comdisco is obtained from publicly available materials provided by the company.

10. Ronald Coase, writing in 1937, introduced the concept of transaction costs which he defined as the "cost of using the pricing mechanism," including searching for prices, negotiation of trades, and the cost of specifying contractual contingencies. He asserted that activities are located within the firm if an entrepreneur, by exercising authority, saves the costs of using markets. See Ronald M. Coase, "The Nature of the Firm," *Economica*, 4, 1937, pp. 386–405.

11. In comparing contracts with vertical integration, Oliver E. Williamson emphasizes costly contract contingencies, performance problems in contracts due to monitoring costs, and the possibility of technological spillovers in contracts. See Oliver E. Williamson, *Markets and Hierarchies*, New York: Free Press, 1975. Williamson states that, "were it possible to write and enforce a complex contingent claims contract between blast furnace and rolling mill stages, the integration of these activities, for thermal purposes would be unnecessary."

12. Oliver E. Williamson argues that from the transaction cost perspective "economizing is more fundamental than strategizing." See Oliver E. Williamson, "Strategizing, Economizing, and Economic Organization," *Strategic Management Journal*, 12, 1991, pp. 75–94, at p. 76. He further maintains that "strategic ploys are sometimes used to disguise economizing weaknesses" and suggests that managers should "get and keep priorities straight" by focusing on costs, contractual relations, and organization, rather than on "the beguiling language of strategizing—warfare, credible threats, and the like." While I agree that economizing is important, I believe that it is an integral part of the strategy process, and that competitive strategy considerations are also very important.

13. See David J. Teece, "Economies of Scope and the Scope of the Enterprise," *Journal of Economic Behavior and Organization*, 1, 1980, pp. 223–247, and "Towards an Economic Theory of the Multiproduct Firm," *Journal of Economic Behavior and Organization*, 3, 1982, pp. 39–63.

14. Oliver E. Williamson, *Markets and Hierarchies*, p. 98.

15. Jim Manzi, "Computer Keiretsu: Japanese Idea, U.S. Style," *New York Times*, February 18, 1994, p. 15.

16. See K. Miyashita and D. W. Russell, *Keiretsu: Inside the Hidden Japanese Conglomerates*, New York: McGraw-Hill, 1994.

17. As noted by Miyashita and Russell in *Keiretsu*, the 189 companies account for 15% of total sales for Japanese companies. They quote a study by the Japanese Fair Trade Commission of companies in which core companies or their subsidiaries hold at least a 10% share. This group of companies includes 12,000 companies, accounting for over one-fourth of total assets and sales of Japanese companies. The authors observe that the study vastly underestimates the number of companies involved and thus misses much of the total sales picture, suggesting that the number may be one-third or more of the aggregate sales of Japanese companies.

18. See Miyashita and Russell, *Keiretsu*.

19. See Paul Sheard, "The Main Bank System and Corporate Monitoring and Control in Japan," *Journal of Economic Behavior and Organization*, 11, 1989. See also Paul Sheard, "The Japanese General Trading Company as an Aspect of Interfirm Risk Sharing," *Journal of the Japanese and International Economies*, 3, 1989, pp. 308–322.

20. See Miyashita and Russell, *Keiretsu.*
21. See T. Ozawa, "Japanese Multinationals and 1992," in B. Burgenmeier and J. L. Mucchielli, eds., *Multinationals and Europe 1992: Strategies for the Future,* London: Routledge, 1991, pp. 135–154, at p. 147.
22. Ibid, p. 148.
23. The information on the Toyota Keiretsu is from Miyashita and Russell, *Keiretsu,* pp. 135–137.
24. James Bennet, "Detroit Struggles to Learn Another Lesson from Japan," *New York Times,* June 19, 1994 Section 3, p. 5.
25. Kathryn Jones, "A Move Along the Food Chain," *New York Times,* July 2, 1994, p. C1.
26. Ibid.
27. See J. Bleeke and D. Ernst, *Collaborating to Compete,* New York: John Wiley & Sons, 1993, p. 7.
28. The list of companies and their contributions is drawn from Krause Reinhardt, "Oracle Serves Multimedia Feast as Vendors Commit," *Electronic News,* 40, February 21, 1994, p. 36.
29. Kim Nash, "Oracle, Novell Pact Aids DBMS on Networks," *Computer World,* 27, December 6, 1993, p. 51.
30. Shawn Tully, "The Modular Corporation," *Fortune,* February 8, 1993, pp. 106–113, emphasis in original.
31. Ibid, p. 112.
32. "Motorola: Training for the Millennium," *Business Week,* March 28, 1994.
33. Alex Taylor III, "Ford's $6 Billion Baby," *Fortune,* June 28, 1993, p. 76.
34. Robert L. Simison and Neal Templin, "Ford Is Turning Heads with $6 Billion Cost to Design World Car," *Wall Street Journal,* March 23, 1993, p. 1.
35. Alex Taylor III, "Ford's $6 Billion Baby."
36. "Wonder Chips, How They'll Make Computing Power Ultrafast and Ultracheap," *Business Week,* July 4, 1994, pp. 86–92.
37. Ibid.
38. Ibid.
39. See Eric von Hippel, *The Sources of Innovation,* New York: Oxford University Press, 1988.
40. Shawn Tully, "The Modular Corporation," p. 113.
41. "What's the Word in the Lab? Collaborate," *Business Week,* June 27, 1994, pp. 78–80.
42. Von Hippel, *The Sources of Innovation.*
43. Ibid, p. 89.
44. The account here is based on Lawrence M. Fisher, "Preaching Love Thy Competitor," *New York Times,* March 29, 1992, Sec. 3, p.1.
45. Ibid.
46. Novell Press Release, April 1994.
47. The description of the three business units is based on Novell's 1993 Form 10-K.
48. "Novell-WordPerfect Workgroup Computing Strategy: An Introduction to Novell GroupWare," Document Number 500-02, April 5, 1994.
49. Ibid.
50. Novell Fiscal Highlights, 1994.
51. Lawrence M. Fisher, "Novell Agrees to Sell WordPerfect Division," *New York Times,* February 1, 1996, p. C.8.

MARKET STRATEGIES

7
ENTRY STRATEGIES

It has been said, "If you build a better mousetrap, the world will beat a path to your door." I believe that if you make paths that bring the world to your door, you can build a better mousetrap. Product design and innovation are crucial, of course. But access to customers helps the firm to determine what products they need, and access to technology enhances product design. Market pathways to suppliers and customers are critical to business performance.

A company wins its markets when customers and suppliers look to that company as their primary source (or outlet) for products and services. They are willing to trust the company with product procurement and distribution. For the firm to gain this position of trust it must provide market services more effectively and more efficiently than its competitors. This involves offering more than low prices and better products, although these can be very important. Convenience is an essential part of the package.

Competitors are not simply companies offering similar products. The company competes with alternative market mechanisms, whether decentralized direct exchange between buyers and sellers, merchant activities provided by brokers and marketers, or different types of stores. Companies that save on transaction costs will win their markets.

Entry strategies take advantage of the company's ability to create and manage markets. This opens up a wide range of strategic alternatives and allows the company to develop its market relationships and profit from its unique knowledge. The MAIN framework provides a novel approach to competition in which the company looks across its markets from the supplier side to the customer side. This expansive panorama suggests ways to out-think competitors who are rooted in traditional customer–market maneuvers and have no perspective on the business as a whole. I do not offer an exhaustive list of strategies. I hope instead to provide companies with a method of arriving at strategies that are best suited to the types of markets in which they operate.

Corporate strategy focuses on the question of what markets to enter or exit. These decisions shape the organization and determine its goals. Entering new markets is not as simple as comparing the expected revenues from entry with the investment costs of setting up new operations and then forging ahead. Rather, entry is a strategic problem. In choosing to enter, the firm's managers must anticipate competitive maneuvers. They should prepare for responses from incumbent firms and challenges from other entrants.

If entrants face costs that are not present for incumbent firms, there is a strategic difference between incumbents and entrants known as *barriers to entry*.[1] One of the key strategic aspects of entry or expansion is the need to make irreversible investments in setting up new operations, including production facilities, marketing, market research, and R&D. Irreversible investments are also known as sunk costs. Sunk costs can be a barrier to entry if entrants need to make irreversible investments in capacity, while incumbents have already incurred these costs.[2] However, there are strategies for addressing and overcoming this barrier.

If an incumbent has already incurred the sunk cost of facilities but entrants have not, this can confer a competitive advantage on the incumbent. The incumbent need only price to recover operating expenses and incremental capital expenditures. An entrant, in contrast, must anticipate earnings exceeding operating costs, incremental investment, and the irreversible costs of establishing its facilities, before it will decide to enter.

With $100 in sunk costs and $2 in operating costs, the incumbent need only earn $2 to stay in business, while a new entrant must anticipate $102 in revenue to justify entry. The incumbent may threaten a price war if another company enters. Such threats are hardly credible. After the entrant has invested in facilities, it is on the same footing as the incumbent firm.

Of course, price wars do occur, and companies do sometimes lose money and exit from industries as a result. Price wars are part of the everyday struggle of companies seeking to win markets. They can result from excess capacity in the industry or from the belief of competitors that they each have what it takes to serve customers at the least cost. If the irreversible investment is embodied in productive capacity, that capacity often stays in service even if the firm that originally constructed the capacity exits the industry. Duplication of investment and either excess or insufficient capacity can occur as a consequence of uncertainty regarding costs, technology, or market demand. When entry creates excess capacity, it often leads to vigorous competition and industry shakeouts that reduce the profits of incumbents.

All competitive markets involve some degree of irreversible investment whether in capital equipment, marketing, or research and development. Entrants commit capital resources in markets where they expect to earn competitive returns on their investments. The differences between the capital investments of incumbents and those of potential entrants may simply be a matter of timing.

Generally, the need to sink cost is not an insurmountable barrier to the entry of new competitors. An entrant with greater cost efficiencies than established companies is well advised to enter a market. An entrant with products that deliver sufficiently greater value to the customer than the offerings of established companies is not deterred by the need to sink costs. Thus, better organization and superior products allow the entrant to compete effectively against the incumbent and recover the set-up costs.

Entrants can reduce the risk associated with making investment commitments in a variety of ways, including contracting with customers before irreversible investments are made and entering into joint ventures or mergers with incumbents. So sunk costs are not a significant barrier to entry when entrants can make contracts with customers: The success of this strategy depends on the costs of contracting. Sunk costs do not deter entry as a general rule, even though some entrants who have high contracting costs may be deterred: By achieving efficiencies in contracting, firms can surmount the sunk cost entry barrier.

Effective entry thus requires efficient performance relative to incumbents: operating efficiencies, differentiated products, or lower transaction costs. Entrants concentrate their best efforts on incumbents' weak points, serving market segments where they create the greatest value added. This suggests that like incumbents, entrants should not spread themselves too thin.

To challenge entrenched incumbents, it is necessary for the entrant to anticipate rival moves. What will be the future strategy of the incumbents? The entrant cannot base the decision to enter on the incumbent's profitability, only on the profits that the entrant will make in competition with the incumbent. The incumbent's performance provides useful information about the costs and earnings of an operating company, yet the entrant must anticipate its own costs and earnings. Moreover, the incumbent will not stand still in the face of entry. Incumbents will anticipate entry and attempt preemptive strategies, such as price cuts or new product introductions. Entrants must make their entry plans in anticipation of these strategic moves. The entrants must even plan ahead for challenges they will face from future entrants.

So, entry strategies involve much more than surmounting entry barriers. The key steps are determining the economic opportunities the target market represents and addressing those opportunities in new ways. Using the MAIN framework (market making, arbitrage, intermediation, and networking) as the building blocks, companies can devise innovative entry strategies. In this chapter, I introduce four entry strategies:

- Go-between
- Bring-together
- Bypass
- Connect

Companies using the *go-between* strategy interpose themselves between sellers and buyers, offering market-making and other services that improve on their direct transactions. The *bring-together* strategy involves offering the products of different suppliers to the same customers, giving them the benefits of one-stop shopping and yielding economies of scale and scope. Companies use the *bypass* strategy to go around their distributors or other intermediaries to get closer to their customers, or to go around their wholesale suppliers to get closer to their initial suppliers, thus rationalizing distribution. Finally, companies use the *connect* strategy to integrate or contract with upstream suppliers or downstream distributors, yielding economies of sequence and improved coordination as means of forming alliances against competitors.

These four entry strategies are based on a broader conception of the firm as more than a product market competitor. Instead, they are founded on a view of the firm as an organizer and manager of markets. Market entry entails more than simply the decision to provide a product to a new set of buyers. The firm targets both suppliers and buyers, so its competitive strategy must improve upon existing market mechanisms.

Go-Between

The go-between strategy requires interposing the company between buyers and sellers who are currently transacting. For the strategy to be effective, the company must improve on the existing transaction costs that buyers and sellers face. The go-between strategy competes with the direct transactions between buyers and sellers (see Figure 7-1). To successfully implement the go-between strategy, companies carry out market making, arbitrage, intermediation, and networking. These activities must be more effective than the direct transactions they replace.

Figure 7-1.
THE GO-BETWEEN STRATEGY

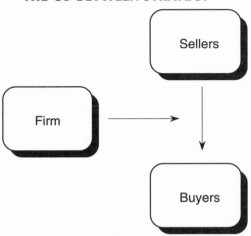

An important part of the go-between strategy is to get close to the customer. The go-between creates a new marketing channel. The closer the company gets to customers, the wider the range of upstream suppliers that the company controls. This means either completely eliminating competing channels or converting companies to being your supplier that were formerly your competitors. By controlling access to the customer, the go-between is in a position to receive economic rents from suppliers seeking to sell their products. This does not mean that the company is a bottleneck receiving monopoly rents. The go-between position is achieved by performing transactions more efficiently. The economic rents earned by the company are the returns to innovations in transactions.

The company pursuing the go-between strategy begins by identifying existing market transactions between buyers and sellers. Then the company surveys its own resources and skills and attempts to create innovative ways to carry out the transactions at less cost. It then seeks to convert existing sellers into suppliers and existing buyers into customers.

The go-between strategy is multifaceted. First, if there are many buyers and sellers and they have high search costs, the go-between can create a central place of exchange, saving the costs of search. Suppliers save on marketing and distribution costs, and customers benefit from convenience and lower time costs of shopping.

Second, the go-between handles the back-office transactions, keeping track of the paperwork for suppliers and for customers. By handling a greater volume of transactions, the firm achieves economies of scale in the back office. This lowers transaction costs for suppliers and customers, who then turn to the intermediary to manage their transactions.

The go-between strategy offers improved market information. If sellers and buyers relied on negotiation, the company offers the convenience of posted prices. The posted prices save on the time costs of bargaining and remove the inherent uncertainty in negotiation. Therefore, by clearly posting prices, the intermediary can attract customers and suppliers away from a high transaction cost market that involves bargaining.

The go-between strategy can create markets when it is costly for buyers to monitor the quality of products offered by sellers. With decentralized exchange, there can be variations in product quality. Consumers are uncertain about the efficacy of pharmaceuticals, the durability of appliances, or the quality of automobiles. Suppliers generally have better information about the products they offer than do their customers. The go-between can test products and certify product quality. A market for a good may fail to grow or even collapse entirely when product quality is difficult to observe. Consumers are unsure of product quality and as a result are only willing to pay for some average level of quality that represents their best guess about the quality they expect to receive. Because they are willing to pay less, high-quality suppliers, who tend to have higher costs than lower quality suppliers, may not be profitable and are driven from the market. This implies that only low-quality suppliers survive—bad products drive out the goods ones. Anticipating this, consumers will only purchase the product if they have a need for the lower quality version.

Product quality testing and certification yield returns for go-betweens. To some extent most retailers gather information about their products. The retailer's reputation is added to that of the manufacturer. Retailers thus obtain returns when they build a reputation for carrying high-quality products. Buyers and sellers both benefit by selling through the intermediary. The company has a greater incentive to invest in monitoring quality than does an individual buyer, since the intermediary buys more goods. In addition, the intermediary's incentive to report the quality of goods accurately stems from the returns to building a good reputation.[3]

The intermediary can have a greater incentive to test and certify products than its suppliers. A retail or wholesale intermediary can offer many different products for sale, and consumers can rely on the reputation of the intermediary without having to investigate the many product suppliers. In particular, intermediaries can serve as guarantors of the product quality of their suppliers through warranties and contract terms.[4] In the case of the manufacturer, the manufacturer's brand name often conveys information to customers who then do not need to know the quality of components purchased by the manufacturer. In this way the manufacturer certifies the components included in its products. Since intermediaries handle the products of two or more suppliers, their incentives to sell a lower quality good differ from those of individual suppliers. The intermediary that sells a low-quality product suffers a loss of reputation and thus loses customers for all its other products.

The intermediary offers immediacy and other market-making services. By standing ready to buy and sell, the firm provides convenience to suppliers and customers. The intermediary smooths out the pattern of purchasing and sales by selling to many customers and buying from multiple suppliers, by price adjustment and inventory management. By consolidating transactions, the intermediary offers an advantage over direct exchange between buyers and sellers.

Auto Markets

Markets for automobiles, both new and used, are undergoing substantial changes. Companies are pursuing go-between strategies to supplant inefficient auto sellers and bring a wide range of intermediation services to the marketplace. Consolidation of the industry by reducing the number of dealerships should bring increased convenience and economies of scale. The number of car dealerships fell from 47,500 in 1951 to 22,400 in 1996 and promises to fall still further.[5] The go-between strategy is increasing the shakeout of auto dealers.

Many companies are pursuing the go-between strategy by interposing themselves between the consumer and traditional automobile dealers. For example, the Consumers Car Club provides brokerage services to auto buyers for a fee, negotiating the price and contract terms with auto dealers. CUC International's AutoVantage service for an annual fee provides its members with fixed quotes on autos from one of its network of 2,000 dealers. AutoVantage handles the process of searching for the auto dealers that have the vehicle the customer wants, informing the dealer of the desired options, and establishing the price. Warehouse clubs such as Wal-Mart's Sam's Club and PriceCostco pursue a similar go-between strategy. PriceCostco charges dealers a fee to be part of its network and the dealers offer fixed prices to warehouse club members.[6] Finally, dozens of Internet-based services such as Dealer's World provide access to networks of dealers and negotiate prices and options for their customers.

In each of these cases, the go-between creates a supplier network composed of existing dealers. Because the network of dealers offers all makes and models, customers have access to the full range of products. Customers benefit from lower prices and lower time costs of search. Because the go-between does the bargaining, customers pay fixed prices and avoid the time and stress of negotiation. The dealers benefit from the go-between's large customer base and its customer referrals. These referrals increase the dealers' sales volume without requiring additional marketing expenditures. The dealers' sales costs are likely to be lower in comparison with direct customer negotiation, since contracting with the go-between standardizes the transaction.

In the market for used cars, many car owners and buyers meet through want ads. Traditional used car dealers come between car owners who sell used cars and buyers of used cars. Car owners often trade in their used cars to new car dealers when buying a car. The new car dealers then resell the used cars through an affiliated or independent used car dealer. Rental agencies also provide a large source of used cars, selling them on to used car dealers.

A new type of used car dealer has entered the market by pursuing the go-between strategy. Used car superstores are coordinating the buyers and sellers of used cars. Circuit City established the Car-Max chain of used car dealerships to fill a gap. H. Wayne Huizenga, who created Blockbuster Entertainment Corp., launched Autonation USA, a chain of used car superstores. Two other entrants are CarChoice and United Auto Group.

The used car chains and other entrants have become new car dealers as well. According to *Business Week*,

> The dreaded auto showroom, with its gilded illusion and sweaty-palmed reality, is fast becoming an endangered piece of Americana. The tradition of smarmy salesmen, high-pressure tactics, and arbitrary pricing continued unchanged for decades following World War II. But now, the forces that have lately revolutionized the rest of retailing are about to transform the way we buy cars.[7]

The used and new car superstore chains are displacing traditional used and new car dealers. Some of the traditional dealers are exploring ways to cooperate while others are selling out to chains.

The used and new car superstores offer a number of ways to lower customer transaction costs. The stores are much larger than typical used-car dealers, offering customers a wider selection and one-stop shopping. Moreover, the stores sell multiple brands side by side, further reducing the costs of shopping. The chains have fixed prices and a no-haggling policy, thereby reducing transaction costs in comparison with traditional used car sales techniques. The superstores track inventory by computer, further simplifying transactions. Sales personnel are paid salaries instead of sales commissions, focusing their attention on service rather than bargaining. The stores have longer hours than traditional dealers and offer amenities such as child care and food.

While customers have taken to the superstores, the reaction of auto manufacturers is mixed. Some, like Chrysler, see an opportunity to improve sales through increased customer value delivered by the superstores. Others, like General Motors, are wary of the chains and are attempting to exercise greater control over their traditional dealer networks.

Figure 7-2.
THE BRING-TOGETHER STRATEGY

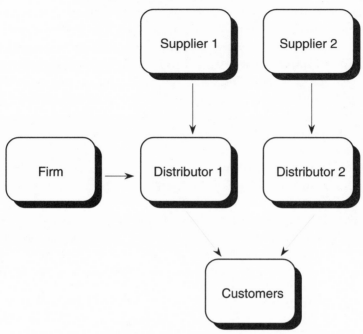

Bring-Together

The market strategy pursued by the automobile superstores has another important dimension: a bring-together strategy. Companies that follow this strategy compete with a fragmented distribution industry (see Figure 7-2). The firm consolidates the distribution by purchasing from both suppliers and reselling to final customers. The firm purchases from both supplier 1 and supplier 2, and competes with both distributor 1 and distributor 2. The firm can outperform the independent distributors by reaping increased efficiency from the bring-together strategy.

With many diverse sellers, the bring-together strategy offers a supermarket approach to distribution, selling a wide variety of products and services. As a distributor, the firm is an impartial promoter of all the suppliers, selecting offerings on the basis of customer demand for the products. Customers gain from one-stop shopping, choosing the best from a wide variety of products by comparison shopping at one central location. Customers that purchase multiple products also gain from the lower costs of putting together a market basket of goods and services. Thus, the bring-together firm has an advantage over competitors that rely on only a subset of suppliers and that handle only a few products or services.

The bring-together strategy allows the firm to achieve economies of scope by handling multiple products. The company saves on the overhead and other costs that multiple distributors would incur. This increased efficiency allows the company to lower prices relative to independent distributors. The bring-together strategy can be accomplished by a new entrant through substantial initial investment to provide a broad range of products and services, contracting with a wider range of suppliers or customers than competing firms. Entrants can merge with or acquire existing distributors to bring their markets together. Alternatively, the strategy can be carried out through targeting a market segment and diversifying the firm's offerings over time.

The returns to the bring-together strategy are evident in the growth of superstores and category killers. Book superstores such as Barnes & Noble bring together in one place the books offered by a host of specialty bookstores. By adding recorded music, Barnes & Noble attracts customers who are buying both books and music, competing with independent music stores. Blockbuster Video has expanded from video rentals to recorded music and video games. Electronic superstores such as Best Buy combine a variety of products, outperforming specialized stores selling computers, cameras, or stereos.

A company can pursue a bring-together strategy to enter into markets that have fragmented distribution sectors. The company can take advantage of economies of scale and scope to combine multiple products and services, outperforming specialized suppliers.

Charles Schwab

Discount broker Charles Schwab & Co. is the master of the go-between and bring-together strategies. To understand how the company operates it is useful to review some of the basics of investment and the intermediaries with whom Schwab competes.

The ultimate intermediary in securities is the stock market itself, where buyers and sellers of stock trade through specialists on the New York Stock Exchange or through dealers in the over-the-counter market. Individual investors must rely on brokers to trade in the stock market.

Everyone knows the first rule of investing: Don't put all your eggs in one basket. Stocks are risky, so the best way to invest is to diversify by holding a portfolio of financial assets including stocks. This is simple in principle, but very difficult to carry out in practice. A small investor would incur almost prohibitive transaction costs in trying to assemble a portfolio of assets that is large enough to diversify sufficiently.

The investor must incur the research costs to track the performance of companies in the portfolio and other companies that might be added in.

The investor must keep track of purchases and sales for investment planning and tax purposes. Individuals can purchase shares directly from companies. A broker can serve as a go-between, providing the individual investor with investment advice and management of investment records.

However, the broker does not fully solve the investor's problems. The individual investor still must monitor the contents of the portfolio. Moreover, the investor must evaluate and act on the broker's advice. In addition, the investor incurs brokerage fees every time a stock is purchased or sold, making it costly to adjust the portfolio to account for new information. It is still prohibitive to assemble a fully diversified portfolio of shares.

Enter the mutual fund. The mutual fund serves as a go-between, purchasing a portfolio of stocks. The investor need only buy shares in the mutual fund to have a portfolio with the same mix of stocks as the mutual fund. The mutual fund is able to earn returns as a go-between as a consequence of its economies of scale in gathering information about the companies whose shares it owns or may purchase. The mutual fund also achieves economies of scale in making trades since it buys and sells stocks in large blocks by aggregating the investments in the fund. Finally, the mutual fund realizes economies of scale and scope in record keeping, allowing it to provide investors with accurate and complete records of the fund's performance and other useful information. The mutual fund also supplies fund managers that pursue various investment philosophies in acquiring and divesting stocks.

Although the investor's transaction costs are lowered significantly by dealing with a mutual fund, the problem of diversification arises again if the investor wishes to purchase more than one mutual fund. Funds differ significantly. Some are centered in one economic sector, such as high-tech companies or transportation companies. Others are based on market indices, holding portfolios that mirror the stocks used to calculate the Dow Jones Industrial Average or the Standard and Poor's 500. Still others seek different combinations of risk and return, striving for income or growth. The individual investor must monitor the performance of a host of mutual funds, seek each fund out individually, and assemble a portfolio of funds.

This creates a role for another type of go-between, the mutual fund family. Companies such as Fidelity, Magellan, and Vanguard maintain a number of different mutual funds, so that an investor can easily assemble a portfolio of mutual funds and move money among them with relative ease. Yet even this innovation is not sufficient, particularly if the investor wants to purchase funds from different families.

Charles Schwab combined the ultimate in go-between and bring-together strategies with its creation of the mutual fund supermarket: a family of families. Through Schwab's Onesource, investors have access to a family of no-load mutual fund families. The funds themselves pay the fees for the transactions, instead of the investors paying Schwab directly. Through its Mutual Fund Marketplace, Schwab offers hundreds of additional no-load and low-load funds, but charges investors fees. Thus, Schwab becomes a fund retailer, and the funds it offers take the position of wholesale suppliers.

With a single account, the investor can choose among literally hundreds of mutual funds. The investor can easily move money across the funds purchased without withdrawing money from the account, providing flexibility and convenience and offering advantages for retirement accounts that hold money for a long period of time. The investor receives a single statement summarizing all account activity.

Schwab has created its own fund family and even funds of funds, which compete with the funds offered by other companies. It has dozens of its own funds, including securities funds, index funds, bond funds, and money market funds. For example, the company established the Schwab 1000 Fund, which is a no-load fund that attempts to match the performance of the Schwab 1000 index of stocks. Schwab also offers Onesource Portfolios, funds that invest in other mutual funds. The fund manager monitors the performance of hundreds of mutual funds and continually updates the fund mix in response to changing market conditions. One fund, called the Growth Allocation Fund, primarily focuses on securities funds, with some bond and money market funds added, while another, called the Balanced Allocation Fund, holds three-fifths securities funds.

While not offering advice, Schwab still offers plenty of information to investors. The most important information is simply in the lists of available mutual funds, which considerably reduce investor search costs. Moreover, investors can obtain printed information on individual companies or funds and some basic investment information from account managers. Schwab also works closely with thousands of independent investment advisers, who provide their customers with financial planning while using Schwab's back-office services to manage their customers' accounts. Thus, in the market segment of investors that seek advice, Schwab is an intermediary between the advisers and the financial markets. At the same time, Schwab is an intermediary between the advisers and their customers through a referral service called AdviserSource. Schwab receives fees from the independent advisers for referrals.

Schwab has garnered millions of customers to become the largest discount brokerage. With its mutual fund supermarket, the company is attracting still more investment assets. The company continues to expand by offering a broader range of investment services. Schwab reaches investors through its 200-plus branch offices. It has established an Internet on-line investment service for handling investment communication and customer accounts. It also has a 24-hour telephone service called TeleBroker. For active traders with a minimum level of assets and frequency of commission trades, the company offers additional brokerage services.

As the go-between closest to the customer, Schwab faces a host of competitors. As the winning discount brokerage, it competes not only with other discount brokerages but with full-service brokerages as well, including Smith Barney and Merrill Lynch. In its alliance with independent financial planners, Schwab competes for customers seeking information with financial planning firms such as American Express. Schwab also competes with the suppliers of fund families such as Vanguard and Fidelity that offer access to other mutual funds in a manner similar to Schwab.

The success of Schwab is not lost on its competitors. The chairman of Fidelity, Edward C. Johnson 3d, told the *New York Times*: "The best place to be is in the distribution business because you have access to everybody else's business." Accordingly, Fidelity withdrew many of its funds from the Schwab supermarket and those of other discount brokers, including its Magellan, Contrafund, and Growth and Income funds, offering them only through direct sale.[8] This is a fundamental change in strategy in which the company places its retail distribution services ahead of its wholesale fund sales business. The repositioning is meant to compete against Schwab's go-between strategy.

The question is, how to get closest to the customer? I have identified at least five types of financial intermediaries in the securities markets:

- Specialists and dealers
- Brokers
- Mutual funds
- Family of mutual funds
- Mutual fund supermarket

Charles Schwab successfully pursued go-between and bring-together strategies with its mutual fund supermarket, getting closest to the customer by offering variety and convenience and significantly lowering transaction costs. Schwab entered the mutual fund business with its OneSource service by going between investors and mutual fund families. It handles a high volume of transactions by offering diverse financial assets, yielding economies of scope in distributing mutual funds. By offering many families of mutual funds under one roof, Schwab offers its customers the convenience of one-stop shopping and product variety that specialized mutual fund families do not offer.

Figure 7-3.
THE BYPASS STRATEGY

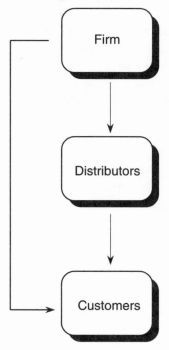

Bypass

Closely related to the go-between strategy is the bypass strategy. The firm bypasses its distributors, takes on the market-making role, and serves its customers directly. Since the firm's distributors earn rents from intermediation, the firm has an incentive to capture those rents by transacting directly with customers. The bypass strategy yields dividends when companies can better tailor their products to customer requirements than could be done through independent distributors. The strategy is illustrated in Figure 7-3.

To carry out bypass competition, the firm must make sure that its services create sufficient value added for its customers that the gains from direct transactions outweigh the benefits of transactions with distributors. For example, a manufacturer can seek to market directly to retailers and bypass its wholesalers. The value added by the manufacturer's market-making activities must exceed those of the wholesaler. The bypass strategy should not be used simply as a way to avoid the distributor's margin. Rather, the upstream firm seeking to bypass must be able to carry out those intermediation services more efficiently.

The bypass can be achieved in a variety of ways. Companies can create internal marketing and distribution systems that supplant market distributors. They can employ new technologies that allow them to reach customers directly. They can take advantage of alternative market institutions for reaching customers.

Manufacturers pursue a bypass strategy through direct sales via in-house distribution systems. This requires manufacturers to set up marketing and sales operations. For example, Dell and Gateway computers sell computers directly to customers, thus bypassing retailers. One advantage of direct sales is that each computer is customized to order. Dell and Gateway are able to tailor their production and inventory to market demand, while incorporating new technologies as the components become available. They can rapidly update their product lines as soon as new microprocessors are shipped from manufacturers.

Technological change offers many opportunities to carry out the bypass strategy. The Internet has allowed manufacturers to bypass traditional retail distribution channels. As Internet sites have proliferated, new intermediaries have emerged to reduce consumer search costs. These entrants compete with traditional distributors.

The airline computer reservation systems such as United's Apollo and American's Sabre systems originally followed a go-between strategy, intermediating between travel agents and airlines. Rather than travel agents contracting airlines directly over the telephone as they had traditionally done, the systems listed airlines' schedules and rates for a fee, and supplied travel agents with computers to speed the reservations process. (See the discussion in Chapter 3.) However, travel agents themselves are intermediaries and airlines must pay them commissions for booking airline trips. If airlines can obtain reservation services at lower cost than the commissions they pay travel agents, they have an incentive to bypass the travel agents. The growth of on-line services and the development of the Internet have created such incentives by lowering the costs of direct interaction with travelers. The airline computer reservation systems pursue the bypass strategy by offering on-line reservation services directly to customers. Airlines pay fees to the computer reservation systems but avoid the fees paid to travel agents. At the same time, many airlines eliminated travel agents' traditional 10% commissions and replaced them with maximum flat-rate commissions per ticket. Airlines also bypass the travel agents with toll-free numbers so that customers can book travel by phone. As a result of these bypass strategies, travel agents have shifted their attention toward booking hotels, rental cars, and cruises.

In the market for natural gas, interstate pipelines have traditionally purchased gas at the wellhead and sold the gas to natural gas utilities, known also as local distribution companies. Deregulation and open access transportation split the merchant and transportation functions of the pipelines. As a result, suppliers of gas were able to bypass the pipeline's merchant function and transact directly with local distribution companies, with customers arranging transportation on the pipeline. Ultimately, brokers and marketers have pursued a go-between strategy, intermediating between gas suppliers and downstream customers.

Insurance companies have an incentive to bypass insurance agents if they can provide market services to customers at lower costs. There are more than 650,000 insurance agents in the U.S.[9] The use of the bypass strategy by insurance companies will lead to a shake-out of insurance agents.

Insurance companies are pursuing the bypass strategy, reaching consumers directly through affinity associations and employers. ITT Hartford, for example, built a substantial business by offering auto and homeowner's insurance directly to the tens of millions of members of the American Association of Retired Persons (AARP), bypassing insurance agents and avoiding costly commissions of 10 to 20% of premiums.[10] ITT Hartford created an organizational division to serve its AARP customers, allowing the company to adjust its services and insurance contracts to the specific needs of the group.

Insurance companies are also setting up Web sites to provide information directly to consumers. Insurance companies with Web sites include CNA, ITT Hartford, Metropolitan Life, Travelers, and Prudential of America. Many insurance companies, such as Blue Cross-Blue Shield of New Jersey, are offering quotes through on-line intermediaries such as Insweb, Quickquote, and Quotesmith Corporation.[11] The on-line intermediaries perform some of the functions of traditional insurance agents by using on-line applications and questionnaires and offering multiple quotations from different companies. These on-line services follow the go-between strategy, interposing themselves between insurance companies and their customers. For insurance companies, using the on-line services lowers their costs compared to using agents and thus represents a bypass strategy.

Some brewers are using the bypass strategy. Brewers traditionally have relied on wholesale distributors to deliver beer to retailers, bars, and restaurants. Distributors operate trucks and warehouses and offer retailers some marketing, sales promotion, and credit services. The distribution system is perhaps better suited for mom-and-pop grocery and liquor stores, but has not kept pace with the growth of discount warehouse stores, such as Wal-Mart's Sam's Club, and the expansion of supermarket chains. Warehouse and supermarket chains incur higher transaction costs when they deal with multiple distributors for a given brand rather than a single distributor. Regional or local distributors are not suited for delivery to these chains, which may operate their own warehouses. Moreover, the brewers themselves have their own warehousing and distribution systems that are prepared to handle a substantial portion of the distribution task.

Because distributors are regulated and protected by state and federal laws, competition between distributors is less than it would be without the restrictions. Distributors may thus impose high markups on top of the manufacturer's prices, charging high wholesale prices to retailers. This is known as the problem of double marginalization.

Brewers have an incentive to bypass wholesalers so as to avoid antiquated distribution systems, to reduce the transaction costs to large customers, and to eliminate double marginalization. A number of brewers, including G. Heileman Brewing Co. (brewers of Special Export, Old Style, and Colt 45; later acquired by Stroh Brewery Co.) and S&P Co. (brewers of Pearl, Pabst, and Falstaff), established contracts with special discount distributors to avoid these problems, delivering directly to large customers.[12] Large brewers will have an incentive to follow suit to reduce transaction and delivery costs for large customers, while continuing to rely on traditional distributors for smaller retailers.

Even though Intel manufactures inputs for computer makers, it succeeded in pursuing a bypass strategy. The company traditionally relied on IBM to reach customers by producing computer chips for IBM computers. Intel eventually pursued the bypass strategy by selling its processors to clone makers. By promoting the computer chips with its "Intel inside" campaign, it reached customers directly, with customers purchasing computers to obtain the next generation Intel chip. Thus, Intel built its brand name despite the fact that its processors are components of the computer. To some extent, consumers began to see clones as generic boxes, simply a means of delivering the branded microprocessor inside. Personal computer makers advertised their products in terms of the features of the Intel processor they contained. Thus, computer makers were forced to compete in other ways, such as discount pricing and customer service, in order to distinguish their products. Motorola and IBM attempted to respond with the Power PC microprocessor, but achieved only limited success. By diversifying its market outlets and branding its product, Intel broadened its market outlets and reached a dominant position in the computer industry.

The bypass strategy recognizes that companies cooperate but sometimes compete with their intermediaries. Companies circumvent their wholesale or retail distributors or manufacturing clients to capture margins and sell directly to final customers. The bypass strategy does not imply the end of intermediation. Rather, it means that competition can quickly change the span of market bridges.

Connect

Companies follow the connect strategy if they wish to forge stronger links with upstream suppliers or downstream distributors. These connections can be through outright merger and acquisition or through contracts. A distributor, in competition with other distributors, may choose to merge or contract with a common supplier, thereby diverting supplies toward their company or obtaining more favorable terms than competitors. A supplier, in competition with other suppliers, merges or contracts with a common distributor, thereby increasing sales to final customers or obtaining more favorable terms than competitors. The connect strategy is likely to be successful if the vertical alliance creates transaction efficiencies.

Vertical partnering or full integration can yield benefits in several ways. The firms have greater incentives to enter into relationship-specific investments in R&D, manufacturing, or marketing when the returns to those investments are captured and shared by the owners of the merged firm or by joint venture partners. Firms create customized products or marketing and sales programs that would not be worthwhile if the relationship lacked exclusivity. Vertical alliances provide incentives for the firms to share technological or marketing data with reduced concerns for security and privacy. Vertical alliances allow the firms to develop communication methods and operational routines that depend on the returns to repeated interaction. Finally, the vertical alliance lets partners coordinate strategy in pricing, product development, and marketing.

Vertical alliances entail costs as well. Distributors and suppliers forego the advantages of independence, particularly the ability to serve diverse suppliers or distributors, respectively. Vertical mergers carry costs of integrating and coordinating distinct organizations. Vertical contracts are subject to the costs of negotiation, monitoring, and allocation of returns shared by all contracts. The competitive returns to organizational integration or long-term contractual relationships must outweigh the benefits of independence.

Vertical alliances address different types of competition. If competition is at the distributor level, distributors may look upstream to connect with a supplier. If competition is at the supplier level, the supplier may look downstream to connect with a distributor. While the structure of the vertical relationship need not depend on which firm initiates the connection, the type of competition the vertical alliance tries to address can influence the form of the alliance. I consider both upstream and downstream connections.

Upstream Connection

Pressed by competition, distributors look upstream to forge alliances with suppliers. The upstream aspect of competition is often ignored by man-

Figure 7-4.
THE CONNECT STRATEGY: DISTRIBUTOR 1 FORGES AN ALLIANCE WITH SUPPLIER

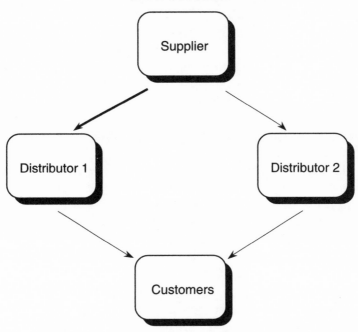

agement strategists due to the usual emphasis on product market competition. Upstream competition can make a difference in the outcome of product market competition. The upstream strategy is illustrated in Figure 7-4.

Many companies compete by outbidding each other for scarce resources. Rivals compete for financing by offering higher returns or different levels of disclosure, through capital structure decisions, and through appointment of skilled managers. Firms compete for skilled labor through wages, benefits, opportunities for advancement, job security, and working conditions. Firms compete for goods and services through price bids, contract terms, and technology transfers. Wholesale and retail firms compete to carry popular brands. Upstream competition is critical when competing firms employ specialized inputs or resell scarce products.

Competition for inputs may raise costs at least temporarily for the downstream firm as it seeks to hire skilled personnel or obtain scarce supplies of capital, goods, and services.[13] Upstream competition may raise the cost of access to certain kinds of technology if a competing buyer is able to obtain an exclusive license. To offset these costs, companies need to forge stronger alliances with critical suppliers as they seek a market advantage over competitors.

A distributor alliance with an upstream supplier through acquisition or attractive contract terms can be used to make a more effective supplier network than competitors can offer. This does not prevent competitors from expanding upstream or from forging their own alliances with suppliers. The main point is that upstream relationships are essential aspects of downstream competition. A company that ignores its supplier relationships will find itself with higher costs, lower quality inputs, and uncertain supplies. Moreover, if competitors achieve economies of sequence from increasing the span of their firms, it becomes necessary to seek similar efficiencies through supplier alliances. The company's success in the downstream competition for consumers is tied to its management of the entire supply chain.

Through its alliances and mergers with upstream suppliers, the firm can induce competitors to seek similar alliances or mergers or to exit the market if they are not successful. For example, a firm may merge with a key parts manufacturer, as a competitive move against a competitor who is also a customer of the same manufacturer. Coordination agreements may be an effective competitive strategy toward rivals that offer the retailers substitute products without additional services.

There is an advantage to vertical alliances if the companies can achieve greater transactional and operational efficiencies as a result. The vertical alliance is desirable if it can reduce costs and improve agility either by bringing repeated transactions within the organization or by formalizing the vertical relationship with contracts.

The agility that can be achieved is illustrated by Ford Motor Company's electronics components plant in Lansdale, Pennsylvania.[14] Each day, the plant produces 124,000 engine controllers, antilock brake sensors, and speed-control units. The plant keeps track of over five million components daily using computers and bar code scanners. Using computerized tracking and design and flexible manufacturing, the plant is approaching a one-day average turnaround time between the receipt of an order and shipment of the finished product. But speed is not an end in itself, nor is it simply a means of reducing inventories and increasing the rate of turnover. Rather, it provides the means for the plant to respond immediately to changing market conditions, in terms of both supplier performance and final customer demand.

If a manufacturing company can react in a matter of hours to suppliers and customers, then product markets become more like financial markets, such as those for securities, options, and international currencies. To succeed in these markets, buyers and sellers must move as quickly as possible to take advantage of even small movements in supply and demand. Moreover, just as financial markets experience constant innovation in the creation of new financial instruments and contracts, firms in the manufacturing and service sectors must continually create new products and contracts to stay ahead of competitors. Companies need to adjust the characteristics of products and services ever more quickly to technological change and to shifts in demand.

Downstream Connection

Suppliers sharing distributors with competitors have some incentives to forge stronger alliances with those distributors. Through downstream contracts a firm may ally itself with a retail chain as a means of competing with a rival that also supplies the chain. The firm may turn to an array of vertical contracts such as exclusive territories as a means of coordinating downstream retailers. The downstream strategy is illustrated in Figure 7-5.

Suppliers depend on the downstream distributor to act as an intermediary in the downstream market. The distributor serving multiple suppliers has divided loyalties. The downstream firm seeks favorable pricing and other contract terms by having the suppliers bid against each other. The distributor has incentives to carry multiple products to obtain economies of scope and to smooth out sales fluctuations as demand patterns change. The distributor wishes to hedge sales risk by carrying a portfolio of brands. The distributor has limited incentive to engage in promotion and sales efforts

Figure 7-5.
THE CONNECT STRATEGY: SUPPLIER 1 FORGES AN ALLIANCE WITH DISTRIBUTOR

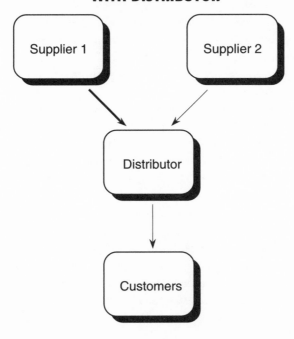

that are tied to one supplier or the other. Moreover, the distributor will prefer generic facilities that allow handling of diverse products and services.

The vertical alliance with a downstream distributor thus provides a number of benefits. Through vertical mergers or contracts, the downstream firm is given incentives to specialize in the products and services of the supplier. The competitive pressures from bidding for supplier loyalty are altered, with competing suppliers given incentives to pursue other downstream alliances or to develop alternative distribution networks. The downstream firm can be given incentives to improve its intermediation efforts on behalf of the suppliers because the alliance can capture the returns. The alliance also gives the distributor incentives to acquire specialized knowledge regarding the supplier's products and services or to invest in transaction-specific facilities. The vertical alliance allows the upstream supplier to brand not only the product itself but also the distribution and service that accompany the product.

The costs of the vertical alliance are that the supplier and distributor have less flexibility in changing trading partners or in maintaining multiple trading partners. The alliance foregoes the benefits of diversification at the distributor level in return for economies from specialization by distributors. If the companies merge, they encounter the usual costs of combining different businesses. If the alliance is contractual, there are costs of negotiation and monitoring.

Companies will incur these costs if the vertical alliance yields sufficient reductions in transaction costs and returns from coordination. The vertical alliance aligns the incentives of the supplier and distributor. This will lead them to pursue a coordinated strategy in pricing, product design, promotion, and sales. The upstream partner will focus more on final customers. The vertical merger increases the span of the firm, with the combined enterprises intermediating between the supplier's input markets and the distributor's customers.

Mergers between investment banks and retail brokerages provide an example of the connect strategy. The brokerage firm Dean Witter Discover merged with the investment bank Morgan Stanley to form a giant financial services company. A major shift in investment decision making by individual investors prompted the merger, as many employers gave their personnel responsibility for managing their retirement accounts. According to the *New York Times*, the amount of money in defined-contribution plans such as 401(k) retirement plans has grown to about $1.5 trillion, exceeding the assets in traditional corporate and union pension funds.[15] In general, individual investors are relying less on banks, shifting savings into the stock and bond markets. The considerable flow of funds through retail brokerages increased their importance as financial intermediaries for investment banks.

The upstream firm, Morgan Stanley Group, specializes in investment banking and asset management. Morgan Stanley is a major underwriter, purchasing new issues of securities from companies issuing the stock and reselling them to investors. Morgan Stanley also participates in the financing of mergers and acquisitions. Although Dean Witter Discover is also an investment banker, it brings to the merger its large market share in the retail brokerage business. The combined firm will be able to intermediate from purchasing securities directly from the issuing companies all the way to the individual investors who purchase stocks, bonds, and mutual funds. The connect strategy pursued by the two firms thus creates market bridges between corporate financing, asset management, and retailing of financial assets.

Dean Witter Discover and Morgan Stanley's connect strategy poses a competitive challenge to other investment banks, mutual fund companies, and brokerages. These competing financial intermediaries can respond with similar vertical mergers. Alternatively, they can retain their present independence if they can achieve better coordination through market transactions.

Acquisitions of bottlers in the soft drink industry are also examples of the connect strategy. As the cola wars between Coca-Cola and Pepsi-Cola heated up, the companies turned their attention to distribution channels. In seeking competitive advantage, both companies reorganized their distribution channels significantly, pursuing connect strategies by capturing and consolidating independent bottlers. While pursuing similar strategies on the bottling side, the two companies diverged in their approaches to fountain sales, with Coca-Cola keeping to a contracting mode and Pepsi-Cola sticking to vertical integration.

The concentrate makers, Coca-Cola and Pepsi-Cola, have long relied on large networks of independent bottlers to handle local and regional marketing, sales, and distribution of their product. As was mentioned in Chapter 5, the concentrate producers asked a lot from their bottlers, including local and regional marketing and sales to supermarkets, convenience stores, and restaurants. Bottlers were expected to invest in plant and equipment, update productive capacity, and maintain product quality, while limiting sales of competing products. In return, the concentrate makers provided national advertising and product innovations and awarded exclusive territories to the bottlers. The concentrate makers also intermediated for the bottlers with suppliers of sugar and packaging materials. The costs of providing contractual incentives and monitoring the performance of the independent bottlers created conditions for a change in the relationship.[16]

The rise of major discount chains such as Wal-Mart and warehouse grocery stores and the growth of supermarket chains posed a major challenge to the distribution system. Negotiating prices and other services with the discount chains and major supermarkets could not be easily coordinated within a fragmented distribution system. As a result, the concentrate makers purchased the bottlers and brought them under direct control. Coca-Cola controls over two-thirds of its bottling volume, through majority and minority stakes in bottling franchises and through its Coca-Cola Enterprises bottling operation, in which it has a 49% stake. Pepsi-Cola also controls over two-thirds of its bottling volume through its subsidiary, Pepsi-Cola Bottling Group.[17] The connect strategy allowed both of the concentrate makers to coordinate marketing and sales strategies with their downstream distribution networks, letting them compete more effectively with each other.

The limits of the connect strategy are illustrated by the other side of the beverage business. Although their bottler strategies have run in a somewhat parallel manner, Coca-Cola has traditionally pursued a different strategy from Pepsi-Cola in the fountain sales market. Coca-Cola has favored contractual alliances with major restaurant chains such as McDonald's, while Pepsi-Cola, in contrast, has operated its own restaurant chains, selling Pepsi to its own companies. This difference in approach gave Coca-Cola an advantage in fountain sales for a few reasons. First, Coca-Cola's attention was focused on the soft drink business, while Pepsi's attention was divided between soft drinks, its Frito-Lay snack food business, and its restaurants. Second, Pepsi-Cola was on both sides of the market, trying to sell Pepsi to independent restaurants while at the same time competing with those restaurants. The restaurants served two potentially conflicting objectives within the company: as restaurant businesses and as outlets for Pepsi products.

Recognizing this conflict, Pepsi-Cola announced that it planned to spin off Pizza Hut, Taco Bell, and KFC (formerly Kentucky Fried Chicken) as a separate business. Moreover, Pepsi-Cola planned to sell its casual-dining businesses, including the California Pizza Kitchen and Chevy's Mexican Restaurants, as well as Pepsico Food Systems, a restaurant supplier. Pepsico's Chairman and CEO Roger A. Enrico told the *New York Times* that Pepsi needed "to bring all our human and financial resources to bear on our soft drink and snack businesses" and to "dramatically sharpen Pepsico's focus."[18] In this way, Pepsi-Cola's strategy on the fountain side came to match that of Coca-Cola. They both recognized the limits of vertical ownership and the advantages of contracting.

AT&T reached a similar conclusion when it decided to spin off Lucent Technologies. AT&T carried out a "trivestiture," splitting into three companies: AT&T, supplier of long-distance and other telecommunications services; Lucent Technologies, maker of telephone equipment and including the former Bell Laboratories; and NCR, manufacturer of computers, automated teller machines, and related equipment. The Lucent divestiture was the largest initial public offering in U.S. history.

As an equipment supplier, AT&T had encountered resistance from the regional Bell operating companies (RBOCs), who would be in competition with AT&T in local and long-distance markets as a result of the Telecommunications Act of 1996. They were reluctant to purchase equipment from a competitor because the purchases would strengthen AT&T and potentially reveal their growth plans. AT&T gained little in terms of economies of sequence from the vertical integration of equipment making and provision of telecommunications services. Also, since AT&T purchased only a limited share of its own switches and other equipment, its costs of vertical integration with equipment manufacturing exceeded the benefits. AT&T carried out its restructuring only a couple of months after the Telecommunications Act was passed. After the spinoff, Lucent's sales of switching, transmission, fiber optic products, software, and wireless equipment to the RBOCs, GTE, and other telecommunications companies soared. Innovation took off as well, with patents going from one per business day to three per business day.[19]

AT&T's exit from telecommunications equipment and computers coincided with its connect strategy in other markets. AT&T planned to vertically integrate local and long-distance services by entering into local exchange telecommunications. It would enter into the local exchange through leasing the unbundled network elements of the local exchange carriers or reselling local exchange carrier services purchased at wholesale discounts under the Telecommunications Act. AT&T also vertically integrated into wireless with its purchase of the largest cellular carrier, McCaw Cellular Communications. In addition, AT&T acquired spectrum licenses to transmit digital Personal Communications Services (PCS), with plans to combine its PCS and cellular operations for a total potential market reach of 217 million subscribers.[20]

GTE Corp. also had incentives to pursue the connect strategy. In the wake of the Telecommunications Act, it reentered the long-distance market, signing up over a million customers in the first year. Next, it entered into a $1 billion alliance with Cisco Systems Inc., contracting for the purchase of data networking equipment. Then it acquired a large share of a national fiber optic network under construction by Qwest Communications Corp., a unit of Anschutz Corp.[21] These purchases were complemented by the acquisition of Internet service provider BBN. The purchase of BBN in particular makes GTE a major player in the national market for data communications. BBN has been called "the Bell Labs of the Internet." As Charles R. Lee, the Chairman of GTE, observed: "We are becoming a nationwide provider of telecommunications services—voice, data and video."[22] At least one of the strategic effects of the connect strategy was apparent: BBN had been under contract with AT&T to supply most of the networking for AT&T's Internet service.[23]

Endnotes

1. This definition of entry barriers comes from George J. Stigler, *The Organization of Industry*, Homewood, IL: Irwin, 1968, p. 67.

2. The definition is commonly applied; see for example William J. Baumol and Robert D. Willig, "Fixed Cost, Sunk Cost, Entry Barriers and Sustainability of Monopoly," *Quarterly Journal of Economics*, 95, pp. 405–431. See Daniel F. Spulber, *Regulation and Markets*, Cambridge: MIT Press, 1989, pp. 40–42 for additional discussion of barriers to entry.

3. This observation is examined by Gary Biglaiser, "Middlemen as Experts," *Rand Journal of Economics*, 24 (2), Summer 1993, pp. 212–223.

4. For further discussion see Gary Biglaiser and James W. Friedman, "Middlemen as Guarantors of Quality," *International Journal of Industrial Organization*, 12, pp. 509–531.

5. "Revolution in the Showroom," *Business Week*, February 19, 1996, pp. 70–76.

6. Ibid.

7. Ibid.

8. Edward Wyatt, "Why Fidelity Doesn't Want You to Shop at Schwab," *New York Times*, July 14, 1996.

9. Joseph B. Treaster, "When the Agent of Change Is a Click of the Mouse," *New York Times*, September 16, 1996, p. C1.

10. Michael Quint, "An Insurer's Dream with No Middleman," *New York Times*, January 23, 1996, p. C1.

11. Joseph B. Treaster, "When the Agent of Change Is a Click of the Mouse."

12. Marj Charlier, "Beer Brouhaha, Existing Distributors Are Being Squeezed by Brewers, Retailers," *Wall Street Journal*, November 22, 1993, p. A1.

13. See Steven C. Salop and David T. Scheffman, "Raising Rivals' Costs," *American Economic Review*, 73, May 1983, pp. 267–271.

14. The account of Ford's parts plant is based on John Holusha, "Industry Is Learning to Love Agility," *New York Times*, May 25, 1994, pp. C1, C5.

15. Floyd Norris, "A Deal Reaffirms the Strength of the Individual Investor," *New York Times*, February 6, 1997, p. C1.

16. See Timothy J. Muris, David T. Scheffman, and Pablo T. Spiller, "Strategy and Transaction Costs: The Organization of Distribution in the Carbonated Soft Drink Industry," *Journal of Economics & Management Strategy*, 1, Spring 1992, pp. 83–128.

17. See Timothy J. Muris, David T. Scheffman, and Pablo T. Spiller, *Strategy, Structure and Antitrust in the Carbonated Soft Drink Industry*, Westport, CT: Quorum Books, 1993, p. 6.

18. Glenn Collins, "Pepsico to Spin Off Its Restaurant Business," *New York Times*, January 24, 1997, p. C1.

19. Lucent Technologies first Annual Report, for first nine months of operation, through September 30, 1996.

20. "Vaulting the Walls with Wireless," *Business Week*, January 20, 1997, p. 85.

21. Seth Schiesel, "GTE Discloses 3 Big Deals in Growth Bid," *New York Times*, May, 7, 1997, p. C1.

22. John J. Keller, "GTE Agrees to Buy BBN for $616 Million," *Wall Street Journal*, May 7, 1997, p. B6.

23. Ibid. See also John J. Keller, "GTE Planning to Buy BBN, Internet Pioneer," *Wall Street Journal*, May 6, 1997, p. 1.

INDIRECT STRATEGIES

Competition is not the objective of the firm; its goal is winning markets. Competition, the means to the end, is an expensive proposition involving lower revenues from price reductions and higher costs for promotion, advertising, and enhanced services. To make money, companies find ways to avoid costly battles with competitors, while taking the actions necessary to win the market. Consumers are not harmed by the avoidance of conflict; quite the contrary. Companies achieve success by meeting unmet needs, serving neglected segments of the market, increasing product variety, and providing innovative goods and services.

The secret to winning the market is *indirection*. Two thousand five hundred years ago in *The Art of War*, Sun Tzu wrote, "In all fighting, the direct method may be used for joining battle, but indirect methods will be needed to secure victory."[1] This does not refer to deception in the standard sense. After all, nothing is more visible than a successful business; companies need publicity to attract customers and investors. However, many winning firms have conquered the dominant players in their markets by taking advantage of the incumbents' blind spots, overlooked opportunities, and bureaucratic inertia.

The indirect strategy not only conserves effort, avoiding the costs of direct confrontation, it also increases the chance of success when competing against a stronger, better-established rival. By eluding competition or surprising rivals, an entrant can best use its assets, including management agility and creativity, while neutralizing the advantages of the larger incumbent, including brand equity, scale economies, and access to capital. Success in serving unmet needs in what is perceived as a niche allows the entrant to build strength in preparation for direct competition.

Managers should prefer indirection to the direct attack on a stronger competitor because the other firm will not sit still in response to a competitive challenge. It will concentrate its efforts, matching or beating price cuts or service enhancements. The competitor will be stimulated to invest in a response that will raise the costs of both companies. It will anticipate the direct attack more easily, and take defensive actions to reduce the effectiveness of marketing and pricing plans.

Indirect strategy refers to the avoidance of direct confrontation. The firm builds its bridgeheads where they are less likely to be observed or understood by competitors. It attacks the undefended territory, maximizing value added. Companies engage in surprise, deception, or simply serving markets in ways that no one had thought to serve before. Indirect strategies aim to win the market, even though they are designed to avoid the battle.

In this chapter, I outline a set of strategies that can be used to win markets by indirection:

- Economy of force
- Undefended markets
- The path of least resistance
- The line of least expectation

I give examples of successful firms that came "from out of nowhere" to win their markets.

Economy of Force

In the words of Sun Tzu, "Those skilled in war subdue the enemy's army without battle."[2] How can a business win the market without battling its competitors? The secret is to serve markets that are not served, or not served well, by competitors. Companies create markets by discerning new opportunities for linking suppliers to customers. When carefully chosen, these market bridges create high arbitrage rents while avoiding direct conflict with other companies.

In economic terms, the notion of economy of force is closely related to profit maximization in competition. Companies choose which markets or market segments they wish to serve. The most profitable market segment may yield low revenues but correspondingly lower costs, so that profits are higher than in hotly contested markets. Alternatively, a high-cost market can be profitable if the costs of service have deterred other firms from providing service.

Seeking economy of force can also guide the types of expenditures that are most productive. A competitive battle with an entrenched incumbent firm could be highly costly in terms of marketing and product design expenditures. The firm might better invest money in developing new products and services for other markets.

Direct confrontation is an expensive proposition. A price war can easily drive prices down to operating costs, causing companies to fail to recover their costs of capital. The ensuing shakeouts bring exit and economic losses to companies exiting the market. Companies should only enter into such a direct battle if they are sure that cost efficiencies, superior product performance, or some other factor heightens their chance of emerging victorious. Winning markets does not mean being the last company left standing. The company's cost and demand advantages should be sufficient for it to be competitive while achieving economic profitability.

Similarly, an innovation race will cause the two companies to sink substantial expenditures into R&D. To the extent that the winning firm can protectively patent its inventions, the loser will not share in the economic returns when the race is over. Similarly, two companies racing to outspend each other for capital equipment to manufacture similar products will end up in a costly shakeout if market revenues cannot support operating all of the new facilities.

Why do firms voluntarily enter into such shakeouts? There are many reasons. Companies may have imperfect information about their rivals' costs or capabilities. Each therefore believes that it has a chance at success, so that its profit expectations are positive. Competition reveals which company has the technological or other superiority.

Another type of shakeout occurs due to uncertainty about the size of the market. Companies continue to enter until an additional firm would drive expected profits below zero. As entry takes place, the size of the market is discovered by those in the industry. A low realization of demand would cause some firms to exit while a high realization would result in additional entry if existing firms faced capacity constraints. A similar effect occurs if companies are using an untried technology. They are then uncertain about *their own costs*. As they begin to operate and the technology turns out to be expensive to run or the learning curve is not steep, the less productive companies exit the business.

Telecommunications capacity continued to expand significantly in the 1980s and 1990s. Additions to transmission facilities include coaxial cable, fiber optics, and wireless facilities. There are already multiple networks operating in most telecommunications markets. Market participants have considerable uncertainty about what is the best technology, what are their rivals' costs, and the extent of demand for new communications services. At the same time, deregulation is tearing down barriers between local and long-distance, cable and telephone, and wireless and wireline service. Companies are entering the industry to stake their claims, but many will ultimately be shaken out.

Some shakeout battles result from a failure to think ahead. The contest escalates until companies find no way out. All companies end up sustaining losses. Companies can sink costs in the early stages and still continue the contest since the benefits to the winner exceed the costs of fighting an additional round. This problem is familiar to auction experts.[3] An auctioneer offers to auction off a dollar. The highest bidder wins but both the highest and the second highest bidder must pay their final bids to the auctioneer. Suppose that there are only two bidders and bids must rise in increments of five cents. If bidder one has bid 90 cents and bidder two has bid 95 cents, the first bidder has a choice between bidding a dollar and breaking even or losing 90 cents. Bidder two then prefers to pay $1.05 for the dollar to lose only 5 cents, rather than losing 95 cents. This logic continues indefinitely as losses escalate and the two parties continue bidding, offering to pay more than a dollar. The reason is that a bidder receives 90 cents by raising the bid by only 10 cents. As a result losses continue to mount. The best solution is to avoid such a contest altogether.

There is a high cost to direct conflict. It is measured in terms of economic returns that companies could have earned by investing their capital and resources in other markets. The key to avoiding direct conflict is to discover opportunities to serve customers not perceived by others. The firm will earn arbitrage rents without costly price wars.

The indirect strategy is closely tied with a strategy of *building strength*. By serving undefended markets or market segments, a start-up company grows. This expansion allows it to defend the newly acquired territory from incursions by future entrants. The company develops expertise in distribution, marketing, production, R&D, purchasing, and financing. As the company becomes established its operating costs fall due to learning by doing. The company identifies talented personnel and managers. It gets to know the ropes and forms market networks of suppliers and distributors. These types of information and market contacts are highly valuable when the firm is ready to expand into new markets. The firm also develops new products and services that can be sold to new customers. Finally, the firm builds up cash reserves or develops sources of financing that will be needed to invest in new markets. Eventually, growth creates sufficient strength to take on established rivals in other markets.

Undefended Markets

The most appealing indirect strategy is to identify customer needs in the market that are not being met. Many entrepreneurs will say that filling a need was the primary motivation for starting their businesses. Of course, to survive, any business must meet customer needs that others do not satisfy. Indirect strategy means identifying needs that competitors do not even dream of satisfying. When you enter the market, competitors still do not understand the purpose of your business. The territory remains undefended, at least in the near term.

Undefended markets translate into gains from trade. If the firm can bring buyers and suppliers together in a new way, selling products and services to customers that have not been served before or purchasing inputs for new types of production or distribution, the firm captures economic rents.

This flies in the face of conventional wisdom in economics. It is reminiscent of the well-known story about two University of Chicago economists walking down the street who spot a $20 bill on the sidewalk. Neither stops to pick it up because they agree that it is simply not there; no one could have passed up a profitable opportunity. The problem with this story is that the $20 bill might have fallen there recently, without anyone else yet having noticed its appearance.

The economy is full of imperfections and asymmetric information. Changes in consumer tastes and technology continually create new opportunities. It is easy to imagine that no other manager has yet observed a particular market opening. Finding such unmet needs takes creativity and talent, which are not available in unlimited supply in business, or in any other endeavor. Moreover, identifying opportunities is costly, requiring market research and technical know-how. If companies differ in their research costs, those with greater research efficiencies will find different opportunities. There is also a large element of chance, so that discerning an unmet need may be fortuitous. This means there are always many unexplored opportunities.

Identifying unmet needs is a crucial skill that eludes many a manager. The undefended territory can be simply bringing new products and services to a geographic region not served by others. Alternatively, it can be a customer group, distinguished by age, gender, or other aspects, whose needs for a particular service are being ignored. The point of entry may be a low-cost generic service or a high-quality service. An undefended territory need not be a niche. A sufficiently innovative product or service for a mass market can be supplied without initially encountering rivals.

The economic returns to serving undefended territories are many. Margins can be higher as companies earn returns to their innovative products and services. Companies can travel down the learning curve, lowering costs or improving services before rivals get wind of new developments. Companies gain a first-mover advantage by committing capital to serve the newly created market. Companies are instant winners when they effectively serve the undefended territory. The company's dominant position continues at least until competitors attempt to imitate the successful entry. This can occur rapidly or slowly, depending upon the agility and insight of competitors.

At first blush, it seems unlikely that any territory can remain an open field for long. If one company discerns an opportunity, will not almost everyone else? If a company creates a market, will not others instantly emulate its success? In a perfect world, companies would respond at once and eliminate all economic profits. But strategy functions in the shadow of economic imperfections. Some companies are organizationally incapable of identifying targets of opportunity. Others, endowed with such insights, are sluggish nevertheless.

Wal-Mart

The idea of taking the undefended territory is best illustrated by the history of Wal-Mart. The late Samuel Moore Walton, known to everyone as Sam, began with a single variety store in a small town. From humble beginnings, he built a $100 billion a year company with about 2,000 stores. He drove an old Ford pickup truck and lived simply, but became the richest man in America by the mid-1980s. Every management guru has offered an explanation for the success of Wal-Mart Stores, Inc. There certainly are many reasons for the company's dominance, not the least of which is the creativity and focus of Sam Walton.

However, one key to making Wal-Mart the number one retailer that has not been given the attention it deserves is the expansion of the company in the small towns of the Midwest and Southern U.S. This was neglected territory, served by small statewide retail chains and local merchants but overlooked by large retailers such as Sears Roebuck and J.C. Penney.

Of course, much strategy is serendipity. The location of Wal-Mart reflected Sam Walton's origins. He grew up in small-town Missouri and graduated from the University of Missouri in 1940.[4] Upon completing school, he declined an offer from Sears and went to work for J.C. Penney in Des Moines where he began to learn about retailing. Walton later met and married his wife, Helen, in her hometown of Claremore, Oklahoma, and served for two years in the Army during World War II. Helen told Sam that since they had moved sixteen times during his stint in the Army, they would have to settle down in a city with no more than 10,000 people. Heeding this request, Walton began his retail career in earnest, operating a franchise for the Ben Franklin variety store in Newport, Arkansas, a town of 7,000 in the Mississippi River Delta. The second franchise store that he ran was in Bentonville, Arkansas, which was closer to his wife's hometown, and as Walton puts it,

> I wanted to get closer to good quail hunting, and with Oklahoma, Kansas, Arkansas, and Missouri all coming together right there it gave me easy access to four quail seasons in four states.

He began to open a series of Ben Franklin franchises in the area. By the early 1960s, Walton had decided that the future of retailing lay in discounting, and in 1962 he established the first Wal-Mart in Rogers, Arkansas, down the road from Bentonville. Rogers was a town of only 6,000 at that time.

That is not to say that no one else had the same idea. Sam Walton observed that 1962 was "the year which turned out to be the big one for discounting." S.S. Kresge started Kmart, F. W. Woolworth established Woolco, and Dayton-Hudson began Target. As Walton marvelled,

> It turned out the first big lesson we learned was that there was much, much more business out there in small-town America than anybody, including me, had ever dreamed of.

During this time, Wal-Mart was "too small and insignificant for any of the big boys to notice."

Competition certainly was present in the small towns, from regional chains and local merchants. Initially, Walton's stores thrived based on his creativity, innovativeness, and relentless discounting of prices. At some juncture, however, his competitive tactics moved from intuitive understanding to grand strategy. After only a few Wal-Marts had been established, Walton's overall conception was clear. He understood where he wanted to go and had few doubts about the potential success of Wal-Mart. The company accelerated its expansion in regional small towns, adding new stores at an increasing rate. By the mid-1980s, over half of the chain's stores were located in towns of 5,000 to 25,000, with a third of the stores in towns or counties not served by competitors.[5]

The other discounters, such as Kmart and Target, focused attention on larger towns. Sears did not embrace discounting until decades later. Wal-Mart escaped scrutiny, even though it reached a half-billion dollars in sales by the mid-1970s and two and a half billion dollars in sales by 1981. Continually building strength, the company was well positioned by then to enter larger and larger towns and challenge the larger chains directly.

Early on, Wal-Mart began construction of a computerized central warehousing system. It implemented cross-docking, a system that allows a warehouse to simultaneously receive and send out preassembled orders for individual stores. With some resistance from its founder, the company nonetheless embraced advanced computer and communications technology as soon as they became available. The technological advances made expansion feasible and conferred competitive advantages on the company, but these operational or logistical strengths should not be confused with strategy.

The strategy was to avoid head-on confrontation, to serve areas not served by others, and to have the "lowest prices always." The company continued to grow, reaching 330 discount stores by 1980, at a time when Kmart had almost 2,000 stores. Within ten years, Wal-Mart had far surpassed Kmart in sales. Other discounters were less successful. Sam Walton noted that 76 of the 100 top discounters that were in business in 1976 disappeared by the early 1990s. The disappearing act continued unabated into the 1990s, particularly among regional chains. In the Northeast, for example, Ames (with 307 stores), Hills (164 stores), Caldor (166 stores), and Bradlees (136 stores) filed for Chapter 11 bankruptcy, and Jamesway (90 stores) liquidated entirely.

Wal-Mart grew out of the discount category to become America's number one retailer. Were other retailers asleep at the wheel? Perhaps it was not worth paying attention to Wal-Mart. After all, at the time Sears opened the Sears Tower in Chicago in 1973, Wal-Mart had only been a public corporation for several years. Sears had long ago cut off its small town roots when it shifted in the twenties from a mail order to a chain store operation. Moreover, retailers had expansion plans of their own. In the 1980s, Sears was diversifying into real estate sales and financial services. Yet at some point, large retailers ignored changes in the retail marketplace. They did not remodel stores or embrace discount prices. The large retailers did not pay sufficient attention to the advantages of up-to-date communications and inventory management technology. By the early 1990s, as Sears fell behind Wal-Mart and Kmart, it reversed its financial supermarket strategy, divesting most of Coldwell Banker real estate and Dean Witter Financial Services Group and part of Allstate Insurance, to focus on the retail business, its main competitor being more clearly in focus.

Kmart, the largest retailer at the start of the 1990s, fell to one-third the size of Wal-Mart by the middle of the decade amid rumors of Chapter 11 bankruptcy. According to Kmart's CEO, Floyd Hall, about half of Wal-Mart's customers drive past a Kmart to get to Wal-Mart. His predecessor, Joseph Antonini, had diversified investment dollars and management attention away from minding the store toward other ventures: OfficeMax, the Sports Authority, and Builders Square. Like Sears, diversification made Kmart take its eye off Wal-Mart. Hall is banking on opening SuperKs, supercenters that combine a discount store with a supermarket. However, Wal-Mart already has 231 supercenters to Kmart's 87, and customers appear to prefer Wal-Mart's better displays and larger inventory.[6] Wal-Mart continues without an effective challenger.

The Path of Least Resistance

To prevail against stronger competitors, take the path of least resistance.[7] Market segments may be served by major competitors, but ineffectively. There are economic rents to be earned by addressing those segments with improved products and cost efficiency. These must be markets in which competitors do not perceive entry to be a threat requiring an extensive response. By dodging competition, it is possible to build strength to the point that the company can prevail in direct confrontation. The company avoids devastating pricing and marketing duels so that it can focus on customer service and controlling costs.

If the company's approach is sufficiently different from those of its established competitors, there is a better chance of pursuing the strategy without substantial opposition. By appearing as a niche player, a specialist, a start-up, the entrant can even appear to be in a different line of business than its potential rivals. Innovative services and different corporate structure conceal long-term intentions and weaken resistance. The company can achieve revenue growth and establish a reputation with suppliers, investors, and customers that will sustain it when direct competition begins.

The price-leadership strategy can be adapted to following the path of least resistance. A company can offer a product at a lower price by reducing its costs or lowering its margins, but it can do so in such a way that its competitors do not immediately perceive the threat of price competition. Without directly challenging competitors, the low-price product can be offered in a different market segment than the incumbent's product. By entering a market at the low end, companies may find they face few initial challenges from higher priced, high-end competitors.

Companies that produce generics provide a good example of the low-end approach. Supermarkets have higher margins on some lower-cost generic products, from prepared foods to detergents. Costs are kept lower through reduced marketing and sales expenditures as well as lower production costs. In many categories, the major producers of brand-name products did not see the generics coming. The major brands did not believe that generics posed a significant challenge to the sales strength and reputation of their brands. Eventually, companies such as Procter & Gamble had to adapt to the incursions of generics by consolidating brands, reducing price variability associated with promotions, and lowering prices consistently.

Products that compete are known as substitutes. Many people misunderstand that products with vastly different features and different prices can compete for customers. One reason for this is that the substitution is not always one-for-one. A consumer might increase usage of one product or service at the expense of another product or service, but the tilt in consumption will not be exactly the same. The consumer may replace one service with a little or a lot of another service, depending on relative prices and the features of the two services. What determines whether products compete is not their physical features, but the services the customer receives, as noted earlier. For example, in telecommunications, customers are indifferent to the mode of transmission, since they only care about the convenience of use. Thus, even though wireless phones use radio waves and pay phones use land lines, the two compete. People will obtain a cellular phone to avoid using pay phones. The extra cost of a cellular phone is justified by its convenience. You can place a call from your car without having to find a phone booth.

Discount brokerage services are substitutes for the services of full-service brokerages, even though they are sometimes perceived as different markets. The full-service brokerages bundle advice and trading services together. The discount broker offers trading services with little advice. The low cost allows the customer to purchase advice from other sources, whether investment advisers or publications. The customer trades off the advantages of one-stop shopping at the full-service broker with the price savings and flexibility of the discount broker. There is no question that discount broker Charles Schwab draws customers away from full-service brokers. It appears that the full-service brokers did not fully understand the nature of the threat to their business until Schwab had built up its strength and become fully established in the market for financial services.

Product differentiation strategies can also be implemented along the path of least resistance by initially avoiding direct comparisons with established brands. The product can excel in several features in comparison with existing products. Its purpose can be disguised by emphasizing that the product is in a different category. Thus, built-in computer fax modems ultimately exceeded sales of stand-alone fax machines. The phenomenon of incumbent managers failing to observe challenges from new technologies is known as marketing myopia. Until incumbents recognize the new product as a direct rather than indirect challenge, the new entrant can build up its customer base, establish supplier links, obtain financing, and build the strength needed for direct competition. Products that are viewed as serving a niche for consumers seeking high quality or particular product features can later be repositioned to contest the market of established brands.

An important way to take the path of least resistance is to exploit the incumbent's weaknesses to create a different product or service. No firm can be all things to all people, so openings always exist for innovative entrants. If the incumbent's goods are too expensive, a low-price, low-end strategy can be successful. By portraying the product differently, it may be possible to appeal to customers while eluding detection by the incumbent.

If the incumbent's service quality leaves much to be desired, emphasize that your company is a service specialist. America Online expanded to become the leading on-line provider of services while offering its customers congested phone lines and long waiting periods. The poor service was outweighed by low "all you can eat" pricing and ease in signing up for the service. This created opportunities for Internet service providers to provide better service, such as customer help lines and reduced congestion.

Companies can achieve a leadership position by concentrating on one aspect of the business and executing that better than the competition. Domino's Pizza is the leading pizza delivery company because it only delivers, having decided early on that combining delivery with restaurants would lower the service quality of delivery. For them, the delivery-only strategy turned out to be the path of least resistance, since other companies were pursuing a combined restaurant and delivery approach.

If the incumbent offers one-size-fits-all service, entrants can offer customized services. This strategy can go undetected until the incumbent discerns that you are pursuing a mass customization strategy. If the incumbent is strictly confined to stores, offer your product through new channels such as catalogs and Internet shopping.

If incumbents offer confusing contracts, cut through the complexity and offer clarity. A simple contract may be sufficient to attract customers without resistance from incumbents. In local and long-distance telecommunications, rates are becoming more complicated as deregulation proceeds. Incumbents can find it difficult to respond quickly to an entrant that targets customers with simplified pricing with no more than two or three options.

MCI mastered the path of least resistance by exploiting the regulatory constraints of incumbents. When it entered into long-distance service, AT&T was bound by price floors, allowing MCI to attract customers with small discounts below the floor, without the incumbent being able to retaliate. After AT&T's price floors were dismantled, AT&T was able to offer competing discounts and customer churning between the carriers began in earnest. MCI carried its strategy into the local exchange, seeking to benefit from continuing price regulation of incumbent local exchange carriers such as Ameritech or Pacific Bell. In the local exchange, continuing rate regulations made it difficult for incumbents to adjust prices in response to competitive challenges. MCI was able to target lucrative business customers in local markets with targeted discounts, just as it had done earlier in long-distance markets.

Southwest Airlines

Southwest Airlines is the Wal-Mart of the air. Its slogan, "The low price airline," alludes to its leadership of the discount carriers. Chairman and CEO Herb Kelleher started the airline from scratch as a regional carrier, taking it to the top of the airline market with substantial earnings while the majors, including American, United, and Delta, were posting losses in the early 1990s. Investment analysts compare the potential of the airline's stock to that of Wal-Mart.[8]

Flights began in the early 1970s from Dallas, competing with local carriers but not directly challenging the majors. There are many reasons that Southwest did not appear on the radar screens of the majors. Southwest flew directly between city pairs, avoiding the hub-and-spoke system that the majors had embraced when the industry was deregulated. Unlike the majors, Southwest followed a regional strategy, flying short-haul routes and sticking to secondary airports including Love Field in Dallas, Midway in Chicago, and the Detroit City Airport.[9] Indeed, its main competitors were passenger cars and other ground transportation. While the majors fly a diverse assortment of planes to fill out different portions of their route structure, Southwest stuck to 737s. Southwest offered no-frills, low-price service, as against the majors who sell a wide range of fares from supersaver to first class, carrying over an emphasis on service from the days of regulation, when airlines coordinated fares rather than competing on price. Finally, Southwest does not sell through airline computer reservation systems, thus avoiding listing fees at the expense of reduced travel agent sales.

All of these factors were later to be identified, along with motivated employees and cost cutting, as competitive advantages. However, in the early years they also served to create a stealth airline, visible to passengers but less well understood by the major airlines, who saw little need to resist the niche carrier. By the time Southwest was perceived as a worthy competitor, the airline had already built its strength in terms of brand recognition, management expertise, a skilled workforce, and investor confidence. The response of the majors has been to imitate Southwest. United introduced a lower-cost clone called Shuttle by United. Yet this approach still misses the point. The Southwest strategy is to build a transcontinental airline that will challenge the majors. Fighting back with clones only postpones the need for the majors to reconfigure their entire operations. Until then, the Southwest strategy continues to be the path of least resistance.

The Line of Least Expectation

Competition requires the element of surprise. For Sun Tzu, "all warfare is based on deception." He continues, "when capable, feign incapacity; when active, inactivity. When near, make it appear that you are far away; when far away, that you are near."[10] The great military strategist Liddell Hart counsels choosing "the line of least expectation."[11] Surprising competitors requires innovation, speed, and deception. Surprise reduces the effectiveness of rival responses. The success of such strategies depends on the creativity of entrants and the limits on perceptiveness of incumbents.

How can such advice be useful in competition? Business is the most open of activities. Companies seek publicity. They invest to build brand recognition. Products and services cannot be sold unless they are well advertised. Companies cannot raise capital without communicating with investors. Nothing is less secret than a successful business venture.

Moreover, deceptive announcements or activities would be fraudulent; advertising and public statements must be truthful.

There are still many ways to surprise the competition. Product introductions can surprise incumbent firms when they represent drastic design changes or jumps in technology. Companies can announce a market entry but still surprise rivals by focusing on only one geographic area or market segment. The best type of surprise is taking advantage of the incumbent's myopia, serving a low-end market segment or out-of-the-way customer that does not even appear important to the incumbent. If the established firm does not even notice the upstart entrant, why explain the details? Just grow the business until the challenge becomes difficult to ignore. At that time the new business will be well established and it will be far too late for the incumbent to mount an effective defense or retaliate.

Surprise

Surprise constitutes doing something new. Companies need not disclose a new production process until it is put in place or a new product until its development is completed. Surprise can take the form of larger-than-anticipated investments or increases in some aspect of performance, particularly speed. An unanticipated strategic alliance or acquisition can stun the opposition. IBM's purchase of Lotus startled Microsoft and other networking software companies. The acquisition combined IBM's marketing powers with the popular networking product Lotus Notes for the client-server market. Lotus Notes would contend with Windows NT and others for the client-server business.

Surprise is vital at the tactical level. Microsoft surprised the software industry and stock market analysts by announcing an early release of its suite of applications for Windows 95. The suite, called Microsoft Office for Windows 95, included a word processor, spreadsheet, and electronic calendar. The suite had been expected about a month after Windows 95. The announcement caught competitors Lotus and Novell by surprise. The early release may have increased the rate of corporate adoptions among those customers unwilling to wait for competing application packages.[12]

Another source of surprise is action in supplier markets. Napoleon Bonaparte first introduced his deadly *manœuvre sur les derrières* (the maneuver at the rear) against Austria and used it 30 more times by 1815. While attacking the enemy with strong forces on his main line, he sent a powerful column to outflank the enemy and attack from the rear, cutting off the lines of supply and retreat with a strategic barrage of other barriers.[13] By forming new alliances and contracts with manufacturers, parts suppliers, and technology labs, companies can create value added and preempt their competitors. Preemptive supplier alliances are a form of encirclement.

Unexpected actions in the supplier markets strengthen your company while disconcerting competitors.

In attempting to anticipate each others' strategic actions, companies will view costly actions as the least likely. It is for this reason that achieving surprise can be very costly. Edward N. Luttwak calls this phenomenon the "conscious use of paradox." He points out that secrecy and deception involve costs of coordination within the organization. Taking the unexpected action is inevitably costly. He illustrates this point with the example of an army choosing between two roads. One is straight and well paved; the other takes a roundabout route and is bumpy and partially obstructed. Taking the first road will get the army to the destination sooner. Taking the second road will take longer, fatigue the troops, and harm the equipment. As a result, the good road will be well defended. The element of surprise calls for taking the second road. The greater the relative disadvantage of the second road, the more it will achieve the element of surprise.[14]

Luttwak cautions against the "failure of success." In war, armies become wedded to a successful offense or defense and continue to repeat it long after its costs have overshadowed its benefits. Also, the more successful a weapon system or tactical ploy, the more effort the opponent devotes to developing countermeasures, diverting their attention from countering other threats. Thus, paradoxically, less effective weapons can have a longer useful life than more successful ones.

Companies continually face this paradox. The more innovative a product, the more competitors will imitate it or develop competing features in their products. This suggests that companies should not rely exclusively on the technical leap. More mundane improvements in the product or in customer service should be implemented alongside the innovation. These small measures will continue to be a source of earnings, even as competitors shift their focus to countering the breakthrough product.

The most important source of astonishment is innovation. By creating new products or developing innovative features, an entrant can capture market share before the incumbent has time to effectively prepare a response. Product innovations create confusion for competitors when they represent drastic discoveries, with features that are difficult to copy and that address customer needs in a different way.

While innovation is a surprise almost by definition, the decision to pursue R&D need not surprise competitors. In fact, innovation is a direct strategy when companies are in a patent race, each sinking large investments into similar research projects to develop related products. The winner of the patent race obtains temporary property rights to the stream of economic returns from the innovation, subject only to imitation and development of related products not covered by the patent. As with direct competition in general, the patent race results in a shakeout, with only one or very few firms achieving success.

Innovation becomes an indirect strategy when competitors do not anticipate the direction or extent of their rivals' R&D efforts. Thus, to take full advantage of innovation requires that the rate and direction of the company's project be distinguished from those in the industry. The advantage gained by surprise from a single innovation can be lost quickly, so the company must pursue a process of continual innovation, keeping competitors off balance as they chase the last breakthrough.

Innovations in production processes, known as process innovations, allow lower prices or higher margins and may be more difficult to imitate in the short run. Speed, as well as stealth, can enhance the success of new product introductions.

Nucor is a minimill that produces steel from scrap. As a small-scale new entrant into the steel industry, Nucor's enterprising adoption of thin-slab casting of steel surprised incumbents such as USX and Bethlehem, both larger-scale, traditional producers of steel. Other steel producers were slow to adopt the new technique despite its cost advantages and widespread publicity by its developer, SMS, a German supplier of steelmaking equipment. So, Nucor's adoption of thin-slab casting helped the company create a sustained competitive advantage.[15]

Ted Turner followed the indirect strategy in his innovative creation of the CNN news network. In contrast to the traditional half-hour evening news format of the (at the time) big three broadcast television networks, Turner saw an opportunity for a different service. The CNN networks would be carried on cable, perceived as less of a threat by the big three since their expectations were based on the history of broadcast television. The CNN format would broadcast news all day, renewing itself every half hour on the headline news channel and including features on another channel.

The leading networks simply doubted that there would be sufficient interest in news all day. Their expectations were based on the experience of everyone watching the evening news during the dinner hour. The reason that everyone tuned in to the evening news was that it was the only source of national news on TV at the time. Customer viewing patterns were following the broadcast services that were available. This did not mean that the viewing time was convenient. With an increasing proportion of families in which both husband and wife were working and more people taking on two jobs, fewer viewers found the evening news time convenient. The CNN format allowed viewers to tune in whenever it was convenient for them. People could watch at night after working late; work-at-home viewers could tune in all day; CNN could update the news regularly during important news events such as the Gulf War and people would stay tuned in all day. The network became the standard source for decision makers in the U.S. and around the world.

The success of CNN surprised the networks and significantly reduced the luster of the network evening news, which had always been flagship programs for the broadcasters. Yet it would be many years after the launch of CNN before rivals geared up to challenge it with cable news channels of their own. The innovative strategy of CNN created a sustained competitive advantage for that network.

The entry of Japanese manufacturers of automobiles, television, and other products perhaps unintentionally followed a line of least expectation. Manufacturers in the U.S. held an image of Japanese companies as low-tech manufacturers of low-quality products, even after their innovation and skill had become apparent to consumers. Television manufacturers were convinced that Japanese television makers were dumping their products on the U.S. market and didn't bother to benchmark competing manufacturing techniques to modernize U.S. television manufacturing. The U.S. auto industry favored voluntary export restraints to control the number of Japanese cars entering the U.S. market, without foreseeing the Japanese automakers' strategy of high-end entry that has made the Lexus and Infiniti such strong brands. The Japanese manufacturers were certainly effective competitors in automotive and electronic products. However, it was the blind spots of U.S. companies that helped create opportunities for the growth of companies such as Toyota and Sony.

Java

Sun Microsystems' Java software is an excellent example of following the line of least expectation. The software surprised Microsoft and a host of other software companies as well as computer makers. According to Sun Microsystems' chairman and CEO Scott McNealy, "the beauty of the fact that not everybody buys into what we're doing is that it gives us a head start."[16]

How did the strategy come about? Bill Joy, cofounder of Sun and its vice president for R&D, set forth a two-part strategy that consisted of preventing any company or product from dominating the Internet and changing the way documents and programs work on computers that are linked to the Internet.[17] He clarifies Sun's innovation strategy, contrasted with the standard-setting activities of leading firms:

> To me, the beauty and significance of the Net is that it is, by its very design, a decentralizing force. Not only does it defy being controlled by any one entity, it doesn't discriminate. There are no 'wrong' types of computers or software for the Net, as long as they follow some very basic communications rules. . . . It's a liberating atmosphere that

encourages more innovation than central planning or strict standards ever could and it's something we don't want the Internet to lose.[18]

The strategy is not accidental. Joy and Eric Schmidt had long ago developed Berkeley Unix, a form of AT&T's operating system software that they adapted to connect with the Internet. According to Schmidt, "We always knew that microcomputers made the most sense not in isolation but when they were connected in networks."[19] Thus, each of the 1.5 million computers ever sold by Sun Microsystems has the hardware and software capability for Internet usage.[20] The problem is how to implement the innovation strategy successfully, particularly for a company that is primarily a hardware manufacturer whose software resources are overshadowed by Microsoft's legions of programmers.

The innovation of the Java software language must be measured against this backdrop. The Java language is constructed to be read by practically any computer operating system, whether IBM, Apple, Unix, or something else, thus transcending operating systems. While the operating system is running the individual machine, the language connects individuals to Web documents. It thus becomes a universal interpreter, that is, an intermediary between the computer's operating system and the Internet. In this position, Java becomes the channel for all transactions between individuals and the Web. Information being sent and received must go through the interpreter. This process supersedes the functions of operating systems, which are meant to underlie applications, the software that carries out tasks. In fact, the language ultimately provides an alternative operating system for the PC.

But more than that, the language changes the nature of applications themselves. Java supplies small software programs called applets that allow a computer user to observe an animated Web page, or even to carry out jobs specific to the Internet site, such as ordering products, calculating the cost of an order, or receiving some type of information-based service.

Java also changes the world of computer operating systems regardless of the Internet because programs run on a Java virtual machine. This means that programs written for Java can run on top of any machine's operating system (OS). Therefore, applications software developers can avoid having to adapt a program to every operating system. They can lower their costs by writing the program only once, in Java. So while other operating system software depends on being run on a compatible machine, Java transcends the equipment.

One way to understand Java is that it is the computer equivalent of an intermediary. Operating systems are software intermediaries, since they stand between your computer and the software applications you use. An operating system interprets the computer code in software applications so they can run on your computer. Thus, every computer must have an operating system. Microsoft benefited from a contract with IBM to provide DOS (Disk Operating System) for its PCs. Providing the operating system is a software go-between strategy, since computers and applications must interact through the operating system.

The Java platform takes the go-between strategy one better, by intermediating between applications and most operating systems. Through its virtual machine, Java interprets applications for the resident operating system. This means that computer users can simply add Java onto their existing machines and be ready for any Java applications, without purchasing additional equipment.

The Java strategy is indirect because it does not appear to compete with other operating system software, but rather works together with it. According to *Byte*, "Java is a stealth platform that propagates entirely in software and coexists peacefully with the native OS."[21] Apple, IBM, Microsoft, Novell, Silicon Graphics, and others are adopting the Java interface, known as a run-time environment. Java virtual machines are included in later versions of Windows, Mac's OS, Unix, OS/2, Netware, and other systems, and in IBM's corporate computers. Java's run-time environment is part of competing operating systems. Also, Web browsers such as Sun's HotJava, Netscape Navigator, and Microsoft's Internet Explorer all include a Java run-time environment.[22] Thus, competitors are helping the propagation of Java onto existing machines, much as the Greeks' gift of the Trojan horse was welcomed into the gates of Troy.

Java appears risk-free to competitors because it is an open system. Companies can write applications for Java as a platform and use the Java language in writing software. However, if Java becomes more popular than the underlying operating systems, Sun Microsystems, the owner of the Java brand, stands to gain market power. This gain occurs at the expense of competing brands of operating systems and microprocessors, which become even more interchangeable.

Deception

Companies can pursue indirect strategies through actions and announcements that alter competitor expectations, thus influencing the line of least expectation. By leading competitors to underestimate your skills or industry knowledge, you may delay or discourage their competitive response. GE's success with the management of NBC may have been helped by perceptions in the entertainment industry that GE executives were engineers who could not run a network.

Taking advantage of naive, credulous, or arrogant opponents has a long history in armed conflict. Companies also use various forms of deception in competition. They have every interest in concealing their intentions as they devise pricing policies or develop new products. While plans are publicized as much as possible to customers and investors, it often makes sense to keep innovative projects under wraps until the launch. In some cases, projects are publicized before they are ready as a means of preempting rivals. Software makers are noted for vaporware, that is, premature announcements of new software products meant to deter rival research and development efforts.

In addition to concealing or revealing their plans, companies use marketing in numerous strategic ways. Advertising provides endless opportunities to put one's products in a better light than those of competitors, highlighting the shortcomings of rival companies. AT&T papered over its decision to invest in outmoded cellular technology acquired through its purchase of McCaw Cellular. In the face of competition from entrants who had purchased spectrum licenses for higher frequency digital personal communications systems (PCS), AT&T responded with a quick fix by simply renaming its cellular service Digital PCS. AT&T purchased PCS spectrum and planned to reconfigure its analog cellular system to handle digital transmission, but the announcement was made long before the rollout. AT&T's announcement was exquisitely timed to highlight the delays of actual PCS providers in getting their systems to work while emphasizing AT&T's readiness to provide service, even if that service was neither fully digital nor fully PCS.[23]

Endnotes

1. Sun Tzu, trans. Samuel B. Griffith, *The Art of War*, London: Oxford University Press, 1963, p. 79.

2. Ibid.

3. Martin Shubik, *Game Theory in the Social Sciences: Concepts and Solutions*, Cambridge, MA: MIT Press, 1983, p. 291.

4. The account given here draws from Sam Walton with John Hewey, *Sam Walton: Made in America*, New York: Bantam Books, 1992.

5. Pankaj Ghemawat, "Wal-Mart Stores' Discount Operations," Case Study, Harvard Business School, 1986.

6. Patricia Sellers, "Kmart Is Down for the Count," *Fortune*, January 15, 1996, pp. 102–103.

7. See B. H. Liddell Hart, *Strategy*, 2nd rev. ed., New York: Meridian. 1991, pp. 341, 348.

8. Kenneth Labich, "Is Herb Kelleher America's Best CEO?" *Fortune*, May 2, 1994, p. 44.

9. Ibid.

10. Sun Tzu, *The Art of War*, p. 66.

11. Liddell Hart, *Strategy*.

12. See Laurence Zuckerman, "Microsoft Is High on News of Software," *New York Times*, July 11, 1995, p. C2.

13. Bevin Alexander, *How Great Generals Win*, New York: Norton, 1993, p. 107.

14. Edward N. Luttwak, *Strategy: The Logic of War and Peace*, Cambridge, MA: The Belknap Press of Harvard University Press, 1987.

15. See Pankaj Ghemawat, "Commitment to a Process Innovation: Nucor, USX and Thin-Slab Casting," *Journal of Economics & Management Strategy*, 2, 1993, pp. 135–161; and

"Competitive Advantage and Internal Organization: Nucor Revisited," *Journal of Economics & Management Strategy*, 3, 1995, pp. 685–717.

16. "Why Java Won't Repeat the Mistakes of Unix," interview with Scott McNealy, *Byte*, January 1997, p. 40.

17. Brent Schendler, "Whose Internet Is It Anyway?" *Fortune*, December 11, 1995, p. 120.

18. Ibid.

19. Ibid.

20. Ibid.

21. Tom R. Halfhill, "Today the Web, Tomorrow the World," *Byte*, January 1997, pp. 68–80.

22. Ibid.

23. AT&T Digital PCS operates in both the 800MHz spectrum and 1900MHz spectrum and involves dual-use phones that provide analog service when digital service is not available. Ian Olgeirson reports that "Despite the name, the venerable AT&T service uses cellular technology instead of PCS," see Ian Olgeirson, *The Denver Business Journal*, November 10, 1997. Stewart Wolpin observes that "AT&T's 'Digital' network isn't all digital. It's actually a patchwork of its own 800MHz digital network, available in 42 markets, complemented with analog and digital agreements with local carriers," as well as AT&T's own digital 1900MHz network, see Stewart Wolpin, "Digital Cells: Not Ready for Primetime, Part 1: They'll be great in about a year," October 13, 1997, "Digital Cells: Far from Functional, Part 2: What no ringer or volume controls," October 20, 1997, "Digital Cells: The AT&T Paradox, Part 3: Best all around service but lacking in many areas," October 27, 1997, www.e-town.com/news/articles.

OFFENSIVE AND DEFENSIVE STRATEGIES

In Chapter 8, I emphasized the value of indirect strategies. Companies can maximize value added by winning markets that are not well served or are even ignored by competitors. Innovative strategies win the battle before it begins. Yet in the long run, direct conflict is unavoidable. Entrants seek out competitors and take them on directly as they grow into new markets or expand their operations to battle incumbents for market share. Companies contemplating entry or expansion must have more than indirect strategies. This chapter presents offensive and defensive strategies.

Captain Liddell Hart summarized the principles of war in a single phrase: "concentration of strength against weakness."[1] For business, this means that when entering a market or challenging a competitor, you should begin by identifying the competition's strengths and weaknesses. Do not attempt to enter a competitor's market segments that are well defended. The entry target should be unexpected, to the extent possible. Then, do not scatter your efforts but instead focus your marketing, product introduction, customer services, R&D, management, and other resources on the desired segment of the market.

Companies earn rents from establishing and managing markets. The components of the MAIN framework provide strategic ideas for managers. By reducing the costs of transacting or making possible new types of transactions, companies take the offensive against less creative competitors. I identify four classes of offensive strategies:

- Market maker
- Arbitrageur
- Intermediary
- Network organizer

The market maker creates and manages markets by providing better deals, greater immediacy, and more coordination services than competitors. The arbitrageur moves faster than competitors to take advantage of price differences or available gains from trade. The intermediary reduces transaction costs for customers and suppliers below those of competitors. The network organizer forges stronger and broader networks than competing firms.

Offensive strategies require overwhelming force to succeed. In business, overwhelming force means greater productive efficiency, lower costs, competitive pricing, higher quality products, skilled employees, and access to financing. The company seeking entry or expansion must be prepared to outperform incumbent rivals in the marketplace.

For the company defending its markets from entrants or the expansion of competitors, the converse holds: Expect entrants to concentrate their strengths against your weaknesses. Entrants' strategies may involve surprise and deception as well. Since you cannot anticipate every challenge, defensive strategies require flexibility of response, with forces held in reserve. An incumbent that is overextended creates an easy target for entrants. Successful companies face continual challenges that require defensive strategies. Sustaining a winning position requires being prepared for the expansion of existing competitors and challenges from new ones.

Competitive advantage is inherently not sustainable. What works today is unlikely to be successful tomorrow as rivals find ways to copy or counter successful strategies. The best solution to this problem is to continually explore ways to improve performance, to create new products and services, and to link suppliers and customers in new ways. Innovation is essential to both offensive and defensive strategies. These strategies are a guide to market actions but they are no substitute for economic performance. To enter markets successfully, companies must outperform their rivals economically, providing their customers with superior goods and services.

Whether strategies are offensive or defensive, companies act in anticipation of rival company strategies. Each manager asks a number of questions. What are my competitors going to do? What are my rival's expectations about my strategy? Given what I expect the other firms to do, is my strategy the best choice? How will the strategic interaction with my competitors evolve over time? Finally, how are market outcomes affected by the strategic interaction between my company and its rivals?

Offensive strategies are used to carry out market entry or expansion against existing competitors. The MAIN framework generates a set of profitable offensive strategies. Companies can outperform competitors in market-making activities. Entrants should continually seek arbitrage advantages over incumbents. Entrants can provide superior intermediation services. Finally, companies can overwhelm rivals by building better market networks.

Offense

Firms continually strive for competitive advantage and leading firms are often replaced by a succession of rivals. The competitor's suppliers may be more efficient or they may offer technological innovations that are reflected in lower costs or better quality products. If the indirect approach cannot be pursued or becomes unnecessary due to superior strength, the firm seeking entry or expansion should concentrate all of its forces on the competitors' weakest point. Effective head-to-head competition requires outperforming competitors through substantially lower costs of production, superior distribution systems, or more innovative products.

Finding the point of attack is intrinsic to the art of competition. The market segment need not be the one least-well-served or least-well-defended, since determining the point of weakness is not an easy calculation. It should be the rival's critical vulnerability, what Clausewitz calls the opponent's "center of gravity." As Robert Leonhard points out, in the game of chess the opponent's source of strength is the queen, but the critical vulnerability is the king. Although the king is a weak piece, its checkmate wins the game.[2]

One means of identifying the competitor's Achilles' heel is to determine whether some segments are cash cows. By operating a high-margin business, a company is vulnerable to more efficient entry. The challenger can offer better deals to customers and suppliers by narrowing the spread between buy and sell prices. Enhancing value added can take away the competitor's high-margin business. Moreover, cutting off the competitor's source of cash will impede the company's plans in other markets.

The center of gravity for regulated companies is often easy to identify. Most regulated rate structures have built-in cross subsidies. For example, large-scale industrial users of electric power subsidize residential rates. Business rates in local telecommunications subsidize residential rates. New entrants in these industries have attracted industrial and commercial customers by offering similar services or innovative services to these high-margin segments that were providing the cross subsidy, bidding away customers. The entrants can obtain high margins even if the entrants' costs exceed those of the regulated incumbent. The regulated company is often taken by surprise by this strategy and accuses the entrant of cream skimming. The problem for the incumbents is that the cross subsidies in their pricing structure create a point of weakness.

The regulated firm is often powerless to respond because regulators continue to enforce distorted rate structures even in the presence of competition. The regulated firm attempts to counteract the cherry picking of its highest-paying customers by dropping its prices in the competitive segment and raising them on the previously subsidized segments. This can also be a mistake if the entrant has become entrenched in the market by developing its service for the high-end segment. Having learned the business and established its facilities in the market, the entrant extends service to the regulated utility's supposedly captive customers after they are dissatisfied over the new price hikes. Thus, the initial beachhead in the high-end segment is extended later to the entire market.

MCI began by attacking selected AT&T business customers. These customers were a major source of revenues for the incumbent—not a position of strength. MCI extended its entry to the entire long-distance market. Then, having built a long-distance network, MCI repeated similar strategic maneuvers to begin its entry into local exchange markets.

The United States Postal Service's productive inefficiencies have made it a sitting duck for entrants. Although the Postal Service created overnight delivery service, Federal Express perfected the service with reliable delivery and modern tracking systems and captured most of the market. United Parcel Service and other private carriers snatched package delivery away from the Postal Service by offering reliability and convenience, which were weak points of the incumbent.

The center of gravity for the incumbent can be a flagship product or cherished market segment. This does not mean that the best-defended market segments should be approached first. On the contrary, the flagship brand may be neglected as the established market leader pursues new projects, leaving open its traditional business. The center of gravity can be on the supply side. Wooing away parts suppliers or research partners can unbalance the competitor's plans and create competitive advantages. Having identified the center of gravity, the approach should not be tentative. The entrant should muster all of its available competitive resources, producing a product that meets stretch targets for quality, effectiveness, and customer value. This means diverting resources from other activities, since low resource commitment increases the likelihood of failure just as it reduces expenditures. Top management may balk at such a concentration of effort. However, half measures in competitive entry greatly reduce the entrant's chances of success.

The market-based offensive strategies that I set forth here go beyond the traditional array of competitive strategies. Michael Porter identified three crucial generic strategies: cost leadership, product differentiation, and focus; that is, high quality and low price in a market niche. These strategies encapsulate the basics of price competition and changing product characteristics. Market-based strategies based on the MAIN framework extend and complement these approaches.

Market Maker

The company's market-making activities generate strategic opportunities. As market maker, the firm can achieve competitive advantage through price setting, coordinating exchange, market clearing, and allocating goods and services.

The go-between, bring-together, bypass, and connect strategies discussed in Chapter 7 can be used to enter new markets and compete against incumbents. By providing one-stop shopping and a focal point for customers and suppliers, companies can outdo established incumbents, particularly in a fragmented industry. Companies can expand and enter new markets by coordinating exchange better than their competitors.

Transaction Costs. Competitive pricing is not simply lower prices. Pricing so as to reduce the cost of transacting for customers and suppliers is an important source of competitive advantage. Discounted pricing not only costs less, it reduces the need for further shopping. Maintaining low prices reduces the returns to consumers from searching for a better price. Consumers avoid the time costs of further search as well as the costs from delayed benefits of consumption. Clear price information reduces the cost to consumers of evaluating the deal. Communicating price information to customers helps them with their budgeting and decision making. These pricing services can confer competitive advantages over competitors with fluctuating or nebulous pricing policies.

Market-clearing activities are a source of competitive advantage when the firm manages its inventories better than its competitors do. Consumer convenience is enhanced by immediacy. Companies easily lose business if customers consistently find a poor selection or cannot obtain an important sought-after item. Simply carrying a larger inventory is costly because the company incurs the interest carrying costs of inventory and the costs of space, as well as the costs of unsold inventory. Therefore, outperforming rivals in providing immediacy requires innovation in the management of inventories, including ordering and tracking systems and information exchange with suppliers.

Closely related to market-clearing activities is the allocation of goods and services across the firm's markets to insure immediacy and responsiveness to changes in customer tastes. Outperforming competitors in market allocation requires organizational flexibility and continual innovation in data processing and communication with customers and suppliers.

To illustrate the competitive strategy aspects of market making, consider the problem of competitive entry into some area of retail or wholesale distribution. The entrant must purchase and sell in a manner that narrows the spread in relation to established firms, which entails either narrower margins or reduced operating costs due to productive efficiency. Alternatively, the entrant must offer increased value added for consumers and suppliers, which requires improving upon existing delivery systems or creating an entirely new distribution method.

Consider for example the business of book distribution. Many readers once relied on mail order catalogs and clubs such as the Book of the Month club. Traditional small booksellers offered consumer services but very limited selection. Booksellers often were inconveniently located as well. Bookselling chains improved location by siting stores in malls and suburban locations, although the chains offered even more limited selection and fewer consumer services, hiring clerks with less knowledge of the books they were selling. The chains offered a popular selection of books by sticking to only the best-selling titles. The next great innovation was the book superstore created by Barnes & Noble, Borders, and discounter Crown Books. These stores offer a greatly enhanced selection, well-trained clerks, computer-aided searches and ordering, as well as poetry readings and in-store coffee bars.

How could a new entrant penetrate the book retailing market? Given the evolution of the industry, the challenge is clear, but the solution is far from apparent. One approach would be simply to do what the incumbents are doing, but to match the size and selection of the superstores would be a costly enterprise with limited chance of success from me-too marketing. A viable solution turned out to be on-line marketing by Amazon.com, replacing the bookstore with a Web site. The company was able to offer discounted pricing by eliminating the bricks and mortar. The number of available titles soared to over 1.5 million, with another million out-of-print books, because the firm can drastically reduce inventories by relying on publishers, in return offering publishers access to a wide range of customers and simplified transactions. The on-line store offers highly trained clerks who are knowledgeable in their fields.

Amazon.com defines itself in superlatives: "Earth's biggest bookstore," "The best selection of books," and "The best prices." It offers discounts of 40% on 500 titles. Most of the books listed are accompanied by additional information such as published reviews. In addition, authors, publishers, staff, and readers can add their own comments. Readers can search the store by author, title, and subject, breaking down the barriers of the bookshelf. The store has its own journal and electronic forums for readers to interact. Readers can sign up for personalized e-mail on topics of interest. By bringing buyers and sellers together in this dramatically innovative manner, the store performs market-making functions that challenge the traditional booksellers and superstores as well.

Gains from Trade and Better Deals. To compete, each company must offer its customers and suppliers better deals in comparison with competitors. The company cannot set its prices on the basis of its own costs. The company should not price to customers solely on the basis of their direct benefits received from the good, and it cannot price to its suppliers solely on the basis of their direct costs of supplying the productive input. Instead, prices must be set on the basis of the best available market alternative for customers and suppliers. This means narrowing the price spread, or increasing buyer or seller gains from trade through greater value added.

Market transactions are voluntary. Buyers only agree to make purchases if their benefits are greater than their payments to companies. Sellers only agree to make sales if their costs are below the payments they are being offered. In general, buyers and sellers only agree to transactions if they receive gains from trade. A company carries out transactions by offering gains from trade to its customers and suppliers.

Competing firms must forge better market bridges. To achieve success companies need to create and manage markets that outperform the alternatives, whether direct trade between buyers and sellers or alternative intermediation offered by direct competitors. Companies must offer the greatest gains from trade to attract the business of customers and suppliers. These gains from trade reflect not just the firm's prices and product features, but the additional costs of transacting with the firms.

Understanding gains from trade is essential to competitive strategy. It is not sufficient to offer the customer a deal with benefits in excess of payments. The company must offer the customer the *best* deal, that is, the transaction that yields greater gains from trade than those offered by the firm's competitors. Put differently, the customer's net benefit from a transaction with your company is the benefit from the product or service, net of the payments, and net of the gains from trade from the best alternative deal. The cost of dealing with your company is the payment for your goods and services plus the net benefits foregone by not purchasing from other companies.

For example, suppose that the consumer values your product at $10. The customer can purchase a similar product from a competitor that the customer values at $9. The competitor is offering the product at the price of $5, so that purchasing the rival product yields net benefits of $4. The most that can be charged for the good is the benefit to the customer

($10), net of the opportunity cost of not buying the rival product ($4). So, your price cannot exceed the consumer's economic benefit of $6:

$$\text{Economic benefit: } \$10 - \$4 = \$6$$

The target for pricing is not the customer's benefit from your transaction in isolation. It is the benefit net of the opportunity cost of foregoing the best alternative. This is the meaning of the best deal.

Similar reasoning defines the best deal for suppliers. Suppose that the supplier's direct cost of providing you with a productive resource or piece of equipment is $2. Otherwise, the supplier could earn revenues of $5 selling a product that costs $4 to produce, for a net return of $1. The supplier's costs are then the sum of production cost and opportunity cost:

$$\text{Economic cost: } \$2 + \$1 = \$3$$

The supplier must be offered at least $3 to induce it to sell the productive resource or equipment to your company. The economic cost to the supplier is the cost of production plus the net returns from the best alternative.

For the business to be successful, the company must be able to make the best deal for both suppliers and customers at the same time. In the simple example above, the company must be able to create a profit spread that supports gains from trade for its customers and suppliers. By asking $6 from customers and offering $3 to suppliers, the company is able to make a profit of $3 on the necessary transactions, thus bridging the two markets.

Pricing strategies in the company's product and input markets are designed to create better deals for customers and suppliers. This does not mean undercutting competitors. Companies whose products deliver greater value to customers can increase prices to the extent permitted by the better deal requirement. Companies can differentiate their products by enhancing the products and the accompanying services, including transaction convenience.

Pricing itself provides a means of differentiating the product. Sears offered "everyday low prices" to differentiate its stores from competitors. Many discounters offer price stability as an inducement to customers. Shoppers may not know the exact price of specific items when they plan a shopping trip, but they will choose a store that has traditionally offered low prices and that keeps its prices relatively stable, avoiding the rapid swings that come with a cycle of sales and markups. Procter & Gamble switched to a policy of steady low prices with less reliance on promotions to compete more effectively with national brands while counteracting the lower-priced generics.

For many companies, discounts, promotions, and sales are used to stimulate interest in their product and service offerings. Department stores feature frequent markdowns for every occasion. These price fluctuations draw attention to the company and are a good marketing device. They separate price-conscious shoppers, who are willing to visit the store to take advantage of the sale, from other customers who buy on impulse whether or not there is a sale, or from customers who consider their time sufficiently valuable that they will not alter their plans to take advantage of a sale.

There is no obvious prescription. A steady pricing policy reduces customer transaction costs. Buyers turn to a company because they are able to rely on past experience as a guide. Companies can then win the market with a low-pricing policy, counting on repeat sales in the future to drive down unit costs, allowing continued low prices. Alternatively, a flexible pricing policy draws attention to the company and allows for a rapid response to market events that suggest raising or lowering prices.

The choice of a pricing approach depends on strategic considerations. When facing low-price competitors, it is necessary to find ways to beat their low prices or to enhance customer value through product and service differences. When facing companies with rapidly fluctuating prices, there are gains to a pricing policy that insure customers against price risk. The problem with a steady pricing policy is that customers will buy from the steady-pricing firm when the rival company's prices are high and not when the rival company's prices are marked down for a sale. The solution to this is to provide guarantees, such as airline frequent flyer programs, that reward customer loyalty with assurances that expenditures will be lower over the long term.

Prices must be easily understood. Companies that confuse potential customers with complex options and discounts on list prices that are difficult to calculate can be outmaneuvered by prices that are simple. In this way, straightforward pricing provides a service to customers by reducing the costs of comparison shopping. Customers will even pay a premium for convenience. For this reason, complex marketing and promotional schemes can be defeated by presenting customers with a basic price plan.

When competitors' prices are excessively high, the company can follow an everyday low-price strategy. When others' prices are complex and difficult for customers to understand, the company should present simple pricing rules that may sacrifice some short-term returns for long-term building of customer confidence. If rivals disguise their prices, or requiring shopping, bargaining, or other time-consuming methods to discover the price, the company should provide easily accessible pricing information. When competitors constantly change their prices, creating risk and uncertainty for customers, the company can offer fixed prices or pricing guarantees, similar to most favored nations clauses. When rivals bundle unwanted goods and services, the company can unbundle, pricing components separately and offering customers the flexibility to create their own options packages.

Input Prices and the Price Spread. When companies compete based on prices for suppliers as well as customers, they simultaneously raise the bid price to suppliers and lower the ask price to customers, thus tightening the bid–ask spread. This is much more difficult than a basic cost leadership strategy. Instead the firm must continually adjust both input and output prices and harmonize the two pricing policies. This requires continual monitoring of the competition in upstream and downstream markets and effective use of information.

The firm can be successful by providing improved coordination of suppliers and customers. New methods of exchange can allow an incumbent to remain a market maker or permit an innovative entrant to bypass the incumbent. Intermediary competition offers the possibility of far more effective use of information. A retailer such as Wal-Mart gains a competitive advantage over other retail intermediaries through its well-developed electronic data interchange system that allows it to pass on information about customer purchasing patterns to its suppliers. This gives Wal-Mart an edge in terms of supplier relationships and allows it to obtain favorable terms compared to competing retailers.

Price Wars. Pricing is at the heart of competitive strategy. Ultimately, companies compete on price relative to value received. The most damaging direct form of competition is the unrestrained price war between firms offering identical products. In the following example, I consider factors that exacerbate and attenuate price wars and explore the effects of these factors on strategic decisions.

To understand price wars, consider the classic example adapted from the work of the French economist Bertrand in 1883. Two mineral water sellers, Marcel and Georges, are offering identical products, bottles of water sold at the well. Their only costs are those of bottling, which are exactly one franc per bottle. How much will each producer charge? Both sellers have sufficient capacity to serve the full market demand at any price at or above one franc.

Neither supplier will charge below one franc, for to do so would mean a loss on each bottle. The question is whether they will charge more than one franc. Total market demand is shown in Table 9-1.

Suppose that both sellers charge 5 francs per bottle. If they each get half of the customers, they will each sell half the demand (5 bottles) and earn a total revenue of 25 francs. Since their costs are one franc per bottle they will each earn 20 francs profit.

Marcel notices that if he cuts the price to 4 francs per bottle, he will greatly increase sales, not only capturing the other seller's customers but increasing total market sales to 12 bottles. The profit earned from such a move would be a revenue of 48 francs net of the cost of bottling of 12

Table 9-1.
DEMAND FOR MINERAL WATER

Price per bottle (in bottles)	Market demand (in francs)
5	10
4	12
3	14
2	16
1	18

francs, which comes to 36 francs. Because it will increase his profit, Marcel cuts the price to 4 francs.

Georges finds that all of his customers have deserted him. He must decide whether to match Marcel's price cut or to undercut further. If he matches Marcel, they split the market, each earning a profit of half of 36 francs, or 18 francs. If Georges undercuts the price, going down to 3 francs, he not only takes away Marcel's customers, he expands demand further to 14 bottles, earning revenues of 42 francs with costs of 14 francs for a net profit of 28 francs. Georges then cuts his price to 3 francs.

Inevitably, Marcel must respond because all the customers have gone to Georges. By matching Georges, Marcel would get half of his profit, only 14 francs. The only alternative is to cut prices to 2 francs, yielding a profit of 16 francs, so Marcel sets a price of 2 francs. Georges is forced to respond and the two sellers end up at the one-franc price, splitting the market demand of 18 bottles and just breaking even.

In fact, if Marcel and Georges understand the game fully, they will immediately offer the same price of one franc. More sophisticated players that repeat the game daily may play differently. They may choose to fasten on a higher common price that is profitable for both. If either seller deviates from that price, the other immediately reverts to the zero-profit one-franc price. Such repeated interaction can allow above-cost pricing to emerge in this very basic competition.

Break-even pricing is the competitive ideal: All sellers earn revenues that cover all of their economic costs. Consumers get the best possible deal because prices have fallen all the way to costs. The problem with this scenario is that break-even pricing offers no incentives to incur any of the other costs that are required to get into the game, such as investment in production capacity or R&D to develop new products. While price wars are by no means rare, there are many factors in competitive markets that attenuate price competition, yielding positive economic returns to competitors. These returns attract new entry into the market and foster innovation.

Price competition reflects the differences in efficiency of the rival firms. Suppose that Marcel and Georges have different costs of producing and bottling mineral water. Let us say Marcel is efficient with costs of one franc while Georges is inefficient with costs of two francs per bottle. Marcel will price just below two francs, earning a profit of about 16 francs and driving out the inefficient competitor.

Product Differentiation. The apparently drastic outcome of the price war between the mineral water sellers changes when market conditions change. One of those crucial conditions was the assumption that the two mineral waters were identical products. When products are truly identical, a small price differential sends all of the customers to the low-priced company. It is almost as if customers were on a frictionless roller coaster, responding only to the gravitational pull of lower prices.

Suppose instead that the products are differentiated in some way; say the two mineral water sellers are Perrier and Evian. If customers perceive a difference, whether due to the characteristics of the products or simply brand recognition, the extreme effects of prices on demand disappear. When products differ, some but not all customers are pulled over to the lower-priced firm. Those customers are on the fence, and at the original prices are close to indifferent between the two products. Any change in the price differential is enough to attract these swing customers, but not sufficient to attract the more loyal customers.

This changes the price competition between the two firms and averts a price war. A firm that contemplates lowering its price faces a trade-off. It would gain by attracting some customers away from its competitor, but it could lose because revenues might fall from the customers that it already had. Each firm balances these two effects in choosing what price to offer. The result is that the two firms make profits because they have no reason to undercut each other's prices. The prices chosen by the two firms still depend on what each thinks the other will offer. However, the competitive prices sustain markups above the firms' marginal costs.

Price wars are still possible with differentiated products. Breakfast cereal makers Kellogg, General Mills, Post Cereal (General Foods), Nabisco Cereals (Philip Morris), Quaker Oats, and Ralston were in a price war in the mid-1990s. The price war was motivated in part by the success of store brand cereals on the low end and various challenges to Kellogg's market leadership on the high end of the market. Under pricing pressure, Ralcorp, maker of Chex, sold its cereal brands to General Mills, retaining its generic private label cereal business.

The extent to which the firms earn returns to their product differences depends on the loyalty of customers to their products and the extent of the differentiation.

■ Products may be physically similar but the companies supplying those products have different locations. Travel is costly for consumers.

Competitors will not undercut each other's prices because travel costs create loyal customers.

■ Products may be distinguished by subjective characteristics such as design, packaging, or brand image.

■ Products can differ in terms of quality or performance measures such as durability, energy efficiency, or ease of maintenance.

■ Products can differ in terms of accompanying services, including the transaction costs of obtaining the product.

Companies choose the extent of product differentiation from their competitors. In some cases, they try to mimic each others' product characteristics to try to capture the other's loyal customers. In other cases, they try to distance their products from those of the rivals to protect against direct competition. Thus, in some markets companies tend toward similar products, which creates the potential for price wars. In other markets, companies tend to emphasize product distinctions, which raises costs while increasing prices.

Another factor that affects pricing strategy is the cost to consumers of switching suppliers. This gives an incentive to firms to offer low introductory prices as a means of attracting customers.[3] If it is difficult to switch products due to customer inertia or because the customer needs to acquire special skills to use the product, such as a word processing program, the firm can raise prices later. Customers who must weigh the benefits of changing to another supplier against the costs of switching become captive for some range of prices. The presence of switching costs intensifies initial price competition as products are introduced and companies seek to build a loyal following. After customers have chosen products, price competition is reduced since price cuts only move some of the customers that have low switching costs. Therefore, switching costs work a bit like product differentiation.

This insight suggests to some that companies should create their own switching costs or do something to increase customer inertia. Thus, airlines offer frequent flyer programs and phone companies offer rewards for frequent callers. These programs are not only costly, they can be overcome by competitors offering switching bonuses to overcome customer inertia. By avoiding the costs of erecting switching costs, entrants can lower prices sufficiently to attract customers from the incumbent that relies on such programs. The entrant can counteract the effects of contracts between customers and incumbents by offering a no-contracts policy to appeal to customer concern over costly commitment to a single supplier.

Capacity Investment. Another factor that limits price wars is the cost of production or distribution capacity. Even if products are identical, the strategy of undercutting the competitor's price to capture their customers is only attractive to the extent that the company lowering its price has enough productive capacity to serve those customers. Also, it is not necessary to lower prices to attract customers if the competitor's capacity limits are already rationing sales and driving customers to your company.

Companies should anticipate the outcome of price competition when they make their capacity investments. Having invested in productive capacity, the price competition begins. If both companies hold sufficient capacity to serve the entire market, then price competition will erase profits. Foreseeing this eventuality, firms will commit capacity that is less than that required to serve the entire market. Price competition then will be attenuated and the firms will earn profits on their capacity investment.[4]

Companies should plan their capacity investment on the basis of how they believe future price competitions will play out. If products are very similar to those of competitors and operating cost differences are small, companies should invest carefully, restraining their capacity commitments. If products are differentiated, the anticipated success in winning over swing customers and the competitor's loyal customers should enter into the capacity investment decision. If the company's product is superior or if it has an operating cost advantage, this suggests an all-out investment strategy to allow sufficient capacity for the company to realize the full returns to its expected product quality or pricing advantages.

Coordination. It does not matter which side of the road people drive on, as long as everyone drives on the same side. In the U.S. people drive on the right; in the U.K. and Japan people drive on the left. The U.S. automakers suffered low sales in Japan for years by failing to recognize this simple fact and attempting to sell left-side driver cars. Coordination of driving habits is a matter of law. In markets, coordination is achieved in many ways, one of which is pricing.

Companies are often intent on advertising that they have the lowest prices, that they are the leaders in price cutting, or that there are no other lower-priced firms. Southwest Airlines says that it is *the* low-priced airline. These pricing practices and the publicity around them are market coordination devices. Consumers seek the lowest-price firm. Going on the basis of reputation, they seek out the firm that had the lowest prices in the past. This makes the low-price leader the high-volume leader, and therefore through economies of scale or cost-reducing investment, the low-cost leader. Being the low-cost leader allows the firm to continue its policy of setting low prices, thereby validating consumers' expectations. Prices have done their job as market coordination mechanisms, helping consumers find the low-cost firm.

Pricing and capacity investment strategies are closely related when consumers base their search decisions on past prices.[5] It is costly for consumers to continually monitor all current prices for many goods. This is particularly true of retailer superstores that offer many different goods. Consumers rely on the reputation stores create from past pricing practices and on impressions formed based on the last time they visited the stores. The prices set by the store therefore affect the pattern of sales in future periods.

Stores face a trade-off between the reduced earnings from lower pricing today and the gains in sales tomorrow that today's low pricing will create. The firm must balance pricing high today for quick earnings today or pricing low today to invest in reputation for higher earnings tomorrow.

If the store prices low today, it will benefit from greater demand for its products tomorrow. That higher demand justifies increased investment in capacity, which in turn will lower the store's unit costs. Increased sales tomorrow will also lower unit costs when economies of scale are present. This further increases the returns to being the low-price leader.

Therefore, today's price competition will determine who is the market leader in the future. Some stores will pursue a high-price strategy, making hay while the sun shines. Others will pursue a reputation-building low-price strategy. Anticipating the increased sales from the low-price strategy will allow the firms to make cost-reducing investments and realize higher sales that will further lower unit costs. This growth will allow today's price leader to remain in that position. Consumers will benefit from the coordination effects of pricing, seeking out the low-price leader based on the company's pricing reputation. Today's low-price leader will win the market tomorrow.

Imperfect Information. Price competition is further influenced by lack of complete information about competitors' costs and product offerings. The many differences between companies' technology, organization, and management practices add complexity to price competition. If the competitor has a clear cost disadvantage it is possible to exploit it by pricing below their costs. If the competitor's costs are not known, the strategic decision is a trade-off between the revenue gains from raising one's price and the potential that the higher price will be undercut by a low-cost rival.[6]

The uncertainty about rival costs translates into uncertainty about their future pricing policies. This transforms price competition into a type of auction as companies bid for customers. Firms offer prices that reflect the trade-off between the revenue gains from offering a higher price and the increased likelihood of winning the bidding war that results from offering a lower price. The company with the lowest costs ultimately will win the bidding. However, all companies mark up their prices over marginal cost, unlike what would occur in a world where rival costs were easy to observe. The size of the markup depends on the number of companies bidding to serve customers and each company's expectations about how much costs vary across the industry.

Repeated competition may narrow markups as companies get to know each other. However, in a market with rapidly changing demand and cost conditions, the bidding for customers need not reveal costs, so that companies can compete repeatedly and still experience uncertainty about rival actions.

Segmenting Markets. Marketers understand clearly the importance of segmentation. Consumer tastes and incomes differ. One-size-fits-all may end up fitting no one. Ideally, companies would like mass customization, reaping the benefits of economies of scale while satisfying individual needs. But customization can entail transaction costs. The solution is to divide customer markets into segments and tailor offerings to each segment.

Pricing must adapt to customer willingness to pay. Charging the same per-unit price to everyone can be inefficient. If there are wide disparities in customer valuations, it makes sense to offer quantity discounts. Large demanders are charged less per unit and increase their purchases in response to the discounts. Both large and small buyers are made better off relative to an average price.

Buyers value quality features differently. Buyer diversity can be addressed by the offering of a product line, with higher cost and higher quality at the top end. The product line is priced with quality discounts, providing incentives for buyers that value the enhancements to travel up the product line. Thus, Federal Express offers a variety of express services, from second-day delivery up to next morning, with price variations reflecting the relative willingness to pay of the market segments being targeted.

The design of a product line is an effective competitive device allowing the firm to address the competition within market segments by targeting product pricing and features to meet and beat niche players. A variety of strategies is possible using maneuvers in the terrain of product features. To compete with a firm offering a single product, a company can respond with a product line that encircles the competitor's product, offering lower-cost models and higher-cost models to capture both the high and low ends of the market. Customers benefit from the increased variety, and they will be attracted by the wider product line. Elements in the product line can be repositioned by changing individual prices and product features without changing the whole line.

Companies offer multiple product lines to target multidimensional aspects of market segments. Customers might be described by both income and product preferences. A single product line might separate the consumers by income but would not be sufficient to address the other product preferences. For example, General Motors' line of midsize cars addresses many competitors. General Motors' midsize cars include the basic Chevrolet Malibu and Oldsmobile Cutlass, the Pontiac Grand Prix, targeted to drivers seeking a sporty midsize car, the Buick Century and Regal, and the upper-end Oldsmobile Intrigue. Each car has base and deluxe variations. The brands of the cars target product preferences and a range of competing midsize cars, such as Ford's Taurus, Toyota's Camry, Honda's Accord, and Chrysler's Concorde.

Pricing a product line allows the company to carry out more complicated competitive strategies. It can simultaneously offer low-price alternatives and high-priced features, competing against low-end and high-end competitors. It can outflank competitors through price leadership on the low end and innovative features on the high end.

Arbitrageur

Companies can outperform competitors by arbitrage, but this offensive strategy is one of the toughest to follow. Discerning arbitrage opportunities means noticing them faster than others and acting faster to capitalize on them. This means that the company must have better market information than competitors through supplier and distributor alliances or better communication procedures. By carefully tracking the prices of productive inputs, the company can take advantage of falling input costs to lower output prices, thus gaining an edge with consumers. If some input prices are rising, the source of cost increases can be identified quickly and purchasing decisions adjusted accordingly.

The company can also achieve arbitrage advantages by building new market bridges, putting together innovative contracts that make new customer–supplier connections. Arbitrage of this type requires working closely with suppliers to improve their inputs to your production process, or searching for the best suppliers. Manufacturing innovative products with new materials and technologies is also a way to carry out arbitrage. The margin on the innovative product is the return to developing the new product.

As firms bid competitively for customers and suppliers, the price spreads narrow and the returns to arbitrage decline. With these slimmer margins, the company needs higher sales volumes to cover its overhead and other fixed expenditures. In businesses without much product differentiation, winning markets depends on the essential element of the high-volume, low-margin strategy. Superstores and category killers in electronics, toys, hardware, and other markets are examples of this strategy. Supermarkets go directly to suppliers to produce generics that are resold at lower cost than name brand products, thereby arbitraging between the wholesale and retail markets for no-name detergents, paper products, or prepared foods. Because competition narrows margins, the pursuit of arbitrage returns leads to rapid adjustment of purchasing patterns and product mix.

Dell Computers exemplifies the arbitrage strategy, assembling computers from components and arbitraging between the market for components and the market for computers. Dell is extending this strategy from personal computers to workstations and network servers. This complements Dell's sales of PCs to business customers. It competes against other equipment makers by narrowing the price spread between these two markets, connecting customers with component makers through its assembly and distribution processes.

Companies achieve competitive arbitrage by bringing products and services to new markets where the products are not currently available. One way is by pioneering exports or imports in international trade. Another way is to distribute products in a new way, through outlet stores or Internet Web sites, for example. Arbitrageurs unbundle when necessary, if consumers want just one or two components but not the whole package. For example, Internet service providers are supplying direct access to the Internet without the additional services that companies like America Online provide. Arbitrageurs bundle products when needed if buyers value the convenience of packaging or if the bundle can be obtained less expensively than individual components. Companies following offensive arbitrage strategies connect markets in new ways, providing a better mix of price and convenience than their competitors.

Intermediary

Offensive strategies based on intermediation attempt to lower transaction costs for customers and suppliers relative to the costs of dealing with competitors. Companies must outperform competitors, whether acting as agent, monitor, broker, or communicator. In head-to-head competition, companies need to lower the transaction costs for customers and suppliers. Back-office processes can be an essential part of the intermediation strategies, because those processes compete with market transactions. The reengineering of operations and office processes was embraced by companies targeting organizational costs. Firms need lower costs of communication within the organization to compete with market transactions.

For consumers, a large cost of purchasing goods and services is the time cost of searching for providers, evaluating goods and services, and in some cases negotiating prices. Retailers should look upon themselves as their customer's purchasing agent. The process of getting the supermarket to order a special item or a bookstore to order a book that is not in stock is altogether too difficult. Companies invest time and effort to study their customers, and yet they sometimes neglect the important information provided voluntarily by individual customers. Companies that are successful as buyer's agents will be those that are most responsive to requests for products and services.

Supervising employees is a service to customers. Companies that rely on customers to do the monitoring for them are not being responsive; they simply raise the cost to their customers of doing business. Companies can outperform others in terms of customer service by continually lowering the costs of dealing with the company's employees. One way of carrying this out is to make sure that financial incentives for employees are aligned with those of customers. Southwest Airlines provides incentives for its employees to respond to customer requests, thereby outdoing other airlines that have noncooperative employees. Improving customer service relative to competitors is an effective offensive strategy when it significantly reduces the cost to customers of interaction with employees.

Companies that offer brokerage services must reduce the costs of supplier–customer interaction to remain competitive. Retailers should make a point of handling customer returns or questions about products. Those that direct the customer to contact the manufacturer increase the transaction costs to the customer. These companies are vulnerable to entrants that handle all of the customer's requests. Resellers can outperform existing sellers if they add value to sales though lower-cost management of the transaction and handling of customer communications.

Companies can pursue a head-to-head strategy of providing better information to customers than their competitors. Thus, clearer price information or product specifications can provide the crucial competitive edge. Long-distance companies have complicated matters with their plethora of pricing plans. The company that offers simplified pricing will gain an advantage in what is otherwise a generic service.

For business customers, most company costs are tied up in financing, hiring, procurement, and technology. Companies that can reduce the costs of these functions relative to their rivals will gain a competitive advantage in serving business customers. The purchasing agents of a business respond not only to price but also to convenience, particularly when they must transact repeatedly with suppliers. By offering to handle inventory management, billing, and other aspects of the transactions, suppliers gain a competitive edge. The switch to Internet commerce to reduce the costs to business customers is accelerating. Business customers are able to shop through interactive Web sites provided by their suppliers that let business customers place orders themselves, monitor the progress of their orders, change the orders, and obtain answers to pricing and technical product questions.

Network Organizer

Entrants can outperform incumbents through the establishment of superior networks of suppliers or distributors. Creation of market networks is an essential part of effective competitive strategy. I have already mentioned how Coke and Pepsi intensified the cola wars by purchasing and reorganizing their bottlers to increase control and to improve their efficiency.

To illustrate the significance of creating market networks as a competitive strategy, it is worthwhile considering one of the leading examples. General Electric Information Services established its Trading Process Network (TPN) as an on-line marketplace. GE originally started TPN as a means of streamlining its own procurement processes. In its first year, GE used TPN to source about $1 billion in business with its own 1,400 suppliers, out of a total of $30 billion in expenditures on supplies.[7] The potential for expansion simply based on GE's own procurement is evident. The benefits of the network to GE are many, including lower bids due to supplier competition, faster response to requests for quotes, better communication with smaller suppliers, and generally lower transaction costs. TPN allowed GE to build an effective supplier network, thereby obtaining a competitive advantage over competitors lacking such a network.

As a result of creating the network for its own purposes, GE realized that it could provide the same service to other buyers and sellers. According to CEO Harvey Seegers, TPN accomplishes three goals for large and small businesses:

1. Increasing productivity in the purchasing arena for buyers
2. Establishing a global reach in marketing for both buyers and sellers
3. Decreasing costs and cycle times in sales efforts for suppliers.[8]

Seegers states that "we are the world's leader in electronic commerce services and manage the world's largest trading community of more than 40,000 companies."[9] The extension of a company's market network to the creation of trading communities shows the significant potential of the network organizer strategy.

The TPN marks the beginning of a shift from electronic data interchange over private networks to Internet-based market networks. Electronic data interchange was ubiquitous among large companies but relatively costly for smaller businesses. Following a common protocol and using the widely accessible Internet allows data interchange to be dictated by business relationships rather than by dedicated networks.[10] Companies setting up market networks face fewer technological limits. The successful networks will be those that provide the greatest transaction cost economies.

Case Study: Microsoft

Microsoft's competitive moves in software markets provide illustrations of both offensive and defensive strategies. Some of the critical offensive strategies are illustrated by Microsoft's entry into corporate computing. While dominant in desktop operating systems, Microsoft faces substantial competition in practically every market segment as the industry in general shifts to network computing. Network computing has two important aspects: Internet applications and corporate intranets. Company personnel have to be able to interact with customers and people in other companies, and the Internet provides the best vehicle for that communication, outperforming proprietary networks. For communication within the company, there has been a move to client-server technology, with Internet-based software holding out promise for standardizing such systems.

Having successfully defended its position as the leading maker of PC operating systems, Microsoft switched to the offensive in at least three major areas:

- Internet browsers
- Operating systems and corporate networks
- Business applications

Microsoft has sufficient strength, in terms of brand awareness, technical talent, and financial backing, to take on a host of competitors simultaneously in direct competition. Yet, while breathtaking in its scope, that kind of simultaneous, multiple-front battle is the most risky of competitive strategies.

Microsoft faces many different entrenched and powerful rivals, not to mention creative startups. Microsoft must have overwhelming strength to pull off its multifront strategy. This means a substantial commitment to investment in research, product development, marketing, and sales to promote a range of products. It will need powerful allies, including Intel in microprocessors, Hewlett-Packard, Compaq, and Digital in hardware, and a host of applications developers. Microsoft's moves provide a fascinating case study of multimarket entry.

Internet Browsers: Internet Explorer. Enter the Internet into the best-laid plans. The potential of network computing began to be realized by the middle 1990s, about a decade after it was established. While the PC excels at moving data across the desktop and local networks linked one desk to another within companies, the Internet connects networks to each other. The Internet poses an important challenge to all makers of computers and writers of software. Microsoft was as surprised as any company and its corporate strategy was out of tune with the growth of the Internet.

A vast expanse of the Internet, known as the World Wide Web, or the Web for short, is a set of locations linked together by a system of cross-referencing that allows rapid movement across the locations.[11] Information at each location is available in the form of documents, a term of art in computers that denotes a method of storing and communicating text, data, sound, and video. This system spawned programs for navigating the Web, creating a generation of Internet surfers. The Web quickly took on a life of its own, with companies and individuals setting up sites for advertising, transacting, and exchanging all kinds of information.

With all of the fervor of a convert, Microsoft positioned itself to be a supplier of network services as it came to recognize the potential of the Internet. It launched Microsoft Network, a service intended to compete with America Online, Prodigy, and CompuServe. As the focus shifted to providing Internet access rather than just a homemade network, Microsoft began the switch to supplying access. Users could initiate access to Microsoft Network, after they installed Windows 95, simply by a click of the mouse on the computer screen.

Netscape was first to market with its Navigator browser program. In only a couple of years, Netscape had come to dominate the market for Internet Web browsers, that is, software that allows people surfing the Web to "read" Web sites. In a very brief time Netscape brought out several versions of its browser program, at an average rate of one every six months. This dramatic increase in innovative speed began to change the rules of the game in software. Compare, for example, Microsoft's standard rate of about two years for new versions of various types of software.

In addition to rapid updates of Navigator, Netscape redefined the speed of standard-setting, coming to dominate the world of browsers in a couple of years through free distribution of test versions of the program. By distributing Navigator on-line, the company avoided the costs of packaging and delivering software in traditional formats such as computer disks. The company delivered corrections and updates on-line as well. The company's program became so successful that it was the second most popular software title, trailing only Microsoft's Windows operating system.

In fact, the growth of Netscape has elements of indirect strategy. The reason is that an Internet browser such as Navigator has many features that are similar to a computer operating system. While designed to surf the Web rather than operate a personal computer, an Internet browser presents a single face to the consumer no matter what Web site the consumer is visiting, much as an operating system does when a computer user employs alternative applications. An Internet browser intermediates between the Web sites, stored on other computers, and the computer on which the browser resides.

Thus, while the computer operating system allows the computer user to perform such tasks as retrieving data from files stored on the computer, Web browser software allows the user to retrieve data from files stored on other computers. Because these two functions are closely related, it is not too hard to see that either type of software can be enhanced to take on the tasks performed by the other type of software. From the user's point of view, it is helpful if both types of information can be retrieved in the same way, whether they are on your computer or on someone else's computer. If the "network is the computer," then the convergence of the two types is not hard to predict.

Yet, the challenge to Microsoft's Windows operating system did not become obvious until the spread of Navigator had already taken place. Microsoft's long-term focus on operating systems had blinded it at least temporarily to the potential of browsers. However, within about a year of Navigator's launching, Microsoft caught on and shifted its strategy to Internet-based computing.

The browser war with Netscape escalated rapidly. Microsoft introduced its Internet Explorer program as a direct challenge to Netscape Navigator. Navigator was a well-entrenched incumbent. To carry out its entry strategy, Microsoft began free distribution of Explorer. Within less than a year, many of the major Internet access providers had shifted from Navigator to Explorer, including America Online, Prodigy, CompuServe, AT&T Worldnet, and MCI. Microsoft included its browser in its Windows operating system, allowing users to click onto the browser as part of the software in a convenient manner. Microsoft attained a successful position in browsers within two years of Netscape's creation. Microsoft's initial success in the browser segment was tempered by the shift in market focus to corporate networks.

Operating Systems and Corporate Networks: Windows NT. Computers are run by operating system software. Microsoft has been the major supplier of operating systems for personal computers, beginning with its Disk Operating System (DOS) and continuing with its Windows programs. Windows is called a graphical interface because computer users employ a mouse to point and click on buttons and other on-screen images to operate applications. The combination of DOS and Windows sets the standard for desktop computer operating systems, with over 80% of the market worldwide.

Yet Microsoft's Windows 95, launched with much fanfare, is the last generation of an operating system that is a couple of upgrades away from retirement. The software maker's plan of continued expansion had two steps. First, it intended to provide the operating systems for corporate networks, including servers, central computers that link PC clients in networks. Second, it eventually hoped to provide operating systems for a host of other technologies, including video game systems, personal digital assistants, office equipment, consumer appliances, TV set-top boxes, network switching equipment, and video servers. Microsoft was prepared to provide operating software for mass market networks whether customers used their TVs or personal computers or both as communications terminals. One aspect of the process of adapting software to different tasks is known as *scaling.* Software for computers is scaled up to handle the many users on a corporate intranet. It is scaled down to reduce memory and processing requirements so that it can operate smaller devices.

Microsoft viewed Windows 95 as a transition to Windows NT that would allow companies writing applications to prepare programs that run on both the current and the more advanced program, and that would allow users time to upgrade their computers to meet the heavier processing and memory requirements of the NT software.[12] Windows NT has an underlying applications programming interface (API) named Win32. An API is used by programmers and interprets the commands of applications software such as spreadsheets and word processing programs.

Microsoft's plans centered around Windows NT (new technology) as the operating system initially for advanced users and later for the mass market, when users had upgraded their systems with sufficient memory and computing power. Introduced early in the 1990s and continually upgraded, Windows NT began to build share in the corporate network market. Windows NT included advanced features for client-server interaction, integration of different software programs, and components that carry out tasks for programmers. Thus, Windows NT was intended to maintain Microsoft's share of the operating system market for personal computers, defending against future alternatives.

Two major developments created an opening for entrants into the corporate network. First, companies turned toward client-server configurations with linked networks of PCs and away from the big iron of mainframes. Second, company networks began to adopt Internet-based standards, moving away from fragmented proprietary systems. Internet standards include the TCP/IP (transmission control protocol/internet protocol) for Internet traffic. This called for operating system software that could operate with a client-server network architecture **and** that included Internet protocols.

If incumbent suppliers of corporate network equipment and software could adapt to the new technology, corporate computing would be a difficult market to penetrate. On the other hand, if these suppliers were slow to adapt or fell victim to technological and marketing myopia, adaptive entrants would have a shot at a huge market.

Despite having missed the first wave of Internet growth, Microsoft was quick to catch on to its implications. Competitors' concerns over Microsoft's success in operating systems had long been evident. Microsoft's Internet strategy only increased their anxiety. Eric Schmidt, chief technology officer of Sun Microsystems, said, "I personally believe that Microsoft is the most powerful economic force in the United States in the second half of the 20th century."[13] Schmidt's view suggested the need for an indirect strategy to challenge Microsoft, and that is exactly what Sun pursued with its Java language, as noted in Chapter 8.

Windows NT for servers and workstations challenged other operating systems: Unix, Novell Netware, and IBM's OS/2. Windows NT, by setting a market standard, presented a clear advantage over Unix, which operates in 34 versions. Since there are so many different flavors of Unix, the transaction costs for companies that use the software and for applications developers are very high. Corporate networks running NT on servers with Intel PCs also posed a challenge to servers and workstations offered by Sun Microsystems, Silicon Graphics, and others.

In the battle for operating software running corporate networks, Microsoft challenged the incumbent, Novell. Novell's Netware had been dominant in corporate networks. However, Novell missed both of the major developments in networking, the Internet and client-server computing. How could these developments have passed them by? Novell's management had focused its attention on divesting WordPerfect Corporation and the QuattroPro spreadsheet it had acquired from Borland. In the aftermath, Novell's CEO, Robert J. Frankenberg, was forced to resign.[14] Finally, Novell introduced the Intranetware operating system to address client-server networks and Internet standards.

A new entrant to the corporate market, Netscape offered another corporate network software product named SuiteSpot for operating servers. Continuing its challenge to Microsoft, Netscape brought out its Constellation software, which provides the user with an alternative interface to Windows, one that combines Internet applications and will run on the PC.

Netscape Communications Corp. formed a joint venture (with Sony, Nintendo, Sega, and others) called the Navio Corporation to develop operating system software for devices other than personal computers, including set-top boxes. In addition, Netscape, Oracle, IBM, Sun Microsystems, and others are exploring ways to develop operating system software for low-cost network computers.

Thus Microsoft, in seeking to defend and extend its markets, took on companies making software for corporate networks and for other types of devices. This opened multiple fronts in the operating systems competition. However, this was just the beginning of the Microsoft offensive.

Business Applications: BackOffice. Building on the widespread usage of its Windows operating system, Microsoft supplied a suite of applications, with word processing, spreadsheets, graphics, and other programs, in the Microsoft Office bundle. That program garnered over four-fifths of the market for such suites, towering over competing Lotus SmartSuite and PerfectOffice, assembled by Novell and later sold to Corel.[15] Ultimately, the operating system, graphical interface, and applications became a unified environment, with users purchasing the integrated software system.

Microsoft effectively served this market segment. However, with the growth of corporate network computing, its position could be maintained only by moving applications into network computing, where the company faced a host of other rivals.

To achieve this, Microsoft intended to build on the success of Windows NT to supply Microsoft BackOffice, a bundle of applications that includes interactive software, database management, systems management, and other business software. Companies can manage files with Windows NT Server, manage databases with SQL Server, manage networks with Systems Management Server, and maintain Internet Web sites with Internet Information Server. Exchange Server handles messaging, groupware, and scheduling, and companies can handle Internet commerce with Transaction Server and Merchant Server, renamed Commerce Server.

Microsoft faced many smaller competitors and three major ones: IBM, Netscape, and Novell. Long a power in corporate computing with its vast corporate sales force, IBM offered a group of programs called Project Eagle. IBM's acquisition of Lotus Notes gave it the capability to provide Internet-based e-mail, scheduling, and database management. Netscape's Communicator works on corporate network servers and has an associated set of applications called SuiteSpot. Netscape includes its Navigator browser within SuiteSpot. As mentioned previously, despite its strong position in corporate computing, Novell was having difficulty adapting to the Internet and client-server computing.

One battle is over groupware, software for sending messages, holding on-line discussions, scheduling meetings, and managing data. E-mail is a mission-critical component of corporate software. Many companies have proprietary e-mail systems that do not communicate easily with other systems. Internet protocols have rendered those systems obsolete. The Internet protocols are designed to handle large amounts of traffic and to allow messages to follow the same format for addressing and routing. Accordingly, some proprietary systems, such as Microsoft Exchange, Lotus Notes, and Novell's Groupwise 5, have included or are based on Internet protocols, while Netscape Communications' SuiteSpot is already an Internet-based messaging program.[16] These companies were ready to battle it out directly, having pushed aside companies not embracing Internet standards.

Internet compatibility was an essential part of the corporate software package. Microsoft bundled its Internet browser with its BackOffice software. Netscape's Communicator bundled its Navigator browser with software for groupware, scheduling, sending e-mail, and making Web documents.

Another set of competitors (or potential allies) existed in database software, including Informix, IBM, Oracle, and Sybase, that works with the Unix operating system. To compete, Microsoft offered SQL Server, which runs on Windows NT. Competitors did not view Microsoft as a threat because of the scalability problem; that is, Unix-based programs could handle large-scale jobs with high-capacity servers. Microsoft's Windows NT could only work on smaller jobs, at least initially.

However, as an entry strategy, it can make sense to come in at the low end, offering fewer capabilities at lower cost and serving smaller businesses. There are many more smaller businesses than there are major corporate clients. This is a way of building market share and earnings. Microsoft, as an entrant into the business market, then can gain strength for a full-scale assault on large-scale corporate computing. It has steadily upgraded Windows NT to handle larger tasks and higher-end servers.

By taking on so many competitors, many of them well established and experienced in the corporate market, Microsoft ran the danger of spreading itself too thin. It would need agility and overwhelming strength to penetrate so many markets simultaneously. Yet to a great extent, a multimarket strategy made sense because of the advantages of standard-setting. A common standard, which Windows NT provided, would lower user companies' hardware and software costs. Moreover, Internet standards would simplify the tasks of running internal networks and linking companies with each other. By embracing Internet standards and offering companies a well-recognized product that inherited the standardization of earlier Windows programs, Microsoft had a chance to set standards in network computing, although each segment would be hotly contested. By creating market networks through its standardization of corporate desktops and embracing the Internet standards, Microsoft could create an effective market network that would lower the transaction costs of corporate computing. This was the basis of its risky but potentially rewarding entry strategy.

Defense

Defensive strategies are used for the protection of market position from competitors entering the market or expanding existing operations. As companies win markets they must be prepared to face constant challenges from innovative competitors. The incumbent can fend off attacks with defensive positions, counterattack competitors with offensive strategies, or stay ahead of the game with continual innovation. I consider innovation strategies in the next section.

In contrast to military strategy, defense of market position is not a sign of weakness. Instead, it is a sign of the incumbent's success in developing markets. By launching products and building a customer base, the incumbent's leading position attracts competitors by signaling potential returns to entry. Although the incumbent should update its prices and product offerings frequently, it cannot challenge all competitors directly.

Offensive challenges to incumbents come in so many forms that it is difficult to anticipate them all. Incumbents should be prepared for both shark and piranha attacks. Sharks will attack head-on, posing challenges to the incumbent's major markets. Piranha will proceed by taking small bites out of the incumbent's market segments; however, these smaller entrants come in large numbers and many little bites soon add up to major losses in market share. The one thing that thriving incumbents need to guard against is complacency.

Incumbents that win markets should be prepared for continual waves of entry and rival expansion. Thus, for leading firms, a defensive strategy is a necessary complement to its own offensive strategy. Companies may find themselves fighting rear-guard actions even as they advance on new markets.

Flexible Response

The classic defensive mistake is maintaining a fixed line of defense. Like the ill-fated Maginot line or fixed fortifications, rigid defense strategies do not prevail in the long run against persistent offensives and innovative challenges. A business cannot expect to resist competitors with tried-and-true routines. Competitors have an easy time with a stationary target. In contrast, continual improvement in pricing and products enhances defense. Yet companies cannot anticipate all competitive innovations. Thus, incumbent firms must be prepared for flexible response.

The market must be won again every day. Competition is continually renewed. Success in the marketplace attracts innovative challengers. Having achieved a dominant market position by outperforming competitors, the firm must then be prepared for the continual entry of niche firms and for major players seeking to wrest away customers. At that point, the firm must consider defensive strategies.

Complacency is an invitation to competitive entry. The best way to maintain market position is to continually improve customer service and to operate efficiently, cutting costs and maintaining lower prices. Repeated introduction of new products keeps the company abreast of new technology and improves customer well-being. These steps are management imperatives, but they do not constitute a complete defensive strategy. Effective defense requires anticipating the types of attacks that will be mounted by actual and potential competitors. Then, the company must be prepared to avoid these attacks, preempt them, or respond to them.

What is a defense? In warfare, according to Clausewitz, defense has two parts: awaiting the blow and parrying it. Defensive measures exist at all levels of warfare: strategy, maneuver, and tactics. The defense is fought on your own ground in response to an offensive by the opponent. Defense includes an offensive response within your theater of operations. After withstanding the enemy assault, a defensive counterassault takes place. Clausewitz argues that "the defensive form of warfare is intrinsically stronger than the offensive" because the defense benefits from preparation time and it capitalizes on the mistakes of the offense. Moreover, the defense is better able to make use of the terrain and to surprise the offense with counterattacks. He concludes that defense is "a means to win a victory that enables one to take the offensive after superiority has been gained."[17]

Napoleon cautioned that "[a] general-in-chief should ask himself frequently in the day, what should I do if the enemy's army appeared now on my front, or on my right, or on my left?"[18] Managers must also be prepared for the unexpected actions of competitors or the sudden appearance of new competitors. Successful companies need an effective defensive strategy to hold market share, and a defensive strategy is of tactical value to new entrants experiencing counterattacks in their market segments from incumbent firms.

Defensive strategy does not mean attempting to erect entry barriers. Market entry barriers are easily surmounted by competitors with greater cost efficiencies, better products, contracts with customers, or simply the willingness to risk capital investment. Moreover, a diversified established firm cannot effectively defend every market segment or, indeed, every market that it serves. A determined competitor can concentrate all of its forces in serving just one market segment. The company can easily end up facing a swarm of niche competitors addressing each of its market segments.

The flexible response strategy requires having forces in reserve. The company needs general resources in management, production, marketing, sales, R&D, purchasing, and finance that can be redirected as the need arises. This involves more than putting out fires. It means flexible manufacturing that can respond to market needs, or creative talent that can be shifted to new projects. Suppliers can provide swing capacity for increased production. Outsourcing services allows the firm to dramatically alter its activity level without holding spare capacity.

Defensive mobility requires a flexible organization. The ability to assemble and manage special project teams becomes essential. The company gains an advantage by quickly employing new technology or market information. It can then respond to entrants by offering its customers an attractive alternative. This rules out rigid adherence to a long-run plan, which is the opposite of a competitive strategy.

Incumbents should attempt to anticipate entry by preemptive actions, such as price cutting, service improvements, and innovation, *before* challenges occur. This is achieved through continual improvements motivated by organizational routines, rather than being surprised by external threats. The company must also be prepared to switch to offensive strategies in response to increased competition: Outperform competitors rather than taking a wait-and-see attitude.

Do Not Overextend

Because competitors will follow the offensive strategy of pitting strength against the incumbent's weakness, incumbents should not be overextended. Trying to cover too many markets at once creates many openings for entrants because the incumbent cannot be all things to all consumers. Incumbents should limit expansion and diversification with defensive strategy in mind. Fledgling operations are appropriate for indirect strategy. Serving market segments that are subject to challenge requires substantial resources. To prepare for competition, the incumbent must be sure that its consumers get the best services it can provide.

The mistake of dispersal of forces was made by food giant ConAgra in its launch of the $1 billion flagship brand, Healthy Choice. The brand appeared almost simultaneously throughout the grocery store, taking on canned soup, dairy products, frozen foods, and other products. While sales jumped, the company faced targeted retaliation by companies dominant in each segment, creating lower returns. Careful maneuvers would have helped, targeting fewer market segments for the launch and then progressively extending the brand to other segments.

Defensive strategies are illustrated by the responses of brand name companies to low-cost alternatives. Supermarkets and other stores offer house brands, also known as generics. For retailers and the producers of generics, entry began as an indirect strategy when companies selling name brands failed to perceive growing competition coming from the low end. The brand name companies seemed to believe that national advertising and a quality differential were sufficient not only to distinguish their products from the generics but also to maintain their market share. However, price-conscious consumers increasingly turned to low-priced alternatives, posing a challenge to Procter & Gamble, Kraft, and other leading suppliers of brand name products. For consumers, generics offered significantly lower prices, low enough to outweigh perceived quality differences from name brands.

Retailers also benefited from the generics because they were able to obtain sufficiently lower wholesale prices so that their margin on the generics was higher than on the name brands. A higher turnover on generics also helped the retailer realize a higher return to its limited shelf space. Moreover, supermarkets and other retailers were able to put their own names on generic products, thereby enhancing the market recognition of the retailers' own brands. A stroll through any supermarket confirms the growth of house brands.

As the name brand manufacturers began to realize the increasing impact of generics, they began to formulate defensive strategies. Name brand prices were lowered to increase consumer value added. Name brand manufacturers made additional marketing expenditures to enhance the perceived value of their brands.

There is such a thing as too much variety. By selling so many brands, companies such as Procter & Gamble (P&G) were spread too thin, with many brands serving ill-defined market segments, often overlapping and competing for customers, a phenomenon known as fratricide. Providing so much variety is costly for manufacturers in terms of manufacturing, marketing, distribution, and transaction costs. The proliferation of stock-keeping units not only increased the costs of multiproduct manufacturers, but increased transaction costs for retailers and within-store search costs for consumers.

To avoid overextension and focus their marketing efforts, companies sold off or retired marginal brands. By the mid-1990s, P&G had cut the total number of its products by one-third, including reducing the number of its shampoos and other hair care products by one-half. It accomplished this by eliminating minor variations of the same product, standardizing packaging, reducing new product introductions, and divesting brands. P&G sold off Bain de Soleil sun care products, its stake in the painkiller Alleve, Lestoil household cleaner, Lava soap, and other brands.[19]

By realizing cost savings from reduced variety, P&G could operate profitably at lower prices, increasing its competitiveness with generics. It could be more effective by concentrating its marketing efforts on fewer brands. With fewer brands, management attention was more focused. By consolidating brands, P&G was in a better position to defend market share on the remaining brands.

In addition to consolidating brands, P&G met the generics by simplifying its pricing. By offering discounts and promotions to stores that varied over time, P&G and other manufacturers had encouraged retailer chains to purchase products based on wholesale discounts rather than on demand patterns. Thus, retailers arbitraged against manufacturers by building warehouses to store the purchases made during promotions, reducing purchases and relying on inventories when a manufacturer's promotions were not available. By switching to "everyday low prices," retailers could smooth out their purchases and adjust them to demand patterns, while at the same time reducing their inventories of manufactured goods, thus avoiding the costs of holding unnecessary inventories.

P&G's defensive strategies targeted not only consumers, through lower prices and increased marketing, but also its retail intermediaries, supermarkets and discount chains such as Wal-Mart. P&G looked for ways to reduce transaction costs for retailers and enhance retailer margins. By concentrating on fewer brands it boosted sales of existing brands, thereby raising turnover for retailers and justifying its shelf space.

The reduction of variety as a defense against generics refutes the view of some economists that companies can deter entry by brand proliferation. Some have suggested that companies can crowd the product space by offering so many brands that there is no room for an entrant to place its own brand in the market because it will go head-to-head with some existing brand with very similar characteristics. This theory is questionable on its face because the potential variations of brands are so large that such crowding is difficult if not impossible. The experience of P&G shows that even if crowding the brand space were possible, it would be a very weak defensive strategy, since entrants will have a easier time concentrating their efforts on an incumbent that is spread too thin. Keeping variety in check allows the company's resources to back up its market-leading brands.

Innovation

Companies must innovate to stay ahead of the game, whether they are pursuing offensive or defensive strategies. Product innovation opens the door to new markets, and process innovation is the way to cost leadership. The distinction between product and process innovation is imperfect, of course. New products often require different production techniques, while changes in production technologies enable product improvements.

One of the important payoffs of product innovation is the ability of the innovator to set market standards. By setting standards, companies dictate the rules of engagement. The standard can determine the compatibility of complementary products, such as computers and peripherals or cameras and film. The standard can confer a competitive advantage on the innovator if competitors have not yet learned the cost-reducing production methods of the first mover. Innovators earn returns if competitors must license the product from them. The best innovation need not set the standard; the experience of Beta losing out to the VHS standard in videotape is the classic example. And companies whose innovations have set standards have not always realized the returns to their innovations. Still, a major path to winning markets is through standard-setting innovations.

Imitation and Sustainable Competitive Advantage

Why do some firms win markets while others are less successful? Is success simply a matter of chance or does some crucial difference between the firms in an industry confer competitive advantage? If firms differ, how do they control those differences? If a firm outperforms others, can it keep the secret of its success or will competitors immediately be able to imitate the winners?

The answers to these questions vary by industry, but one thing should be clear: Companies differ. At a minimum, the individual characteristics of each firm's personnel, particularly managers and technical staff, certainly affect the firm's perspective, body of knowledge, and decisions. In addition, firms can have unique histories, which are preserved by choice or inertia in the firm's organizational form, incentive programs, decision-making procedures, corporate culture, and company traditions. Moreover, companies acquire technical and market knowledge through production, purchasing, and sales activities. They develop brand recognition or company reputations with customers and suppliers. Corporations differ in terms of their ownership structure, capital structure, and other legal aspects of incorporation. Companies can differ in terms of their assets, which can include land, natural resources, and patents.

These differences suggest that success is more than a matter of chance. Just as some athletes consistently win, the talents of one company's personnel may simply be greater than those of a competitors' employees. Other resources owned or controlled by the firm can be the key ingredients of growth.

Company actions can easily differ simply because there are so many alternatives that no set of companies can cover all the bases. Companies make their own assessments of demand and supply conditions and technology. They make their predictions about market change and select the best alternatives. But potential variations in prices and product characteristics are endless. The choices of companies in the marketplace represent optimization given the information available. Moreover, companies are fallible, so that many choices could be the result of myopia or imperfect use of information.

Not surprisingly, management strategists have spent much time and energy debating what the key resources are. If these resources could be identified, would not the company that acquired them earn higher than normal returns? The problem is that if the ingredients were so well known, all companies in the industry would try to get them, and the competitive advantages they yielded would be neutralized rapidly. This suggests that the route to competitive advantage lies in developing resources that cannot easily be imitated. The company can innovate to pull ahead of competitors, but innovations can be copied. Some suggest that it is the ability to innovate rather than the innovations themselves that is key to success, because the innovator can always stay ahead. This line of reasoning can get a bit absurd. If the innovation process itself can be copied, then the firm that creates new ways to innovate prevails, et cetera.

The question of imitation and sustainable advantage can be resolved to some extent by noting that imitation is costly. There are transaction costs to doing what another firm is doing. Even if another company's personnel seem more talented, discerning who the key employees are is difficult for outsiders and raiding personnel can be a costly exercise.

Copying innovations is difficult as well. It is difficult to reverse engineer an innovation and there are costs to inventing around patent protections. Emulating a competitor's distributor or supplier networks entails transaction costs of search and negotiation. These costs suggest that imitation only occurs if the entrant's economic rents outweigh the transaction costs of imitation.

When imitation is costly, incumbents can earn rents to their innovations. Then, entrants are likely to be better off innovating themselves instead of copying others. Entrants may differ in their ability to imitate or innovate, which is another reason why entrants into an industry pursue diverse strategies. Innovation certainly contains an element of chance, although the *rate* of innovation can be altered through investment in R&D.

Innovative success also depends on the *direction* of R&D. This is subject to control through company alliances with sources of R&D, whether start-up companies, private labs, or university researchers. Moreover, gathering customer information about desired products and services is vital to controlling the direction of the company's research efforts. The role of transaction costs in determining the effectiveness and imitability of innovations suggests that the market-making and related activities of firms are also important to innovative success.

R&D Competition

Within the limits of science and creativity, management of R&D can change the rate and direction of innovative activity. To some extent innovation is a race. Companies that invest in similar projects struggle to be the first to the finish line. The returns to being first are patent protections and first-mover advantages in the market. The returns to being late are the possibility of improving on earlier innovations by others and the cost savings from scaling back projects. With rapid diffusion of technological knowledge, the returns to being first are reduced. Companies trade off the cost of investment against the returns to more rapid innovation. Early innovators might set standards but later innovators can leapfrog to next-generation technology.

If companies are racing for a prize, then R&D looks a lot like a price war, with each company upping the ante until the investments in R&D exhaust the returns to innovation. The investments in an R&D race are sunk costs and to some extent duplicative, although multiple attempts at the same project can increase the overall chance of a successful innovation.

Just as a number of factors alleviate price wars, similar factors modify R&D races. If R&D projects at different companies yield distinct innovations, the companies are in a race with many prizes. This makes a winner-take-all outcome less likely. Similarly, if the innovations are made by companies that offer differentiated products, each of their R&D projects can realize market returns. Innovation becomes just one more competitive instrument for each company, but not the only determinant of success or failure.

Given the uncertain nature of technological change, companies are likely to have incomplete information about the progress of their competitors' projects. This incomplete information gives R&D a bit of an auction flavor. Companies have an incentive to participate in the race because they do not know the progress or abilities of their competitors. Each player has some initial chance of success. Investment in R&D trades off the cost against the likelihood of winning the race. However, companies will proceed cautiously to the extent they feel that each of them is only partly informed about the expected value of the innovation. Winning the R&D race by investing heavily may not be desirable if it entails the winner's curse. When companies fear the winner's curse, they are more likely to invest in R&D joint ventures or to seek independent sources of research.

Iain Cockburn and Rebecca Henderson studied R&D in the pharmaceutical industry.[20] They looked at a sample of U.S. and European manufacturers that collectively accounted for over a quarter of worldwide R&D and sales for the industry, and focused on cardiovascular drugs. They found that R&D strategies do not appear to be driven by tit-for-tat responses, but rather by each firm's own research productivity. This suggests that there are research spillovers across firms, as companies benefit from the discoveries of others. They also suggest that the returns to innovation depend more on the different capabilities of the companies doing the research than on outdoing rival R&D programs.

An R&D success may explain how a company gains competitive advantage. However, more fundamental company differences explain repeated R&D success. Ultimately, the market contacts and networks established by the firm appear to be a source of competitive advantage. Customer interaction provides important information about the direction of technological change. Knowledge of technology markets provides insights that help guide the company's R&D efforts. Market makers provide the crucial links between technological development and customer applications.

Market Intelligence

Market intelligence is a key component of both offensive and defensive strategies. The task of gathering intelligence must be systematic, rather than the random process it often is in many companies that rely on informal monitoring of their markets. In addition to gathering intelligence, it is useful to have formal mechanisms for propagating knowledge within the organization.

The firm should gather economic information about its customers. Market research should include careful estimation of customer demand patterns, including price responsiveness and measurement of demand differences between market segments. Advances in computer storage allow companies to warehouse and mine vast quantities of consumer demand data. Advances in communications, including data transfers over private networks and the Internet, speed the transfer and usage of this data in the companies' pricing and strategic decision making. Companies have set up such programs as frequent flyer mileage awards, retail discount cards, and warehouse clubs in part as ways of keeping track of consumption patterns. Armed with this demand data, companies can tailor prices and product offerings to individual segments.

Companies should apply formal data collection methods to the understanding of their suppliers and input markets, including labor services and capital markets. Electronic data transfer and Internet marketplaces facilitate the gathering and usage of supplier information. Effective arbitrage is based on combining the firm's knowledge of its supplier and customer markets.

Firms must be aware not only of competitors' characteristics but also of market bridges being built by the competitor. Who are the competitors' customers and suppliers? Who are the potential entrants into the industry? Are those entrants replicating your company's market bridges or are they pursuing different strategies? Companies must anticipate competition from companies pursuing the go-between, bring-together, bypass, and connect strategies discussed in Chapter 7. These can be difficult to predict because competitors will serve the market in substantially different ways from the incumbent. Companies should also be alert to competitors pursuing indirect entry strategies. While their entry poses only a remote threat, indirect entrants are building strength and are likely to be among the firm's future direct competitors.

Competitors need not look like incumbents. They are likely to look quite different as they produce innovative products and services and ally with different suppliers. Market intelligence should focus on the costs of transactions to the company's customers and suppliers, since transactional efficiencies open the door to competitive entry.

Overview

Companies continually strive for growth, whether through expansion within existing markets or entry into new ones. Winning markets means attaining superior performance as compared to rivals, in terms of market share, profitability, product quality, and other performance measures. Winning also means being recognized as the leading creator and manager of one's markets.

Markets must be won against competitors and won again repeatedly against new entrants. Companies should undertake offensive strategies only when they are significantly stronger than their competitors. Otherwise, they should pursue indirect strategies and build up their strength. When pursuing offensive strategies, a company should concentrate its strength against the opponent's weaknesses, improving customer service, pricing, and customer convenience in critical market segments. The company's market position must be continually defended against existing competitors, new entrants, and substitute products and services. Steady improvement of one's own products and services is the antidote to complacency. Innovation is critical to the success of both offensive and defensive strategies.

Market entry requires a clear understanding of the critical differences between firms that allows the company to achieve a competitive advantage. Challenging incumbents requires that entrants have substantial strength. The market-based strategies outlined in this section are useful for entrants seeking competitive advantage over incumbent firms. Successful offensive and defensive strategies are founded on providing the most efficient transactions. Entrants can distinguish themselves from incumbents using the go-between, bring-together, bypass, and connect strategies. They can gain competitive advantage by acting for their customers and suppliers as market maker, arbitrageur, intermediary, and network organizer.

Endnotes

1. B. H. Liddell Hart, *Strategy*, 2nd rev. ed., New York: Meridian. 1991, p. 334.
2. Robert R. Leonhard, *The Art of Maneuver*, Novato, CA: Presidio Press, 1991, pp. 20–21.
3. See Paul Klemperer, "Markets with Consumer Switching Costs," *Quarterly Journal of Economics*, 102, 1987, pp. 375–394.
4. See David Kreps and Jose Scheinkman, "Quantity Precommitment and Bertrand Competition Yield Cournot Outcomes," *Bell Journal of Economics*, 14, 1983, pp. 326–337.
5. See Kyle Bagwell, Garey Ramey, and Daniel F. Spulber, "Dynamic Retail Price and Investment Competition," *Rand Journal of Economics*, 28, Summer 1997, pp. 207–227 for additional discussion.
6. See Daniel F. Spulber, "Bertrand Competition When Rivals' Costs Are Unknown," *Journal of Industrial Economics*, 43, 1995, pp. 1–11.
7. "A Survey of Electronic Commerce: Big, Boring, Booming," *The Economist*, May 10, 1997.
8. GE Trading Process Network Web site, May 20, 1997.
9. Ibid.
10. "A Survey of Electronic Commerce."
11. The cross-referencing process is Hyper Text Markup Language (HTML) that allows the user to point and click on a highlighted word or icon that immediately connects to other documents.
12. For additional discussion, see Tom R. Halfhill, "Inside the Mind of Microsoft," *Byte*, August, 1995, pp. 48–52.
13. James Gleick, "Making Microsoft Safe for Capitalism," *New York Times Magazine*, November 5, 1995, p. 50.
14. Lawrence M. Fisher, "Flummoxed by the Internet, Head of Novell Resigns," *New York Times*, August 30, 1996, p. C1.

15. Halfhill, "Inside the Mind of Microsoft."

16. Michael Nadeau, "Your E-Mail Is Obsolete," *Byte*, February, 1997, pp. 66–80.

17. Carl von Clausewitz, *On War* (1832), Princeton: Princeton University Press, 1976, p. 370.

18. David G. Chandler, ed., *The Military Maxims of Napoleon*, London: Greenhill Books, 1987.

19. "Make It Simple," *Business Week*, September 9, 1996, pp. 96–104.

20. Iain Cockburn and Rebecca Henderson, "Racing to Invest? The Dynamics of Competition in Ethical Drug Discovery," *Journal of Economics & Management Strategy*, 3, Fall 1994, pp. 481–519.

CONCLUSION

If you have ever watched cooking shows on TV, you have probably seen great chefs demonstrate the preparation of the day's recipe. All of the ingredients are set out on the counter. The fruits, vegetables, spices, and other ingredients are already chopped up, measured out, and waiting in small containers. The chef explains the recipe, jokes about each ingredient, and combines them to make the perfect dish. I sometimes think that the most interesting part of the show takes place offscreen. The recipe has been tested many times and perfected. Then a small army of sous-chefs has already prepared the ingredients before the cooking gets underway. Most importantly perhaps, the chef and the assistants have done their marketing to purchase the freshest ingredients. The chef tells the viewers how easy the dish is to prepare. It never seems so easy at home, when you have to visit at least half a dozen stores to round up the ingredients. As any chef will admit, the hard part is doing the marketing.

Paul Bertolli, chef of the legendary restaurant Chez Panisse in Berkeley, observes:

> Good cooking begins with good ingredients—fresh, ripe, seasonal, unadulterated raw materials. The challenge in creating a nightly changing menu at Chez Panisse lies less in dreaming up abstract and novel combinations than in keeping apace with the season and wel-

coming its produce. Responding in this manner yields concreteness, continuity and ease to the cooking.[1]

In his cookbook, Chef Bertolli expresses his thanks to his suppliers, including Monterey Fish, the Chino Ranch, Monterey Market, ranchers, various organic farms, and a "mushroom sleuth."

Even the best dishes with the freshest ingredients count for little without the warm and friendly ambience of the restaurant. It must be a place where customers feel at home and come back for the accommodating service. Chez Panisse offers a different menu every night to draw customers back repeatedly. Chef Bertolli notes that many restaurants have a fixed menu because they assume that the same people will not be back the next night. He brings back his customers by delighting them with ever-changing menus filled with extraordinary dishes.

The tasks performed by firms are very much like the work of the best chefs. They do much more than combine inputs to produce their products and services, just as chefs do more than combine ingredients to follow recipes or concoct new ones. If you only look at the recipe (the production technology) or the cooking process (operations), you can easily miss the big picture. How do chefs assemble their ingredients from the various suppliers? How do they attract and retain their customers?

Firms are much more than production technologies or operations. They build market bridges between complicated market networks of suppliers and customers. The firm's relationships with suppliers are keys to the business. They must obtain capital investment to build the business, skilled and motivated employees to operate the business, high-quality supplies to aid manufacturing, and the latest technology to function innovatively. The firm's relationships with distributors and final customers provide the business with its reason for being, guiding its decisions about what products and services to provide, when and how to provide them, and at what prices.

As I have emphasized in this book, successful firms build bridges between their suppliers and customers. They provide market-making services by standing ready to buy from suppliers and sell to customers. They earn returns by discerning arbitrage opportunities, combining customer willingness to pay with supplier opportunities to generate the greatest value added. They intermediate between suppliers and customers, acting as agents in the marketplace by negotiating contracts and monitoring productivity. Finally, they construct market networks of reliable suppliers and satisfied customers.

The market makers create the most effective transactions for their customers and suppliers. They outperform competitors by offering transactions that are faster, more convenient, and less costly. Efficient transactions are intrinsic to supplying high-quality products and services. These companies retain their customers by providing convenience and immediacy. They expand their market share and enter or establish new markets by developing innovative transactions.

By mastering the workings of markets, companies generate new competitive strategies, going between buyers and sellers to enhance the value added from exchange, bringing together different products and services for the convenience of one-stop shopping, bypassing less efficient suppliers or distributors, and connecting customers and suppliers in innovative ways. Companies that appreciate the value of transactions are companies that understand how to serve customers and suppliers neglected by competitors and how to outperform established rivals. Like master chefs combining the finest ingredients, leading companies create and win their markets.

Endnotes

1. Paul Bertolli with Alice Waters, *Chez Panisse Cooking*, New York: Random House, 1988, p. x.

INDEX

Abegglen, James, 36
Adverse selection, and agents, 130-33
Advertising, and brand recognition, 40-41
Aetna Life & Casualty, 174
After the Trade Is Made (Weiss), 86
Agents, 119, 120-38
  and adverse selection, 130-33
  companies as, 122
  contracting costs, 125-26
  incomplete contracts, 126-27
  as intermediaries, 121
  in law, 121
  moral hazard, 127-30
  multiple, principals with, 135-38
  with multiple principals, 133-35
  principal-agent relationship, 121-25
    agent responsibilities, 124
Airline computer reservation systems, 37,
    83-85, 233
AIX, 44
Alchian, Armen, 141
Alcoa, 10
Alletzhauser, 101
Alliances, 198-200
  focusing on technological/marketing
    complementarities, 199
  growth through, 192
  international, 194
  and market leadership, 43-44
  strength of, 194-95
  vertical, 204
  See also Joint ventures
Amazon.com, 270-71
American Airlines, 52
  Sabre computer reservation system, 37,
    83-84, 233
American Express, 173, 231
American Stock Exchange (AMEX), 81
America OnLine, 160, 254, 286

Ameritech, 255
Ames, 252
Anderson Consulting, 134-35
Apollo computer reservation system, United
    Airlines, 37, 83, 233
Apple Computer, 43-44, 178, 198
Arbitrage, 5, 17-18, 95-117, 281-82
  advantage of, 97
  defined, 95
  dynamic, 101-7
  risk, 107-12
  spatial, 98-100
  technological, 112-16
Art of War, The (Sun Tzu), 245, 246, 256
Asea Brown Boveri, 158-59
Asynchronous Transfer Mode (ATM), 160
AT&T, 33, 135, 160, 178, 207, 255, 263, 268
  and international alliances, 195
  spin-off of Lucent Technologies, 242-43
A. T. Kearney, 135
Aucnet Inc., 163
Auction markets, 79-81
Auto dealers, pricing of, 73
Automakers, 190-91
Automatic teller machines (ATMs), 164

Bar coding, 159
Barnes & Noble, 82, 270
Barnett, Gary, 29
Barriers to entry, 220
Bergen Brunswig, 176
Berkeley Unix, 261
Bertolli, Paul, 303-4
Biglaiser, Gary, 142
Biogen, 205
Bleeke, Joel, 194
Blockbuster Video, 37, 102-4
Blue Cross-Blue Shield of New Jersey, 234
Booz Allen & Hamilton, 135

Borders, 82, 270
Boston Consulting Group, 135
Bradlees, 252
Brand recognition, 39-42
    and advertising, 40-41
Breakfast cereal makers, price wars, 276
Brennan, Edward A., 129
Briggs & Stratton, 33
Bring-together strategy, 222, 227-31
    Charles Schwab & Co., 228-31
Brokers, 119, 145-55
    marketing information, gathering, 152-55
    negotiation, 146-50
    value added, 150-52
Brooks Brothers, 201
Builders Square, 252
Bundling products/packages, 199
Buyer diversity, 280-81
Bypass strategy, 222, 232-35
    airline computer reservation systems, 233
    and brewers, 234-35
    and insurance companies, 234
    and Intel Corporation, 235
    and manufacturers, 233

Caldor, 252
Calhoun, George, 162
California Federal Bank, 174
California Pizza Kitchen, 242
Canon, 177, 207
Capacity investment, 277-78
Capital markets, and recognition, 42-43
CarChoice, 226
Carlton, Dennis, 91
Car-Max, 226
Caston, Art, 114-15
Catalog shopping, compared to computer
        shopping, 163
Chandler, Alfred D., 52
Charles Schwab & Co., 228-31, 254
    AdviserSource, 230
    Balanced Allocation Fund, 230
    competition, 231
    funds of funds, 230
    as go-between, 231
    Growth Allocation Fund, 230
    growth of, 230-31
    mutual fund supermarket, 229-30
Chen, Steve, 115-16
Chevy's Mexican Restaurants, 242
Chicago Board of Trade, 80
Chicago Mercantile Exchange, 114
    GLOBEX system, 80
Chiron Corp., 205
Chrysler Corporation, 190, 207, 226
Circuit City, 163, 176, 226

Citicorp, 10
Clark, James, 162
CNN (Cable News Network), 259-60
Coca-Cola, 33-34, 39-40, 91, 144-45, 241-42
    diversification, 196
Columbia/HCA Healthcare, 10, 175
Comdisco, Inc., 178-80
Communicators, 119, 155-64
    electronic market bridges, 162-64
    information:
        supplied to consumers, 156-58
        supplied to producers, 158-59
    information networks, 159-62
Compaq Computer, 83, 177, 186, 285
Competition, identifying, 23
CompUSA, 38, 39, 82
CompuServe, 286
Computer networks, as centralized market-
        places, 83
Computer reservation systems (CSRs), 37,
        83-85, 233
Computer shopping, 163
ConAgra, 294
Connect strategy, 222, 236-43
    downstream connection, 239-43
    upstream connection, 236-39
Consolidation, returns from, 47-48
Consumers, information supplied to, 156-58
Consumer's Union, 157
Contracts, 192
    external, 203
    incentive, 203
Coopers & Lybrand, 134
Cooper Tire and Rubber, 10
Coordinating exchange, 79-86
Corporate strategy, 23
Cost economies, 52-53
    and growth, 53
Crandall, Robert, 8
Cray Research, 115-16
Cross-price elasticity of demand, 49
Crown Books, 270
CSC Consulting, 135
CSX, 33
Customer recognition, 39-42

Daihatsu Motor, 189
Dai-Ichi Kangyo (DKB), 187
Dayton-Hudson, 251
Dealer markets, 79-81
Dealers, firms as, 81
Dean Witter Discover & Co., 173, 240-41
Deception, 262-63
Defensive market strategies, 291-96
    flexible response, 292-94
    overextension, 294-96

Delay, costs of, 25
Dell Computer, 78, 83, 112-13, 177, 233
Dell, Michael, 112
Demand, elasticity of, 48
Demsetz, Harold, 141
Deutsche Telekom, 195
Digital Equipment, 178, 285
Discount brokerage services, 254
Discounters:
  distribution system, 241-42
  and pricing, 72-73
  wholesale buying clubs, pricing of, 72
Distribution, 159
  outsourcing, 201
Distribution capacity, 277-78
Distributors, and recognition, 43
Diversification, 195
  Coca-Cola, 196
Dojima, 101
Dominick's supermarket chain, 69
Domino's Pizza, 255
Dow Chemical, 91
Downstream connection, 239-43
Drive to win, 8-10
  competition compared to, 9-10, 12
  in international relations, 9
DuPont, 91, 135
Dynamic arbitrage, 101-7
  defined, 101
  financial intermediation, 104-7
  purchase/resale of commodities over
    time, 102
Dynamic consolidation, 47-48

Economic value added (EVA), 33
Economies of scale, 53-54
Economy of force, 246-48
Eddie Bauer, 82
Elasticity of demand, 48
Electric utilities, pooling of capacity, 89
Electronic data interchange, 159, 186
  growth of, 202
Electronic Data Systems, 176
Electronic market bridges, 162-64
Eli Lilly, 33
Ellison, Lawrence, 198
Employee activities, changes in, 45
Employee morale, 42
  and job security, 45-46
Employee recruitment, and recognition, 42
Enrico, Roger A., 242
Entry market strategies, 219-44
  auto markets, 225-26
  barriers to entry, 220
  bring-together strategy, 222, 227-31
  bypass strategy, 222, 232-35

and certification, 224
connect strategy, 222, 236-43
go-between strategy, 222-26
  getting close to the customer, 223
  market-making services offered by, 225
  multifaceted nature of, 223-24
  and product quality testing, 224
Ernst, David, 194
Expansion, 30, 192-93
External contracts, 203
Exxon, 10, 188

Federal Express, 126
  offensive strategy, 268
Federal Home Loan Mortgage Corporation
    (FHLMC) (Freddie Mac), 174
Federal National Mortgage Association
    (FNMA) (Fannie Mae), 173-74
Financial assets, 110
Financial intermediaries, 110
Financial intermediation, 104-7
Financial markets, 168-69
  matching in, 172-74
Firm:
  boundaries of, 46-61
    scale, 46-47, 53-55
    scope, 46-47, 55-56
    span, 46-47, 56-58
    speed, 46-47, 58-59
  consolidation, returns from, 47-48
  cost economies, 52-53
  incremental revenues, 48-50
  objective of, 31-32
  risk reduction, 50-52
Firms, as dealers, 81
Fleming of Oklahoma City, 176, 193-94
Ford Motor Company, 177, 188, 190, 204-5,
    207
  and economies of speed, 58-59
Forstmann Little & Co., 106
Fort Howard Corporation, 186
France Telecom, 195
Frankenberg, Robert J., 209, 289
Franz Haniel & Cie, G.m.b.H., 193
Fuji Motors, 189
Fujitsu, 194
Full-service brokerages, 254
  discount brokerage services compared to,
    254
Fuyo, 187
F. W. Woolworth, 251

Gap, The, 90
Gateway, 233
Gemini Consulting, 135
Genentech, 205

General Electric, 10, 33, 204, 262, 284
General Foods, 276
General Instruments, 198, 207
General Magic, 198
General Mills, 276
General Motors, 56, 74, 141, 188, 190, 207, 226, 280-81
Georgia Pacific, 33
G. Heileman Brewing Co., 235
Glendale Federal, 174
GLOBEX system, Chicago Mercantile Exchange, 80
Go-between strategy, 222-26
Goizueta, Robert, 33-34
Goldern Western Financial Corp., 174
Goods/services, allocation of, 90-93
Goodyear Tire, 10
Government National Mortgage Association (GNMA) (Ginnie Mae), 174
Great Western Financial corp., 174
Grove, Andy, 59
Growth, and cost economies, 53
GTE, 135
Guarantees:
    and consumer reassurance, 129
    and consumer recognition, 41

Hall, Floyd, 252
Hammacher Schlemmer, monitoring by, 143
Harris, Everette Bagby, 114
Hart, Liddell, 256, 265
Health care companies, as labor intermediaries, 175-76
Healthy Choice, 294
Hewlett-Packard, 177, 178, 207, 285
H. F. Ahmanson, 174
Hills, 252
Hino Motors, 189
Hirshman, Albert O., 156
Home Depot, 39, 176
Home Shopping Channel (HSC), 163
Honda, 36, 189
Horizontal consolidation, 47-48
Horizontal *keiretsu*, 187, 199
Horizontal mergers, 192
Hot Java, 262
Hout, Thomas M., 89
Huber, Peter, 162
Huizenga, H. Wayne, 102-3, 226
Humana, 175
Hunt, Johnnie Bryan, 145

IBM (International Business Machines), 43-44, 83, 160, 176, 177-78, 188, 235, 257
    technology alliances, 207
Incentive contracts, 203

Indirection, 24
Indirect market strategies, 245-64
    economy of force, 246-48
    line of least expectation, 256-63
        deception, 262-63
        Java, 260-62
        surprise, 257-60
    path of least resistance, 252-56
    undefended markets, 248-52
        Southwest Airlines, 255-56
        Wal-Mart, 250-52
Information networks, 159-62
Information sharing, with suppliers/distributors, 104
Information sources, for consumers, 156-58
Information superhighway, 159-62
    development of, 160
Innovation, 296-301
    and economies of scale and scope, 58
    imitation and sustainable competitive advantage, 296-98
    market intelligence, 299-300
    R&D competition, 298-99
Innovative transactions, 21-22
Intel Corporation, and bypass strategy, 235
Intellectual property rights, 170
Intermediation, 5, 18-19, 30, 37-38, 119-66, 282-83
    agents, 119, 120-38
    brokers, 119, 145-55
    communicators, 119, 155-64
    monitoring, 119, 139-45
Internal expansion, 192-93
International alliances, 194
Internet Service Providers (ISPs), 160
Isuzu, 189
ITT Hartford, 234

Jamesway, 252
Java, 260-62
J. B. Hunt company, 145-46
J. Crew, 82
J.D. Power & Associates, 163
Jewel supermarket chain, 69
Job security, and employee morale, 45-46
Johnson & Higgins, 186
Johnson & Johnson, 10
Johnson, Edward C. 3d, 231
Joint ventures, 195-200, 203-4
    vertical, 203-4
Joy, Bill, 260-61

Kaleida Labs, 198
Kampouris, Emmanuel, 34
KDD, 195
Keiretsu, 187-91

Kelleher, Herb, 255
Kellogg, 276
Kelly Services, 175
KFC (Kentucky Fried Chicken), 145, 242
Kmart, 11, 72, 193, 251, 252
Knowledge opportunism, 184-85
Kodak, 91
Kohlberg Kravis Roberts & Co., 106
Kraft, 294
Kresge, S. S., 251
Kroger, 176

Labor market intermediaries, 110
Labor markets, 168-69
    matching in, 174-76
Lacy, Herman E., 114
Laminar network, 162
Lands' End, 73, 82
Lateral consolidation, 47-48
Lateral mergers, 195-97
LBOs (leveraged buy-outs), 106
Leonhard, Robert, 267
Line of least expectation:
    deception, 262-63
    Java, 260-62
    surprise, 257-60
L. L. Bean, 82
Lloyd, Edward, 107
Lloyd's of London, 107-8
Lombardi, Vince, 9
Lotus Notes, 257
Lucent Technologies, 242-43
Luttwak, Edward N., 258

McCaw Cellular Communications, 243, 263
McColl, Hugh L. Jr., 3-4
McDonald's, 39, 54, 242
    pricing, 76
McKesson, 176
McKinsey Consulting, 135
McNealy, Scott, 260
MAIN framework, 5-6, 12-22, 265-66
    arbitrage, 17-18
    intermediation, 18-19
    market making, 13-17
    networking, 19-22
Manpower, 175
Manpower, Inc., 110
Manzi, Jim, 186
Market bridges:
    building, 12-22
        See also MAIN framework
    electronic, 162-64
Market centralization, 16-17
Market clearing, 86-90
    and pricing, 71-72

Market coordination, 79-86
    managing transactions, 85-86
    and value, 81-85
Market definition, 167-68
Marketing claims, and pricing, 73
Market intelligence, 299-300
Market makers, 5
    dealers as, 80
Market making, 13-17, 65-94
    coordinating exchange, 79-86
    goods/services, allocation of, 90-93
    market clearing, 86-90
    pricing, 66-79
Markets:
    finance, 168-69
    labor, 168-69
    products, 169-70
    search, 79-81
    structure of, 79-81
    technology, 169-70
    undefended, 248-52
Market segmentation, and pricing, 77-79
Market strategies, 22-25
    entry, 219-44
    indirect, 245-64
    offensive/defensive, 265-302
Market value added (MVA), 33
Mastercard, 173
Matching, 167-68, 172-80
    in financial markets, 172-74
    in labor markets, 174-76
    in product markets, 176
    in technology markets, 176-77
Maytag, 40
Mazda, 189
MCI, 160, 195, 255, 268
    offensive strategy, 268
Mercer Management Consulting, 135
Merck, 33
Mergers, 192-94, 203
    and connect strategy, 240
    consolidation through, 193
    horizontal, 192-93
    lateral, 195-97
    and market leadership, 44
    and transfer of technological knowledge,
        208
Metropolitan Life, 174, 234
Microsoft, 33, 44, 160, 176, 199, 257
    BackOffice, 289-91
    electronic publication on CD-ROM, 138
    Internet Explorer, 262, 285-87
    offensive market strategy, 284-91
    Windows NT, 287-89
Middleware, 162

M.I.T., 207
Mitsubishi, 187-88
Mitsui & Co., 187, 188
Mitsui Fudosan, 188
Mixing, 168, 172-80
  defined, 177
Monitor, 135
Monitoring, 119, 139-45, 203
  and contracts, 139-43
  defined, 139
  delegated, 139-41
  of monitors/potential monitors, 143-45
  and outsourcing, 141
  retailers/wholesalers as monitors, 142
Moore, Gordon E., 205
Morgan Stanley, 173, 240-41
Mosaic, 162
Motivation, and recognition, 44-46
Motorola, 44, 204, 235
Multiple agents, principals with, 135-38
Multiple principals:
  agents with, 133-35
  and uniform commissions, 134

Nabisco Cereals, 276
Nasser, Jacques, 205
National Association of Securities Dealers
      Automated Quotation system (NAS-
      DAQ), 81
National Association of Temporary and
      Staffing Services, 175
National Center for Supercomputing
      Applications (NCSA), 162
National Medical Enterprises, 175
National Securities Clearing Corporation, 86
NationsBank, 3-4, 6, 11, 24
Navio Corporation, 289
NBC, 207, 262
Negotiation, 146-50
  breakdown of, 147
  failures, 146-47, 148
  and reputation, 149-50
  seller's dilemma, 147-48
Netscape Communications Corp., 162, 289
Netscape Navigator, 262, 286-87
Network complementarities, 197-98
Networking, 19-22, 167-216
  matching/mixing, 172-80
  organizational boundaries, 191-214
    Novell case study, 208-14
    scale, 191-95
    scope, 195-200
    span, 200-204
    speed, 204-8
  and organizations, 180-91
    information, 183-87
    keiretsu, 187-91

transaction costs, 181-83
suppliers/customers, 168-72
Networks, 161-62
New England Power Pool, 89
New York Futures Exchange, 80
New York Life, 174
New York Mercantile Exchange, 80
Nissan, 189
Noorda, Ray, 209
Novell Inc., 176, 199, 208-14, 257
Nucor, 259

Offensive market strategies, 265-91
  arbitrageur, 281-82
  Federal Express, 268
  intermediary, 282-83
  market maker, 269-81
    capacity investment, 277-78
    coordination, 278-79
    gains from trade/better deals, 271-73
    imperfect information, 279-80
    input prices/price spread, 274
    price wars, 274-76
    product differentiation, 276-77
    segmenting markets, 280-81
    transaction costs, 269-71
  MCI, 268
  Microsoft case study, 284-91
    BackOffice, 289-91
    Internet Explorer, 285-87
    Windows NT, 287-89
  network organizer, 283-84
OfficeMax, 252
Ohmae, Keniche, 31
Olsten Corporation, 175
Opportunism, 181-85
  knowledge, 184-85
Optional pricing, 77-78
Oracle Corporation, 160, 198, 199
Outsourcing, 201-2
Overpricing, 79

Pace Membership Warehouse, 193
Pacific Bell, 255
Pepsico, 39, 91, 135, 144-45, 241-42
Personal computers (PCs), 161
Philips Electronics, 207
Pizza Hut, 145, 242
Point-of-sale (POS) terminals, 164
Post Cereal, 276
Power Information Network, 163
Preferred provider organizations (PPOs),
      175-76
Price competition, 135-37, 278-80
PriceCostco, 225
Price-response function, 75
Price wars, 274-76

Pricing, 66-79, 269, 272-73
  adjusting the price, 75-76
  and communication of information, 72-74
  and control, 68
  and coordination, 68
  cross-effect of prices, 76
  living on the spread, 66-68
  low introductory offers, 75
  and market clearing, 71-72
  and market information, gathering of, 74-77
  and marketing/purchasing policies, 71
  and market segmentation, 77-79
  optional, 77-78
  option bundles, 78
  and perception, 68
  price competition, 135-37
  price-response function, 75
  price responsiveness, 75-77
  and product line, 78
  quantity discounts, 78
  and reaction, 68
  seasonal items, 75
  as a service, 68-69
  setting the spread, 70-71
Principal-agent relationship, 121-25
Procter & Gamble (P&G), 10, 253, 272, 294-96
  pricing decisions of, 49
Prodigy, 286
Producers, information supplied to, 158-59
Product differentiation, 254, 276-77
Product information, 156-58
  acquiring, 157
Production capacity, 277-78
Product line, and pricing, 78
Product market intermediaries, 111
Product markets, 169-70
  competitive strategy in, 171-72
  matching in, 176
Prudential of America, 174, 234

Quaker Oats, 33, 276
Quantity discounts, 78
Quickquote, 234
Quotesmith Corporation, 234
QVC, 163

RalCorp, 276
Ralston, 276
Recognition, 38-42
  capital markets, 42-43
  customer, 39-42
  employee recruitment, 42
  making the rules, 43-44
  motivation, 44-46
  suppliers/distributors, 43

Research consortiums, 207
Research and development (R&D), 54-55, 205-8
Risk arbitrage, 107-12
  allocation of risk, 108-9
  markets for risk, 109-12
  and R&D process, 111
Risk reduction, 50-52
  and scale, 50-51
  and scope, 51
  and span, 51
  and speed, 51-52
Roberti, William, 201
ROLM, 178

S&P Co., 235
Sabre computer reservation system, American Airlines, 37, 83-84, 233
Sakura Bank, 188
Salomon Brothers, 174
Sam's Club, Wal-Mart, 225, 234
Sanwa, 187
Sarnoff Research Center, 207
Scale, 30-31, 46-47, 53-55, 191-95
Scaling, 287-88
Scarce resources, allocating, 91-93
Schmidt, Eric, 261, 288
Scientific Atlanta, 198
Scope, 30-31, 46-47, 55-56, 195-200
Search markets, 79-81
Sears, 11, 129, 135, 252, 272
  catalog, 82
Securities transactions, processing of, 86
Seegers, Harvey, 284
Sega America, 198
Shakeout battles, 247-48
Sharp, 198
Singapore Telecom, 195
Size, and risk reduction, 50-51
Smith, Adam, 54
Snow, John, 33
Software suits, 199
Software Transformation Inc., 211
Southwest Airlines, 24, 255-56, 278
Span, 30-31, 46-47, 56-58, 200-204
Spatial arbitrage, 98-100
  and Wal-Mart, 100
Speed, 30-31, 46-47, 58-59, 204-8
Sports Authority, 252
Sprint, 160, 195
Stalk, George Jr., 36, 89
Stocker brokerage firms, agency roles, 123
Sumitomo, 187-91
Sun Microsystems, 178, 260, 289
Supercrown, 82
SuperKs, 252
Supermarkets, and market making, 14-16

Supervalu, Inc., 176, 193
Suppliers/distributors:
  information sharing with, 104
  and networking, 168-72
  opportunism, risk of, 202-3
  and recognition, 43
Surprise, as indirect strategy, 257-60
Sysco, 176

Taco Bell, 145, 242
Taligent, 44
Tapscott, Don, 114-15
Target Stores, 251
Tarmarkin, Bob, 101
TCP/IP, 160
Teachers Insurance and Annuity Association, 174
Technological arbitrage, 112-16
  and manufacturing/assembly activities, 114
  profit from, 113
  sources of, 115
  and spread, 115
  and transaction costs, 116
Technology markets, 169-70
  matching in, 176-77
Television-shopping channels, 82-83, 163
Telser, Lester, 144
Tenneco, 33
Temporary service agencies, 175
Texas Instruments (TI), 202
Thomson Consumer Electronics, 207
3DO, 198
Toshiba, 188
Toyota, 38, 89-90, 188, 190
Toys "R" Us, 39, 82, 176
Trading Process Network (TPN), 284
Transaction costs, 181-83, 202
Transmission, 159-60
Travelers Inc., 173-74
Tully, Shawn, 202
Turner, Ted, 259
Two-product monopoly, 49

Undefended markets, 248-52
  Southwest Airlines, 255-56
  Wal-Mart, 250-52
Underpricing, 79
Unisource, 195
Unisys, 178
United Airlines, Apollo computer reservation system, 37, 83, 233
United Auto Group, 226
Upstream connection, 236-39
U.S. Healthcare, 175

U.S. Robotics, 204
Utilities, pooling of capacity, 89

Value, and market coordination, 81-85
Value added, 150-52
Vandiver, F. William Jr., 3
Vaporware, 263
Vertical alliances, 204, 236, 240
Vertical consolidation, 47-48
Vertical integration, 203
Vertical joint ventures, 203-4
Vertical *keiretsu*, 187, 189
Visa, 173

Wal-Mart Stores, 10, 11, 24, 33, 56, 72, 176, 241-42, 274, 295
  and economies of scope, 56
  and economies of span, 57-58
  expansion of, 192-93
  market value of, 11
  Sam's Club, 225, 234
  and spatial arbitrage, 100
  telecommunication/computer links with suppliers, 88
  and undefended markets, 250-52
Walton, Sam, 250-51
Warehouse clubs, 225
Warranties:
  and consumer reassurance, 129
  and consumer recognition, 41
Weiss, David M., 86
Wetterau, 193
Wholesale buying clubs, pricing of, 72
William, Oliver, 181
Williams, Jeffrey, 101, 113
Windows NT, 287-89
Winning:
  profits, 32-34
  size and profits, trade-off between, 35-37
  tournaments, 34-35
  value of, 29-61
Winning markets, 6-12, 168
  defined, 8
  and dominant market share, 11-12
  drive to win, 8-10
  market strategy, 22-25
  setting the target, 10-12
  through innovation, 11
Workplace transformations, 45
Worldcom, 160
World Partners, 195

Xerox, 91, 178

Yield management, and airline industry, 91

Zenith Electronics, 207

About the Author

DANIEL F. SPULBER holds the Thomas G. Ayers Chair at Northwestern University's J. L. Kellogg Graduate School of Management, where he teaches management strategy. He is ranked among the Top Ten economists in the United States by *Economic Inquiry* based on publications in leading economic journals and has received eight National Science Foundation grants for economic research. Spulber is the founding editor of the *Journal of Economics & Management Strategy*, and the author of several books and numerous articles.